The Informal Sector in Ecuador

This book looks back over the last forty years of change and development in Ecuador, showing how macro level changes have impacted families and workplaces on the local level. Traditionally a dependent economy reliant on agricultural exports, the impact of neoliberalism and new sources of income from oil have transformed the informal and artisanal sectors in Ecuador. Exploring these dynamics using a combination of micro and macro analyses, this book demonstrates how the social relations of the sector are connected to the wider social, economic and political systems in which they operate.

The book dives into the links between micro-production and the wider economy, including the relationships between different types of artisanal enterprises and their customers, their connections to the private sector and the state, the importance of social networks and social capital and the relevance of finance capital in microenterprise development. Overall, the analysis investigates how artisans, entrepreneurs and family-based enterprises seek to protect their interests when faced with neoliberal policies and the impacts of globalisation.

This remarkable longitudinal study will be of considerable interest to researchers of development studies, economics, sociology, anthropology, geography and Latin American Studies.

Alan Middleton is Emeritus Professor of Urban Studies at Birmingham City University, UK, Leverhulme Emeritus Fellow and Chief Executive Officer of the Governance Foundation.

Routledge Studies in Latin American Development

The series features innovative and original research on Latin American development from scholars both within and outside of Latin America. It particularly promotes comparative and interdisciplinary research targeted at a global readership.

In terms of theory and method, rather than basing itself on any one orthodoxy, the series draws broadly on the tool kit of the social sciences in general, emphasizing comparison, the analysis of the structure and processes, and the application of qualitative and quantitative methods.

The Informal Sector in Ecuador
Artisans, Entrepreneurs and Precarious Family Firms

Alan Middleton

Routledge
Taylor & Francis Group

LONDON AND NEW YORK

First published 2020
by Routledge
4 Park Square, Milton Park, Abingdon, Oxon OX14 4RN
605 Third Avenue, New York, NY 10017

First issued in paperback 2023

Routledge is an imprint of the Taylor & Francis Group, an informa business

British Library Cataloguing-in-Publication Data
A catalogue record for this book is available from the British Library

Library of Congress Cataloging-in-Publication Data
A catalog record has been requested for this book

ISBN: 978-1-03-257072-3 (pbk)
ISBN: 978-0-367-19210-5 (hbk)
ISBN: 978-0-429-20109-7 (ebk)

DOI: 10.4324/9780429201097

Typeset in Goudy
by Newgen Publishing UK

Visit the eResources: www.routledge.com/9780367192105

Publisher's Note
The publisher has gone to great lengths to ensure the quality of this reprint but points out
that some imperfections in the original copies may be apparent.

In memory of:
Gonzalo Abad Ortiz, 1944–2017
and
Tommy Middleton, 1947–1967

Contents

Figures

Tables

Online tables and figures

These tables and figures are available at www.Routledge.com/9780367192105

Acknowledgements

The research for this book was financed by a Leverhulme Trust Emeritus Fellowship. The ESRC and the Carnegie Trust funded some of the earlier work and throughout the process the investigation was supported by the Latin American Faculty of Social Sciences (FLACSO) in Quito.

Over 40 years, many people provided material and moral support. I am indebted in particular to Gonzalo Abad Ortiz, who introduced me to Ecuador in 1975, provided a desk in the National Planning Board (JNP) and invited me to join him in FLACSO as a researcher. He supported the research throughout, as a friend and a colleague, and he is sorely missed.

One of the people Gonzalo introduced me to was Fabian Sandoval, who worked at the JNP at the time. This research would not have been possible without the support of Fabian and his family over the decades. Other friends and colleagues who I met at that time and who have helped me over the years include Iván Fernández, Luciano Martínez, Edgar Pita, Cecilia Banda-Abad, Francisco Pareja, Eduardo Kingman, Fernando Carrión and Diego Carrión. Special mention must be made of Ana María Goetschel who, from the early days of FLACSO in Quito, provided assistance and support whenever she could, while pursuing her own academic career.

The survey work has benefited from the participation of Helena Santamaría, Guido Coloma, Mayra Aguirre, Lastemia Jumbo, Augusta Hidalgo, Clara Hidalgo, Silvana Silva, Augusta Sandoval, José Barrera, Rogelio García, Byron Barahona, Meri Silva, Luis Miguel Arroyo, Ángel Lozano, Jackeline Antunish, María Tatiana Crespo, Susana Quiroz, Sara Larrea, Silvana Moreno, Giovanny Costales, Alejandra Abad, María José Flor Agreda, Belén Cuesta, Jessica Morales, Mario Romero and Camilla Ulloa.

I would like to thank Andy McArthur for helping me reduce the material to a manageable length.

Thanks also to my wife Patricia and my daughter Jacqueline, who have been part of the story from the beginning, offering encouragement and support.

The errors are mine.

1 Artisans and the informal sector in Ecuador

Introduction

When the first phase of the research for this book began in 1975, neoclassical economics and the orthodox Marxism of the developed world were agreed about one thing – that small-scale production would disappear with the evolution of capitalism in developing countries. With the spread of dependency theory from Latin America (Frank, 1967; Cardoso and Faletto, 1969; Nun, 1969) and a growing interest in the 'informal sector', 'marginality' and 'petty commodity production' across the South (Hart, 1973; ILO, 1972; Quijano, 1974; Le Brun and Gerry, 1975; PREALC, 1976a&b), alternative views began to emerge. It is over forty years since Anibal Quijano argued that, rather than disappearing, petty production was being expanded and modified by its new mode of articulation in the overall economic structure (Quijano, 1974, 403). Similarly, Le Brun and Gerry argued that while in the developed countries petty production is residual and tends to disappear, in peripheral economies 'it seems to be the conservation aspect which predominates' (Le Brun and Gerry, 1975, 9).

Contrary to previous thinking, which was based on the experience of nineteenth-century Britain and which assumed that traditional forms of production would decline with economic development, the experience of developing countries in the late twentieth century was leading economists to the conclusion that 'petty producers' in the 'informal sector' would grow in numbers and that this was leading to a persistent bifurcation of the economy. The popularisation of formal–informal dualism, however, was criticised by *Structuralists* as being an inadequate and overly simplistic theoretical imposition on a much more complex reality (Breman, 1976; Bromley, 1978, 1979). The *Dualist* approach was clearly inadequate for conceptualising the heterogeneity of the economic reality in developing countries. Nevertheless, academics have continued to insist that 'dualism is a pervasive feature of the manufacturing sectors of most developing economies' and that this dualism is a major source of inequality (Kathuria et al., 2013, 1240).

It has also been pointed out that wherever studies of the informal sector examined different branches of activity, there were substantial differences in economic and social characteristics (Little et al., 1987; Anheier, 1992). There were different organisational forms, firm characteristics and business behaviour, in part relating to different structures of supply and demand. Tokman argued that the evolution of the informal sector was accompanied by changes in its structure and that 'the structural changes expected to occur would be due to the future expansion of some informal activities (primarily business services), while others facing greater competition (for example manufacturing) would probably reduce their market participation' (Tokman, 1993, 134).

The heterogeneous nature of the informal sector and the relationship between small-scale enterprises and the global economy led to the development of concepts such as 'heterogeneous subordination' to describe the variety of possible relationships (Tokman, 1978, 1993). This shaping of informal activities by the wider economy in which they operate also took the analysis beyond urban and national structures, into the realm of dependency theory. Influences on informality included global capitalism's relationship with the Third World (Portes, 1985; Castells and Portes, 1989).

If informal activities were being expanded and restructured in a global context, however, there was little evidence to explain how this was taking place. Questions arose, and were largely ignored, about changing structures within small firms and between these firms and the rest of the economy. If the micro-firms were being modified internally, in what sense? Were there, for example, changes in relations of production through variations in family/non-family and paid/unpaid labour? Were all petty production activities being expanded or were some types of activity expanding and others declining, with the net result being a growth in numbers? If the latter, how was the structure of 'the sector' changing? Were the external relations of micro-firms with other enterprises, particularly but not exclusively with large-scale capitalist firms, undergoing change?

What precisely was happening in this process of change and what were the external influences, including the direct relations with other sectors of the economy and local political, social and cultural pressures? Internationally, would changing political and economic theories have an effect, along with factors such as changing technology in a globalising world? Is it even possible to understand the complex movements of a global system of changing social relations of production and exchange and to critically analyse the changing place of small-scale 'informal' firms within it?

The theoretical issues were not addressed in longitudinal empirical research. Policymakers were left with a broad unsubstantiated consensus that small-scale economic activities were unlikely to decline in importance in the way that they had done in the developed countries and they generally accepted that the dynamics of change could not be explained. Our understanding of the complex nature of the conservation or dissolution of small-scale production in developing countries, which should have been of central importance for the elaboration of policies for the elimination of urban poverty and the promotion of economic growth, remained clouded by a global struggle between competing theories that evolved into ideologies. A dominant neo-Keynesian perspective in the 1970s was replaced by a neoliberal one in the 1980s, without the benefit of adequate information about the process of economic change. At the same time, in countries such as Ecuador, this ideological conflict was manifested in a local struggle for power over economic resources.

The impact of neoliberalism

After the ascendency of neoliberalism and the introduction of structural adjustment by the World Bank and the governments of developing countries, the relevance of the theoretical questions remained for academics, but they became less important for policymakers. The informal urban poor became rebranded as entrepreneurs and it was argued that they were the future of capitalism (de Soto, 1986, 1989). Despite a recognition that urban poverty had become particularly problematic in countries undergoing macro-economic adjustment (World Bank, 1991), lack of evidence about the debilitating impact of structural adjustment on small firms left the door open for neoliberals and the new right to return to, reinforce and develop the traditional neoclassical interpretations of the future of petty producers, characterising them as *micro-impresarios* who could be the golden future of capitalism in Latin America (de Soto, 1986).

Setting aside the ideologically driven notion that the urban poor who clean the shoes and the cars of the middle classes, or who sell small amounts of foodstuff or cigarettes on street corners, are micro-entrepreneurs who are to be applauded as the embodiment of the spirit of free capitalism, the fundamental question for neoliberal economists with respect to small-scale producers was 'why are they not growing into capitalist enterprises?' According to their perspective, small-scale producers in the 'informal sector' *should* have been developing into large-scale formal enterprises and since this was not happening, there must be barriers to their growth. De Soto's *Legalist* interpretation of the process of change, or the lack of it, assumed that small-scale producers were part of a restricted sector of the economy which could be the engine of growth if they were freed from the constraints of government regulations (De Soto, 1989; Bromley, 1990; Middleton, 1991). This interpretation, which found immediate favour with the re-emerging free-market theory of growth of the 1980s, presented the 'informals' as a new business class who would make a full entrepreneurial contribution to economic growth if the bureaucratic rules and regulations of the state were to be removed. Part of the solution was thought to lie in the application of neoliberal adjustment policies, which sought to free up markets and reduce the role of the state in the economy.

Around the same time, it began to dawn on some neoliberal economists that not all large-scale capitalist firm were playing the game according to the rules. Many of the workers in these firms were being denied access to workplace benefits to which they were legally entitled and, in many developing countries, laws did not exist that afforded them the same rights as those enjoyed by workers in the developed world.[1] A large swathe of the capitalist workforce, in the absence of legal protection, access to healthcare, pension rights and other benefits, were reclassified as 'informal' workers. In both neoliberal and neo-Keynesian theory, the small firms of the informal sector became subsumed under the banner of the 'informal economy' (ILO, 2002; Maloney, 2004; Perry et al., 2007, ILO, 2013a&b).

These 'micro-firms' did not go away. By all accounts they continued to increase in numbers, but this troublesome category merely became less important in the theoretical scheme of things because, rather than fade away with the passage of time, with the right encouragement they would grow into formal capitalist enterprises. In this process, there would be 'creative destruction' of some inefficient firms as other efficient and competitive micro-firms became capitalist in scale.

There are a number of underlying assumptions in the neoliberal view of small-scale producers which have persisted, which are questionable and which we will deal with in this book. These include the assumption that the sector is homogenous; that neoliberal policies will benefit small-scale non-capitalist enterprises; and that firms in all sectors of the micro-entrepreneurial sub-economy have potential for growth (Loayza et al., 2006; Taymaz, 2009; La Porta and Shleifer, 2014). In this research, we are not only concerned with growth and decline in the numbers of informal firms but, as the economy develops or declines, what happens to the social relations of production and exchange. This includes not only the internal dynamics of firms and households involved in petty production but also the structure of external relations on two levels: between firms in the informal sector; and between the informal firms and other formal sector organisations, including the state. We are particularly interested in how neoliberal economic policies have affected economic change in the national economy and how this has impacted on the local structure of micro-production. National governments become the filters for global theories or ideologies, but their subsequent policies are framed in the specific dynamics of the national economic context. In Ecuador, this context has been dominated by oil since the 1970s.

The research in its national context

When the research began in 1975, the population of Quito was a mere 600,000. It was, however, growing rapidly – particularly after oil began to flow from the Amazon region in the east of the country in 1972. The subsequent wealth was channelled through the capital where there was an expansion of government jobs, growth in all sectors of the economy, and a new middle class was emerging with spending power that was previously unknown.

In the 1970s, the Historic Centre of Quito (HCQ) was known as the Colonial Centre or the Commercial Centre. It was apparently trapped in a process of economic decline as the offices of both the government and the nascent private sector moved north. The grand houses of the country's elite were falling into disrepair as these families also moved to the north of the city, to areas such as Quito Tennis, Bellavista and the area around the Hotel Quito. At the same time, the popular barrios of the south of the city began to grow. As the city expanded both north and south, some of the economic demand, including the markets for micro-production and personal services, followed the people. As the old houses crumbled, however, artisans and traders continued to occupy the spaces at street level, serving a passing trade that still sought out their products and services. Shops, workshops and patios with direct access to the streets were bustling with economic activity as the economy and the population grew and demand for artisan production in the old centre expanded.

By 1975, Ecuador had had three years of military rule under the reformist Revolutionary Nationalist Government of General Rodriguez Lara. Fearing a struggle for control of the new oil wealth between different factions of the oligarchy, he had taken over when the oil began to flow from the northern Amazon region, promising a more equitable social and economic development, through the redistribution of wealth and the incorporation of the marginal masses into Ecuador's modernising economy (JNP, 1972b). The aims of Rodriguez Lara's National Plan coincided with the United Nations Second Development Decade, which put the generation of employment at the heart of the International Development Strategy.

This raised the question as to how strategies that had been designed for combating poverty and inequality would fare in the context of a dependent economy that had been traditionally reliant on exporting agricultural products and where, unlike most developing countries, there were now funds available for financing a new type of development. How would the un-enumerated substructure of informal activity, which provided incomes for the urban poor and created goods and services for the marginal population and the middle classes alike, benefit from this new socio-economic orientation? Just as important, how would the different sections of the ruling class, itself divided between coastal and sierran factions, respond to policies that threatened their historical struggle for hegemony, which had run from colonial times through Independence to the present day?

Just three years after the oil began to flow, the revolutionary-nationalist model associated with the technocrats of the government of General Rodriguez Lara was already failing (Middleton, 1979). The beneficiaries of the new wealth were the expanding middle classes and the government bureaucracy, whilst the relative position of the poor deteriorated and the situation of the poorest sectors of the self-employed declined absolutely. In addition, large increases in national and international capitalist investment in factories producing textiles, clothing and leather products between 1972 and 1976 threatened the future of artisans in these sectors. Investment from above, rather than growth from below, was driving manufacturing growth.

An organic methodology

In 1975, the physically deteriorating Colonial Centre, along with the area immediately around it and the expanding popular barrios to the south, were at the heart of the 'informal sector' of the economy. The lively economic activities that occupied this space in the centre and south of the city were changing rapidly, but the area continued to represent the core of informal activity in the capital. When the first survey was carried out in Quito, it included the small shops and workshops that were distributed through three sub-areas that had quite different physical and spatial characteristics, which at that time were identified as the Colonial Centre, the Peri-Centre or the South (Figure 1.1).[2]

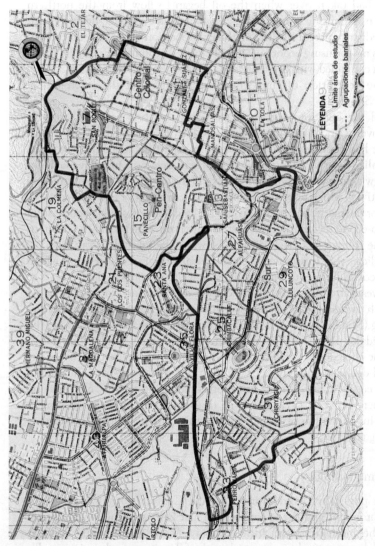

Figure 1.1 Map of the study area. As detailed in the key ('Leyenda'), the solid line represents the 'Edge of the study area' and the dotted line represents the edges of three 'Neighbourhood groupings'. These three neighbourhood groupings are identified as Colonial Centre ('Centro Colonial'), the Peri-centre ('Peri-centro') and the South ('Sur').

Map prepared by Valeria Vegara and the *Instituto de la Cuidad*, Quito.

These three sectors included the popular barrios around the core of the old city – stretching from El Placer and La Libertad, skirting around the Panecillo and passing through Calles Loja and Ambato to la Recoleta. This was a hive of informal economic activity. By way of Avenida Maldonado, which was full of small shops, workshops, bars and restaurants throughout its length, the central area was connected to the 'south' of the study area. The southern section stretched from Luluncoto through Chimbacalle, Chiriyacu, Chaguarquingo and El Camal to what was then Ferroviaria Baja and Ferroviaria Alta.[3]

The barrios around the Colonial Centre and those in the south of the study area are now identified by many *Quiteños* as being in the centre of Quito, but at the time they were marginal, in terms of their geography as well as economically and socially. They were also different from each other in terms of their history, the types of housing, and the economic activities pursued.

There was, of course, no record of this informal activity in 1975. Despite a national census of urban artisans that was carried out in 1961 (Stanford Research Institute, 1963), no one knew how many enterprises there were, what they made or how many people worked in them. Beyond anecdotal evidence, there was no information about the relationship between the home and the workplace, the sources of raw materials and tools, the relationship between different types of artisans and their clients, the role of paid and unpaid labour, and how the health and welfare of artisans and their families was sustained. Knowledge of the social relations of this sector of the economy, and how these relations connected to the wider social, economic and political systems, was extremely limited.

Before the research could be carried out, all the fixed-place economic activities in the study area had to be mapped. The creation of a sampling frame required a census of the artisans and traders in the study area, which was completed by walking the streets, observing, inquiring and noting the locations of their economic activity.[4] All small firms employing up to seven persons, including the owner, were included. A subsequent random survey investigated some of the deeper social and economic issues confronting tailors, shoemakers, carpenters, mechanics, painters, jewellers, printers and others.[5]

Over the next 40 years, the study was repeated and extended for the artisans. In 1982 1995, 2005 and 2015, the activities were remapped to take account of new artisans who had appeared as well as those who had disappeared. Where artisans no longer existed, we tried to find out what had happened to them by interviewing their neighbours or the new people who occupied their homes and workshops. In 2015, a number of life history interviews were carried out with older artisans, encouraging them to speak about their experiences over the 40 years covered by the research.

As the research progressed, the circumstances of the artisans, including their social relations in the family and at work, responded to changes in the wider social, economic and political systems. The production of oil in the Amazon region provided a new dimension in the economy, a new opportunity for either elite capture or the distribution of wealth and, therefore, an impetus for a variation in the historical struggle for power in Ecuador between the dominant elites of the Sierra and the Coast (Abad, 1970; Cueva, 1974). As the oil bonanza gave way to structural adjustment and other neoliberal policies, and then to a socio-political reaction to the harshness of these years, the micro-workshops declined, restructured and evolved into new forms of production and exchange.

As we will see in Chapter 4, the inter-survey periods cover distinct phases of Ecuador's development over the 40 years. The periods can be characterised as:

1975–1982	The oil boom
1982–1995	Neoliberalism and structural adjustment
1995–2005	Globalisation and the crisis of neoliberalism
2005–2015	Anti-globalisation and populist socialism

In each of these phases, the impact of the changes in the macro-economy on the artisan workshops can be traced and analysed. At the same time, there was also an impact on the political stability of the country as different segments of society struggled for power and the right to either implement self-interested economic policies or defend themselves from policies they perceived as detrimental to their interests.

When I first returned to the field in 1982, the main objective of the research was to further investigate the fate of the small-scale manufacturers in the context of an economy that was still growing, albeit at a slower pace than in the mid-1970s, and a politico-legal system that encouraged the protection and growth of these small-scale enterprises. A constant criticism that has been made of Third World Governments is that they recognise the 'formal' capitalist section of the economy but ignore the 'informal' activity. Their policy contains too few elements of positive support and promotion and too many elements of inaction, restriction and harassment (ILO, 1972; de Soto, 1989; Perry et al., 2007; ILO, 2013a&b). In Ecuador, however, state recognition of and support for the artisans of the informal sector goes back to 1953 (Gobierno del Ecuador, 1953), continued through the 1960s (Gobierno del Ecuador, 1965) and was an integral part of the National Development Plan from 1972 onwards (JNP, 1972a).

The expansion of microenterprises into small industries was a major goal of both the state and of the organisations claiming to represent the small-scale producers. One assumption of the ILO (and later the World Bank and others) was that state support for the urban informal sector would go a long way towards solving the problems of those who work in that sector. In Ecuador we should therefore have expected the goal of expansion into small industry to be at least partially realised through the conservation and growth of small-scale production. This research set out to demonstrate that the forces behind the development of micro-production were rather more complex than the models of the ILO and others would suggest. It found that none of the main goals were being realised.

In the literature of the time, the question of conservation or dissolution of small-scale enterprises was considered mainly in terms of the numbers of enterprises. In the original research in 1975, we were not particularly concerned about the numbers of artisans. We carried out a census of petty enterprises in the study area, but its purpose was to provide a sampling frame for an investigation of the structure of the social relations of production and exchange. When we returned to the field in 1982 the number of artisans was still not a major issue, but once the fieldwork started it came to the fore. The research cast some light on the above debate by its investigation of the growth or decline of different types of enterprise and relating this to the wider socio-economic context (Middleton, 1989). In spite of an expanding market for their goods, the numbers of small-scale producers of the means of subsistence were in steep decline, displaced not by the organic expansion and growth of some small firms to the exclusion of others ('creative destruction') but by the international investment from above.

The question of numbers of small informal enterprises is only one aspect of their conservation and dissolution. Various authors had raised questions about the changing internal structure of the enterprise and their relationship to the wider economy. It was in this context that the 1982 research set out to discover whether there was a tendency for conservation that was related to either internal restructuring of enterprises or increased subordination to the capitalist sector. This led us to ask whether relations of production and the external linkages to the rest of the economy change over time and, if so, for what types of enterprise? We set out to discover whether there was a change in the internal structure of the enterprises that was related to the growth or decline of different types of employment. For example, does the importance of one-person enterprises decline as petty manufacturing becomes more fully capitalist in form and employ more wage labour? With respect to external relations we wanted to test the suggestion that there was a conservation of micro-producers through an increase in outwork in its various forms. All of these questions were considered to be important for the elaboration of policy which would have some impact on urban poverty in peripheral economies.

We were also conscious of the fact that petty producers were not passive victims of some greater power. In Ecuador, artisans have a history of organisation that goes back to early colonial times, a proven capacity to organise for the defence or promotion of their interests. The research sought to identify whether or not these interests had changed over time in the perceptions of the leaders of the organisations who claimed to represent artisans. The hypothesis was that the organisations were becoming increasingly dominated by small-scale capitalists and they had become irrelevant to the mass of artisan producers.

Early findings in the field showed a far greater disappearance of petty manufacturers than was anticipated but, through the opening of new firms, there was no substantial change in the total number of enterprises. In 1975, 42% of firms had been in existence for more than ten years, pointing to a considerable level of stability and endurance. After seven years of rapid national economic growth on the back of the new oil exports, 63% of the firms had disappeared. Most of the producers of subsistence goods – tailors, shoemakers and carpenters – no longer existed. The total number of small workshops was slightly higher (by 3%) and the decline for subsistence producers was offset by an increase in the number of firms that could contribute goods or labour to the expanding capitalist sector.

The decline in the number of enterprises was similar for both types of firms but the replacement rates for the 'producers of the means of production' were much higher than for the 'producers of the means of subsistence'. Since the original research had indicated a high level of stability, it was clearly important to try to explain this apparently new phenomenon. We not only sought to identify the changing numbers of artisans, but also to try to find out what had happened to those that had disappeared – in terms of whether they had moved or closed down, whether or not they had expanded if they had moved, why they had moved or closed down, and where were they located now. The overall relative stability in the numbers was hiding a significant change in the structure and nature of the small firms: not only a shift from the production of the means of subsistence to the production of the means of production, but also distinct patterns of change in different areas of the city and internal developments in the nature of some activities (such as shoemakers becoming trading outlets for shoes, including those that were factory-made).

The restructuring of the artisans continued through the following decades, but not always in the same way. When I returned to the field in 1995, the main aim was to investigate the extent of conservation or dissolution of artisans over the 20-year period between 1975 and 1995. The first phase of neoliberalism began in 1982 and, after 13 years of structural adjustment in Ecuador, the principle objectives were to identify the extent to which the numbers of small firms had increased or declined, and in what subsectors of manufacturing; assess the extent to which the internal organisation of production had changed in different subsectors; examine whether the forward or backward linkages of the small firms had changed over time, including whether outwork or subcontracting had grown or declined in different subsectors; and analyse the extent to which the national artisan federations represented the interests of the small-scale producers. We found that, after 13 years of neoliberalism, there was now a generalised decline across all sectors of artisan production, including those that had grown in number during the years of the oil boom between 1975 and 1982.

While the survey methodology remained the same, the main objectives of the research were elaborated and developed in the course of the research, reflecting changing international theoretical considerations and developments in the world economy. Some new questions were added, but the original questionnaire could be used to address developing concerns in the literature. For example, in considering the internal organisation of production, we not only concerned ourselves with the extent to which family labour, wage labour etc. was used, but also started to try to analyse the extent to which firms were home-based or family-based and what the relationship was between these two types of enterprise.

The question about forward and backward linkages was extended to investigate whether home-based enterprises were different from others. In addition, a distinction was made between horizontal and vertical linkages, in order to investigate relations of cooperation and solidarity amongst artisans, which were indicators of social capital. The objectives were met by using a variety of research techniques. While the mapping exercises and surveys of small firms continued, there were other structured and semi-structured interviews with artisans, their leaders, traders and public sector officials who had been concerned with promoting artisan development over the years.

By the time I returned to the field in 2005, the world capitalist economy had seen crises in East Asia, Russia, and other parts of South America. In Ecuador, the local neoliberal experiment had crashed into rampant inflation, a financial meltdown and the dollarization of the currency, whilst globalisation had introduced cheap and shoddy Chinese manufactured products to compete with local artisans. All of these factors had an impact on the artisans, as became clear following the introduction of new questions about these issues in the survey. As we will see, they had serious negative consequences for Ecuadorean artisans.

In 2007, Ecuador elected the anti-globalisation and anti-neoliberal government of Raphael Correa. In 2015, using the same basic methodology that had been used since 1975 but supplemented by a series of artisan life-histories, the fieldwork captured the extent to which the new government had been able to improve the circumstances of this section of the urban poor. There is some evidence that this improvement did happen. In spite of their anti-neoliberal intentions, however, they adopted the World Bank and ILO advice about the desirability of formalising the informal economy. With this drive to formalise the artisans, however, they effectively pushed some small firms further underground, reducing the willingness of some to employ wage labour, encouraging others to employ their spouses in fictitious employment, and causing an increase in a variety of ways of avoiding the growing tax burden.

After 40 years of research, the book provides an analysis that places the artisans of the informal sector in the context of changes in globalisation, the structure of the national economy, the configuration of social classes, and the distribution of power in society. The analysis also locates the artisans and other small enterprises in a theoretical framework that is both historical and structural. The remainder of the book is structured as follows.

The contents of the book

The second chapter is a discussion of the evolution of the conceptual frameworks that have been used by academics and international institutions (such as the International Labour Organisation, the World Bank, the IMF and global charities) as they try to understand the enduring phenomenon of the urban working poor in developing countries. We will look at the theoretical roots of different academic approaches to the 'informal sector'. We will see how neo-Keynesian and neo-Marxist perspectives of the 1970s, which emphasised the poverty of the informal sector, gave way to a global neoliberal consensus, in which the same artisans were presented as entrepreneurs who were being held back by the regulatory state. It will be argued that this neoliberal theory is no more than a culturally embedded ideology that does not stand up to the scrutiny of empirical evidence. Historical-structural analysis will be used to analyse the changing role of artisan production in the process of global development. This will provide the theoretical framework for the critique of neoliberalism that is inherent in the empirical evidence and the experience of the artisans.

In Chapter 3, we will see how the structure of artisan production in Ecuador has evolved over time. In the context of changing national and international economic policy over a period of 40 years, the numbers of different types of artisan activities have developed, resulting in changes in the structure of production. These developments map onto the four phases of economic policy and practice: the oil bonanza, structural adjustment, the neoliberal crisis and anti-globalisation. We will suggest that the fortunes of artisans through these phases are linked to competition, technology, skills, and the capacity of the formal sector to provide both intended and unintended opportunities for artisans. This has led to a substantial restructuring of the types of workshops that are found. In particular, the relationship with capitalist production has decimated some activities though competition and has altered the internal nature of other artisan work, producing a shift from manufacturing to repair. This shift, however, has been neither lineal nor uniform for all activities and geographical locations.

In Chapter 4, in support of the argument in the previous chapter, we will look more closely at the national and international economic context. The major changes in the economy are discussed in relation to the inter-survey periods and the four major development phases over the 40 years. The chapter traces the transformation of the economy from the oil boom years through two period of neoliberalism (structural adjustment between 1982 and 1995 and the end-of-millennium financial crash) to the anti-globalisation of President Rafael Correa. It discusses the nature of neoliberalism in Ecuador before going on to analyse the politics of debt, fluctuations in the rate of growth and the performance of key sectors of the economy. The neoliberal experiment resulted in the failure of the banking system, the dollarization of the economy and serious pressure on the businesses and the lives of artisans – the very 'entrepreneurs' who should have prospered under the experiment. The main victims of the crisis of neoliberalism were small family businesses whose savings were in sucres and who saw demand sucked out of the economy. On the other hand, the coastal agro-exporting oligarchy were the main beneficiaries before the crash, by which time their dollar earnings had been banked offshore.

A considerable amount of intellectual energy in recent years has gone into discussion of the links between the formal and informal sectors and the extent to which informal workers have been excluded from or have chosen not to join the formal economy. Much of the exclusion/choice debate has been based on the assumption that those in the informal sector care about such matters. We will argue in Chapter 5 that they do not. Rational choice theory, which is at the heart of neoliberalism and its position on the informal sector, does not apply. The stories the artisans tell are about entering a trade in the informal sector as children, the affinity they have with this trade in the face of economic adversity, and the transition towards treating it as a hobby in their later years.

Another issue is whether the formal–informal model provides a true representation of the relations between two distinct segments of the economy. It has long been recognised that even those activities that are least capitalist-like in their form are intimately linked into the capitalist system. From street vendors who sell the products of international tobacco companies to recyclers whose glass and metal re-enters the capitalist production process, there are backwards and forwards linkages that tie the informal to the formal. We will see in Chapter 6 that artisans rely on the formal sector for their inputs, such as tools and raw materials, but that this relationship has changed over time. Technology and materials have changed and these have had an impact on relations with suppliers. A significant aspect of their experience, however, has been the decline in the quality of some of their inputs as a result of globalisation and the spread of low-quality Chinese tools and materials.

As distinct from what is reported or assumed about the situation elsewhere in the world, there are few forward links to the formal sector and international markets through the global supply chain, via the purchase of micro-firm outputs or labour (Chapter 7). There are cases of subcontracting, direct contracting and buying up, and these have also been changing over time. However, less than 3% of artisans produce for intermediaries. The concept of subcontracting, or homeworking, has been an important one in the recent literature on the role of the informal sector in global supply systems and there has been a steady increase in the small numbers of artisans producing for the private sector in Quito. These customers, however, are mainly small-scale traders and other artisans, not enterprises that are part of the global supply chain linking petty producers to markets in the developed world. For the older artisans, the customers remain overwhelmingly individuals, many of whom have been clients for over 40 years and who are now dying off, along with the artisans themselves.

Neoliberal theory assumes that the owners of family businesses are entrepreneurs who, because of the extent of their involvement in new venture creation, should have benefited most from neoliberal policy. In Chapter 8, we look at what happened to family businesses over the 40 years and discuss their fortunes in relation to the thinking and policies of international organisations such as the ILO and the World Bank. Defining family-based enterprises as those employing family labour (rather than by ownership alone, since all artisan firms would be family firms under the ownership definition) we will see that there is no correspondence between family-based enterprises (FBEs) and home-based enterprises (HBEs), that the concepts that are applied by the international organisations are more confusing than helpful, and that the variations in the fortunes of home-based and family-based working were not as expected. Instead of the emergence of artisans out of their homes into independent and expanding workshops and factories, artisans were more likely to locate their workshops inside the home during the neoliberal phases, precisely because times were hard. It was only in the initial years of the oil bonanza and the period when globalisation and neoliberalism were rejected that home-based working declined.

Social capital amongst artisans has a long history in the federations of tailors, shoemakers and others. Since early post-colonial times, these organisations have defended their interests and provided social support through difficult periods in the lives of their members. In Chapter 9, we will see how these artisan associations have been captured and used by small-scale capitalist firms to promote their interests, mainly by denying their workers the rights enjoyed by workers in the formal sector and taking advantage of artisan benefits that were accorded to them in the 1950s. As part of the political system in Ecuador, artisan organisations have been fought over by national political parties and manipulated by foreign governments. Across time, however, artisan membership has declined to an historic all-time low. The organisations continue to promote themselves as the defenders of artisan interests, but only a small minority of artisans believe that this is the case. Social capital is more likely to be found in their relations with people who have supported them in times of crisis, some of whom may have risked their own economic interests to do so.

If the federations do not represent them, the government is worse. In spite of a raft of policies and regulations adopted to encourage the defence and growth of artisans since the 1950s, the common and consistent view over time is that successive governments have done nothing for the artisans. We will see in Chapter 10 that this was true pre- and post-neoliberalism, although the feeling was at its highest at the end of the neoliberal period, and it was true of both local and national governments. The most negative responses were following the neoliberal years of structural adjustment, when the rhetoric and policy framework were expressing most support for entrepreneurs; and the most positive were during the anti-globalisation period of the populist government of Correa, when neoliberal policy was rejected. One policy that Correa did adopt from the international organisations was the regularisation of the informal sector – formalising the informal. The impact of this was to reduce non-family wage labour, increase paid family labour (sometimes by falsely claiming a spouse as a paid worker to reduce taxes and increase family benefits), and drive some small firms even further underground in order to avoid the modernising state. There remains an overwhelming scepticism about any government's capacity or willingness to assist them.

Another major concern of international organisations under the influence of neoliberal theory has been how to provide the finance that entrepreneurs need in order to grow. The most striking feature of the artisan's relationship with the financial sector, however, has been their almost universal distrust of the banks. This was true before the financial crash of 1999 and it increased after they lost their savings in the neoliberal end-of-millennium crisis that resulted in hyper-inflation, bank failure and dollarization. In Chapter 11 we will see that the concern of economists about access to finance is based on the false assumptions that the artisans have a burning desire to grow their businesses and that lack of access to finance is holding them back. Being the owner of a large business is a dream of many, but it is no more than a daydream. Artisans are much more pragmatic.

In the words of the artisans themselves in Chapter 12, we will see that the reality of their world is saving for the purchase of tools and machinery, sometimes with family and other support; credit is provided by suppliers of raw materials; and there is a constant struggle to earn enough money to pay the rent of their workshops, for which no bank would ever provide a loan. They express little desire to employ more workers and even less to risk their businesses in entanglements with banks.

Chapter 13 looks at the issues of the recent past in each of the years of the surveys and shows how these evolved in relation to the neoliberal or anti-globalisation policies of successive governments. The words of the artisans tell a story that does not fit the dominant narrative. We will see that the burden of regulation that is at the heart of the neoliberal narrative hardly gets a mention from the micro-firm owners. Their concerns are with the effects of the financial crises and with unfair competition, which has been encouraged by globalisation policies. Their vision of the future is more likely to involve their families than their businesses. A main feature of the motivation of artisans is the education of their children. Very few children will take over from their parents and this is a cause some regret, but this is far outweighed by pride in the number of children who have become professionals such as doctors, orthodontists, engineers, teachers, and so on. Economic 'man' is secondary to family 'man', and this is true across genders.

In the final chapter, we will discuss what the findings mean for neoliberal theory. We will challenge some of the assumptions of Adam Smith and, more importantly, how his thinking has been interpreted. Similarly, we will discuss Schumpeter, particularly the way his work has been woven into the neoliberal narrative. The contributions of Hayek, Joseph, Friedman and others will be confronted with the evidence, some of it from the mouths of elderly utilitarian artisans in a developing economy.

Notes

1 This was before the growth of precarious work in developed countries was seen as an issue.
2 The solid line on the map delineates the study area and the dotted lines identify the three geographic subsectors. The Colonial Centre is identified as the '*Centro Colonial*' in Spanish. This area became the core of the Historic Centre of Quito (HCQ), the first city centre inscribed on UNESCO's World Heritage List in 1978. The Peri-Centre ('*Peri-Centro*' in Spanish) is the area immediately around the HCQ, including all or parts of La Libertad, San Roque, El Tejar, El Placer, San Diego, San Sebastián, El Panecillo, La Recoleta, El Sena. As the city expanded over 40 years, the South ('Sur' on the map) became more central.
3 As Ferroviaria expanded up the cordillera, the area defined as Ferroviaria Alta also moved up.
4 Street traders and fixed-stall market traders were not included. It was impossible to count the former and work on the latter had recently been carried out (Bromley, 1974).
5 Artisans will be defined more precisely in Chapter 3, Table 3.1. The methodology is more fully explained in the online Appendix.

2   Informals, entrepreneurs and artisans

Analysing the informal sector

When the concept of the informal sector was introduced in the early 1970s, the dominant neoclassical and neo-Marxist perspectives held that small-scale non-capitalist forms of production, such as artisans or other members of the 'reserve army of labour', would disappear with the development of capitalism in Third World cities (Lewis, 1954; Fei and Ranis, 1964, Marx, 1967). The emerging neo-Keynesian perspective was that this small-scale economic activity represented 'informal income opportunities' (Hart, 1973) that were characterised by 'ease of entry, reliance on indigenous resources, family ownership of enterprises, small scale of operation, labour intensive and adaptive technology, skills acquired outside the formal school systems, and unregulated and competitive markets' (ILO, 1972, 6).

The concept was thought to be important for explaining how the poor survive and adapt to their circumstances (Hart, 1973), how cities continue to function and support their populations at minimal standards of living (Roberts, 1976) and, somewhat contradictorily, why the poor are poor (ILO, 1972). Some agreed with Portes that it was a 'fundamental concept' for understanding world capitalism, while others agreed with the more modest claim that it contributed to our 'understanding of the causes of under-development and the possible ways towards development' (Portes, 1978, 1; Tokman, 1977, 1).

On the other hand, others argued that the concept was analytically inadequate since the informal sector 'cannot be demarcated as a separate economic compartment and/or labour situation' (Breman, 1976, 1871) and there was 'complete confusion about what is actually meant by the informal sector' (Moser, 1977, 31). The heterogeneity of the concept continued to plague the attempts to assess the relevance of the concept of informality over decades (ILO, 1993, 2013a; Sindzingre, 2006; Chen, 2014).

Analyses evolved from discussions of traditional-modern dualism towards a new formal–informal dualism, which recognised the dynamic interaction of modern capitalism with local economies and argued that what had been characterised as 'traditional' in the past was, in fact, a product of this interaction and in consequence, a modern phenomenon. The work of the ILO and others, however, was strangely devoid of any empirical analysis of the historical development of the pattern of accumulation or of the role wealth and power for the continuation or change of that pattern.

Work that followed on from that of the ILO was bedevilled by the fact that the 'informal sector' concept came to have a wide variety of meanings for a large number of authors. The concept was used as synonymous with 'the urban poor', 'people living in slums', and 'migrants to the cities' (Moser, 1977, 31–9). These orientations referred to the insertion of individuals in social, economic and spatial structures but there was no common agreement as to whether the concept referred to individuals (PREALC, 1976a&b), enterprises (Harriss, 1977), types of occupation (Hart, 1973) or a bifurcation of the labour market (Mazumdar, 1975). In some studies, the authors cautiously did not attempt to define the concept (Tokman, 1977) and in others different definitions were used in different parts of the investigation (PREALC, 1976a&b, 1978). There was no agreement about the 'target group', which included heterogeneous sets of activities and people with no identifiable or analytically useful common characteristics (Moser, 1977, 31)

If the informal sector was concerned with economic activity (rather than people) there was then the question of whether we should be interested in relationships within and between production units; and/or concerned to analyse the activity in terms of an individual's insertion in the labour market. If informal sector analysis seeks to classify activities, should the unit of analysis be the activity of the individual or of the enterprise? Even where enterprises were identified as the unit of analysis, there was no agreement as to what the indicators of informality should be. They included the number of workers employed in the enterprise, the internal organisation, the use of electricity, the legality or illegality of the enterprise, some characteristic of the workforce, pre-categorisation as traditional or modern, links with formal institutions or the state, and whether or not the enterprises entered government statistics (Joshi et al., 1975; Weeks, 1975; Sethuraman, 1975a&b; Sethuraman, 1976; Harriss, 1977; Souza and Tokman, 1976). The concern that the informal sector firms did not enter government statistics was compounded by the fact that they appeared to evade government regulations, an issue that was to dominate later debates about the sector.

Given the heterogeneity of the types of activity and considering the variety of the relationships between different activities and the wider economic system, the search for a single defining characteristic that would cover every case appeared to be utopian, something that was recognised by World Bank economists. In 2004, they conceded that: 'Three decades of research have not yielded consensus either on the definition of the informal sector or its *razon de ser*' (Maloney, 2004, 1159). The Bank did decide that they were primarily dealing with firms, rather than individuals, and that within these informal firms there was a disadvantaged labour force. However, because of the multiple measures of informality, 'we are not clear on exactly what it is and what we should be studying' and, as a consequence, it is arguably an 'unhelpful, umbrella term' (Perry et al., 2007, 1).

The ILO, on the other hand, focusing mainly on individuals and jobs, continued to broaden the definition of informal. The ILO's 1993 definition of the informal sector was based on economic units and it referred to employment and production that takes place in unincorporated small or unregistered enterprises (ILO, 1993, 52–5). Since 2002, they have distinguished between the informal sector and the informal economy (ILO, 2002). Part of the reason for the growth of the popularity of the concept of the informal economy over the informal sector was the influential paper by Chen et al. who preferred the former term because the formal and informal were 'so interlinked that it is misleading to think of two distinct sectors of the economy' (Chen et al., 2002, 2). Informal employment exists in both and informality exists in all labour markets, in both developed and developing countries (ILO and WIEGO, 2013, 1):

> The *informal economy* comprises diverse workers and entrepreneurs who are not often recognised or protected under national legal and regulatory frameworks ... [It] can be seen to encompass a broad range of vulnerabilities, such as limited access to social protection, denial of labour rights, and lack of organisation and representation.

Focusing on the individual and the conditions of his or her employment, the International Labour Conference of 2002 therefore broadened the concept of informality (ILO and WIEGO, 2013, 1):

> moving beyond the narrow, enterprise-based notion of the 'informal sector' to a broader concept of 'informal employment' which comprises all employment that lacks legal or social protection, whether in informal enterprises, formal enterprises or households.

There is, however, disagreement within the ILO about the usefulness of the concept of the 'informal economy'. Statisticians rejected the concept in their 17th Conference in 2003 and the current manual on measuring informality refers to its 'non-use as a statistical term' and 'prefers to use the terms "informal sector" and "informal employment"' (ILO, 2013a, 44). Nevertheless, the report of the 19th Conference in the same year stated that 'statisticians have now accepted the term of "employment in the informal economy" to include the sum of employment in the informal sector and informal employment' (ILO, 2013c, 6).

The widening of the definition has been accepted by NGOs working on 'informality'. For the ILO and WIEGO, the informal economy comprises 'entrepreneurs' and workers who are not recognised or protected under national legal and regulatory frameworks – such as social protection, labour rights and representation (ILO and WIEGO, 2013, 1). Over time, the owners of informal firms have become classified as 'entrepreneurs' and workers in formal capitalist firms that do not receive pay and benefits according to the law have become 'informal' workers. In the latter case, falling into line with the World Bank, *illegal* practices are redefined as *informal*.

For the purposes of national accounts, however, the workers in the informal sector are classified under 'household unincorporated enterprises', which basically means that the informal sector is regarded as being composed of enterprises that are owned by households whose production is indistinguishable from household consumption. This is no more than an erroneous administrative convenience that has not changed since 1993:

> Production units of the informal sector have the characteristic features of household enterprises ... expenditures are often indistinguishable from household expenditures [and] capital goods such as buildings ... may be used indistinguishably for business and household purposes.
>
> (ILO, 1993, Resolution II, para 5.2)

The ILO's 2013 manual for measuring informality adopted the 1993 ICLS definition of the informal sector:

> The informal sector may be broadly characterized as consisting of units engaged in the production of goods or services with the primary objective of generating employment and incomes to the persons concerned. These units typically operate at a low level of organisation, with little or no division between labour and capital as factors of production and on a small scale. Labour relations – where they exist – are based mostly on casual employment, kinship or personal and social relations rather than contractual arrangements with formal guarantees.
>
> (ILO, 2013a, 14)

This definition contains a number of erroneous assertions and assumptions about what is 'typical' for the informal sector. In reality, in informal production units such as artisan workshops, there will always be contractual arrangements – guarantees by word of mouth, rather than in writing. Business expenditures (on tools and raw material) are clearly distinguishable from household expenditures. The use of buildings varies across different areas of the city, depending on the space that is available in and around the home and whether or not the location offers or constrains access to customers. Different activities have different space needs and, as the structure of micro-activity evolves over time, so does the overall relationship to the home. The ILO goes on to argue that 'typical' informal sector activities, such as unpaid work in a family enterprise, casual wage labour and home-based work, provide many poor people with the only opportunity they have to secure the basic needs for their survival. We shall see later that these 'typical' activities are in fact minority activities. The need for the statisticians to incorporate the informal sector into the national accounts has also led to further confusion about the role of the household and the family, which we will return to in Chapter 8.

In response to a resolution calling on the ILO to prepare technical guidelines on measuring the informal economy, the organisation produced the statistical manual on measuring informality in 2013 (ILO, 2003, 2013a, 2013b). There were, however, now three related official terms and definitions, which were used 'imprecisely and interchangeably' in discussions of informality (Chen, 2014, 400):

> The *informal sector* refers to the production and employment that takes place in unincorporated small or unregistered enterprises; *informal employment* refers to employment without legal and social protection, both inside and outside the informal sector; and the *informal economy* refers to all units, and workers so defined and the output from them.

The acceptance of the administrative convenience that allows statisticians to include the 'informal' in national statistics, combined with an ever-expanding definition of the term, has led to greater confusion over precisely what is being measured. It has also not helped our understanding of the causes and consequences of poverty and the uneven distribution of wealth in developing countries. Through an increasing number of household and labour market surveys, data on more countries has become available. Unfortunately, these datasets do not measure the same concepts and they tend to exclude the unregulated micro-firms that were initially the focus of interest. The data are just not available. In addition to the definitional difficulties, there are a number of other reasons why this data is not always compatible. The conceptual distinction between 'employment in the informal sector' and 'informal employment outside the informal sector' (ILO, 2003, 4) leads to two different methodologies: the investigation of employment in the informal sector is based on the *enterprise* as the unit of observation and research on informal employment outside the informal sector is based on *jobs*. Reconciling these methodologies within nation states is difficult, as the case of measuring productivity in the UK demonstrates (Middleton, 2014). Reconciling them across national boundaries with different definitions, regulations and laws is many times more so.

An assumption behind much of the ILO's thinking is that workers in the informal sector are perpetually seeking formal jobs but, as we will see in Chapter 5, formal sector employment is not a choice that many artisans aspire to. The ILO accepts that the informal sector plays a key role in poverty reduction but proposes that many are not able to work their way out of poverty. This is thought to be because their conditions of work perpetuate the poverty in which they live. In fact, as we will see in Chapters 3 and 4, changing global conditions reinforce this, driving down the income-earning opportunities of artisans through both national development and spreading globalisation.

Across the North, as the formal sector is being transformed by global integration, more decentralised work, flexible work, and specialised economic units, more complex forms of 'informal' employment relations are replacing full-time wage employment. Some of these are recognised by the ILO, while others have been emerging since 2013: part-time work, temporary work, fixed term employment contracts, zero-hours contracts, agency working, bogus self-employment, casual employment, subcontracted labour, outwork and home-work. Through a reconfiguration of formal labour markets, workers are increasingly excluded from national labour legislation, social protection, employment benefits and pensions. Growing informal employment encompasses all categories of workers: employers, employees, the self-employed and family workers, both paid and unpaid.

The ILO says that the above complex characteristics are responsible for the 'precarious nature' of 'informal *employment*' outside the legal and institutional structure of the modern economy and that they are excluded from the international definition of the 'informal *sector*', no matter how 'precarious their employment situation may be' (ILO, 2013a, 4 and 16). Twenty years before, the ILO recognised that information on various forms of 'precarious employment outside the informal sector' needed to be obtained along with data for the informal sector (ILO, 1993, para 22.4). It is unfortunate that the ILO has arrived at a position of using the same adjective, informal, to describe two quite different sets of circumstances.

The concept of 'precarious employment' refers to a growing phenomenon in the developed and developing world, where workers are increasingly subcontracted to global corporations (Standing, 2014). Precarious employment bridges the informal and formal sectors. While it is true that the informal sector definition adopted by the 15th ICLS Resolution did not capture the 'non-standard, atypical alternative, irregular or precarious types of employment in the formal sector' (ILO, 2013a, 5), labelling them informal has contributed to the informal sector being marginalised in the ILO's considerations.

The ILO's search for statistics that will improve labour market data and national accounts, as well as assist macro-economic analysis and lead to the formulation of policies for social and economic development, appears to have recognised that information that also leads to specific policies in support of the informal sector is extremely difficult to obtain. The statistical needs of the national accounts have not entirely eliminated the need for informal sector data, for this is still required if increases in the productive potential, income-generating activities, employment and the local stock of wealth are to be achieved, along with improved working conditions and social protection. In the pursuit of these aims we see the neoliberal project confound the small business owner with the concept of the entrepreneur and the emergence of the ideology of the entrepreneur as hero.[1]

Entrepreneurs and small businesses owners

There is no consensus on how entrepreneurship should be defined. In the definitions that are based on the work of Schumpeter, the entrepreneur is innovative and a driver of the growth of the business:

> the function of entrepreneurs is to reform or revolutionise the pattern of production by exploiting an invention or, more generally, an untried technological possibility for producing a new commodity or producing an old one in a new way, by opening up a new source of supply of materials or a new outlet for products, by reorganising an industry and so on.
>
> (Schumpeter, 2003, 132)

At the heart of his definition of entrepreneurship is the concept of innovation in the pursuit of wealth. S/he can be distinguished from other economic actors by the fact that s/he creates wealth through introducing innovative products to the market, creates new production processes, or finds new ways of taking the products to markets. They will not necessarily be innovative/entrepreneurial in every aspect of their work but they will demonstrate innovation in at least some aspects.

Schumpeter stimulated the type of research on entrepreneurship that is concerned with why entrepreneurs innovate and what policies and institutions are needed to support their creative impulses. However, most research in recent years, by focusing predominantly on new start-ups or the extent of self-employment as the main measures of entrepreneurial activity, has ignored Schumpeter's warning that entrepreneurs and the self-employed are not the same thing. A consequence of this is that the role of innovation in developing countries has been under-researched (Naudé, 2011), as has the impact of national and international institutions on entrepreneurship. In addition, we will argue, by concentrating on numbers and assuming that all small firm owners are entrepreneurs, the self-employed urban poor have been misrepresented and their development potential has been exaggerated.

The innovation displayed by the small business entrepreneur will be greater than that which most small business owners will exhibit. The innovation will give the entrepreneur a competitive edge, leading to substantial wealth creation. This is distinct from running a small firm to generate income levels that will provide subsistence for the family and education for the children. Entrepreneurship usually involves considerable risk in the development of new products for uncertain markets, particularly if this also means creating new production processes that need to be financed. The entrepreneur is not merely pursuing an income stream to support the firm owner and his/her family, s/he is also risking an existing stock of wealth in order to create substantial new wealth. The wealth that already exists for the innovative small firm owner does not necessarily all belong to the entrepreneur, for it may involve convincing a bank to put up some of its funds in support of a venture on the promise that it will produce rapid growth and short-term returns to investment. In this process, the bank becomes a co-owner of the stock of wealth.

Neoliberals claim success for the impact of their economic theory and practice by pointing to the creation of millions of new firms and insisting that this is evidence of the growth of entrepreneurship and wealth. There is no doubt that in most countries across the globe, the numbers of the self-employed have increased through the dominance of neoliberalism over decades. However, these are not mainly entrepreneurial firms. Indeed, large swathes of innovative small firms, such as artisans who create bespoke products for their clients, have been wiped out. In a globalised world, this is not the result of the creative destruction that Schumpeter predicts, as we will see in Chapter 3.

In addition, as we will also see in Chapter 3, there has been a growth of repair services amongst artisans. It is clearly possible to be entrepreneurial in repair services, as the success of a firm such as Kwik Fit in the UK demonstrates, a case of process innovation in the auto repair sector, but most mechanical repair workshops do not aspire to this level of achievement. Their work is conditioned and limited by the built-in failures of the products of capitalist enterprises. The manufacture's manual for the product, such as an automobile or a refrigerator, predetermines the spare parts to be used and the process to be followed in the repair of the product. In this process of transformation of small firm activity from production to repair, involving the decline of innovative artisans whose bespoke products are newly designed in every case and the growth of artisans whose function is to repair the products manufactured by capitalist enterprises, innovation is destroyed and entrepreneurial activity is suppressed.

Academics using a Schumpeterian conceptual scheme do not consider the average small firm to be entrepreneurial (Gartner, 1990). The majority of the self-employed are not innovative and they are permanently small, more likely to die young than grow into large-scale enterprises (Henrekson and Sanandaji, 2013). In a great deal of small business research, however, the concept of the entrepreneur is applied to all owners of small firms, irrespective of whether they are innovative or aspire to grow their firms.

The idea that entrepreneurship can be measured by counting business start-ups finds its most influential expression in the Global Entrepreneurship Monitor (GEM) (GEM, 2017, 21):

> The central indicator of GEM is the Total Early-stage Entrepreneurial Activity (TEA) rate, which measures the percentage of the national population (18 to 64 years) that are in the process of starting or who have just started a business.

This assumed association between entrepreneurship and new firm formation can also be found in the recent literature that discusses the relationship between entrepreneurship and ethnicity (Awaworyi Churchill, 2017), gender (Adachi and Hisada, 2017), culture (Fritsch and Mueller, 2007; Stuetzer et al., 2016; Audretsch et al., 2017; Fritsch and Wyrwich, 2014), personality/psychology (Audretsch et al., 2017; Caliendo et al., 2016) and regional development (Fritsch and Storey, 2014). Other authors who are concerned with gender differences in entrepreneurship highlight the different levels of self-employment for females and males (Sauer and Wilson, 2016; Bernat et al., 2017).

The GEM survey provides information on the characteristics, motivation and ambitions of people starting their own businesses in 64 economies across the globe. It provides data on new firm creation that has been an important source for hundreds of academic papers. However, since new firm foundation is confounded with entrepreneurship in almost all of these papers, they contribute to the ideology of the entrepreneur as hero. The GEM also contains information that would support the argument that these small business start-up owners are not entrepreneurs in the classical sense, but this information is not reported in the

GEM annual report. The reasons for starting a business in developing countries are not given the attention they are due.

The report shows that Total Early-stage Entrepreneurial Activity (TEA) rates are highest in the least developed economies.[2] The average TEA rates in LDCs are almost double the rates in the most developed countries and, at the regional level, they are highest in Latin America and the Caribbean and Africa (GEM, 2017, 8). In Burkina Faso, ranked in the bottom 5% of countries in terms of per capita GDP, there is a very high level of business ownership, with two-thirds of working age adults starting up or running their own businesses. What appears to be happening here is that those in the informal sector are being counted as entrepreneurs because they are setting up their own micro-firms, irrespective of their motivation.

When asked if they were involved in a start-up to take advantage of a business opportunity or because they have no better choices for work, around three-quarters said it was to pursue a perceived business opportunity. In the richest countries the figure was 79%. However, around one-third in the poorest countries said it was because they had no better choices. The poorer the economy, the more likely they were to say they had no other options.

The decision based on perceived business opportunities is taken as evidence of entrepreneurship, but it could also be the perception of an income-earning opportunity, rather than the establishment of a business that would introduce new products or processes, create new markets, borrow money, invest in capital and expand its workforce. Those who said they chose to pursue a business opportunity were then asked about their most important motive for this, including the pursuit of independence to maintain or increase personal income, but the GEM Report did not analyse the responses to this question.

Hurst and Pugsley (2011) point out that self-employment is not synonymous with entrepreneurship in the United States, for less than 20% of small firms report any innovative activity and three-quarters have no ambitions to grow their firms beyond what they consider to be a small manageable size: 'The vast majority of small business owners do not expect to grow, report not wanting to grow, expect never to innovate … and report not wanting to innovate' (Hurst and Pugsley, 2011, 112). Only around one-third of new owners said they started their business because they wanted to bring a new product to market. Most common was the existence of non-financial benefits such as independence and flexibility. They had little desire or expectation to grow their businesses beyond a few employees. Most small business owners are very different from the entrepreneurs of neoliberal theory.

There is little evidence that the people starting their own businesses in the least developed countries are creative and innovative entrepreneurs, aspiring to grow their businesses. In the least developed countries, around half of the 'entrepreneurs' operate in the wholesale or retail sectors, most likely as street traders or market stall owners. This compares to 46% in the richest countries who work in information and communications, financial, professional and other services. In countries at all three levels of development, around 45% of 'entrepreneurs' do not anticipate creating any jobs in the next five years. Only 20% of those in the least developed and developing economies expected to be employing six or more people (GEM, 2017, 9). In Latin America, the figure was 17% and in Burkina Faso it was 15%.

As we saw in the case of measurement of the informal sector/employment/ economy, there is a lack of consistency in the measurement of the entrepreneurial activities of firms across national boundaries. Nevertheless, the OECD-Eurostat Entrepreneurship Indicators Programme (EIP) claims to have developed measures of entrepreneurship that can be applied internationally (OECD-EUROSTAT, 2010). The EIP focuses on new firm creation and enterprise failure as the main indicators of entrepreneurship. The EIP concedes that the records on new businesses and failures are not comparable across countries: registration and de-registration are based on different procedures in a variety of national organisations; in many countries, the registration process does not include certain legal forms of enterprise, such as sole proprietors or firms below a certain level of turnover or employment; in some cases, the concept of new firms can include mergers, changes of ownership, changes of name or changes in the type of activity they are engaged in; new enterprise creations can refer to establishments (including branch plants and offices), rather than enterprises; and business registers can include inactive firms. What the EIP does not concede is that most new firms are not entrepreneurial in the Schumpeterian meaning of the concept.

This is in spite of a considerable amount of OECD intellectual endeavour going into an analysis that differentiates entrepreneurial activity from 'ordinary' business activity, which points to the importance of enterprising human activity that creates value through innovation. Ahmad and Seymour (2008, 14) conclude that:

> Entrepreneurs are those persons (business owners) who seek to generate value, through the creation or expansion of economic activity, by identifying and exploiting new products, processes or markets.[3]

In practice, the EIP measurement of entrepreneurship focuses on new firm formation. It argues that encouraging the birth of new enterprises is a key element of policies promoting entrepreneurship, but this can only be true if new companies are 'entrepreneurial'. If they are not, promoting the formation of new firms will not promote entrepreneurial activity.

We cannot know a priori if a self-employed individual, setting up a small firm for the first time, is creative and innovative – aspiring to grow their business capital and create employment through new products, processes or the creation of new markets. Some will fit this profile, others will not. The balance between innovating expansionists and survivalists is an empirical matter in any economic context at a particular point in time.

One might assume that the individual who sets up a new firm with an innovative product or process might be worth encouraging but, astonishingly, the EIP entrepreneurship statistics exclude the self-employed individuals (that is, business owners who do not employ any workers). Self-employed entrepreneurs and survivalists are both excluded from the measurement and discussion of entrepreneurship. In an attempt to harmonise non-comparable data internationally and in recognition of the difficulty in obtaining data for self-employed, the EIP only collects data on 'employer enterprises', those with at least one employee. The main reason that self-employed individuals, who are 'typically very numerous' are excluded is that (OECD-EUROSTAT, 2010, 6):

> The employer enterprises are economically more relevant than non-employer firms and more closely related to the notion of entrepreneurship as a driver of job creation and innovation.

No evidence is offered to support this. It is not clear why individuals who start up their businesses alone and who would qualify as 'entrepreneurs' under the OECD's own adopted definition should be excluded, other than as another administrative convenience. In the EIP, as we saw earlier in the case of the statisticians of the ILO, 'comparability is paramount' (OECD-EUROSTAT, 2010, 6) and this drive to standardise data for international comparison has led to the complex notion of entrepreneurship to be reduced to counting a limited number of start-ups and failures.

It is also claimed that the main determinants of entrepreneurship are a country's regulatory framework, market conditions and access to finance and that this is identified in the conceptual framework of the EIP. However, no one has been asking the micro-firm owners whether any of this is true.

The confusion of entrepreneurship with the ownership of new small businesses has been transformed into an unstated assumption of neoliberal research on small enterprises. Levels of entrepreneurship are measured by start-ups, all people who start businesses are referred to as entrepreneurs and, in spite of the EIP's inability to gather coherent information about small firms, the self-employed 'entrepreneur' is hailed as hero. Hence, in the work of de Soto and others, even street traders and black marketeers who are surviving on the margins of society are celebrated as entrepreneurs (de Soto, 1989). However, as the reality of their marginalised struggle for subsistence is taken into account, new categories of entrepreneurs have been appearing.

Out of the concept of 'informal entrepreneurs' (Maloney, 2004) we have new concepts emerging such as 'survival' entrepreneurs (Bennett, 2010), 'penniless' entrepreneurs (Banerjee and Duffo, 2007), 'replicative' entrepreneurs (as distinct from innovative) (Baumol et al., 2007), and 'necessity' entrepreneurs (compared with opportunity entrepreneurs) (Naudé, 2011). A critical approach to these concepts would point out that these 'non-entrepreneurial entrepreneurs' exist alongside clear evidence that there are many new 'start-up entrepreneurs' that do not contribute to economic growth (Wong et al., 2005). In the face of all the evidence that most start-ups and the majority of the self-employed in developed and developing countries are not entrepreneurs in the classic meaning of the word, neoliberal theory and practice continues to force them into this category and rejoice in their *assumed* expansionist plans for the future. The widespread misconception in the development economics literature that all small businesses want to become big businesses leads to inappropriate policy outcomes, such as entrepreneurship training and a variety of other small firm support programmes, which mainly benefit university-educated business consultants.

We will see that, in Ecuador, few want to expand their businesses and even fewer want to incur debt to do so. The idea that improving access to finance will help is also erroneous. It might help a handful of small firm owners, but not in the way the theory predicts. We will see that, rather than use loans to expand the business, the most common use of funds would be for non-expansionist current expenditure, such as the purchase of raw materials.

The neoliberal ideology of the self-employed individual as expansionist entrepreneur is now culturally embedded, to the extent that people will proclaim that they want to expand into large-scale enterprises, even if this is logically impossible. The theory has become a powerful ideology that finds its expression in the unrealistic aspirations of some small business owners. While few want to expand their businesses in the way that the ideology suggests, there are some who commit to the expansionist belief system in a way that cannot be realised. It is expressed by business owners who want to expand their businesses into larger industries in sectors of the economy where this would not be possible. This is observable in the small number of hairdressers who say they want to expand their beauty salons into 'small industries' in this sector of the economy. Note, not franchised salons, but 'small industries' in a sector that does not have such a category.

In empirical research, in addition to owners of start-ups, the long-term self-employed and the ageing owners of existing small businesses are often taken to be proxies for entrepreneurs. The characteristics of entrepreneurs are assumed to be applicable to all small business owners. Small firm data on the size and growth of self-employment are often used to examine theories of entrepreneurship and there is a resistance to any evidence that questions the ideology. If these groups show no inclination for innovation and growth, there is no justification for either the assumed relationship between size/newness and innovation/growth, or indeed for most policy interventions to promote small firm growth. However, when the research of Hurst and Pugsley (2011) demonstrated that that self-employment was not synonymous with entrepreneurship, critics writing in the same volume of the *Brookings Papers on Economic Activity*, argued that the methodology was faulty, the authors should have asked a different question, or the respondents were either lying or deluded. It was argued that some will have given non-pecuniary reasons for setting up when, in reality, they did it for financial reasons. Contributors to the general discussion of their paper mainly searched their own theory for reasons why Hurst and Pugsley could not be right.

Not everyone agreed with these critics. Schoar (2011, 137) pointed to the misconception that all small businesses want to become big businesses and Wolfers (2011, 140) objected to the 'beatification' of non-entrepreneurial small businesses: 'These businesses create few jobs and often mistreat those that they do employ; they are exempt from or can circumvent workplace safety, family leave, minimum wage and anti-discrimination laws and regulations' – and many of them cheat on their taxes.

One issue for the Hurst and Pugsley research is that it offers a snapshot at one point in time, which can be rejected as an outlier by believers in the ideology. It may be the case that an attachment to growing one's business changes over time, responding to business cycles in the wider economy. When the economy is growing, the owners of small firms may feel more confident about pursuing the growth of their own firms, than in periods of economic stagnation or decline. To investigate this possibility requires historical research that addresses this issue.

Historical-structural analysis

The accumulation of individual and family wealth does not proceed in an even manner. It advances through the resolution of contradictions that arise with the development of capitalism and which have their social expression in class antagonisms – between factions of the ruling class, between capitalists and petty producers, between master-artisans and wage labourers, between capitalists and wage labourers, and between producers and merchants. The control of the state is a central ingredient in the working out of such conflicts. These conflicts and their resolution make the logic of accumulation dialectical rather than formal. There is no deductively inevitable outcome, for it is a logic which can be influenced by social action. It is with such action in mind that empirical investigation within a historical-structural framework takes place.

In this book, artisan production is seen in a global context, which is characterised by a particular structure of production in a process of change, and a corresponding power structure which allows certain social groups and classes to impose their interests and values on society. Within this historical and structural context, the changes that occur in the situation of artisans are consequences of changes that take place at the level of the wider structures of production and domination. The development of small-scale production is a part of the social process of change in a society and it cannot be studied separately from this process. There is a social structure of power, in which classes and social groups try to impose their economic projects and the course of development of that society on other groups and social classes.

As we will see, however, the lack of development of micro-production cannot be explained by reference to *direct* relations of subordination whereby surplus is extracted through direct interaction with capitalist enterprises (Chapters 6 and 7). On the other hand, later chapters are dedicated to explaining how different classes and fractions of classes have different capacities to wield power and to influence the state, and thus to obstruct or promote changes in the structure of production. Artisans have little capacity for promoting or protecting their interests and even policy changes that are apparently in their favour are, in reality, detrimental to the vast majority of them.

Within this general orientation, the concept of the structure of production at the macro level refers not only to the structure or distribution of employment in the rural and urban areas but fundamentally to the different social relations or production and exchange. Changes in the social relations of production occur both within and around micro-production. In investigating the structure of production, I am looking to the interdependence of changing internal and external structural conditions which relate to the development or decline of artisan activity in Ecuador.

In order to carry out this type of analysis, one needs to coordinate macro and micro investigation. First, at the macro level, existing secondary data are used to analyse the spatial distribution of petty production and trading, their relationship to agriculture and to large-scale industry, and how this configuration responds to changing patterns of production on a world scale. This type of analysis is used to investigate aspects of the changing peripheral social formation and pattern of capital accumulation. Unfortunately, available secondary data are not organised in a manner which is perfectly consistent with the needs of our type of analysis. The census and survey information of national and international organisations are not gathered within this theoretical framework. Nonetheless, they do provide valid insights for the type of investigation that is being pursued and they throw up questions and pointers for further micro investigation.

The second level of research is concerned with the internal relations of production of households and enterprises and the structural relationships of the latter with other elements of the productive system. It is against this background that the core of the historical empirical research is carried out on the characteristics of labour force in microenterprises, their insertion in the overall structure of production, their ideology and aspirations, and their capacity for effective organisations with a view to improving their situation.

This, perhaps rather crude, separation of micro and macro does not mean that the two types of methodology are to remain separate and to lead to poorly coordinated analyses. Rather, they should feed into each other and fuse together through the historical investigation of state policy formulation and such political manoeuvring of different social classes as is relevant for the development of the groups under investigation. The changing structure of households, families and small firms are located in the development of the macro economy and society. Through such an overall methodology we should be able to discover the fundamental forces that act on the conditions of these groups and to assess the possibilities for development or decline in the future.

Artisan social relations of production and distribution

There is a need for a reconsideration of the concepts being used in the analysis of artisans, entrepreneurs and the informal sector. First, there are differences between capitalist and non-capitalist forms of production. A distinguishing characteristic of non-capitalist forms of production is that in the owner of the means of production is *also a producer*. The artisan master in a workshop employing up to six people, for example, is normally an owner, a manager and a manual worker. He or she is not alienated from the tools that are essential for the practice of the craft. This is true whether wage labour is employed or not. In a capitalist enterprise, the owner of the means of production will be concerned only with the organisation of the workforce and other administrative tasks, and will *not* be directly involved in the transformation of raw materials into new commodities through the use of tools and machinery.

In small-scale capitalist commodity production, production is for the market with a view to accumulating wealth rather than merely replacing the fund of labour. Wage relations are developed and the owners of the means of production appropriate the surplus created. This is effectively a workshop that is run by an owner-manager who is no longer a manual worker. There may be occasions when this is an end-point of a transition from artisan to capitalist entrepreneur, but it seldom works out this way. As markets expand and capitalism develops in any branch of activity, it is much more likely that capital investment from above will displace the artisan. Middle-class and upper-class wealth already accumulated in other sectors of the economy, usually in the professions, commerce or landownership, will be invested in new technology in firms that fit the size criteria for artisans. This allows non-skilled owners to lay claim to the benefits that have been conceded to artisans, which, during the period of the research in Ecuador for example, have included lower wage levels and freedom from regulations around workers' well-being, pensions and other health and welfare benefits.

As we will see when we turn to the empirical evidence in Chapter 3, *within* non-capitalist production there are a variety of social relations of production, including people working alone and others employing different combinations of wage labour, apprentices, and paid and unpaid family labour. Some are household enterprises and some are not. A few are entrepreneurs in the Schumpeterian sense. Very few are part of a manufacturing supply chain for capitalist manufacturers, whereby artisan outputs become part of the final product of the larger producer. None of them are the sweatshops that exist in places such as Bangladesh to supply footwear and clothing for global brands in Europe and the United States.

Historically, the distinction between traditional artisans and other producers of commodities would have been made at the level of the relations of distribution: the artisan producing for clients and the others producing for the open market. This distinction was important, but nowadays the majority of small manufacturers produce for both bespoke clients *and* off-the-shelf customers. In addition, there are firms that provide ancillary goods and services for other enterprises and an ever-increasing number that offer skilled labour for the repair of goods that have been produced by firms in the capitalist sector. All of these non-capitalist forms of production are referred to as artisans in this research and we will return to discuss this further in the Ecuadorean context in the next chapter.

Informal sector analysis adopted the problems of stable employment and income as the most compelling aspects of reality in the developing world, but failed to elaborate a coherent framework for the explanation of the current situation or for the formulation of policy relevant to the solution of the problems. The 'entrepreneurship' perspective confounded all small firms with entrepreneurs. The petty commodity approach, as a theoretical response to the weaknesses of informal sector analyses, tended to emphasise one aspect of small-scale economic activity when there had been a need for a methodology involving the dialectical interaction between empirical evidence and the theory of capitalist accumulation. The question arises as to whether our basic conceptual apparatus will fare any better than those we have criticised. The answer to this question should become clearer as we progress through the book, using and building on the basic concepts in the process of investigating the reality of the development of artisan production in Ecuador.

What we are proposing is the retention of a first order distinction between capitalist and non-capitalist forms of production and an investigation of the social relations of production and exchange in non-capitalist enterprises. We will see in Chapters 3 and 8 that these relations change over time in response to the changes in the wider economy. The artisan sector and firms within it have been restructured over time. Our formulation of non-capitalist or artisanal forms of production should be understood as an emphasis on the core critical aspects of these forms of production. These aspects will be highlighted in order to analyse concrete reality and extend our knowledge about the creation and continuation of poverty in the context of peripheral capitalist accumulation. However, it has to be acknowledged that empirical reality changes over time. Changes took place through the course of this research that were impossible to anticipate. In particular, I had underestimated the impact of neoliberalism, globalisation, competition from cheap imports from Asia and the way in which artisans would respond to their changing environment.

Earlier authors incorporated the notions of process and change in their definitions of artisans, petty commodity producers and small-scale capitalist producers such that analyses were offered in terms of the ongoing development of capitalism. To relate these definitions so closely to an evolutionary scheme, however, was to pre-judge the reality of the process of capitalist development in the periphery. Rather, in this research our concern has been to identify concepts that can be used to analyse the ongoing processes. This requires consistency in the use of key concepts, which we will return to in the next chapter.

In order to understand the production and reproduction of wealth and poverty we must begin with the empirical investigation of the historically specific process of accumulation in distinct peripheral economic formations, which themselves must be seen in the context of global capitalism. In the next chapter, we will also look at how the development of artisans in Ecuador over 40 years has been influenced by four distinct phases of global capitalist development.

Notes

1   The neoliberal narrative has been unable to decide whether the sector is unregulated or over-regulated (Maloney, 2004; de Soto, 1989).

2   The GEM uses the World Economic Forum's development phases of factor-driven economies (those dominated by subsistence agriculture and extraction businesses), efficiency-driven economies (more competitive with more efficient production) and innovative economies (more knowledge intensive and an expanding service sector). These are taken as proxies for least developed, developing and advanced economies.

3   They also argue that 'entrepreneurial activity is the enterprising human action in pursuit of the generation of value, through the creation or expansion of economic activity, by identifying and exploiting new products, processes or markets. Entrepreneurship is the phenomenon associated with entrepreneurial activity.'

3   Artisans in Quito, 1975–2015

Antecedents

The history of artisans in Quito begins in colonial times, when they were brought to the Americas by the Conquistadores. They were lower-class Spaniards, and later mestizos, who throughout the colonial period provided goods and services for local elites. There were blacksmiths, locksmiths, gunsmiths, sculptors, swordsmiths and saddle-makers, most of whose skills have either disappeared or changed substantially. There were also tailors, shoemakers, carpenters, hat-makers, barbers, stonemasons, silversmiths and slaughtermen, whose activities persisted in Quito through to 1975, when the research for the book began.

In colonial Quito, their lives were dominated by the ruling classes and their activities were controlled by the colonial state. Artisans were not free to charge the market rate for their products and services. Their activities were tightly controlled by upper-class Spaniards through the *Cabildo* (Council) of Quito, which was composed of landowners, mine owners and the owners of *obrajes*, the colonial textile factories that depended on the forced labour of the indigenous population. There was an extreme shortage of all types of skilled labour and these powerful groups benefited from the control they exercised over artisan activities. It was the *Cabildo's* responsibility to hold down artisan prices (Hurtado and Herudek, 1974; Efren Reyes, 1974) and to ensure that they did not follow the dictates of market forces, which would have been detrimental to the economic interests of the elites of the period.

The organisation of the artisans, the operation of their workshops and the training of apprentices were also controlled by the *Cabildo*. It was this ruling authority that imposed a system of guilds in Quito (Robalino, 1977, 34–41). The function of these guilds, which were basically organs of the state and the forerunners of the modern artisan federations, was not to represent the interests of the artisans, but to control them. The *Cabildo* appointed the leaders of each guild and it was the function of these leaders to ensure that the work was fairly distributed, that quality was maintained and that the prices fixed by the *Cabildo* were adhered to (Hurtado and Herudek, 1974, 59–60; Robalino, 1977, 34). The ideological justification for this was the belief that artisans were committed to providing a service, not making a profit. While the artisans indirectly contributed to the accumulation of wealth by those who controlled the prices of their products, their work was not deemed to be for their own profit and accumulation.

It did not take long for the elites to impose their interests on the artisans, nor for the artisans to respond. Rate-fixing is recorded as early as 1537, three years after the arrival of the Spaniards. These rates, however, clearly did not correspond to the needs or desires of the artisans and they were not slow to make this clear. The first strike in Ecuador dates as far back as 1550, when tailors presented a list of grievances to the *Cabildo* and then withdrew their labour (Hurtado, 1977, 59; Robalino, 1977, 34–5). The power of the elite over the lives of artisans, however, extended beyond their workshops and prices. The *Cabildo* was also responsible for ensuring that the artisan did not leave the City without permission (Robalino, 1977, 39).

After Independence from Spain in 1822, the *Cabildo* ceased to control artisans' prices and they moved towards a free market situation, producing for a range of local clients. Their small-scale client-oriented form of production, however, languished in competition with the cheaper production of the British industrial revolution. Nevertheless, they did not disappear, surviving alongside the development of small-scale capitalist manufacturing that was providing raw materials for artisans and other goods for the local market. The basic non-food needs of the urban population continued to be met by artisan production of subsistence goods, and they also produced a range of other goods and services for local consumption, including art and luxury items such as jewellery.

In the second half of the nineteenth century, artisans began to organise in mutual benefit associations to protect their interests (Robalino, 1977, 70). At the same time, wage labour was emerging as a social force. The fact that capitalist enterprises were increasingly manufacturing the raw materials for artisan production, whilst the production of finished consumer goods was almost wholly carried out by artisans, meant that wage rises in factories increased the input costs for artisans and prices for their clients. This bifurcation of the manufacturing process created both common interests and tensions between the wage labourers and self-employed artisans (Middleton, 1982).

In the twentieth century, stagnation in factory production existed alongside the expansion of small-scale production. The latter offered one of the few ways of providing for subsistence needs in Ecuador, as the country moved from one period of economic crisis to another. This type of production, however, was not principally client-oriented. Rather than artisanal production in the traditional sense, there was the development of small-scale capitalist production for an open market in which customers bought ready-made goods off-the-shelf, in place of made-to-measure.

Another important aspect of the history of artisans in Quito is the impact of migration from the rural areas. In 1975, 60% of artisans were Quiteños (Middleton, 1979) but many of the older artisan in the capital had escaped from the cruelty of the socio-economic conditions in the rural areas in the 1930s. Debt peonage, enforceable by imprisonment and passed down from father to child during the colonial period, continued to exist through the 1930s and it persisted in pockets of the Sierra in less extreme forms into the second half of the twentieth century. For many of the small workshop owners in Quito, learning an artisan trade was the only way out of the rural poverty of their parents' generation.

Although artisan activity was almost exclusively an urban phenomenon in colonial times, since then artisans have also been involved in a form of rural manufacturing. Attached to systems of agrarian production that were dominated by the hacienda and plantation owners of the Sierra and the Coast, they were linked to urban markets through intermediaries (Martínez, 1994). Nevertheless, the artisans were an important urban political force during democratic interludes between military rule; and their ties to the church were used by conservative forces to confront the emerging power of organised wage labour in capitalist units of production. In 1953, President Velasco Ibarra and the Conservative party introduced the Law for the Defence of the Artisans (Defence Law), which offered artisan masters a privileged position with respect to the employment of labour, compared to the employment and social security laws that applied to capitalist industries (Gobierno del Ecuador, 1953).

By the early 1960s, artisan production dominated the manufacturing sector in Ecuador but by then it was a mainly rural activity. In 1961, it was estimated that artisans constituted 89% of the manufacturing labour force (JUNAPLA, 1962; Stanford Research Institute, 1963) and many of them were part-time women supplementing peasant household incomes. Less than a third were full-time artisans in the urban areas. Nevertheless, these urban workers represented more than three times the total number of factory workers in the entire country. By 1975, there were still twice as many artisans in manufacturing than there were factory workers (Middleton, 1979).

In the early 1970s, however, the main beneficiaries of the new oil wealth were the urban middle classes, who created a new market for manufactured goods, initially from the artisans but later, as the demand expanded, from a growing capitalist system of production. The new middle classes threatened the stranglehold on power of the traditional elites, but they were not capable of tackling the entrenched issues of the distribution of power and wealth in Ecuador.

The fact of the highly unequal distribution of income in Ecuador before 1972 is well documented (Abad, 1970; Moncada, 1973; Galarza, 1974; Cueva, 1974). A comparative study of 66 countries demonstrated that, in 1970, Ecuador had the highest concentration of income in the countries studied (Moncada, 1973). The new oil dividend promised Ecuador 'a privileged position among the developing countries, in terms of opportunities for economic development and social progress' (IBRD, 1972, 11). Amid a clamour for the benefits of the oil revenues among the different sectors of the Ecuadorean upper class (Galarza, 1974), the Revolutionary Nationalist Military Government of Rodriguez Lara came to power in February 1972 and promised to carry out the reforms that would lead to a more equitable development. It considered itself to be 'Revolutionary', 'Nationalist', 'Social Humanist' and 'Disciplined' and it thought that it was absolutely necessary 'to act quickly and energetically against the socially and economically privileged groups'

(JNP, 1972b, 5). It presented itself as 'anti-feudal' and 'anti-oligarchic' and within its proposals the distribution of income was a central objective. A fundamental aim was to end the 'irresponsible management of matters of state' by the feuding sectors of the dominant classes in the Coast and Sierra.

To bring about a redistribution of power and wealth, the Government committed to achieving 'the total transformation of the system' and a principal objective of the fiscal policy was to be 'a more just and humane distribution of national income' (JNP, 1972b, 12). The Government also proposed a series of restrictions on multinational corporations, designed to stimulate national savings and investment. The fundamental orientation was improving the conditions of the 'marginal' groups, including artisans (JNP, 1972a). While the IBRD noted that it would probably take *some time* before the benefits of the oil revenues reached the majority of the population, the National Planning Board recognised that the oil bonanza would *not* lead automatically to improvements in the living standards of the poor. A major issue was the distribution of power in society.

Development required profound structural transformations, destined to modify the traditional operation of the economy and society. In this regard, there were similarities between the proposals of the Revolutionary Nationalist Government and those of the ILO and the World Employment Conference of 1976 (WEC). It is not important that the ILO should conceptualise the poorer sectors of the population as the 'informal sector' and that the Ecuadorean Government should refer to them as the 'marginal masses'. Quito's artisans fitted both categories and the Ecuadorian government was four years ahead of the World Employment Conference, when the ILO's thinking became more clearly defined.[1]

The *Plan* was proclaimed a success in every area with the exception of land reform and regionalisation. That is, the Government was least successful where they had to deal with the entrenched interests of the landed oligarchy and promote the economic development of the rural areas on the Sierra and the Coast. In January 1976, before the ILO's WEC was underway, Rodriguez Lara was deposed by a military coup, led by a triumvirate of the most senior officers in the armed forces and supported by the CIA and warring factions of the coastal and sierran oligarchy. The traditional power of the ruling class was re-asserted, neoclassical economics re-emerged stronger than ever, and the powerless marginal mass, including the artisans, were excluded from the feast of oil that followed.

In the 1970s, an economy that was dominated by the export of bananas was transformed into an oil-producing economy, whose poorly developed manufacturing sector entered a phase of rapid industrialisation. A new market for consumer goods was created which led to increased investment in the modern sector of the economy and, paradoxically, as we will see, a decline in the demand for artisan production of subsistence goods (Middleton, 1989). In this developing context, the artisans' relationship to the wider economy was undergoing a transformation and there were changes in the internal structures of their workshops.

Artisans in the structure of production and exchange

It was argued in the previous chapter that capitalist and non-capitalist forms of production can be distinguished on the basis of the owners' relationship to the means of production: in non-capitalist firms the owners of the means of production are also manual workers. That is, the owner of the means of production also participates in the process of conversion of raw materials into other goods. The artisans in this study are firmly located in the sphere of non-capitalist forms of production. They are also the owners of firms that employ up to seven people, including the owners. As the size of the workshop approaches this maximum size, the artisans cease to be the operators of tools and they have to dedicate themselves to the management of the workshop: that is, the workshops become capitalist in form. As we will see, even in these small workshops, the social relations of production and exchange evolve over time, this evolution is uneven, and it has been conditioned by national and global forces aligned to the neoliberal project.

The traditional classification of artisans is based on the raw materials with which they work – textiles, leather, wood, ordinary metals, and so on. Examples of the types of activities that correspond to these materials can be seen in Table 3.1. In each of the classifications by material, there tends to be a dominant type of activity. For example, the majority of artisans who work with textiles are tailors, those who work with leather are mainly shoemakers, and so on. When the people of Quito refer to the artisans, they tend to refer to the skills that the artisans possess, as tailors and shoemakers, rather than the formal classification according to the materials they use.

Our theoretically based defining characteristics have never been used by policymakers in Ecuador. In order to link the original field research to government policies for artisans in Quito, it was necessary to make them identifiable in a way that was consistent with both their heterogeneity and how they have been defined in law. As was the case for the international definitions of the informal sector, however, official classifications of artisans in Ecuador have been fraught with inconsistencies and contradictions. Over 60 years, they have been defined and redefined into confusion and, as we will see in Chapter 10, at any one time the government can be using multiple definitions, depending on the ministry involved.

In this study, we use the categories in Table 3.1, assigning the artisans to classifications 1 to 8, but we follow the popular narrative, referring to tailors, shoemakers, carpenters, etc. This means, therefore, that we are using a human being, identified by his or her skill set, instead of the formal physical categories of the raw materials that are used. However, the study is also based on surveys of artisan owners of workshops – and defining an artisan 'workshop' is also problematical. It is a contested concept about which there is widespread disagreement.

Following the definition of an artisan used in the Law for the Defence of the Artisan between 1953 and 1974 (Gobierno del Ecuador, 1953), artisan workshops in this study have been consistently defined as small-scale businesses

Table 3.1 Classification of artisan activities

International classification	Type of activity
1. Textiles and Textile Products	Tailors, dressmakers, weavers of wool rugs and straw hats, and knitters
2. Leather and Leather Products	Shoemakers and those who make other leather products, such as briefcases, wallets, suitcases and saddles
3. Wood Products and Furniture*	Carpenters, cabinet and furniture makers.
4. Ordinary Metals	Car mechanics, radio and TV repairers, electricians, general mechanics, locksmiths, tinsmiths, plumbers and ironworkers.
5. Stone and Marble	Painters, signwriters, masons, glaziers, ornament makers, stone cutters.
6. Fine Metals	Jewellers, watch repairers, makers of gold and silver ornaments.
7. Printing	Printers, bookbinders, photographers
8. Others	Bakers, food processors,** barbers, hairdressers, tyre repairers, upholsterers, mattress makers, etc.

* The sample includes producers of doors and window frames but not installers of these products.
** Excluding the owners of bars and restaurants.
Sources: Stanford Research Institute, 1963, 12; Middleton, 1979, xiii.

that employed up to seven workers, including apprentices and the owner. This definition sits uneasily in two different conceptual contexts: an academic context and an evolving statutory context. Both academic and legal definitions are characterised by conceptual evolution over time, which has led to confusion and uncertainty.

As we saw above, at the beginning of the study Quito's artisans were theoretically located within the 'informal sector' (ILO, 1972; Hart, 1973). As theoretical fashions changed, they could have become disguised wage labourers, petty producers, petty commodity producers, small firms, micro-firms, small-scale producers, entrepreneurs, micro-entrepreneurs, the owners of family firms and precarious workers. As the 'informal sector' became the 'informal economy', informality expanded to include capitalist enterprises that ignored labour legislation and evaded taxes, groups involved in illicit drugs and arms trade, as well as the unlawful activities of the international finance system that benefited from criminal, corrupt and immoral enterprise (Perry et al., 2007; ILO and WIEGO, 2013; ILO, 2015). Throughout, the artisans in Quito remained resolutely informal in the original meaning of the concept and, as the study progressed, the definition that was used did not change: they are non-capitalist form of production, employing up to seven people including the owner.[2]

In our study, the focus on workshops where up to seven workers are employed is close to the Ecuadorian traditional definition of an artisan workshop. As legal definitions have changed, ours has been consistent. However, the type of work that is done by artisans has changed dramatically over 40 years, as has the balance of genders and the type of labour that is employed. The structure of activities has changed, the social relations of production have evolved, and national non-capitalist production is gradually being replaced by the repair of goods produced by international capitalist firms. The basic structure of artisan production and how it has changed over time was captured in the censuses that were carried out in each year of the fieldwork. The changing internal relations of production and the evolving relationships of the artisans to the wider socio-economic system emerged through the surveys and other interviews that were carried out in each of these census/survey years.

The changing structure of artisan production

Throughout the changes that have been taking place in the social, economic and political environment, artisan activity in Ecuador has declined and has been restructured, but many have adapted and survived. In Quito as a whole, as the city has expanded geographically, there is little doubt that the total number of artisans will have increased along with the growth in population since 1975. New markets will have been created by the increase in consumers. The type of artisan activity in the city, however, has changed considerably (Figure A.3.1). Our evidence suggests that the number of artisans per head of the population will have declined, but more significantly, the restructuring of the artisans is based on a dramatic decline of some activities as well as the growth of others. The ways in which artisanal activity has changed can be seen in the following tables and figures.

In Table 3.2, we can see that in the study area:

1. Tailors and shoemakers accounted for almost half of all artisans in 1975. By 2015, they were less than a quarter.
2. The number of tailors/dressmakers fell by almost 60%.
3. The number of shoemakers fell from over 500 in 1975 to less than 70 in 2015, a decline of 86%.
4. The number of carpenters also declined, in this case by 72%,

These three types of artisans were the main producers of manufactured consumer goods in Quito in 1975. They accounted for almost 60% of all artisans and they provided the majority of *Quiteños* with their principal means of non-food subsistence. They have declined dramatically in the study area over the 40 years, in spite of the growth of the Ecuadorian economy. Their apparently unassailable position as the prime producers of Quito's means of subsistence in 1975 is now history.

The only growth areas have been amongst mechanics and 'others', both of which can also be classified as 'service' activities. This is often taken as evidence of a transition from a manufacturing to a service economy, but to say no more

Table 3.2 The changing structure of artisan activities, 1975–2015

	1975		1982		1995		2005		2015		% Change 1975–2015
	No.	%	No.	%	No.	%	No.	%	No.	%	
Tailors	594	25.7	501	21.1	293	16.4	216	16.6	241	17.7	-59.4
Shoemakers	504	21.8	427	17.9	235	13.2	118	9.1	69	5.1	-86.3
Carpenters	272	11.8	218	9.2	153	8.6	83	6.4	75	5.5	-72.4
SUBTOTAL MoS	1370	59.4	1146	48.2	681	38.1	417	32.1	385	28.2	-71.9
Mechanics	341	14.8	377	15.8	316	17.7	286	22.0	381	27.9	11.7
Painters/Masons	90	3.9	131	5.5	93	5.2	70	5.4	78	5.7	-13.3
Printers	79	3.4	137	5.8	132	7.4	86	6.6	74	5.4	-6.3
SUBTOTAL MoP	510	22.1	645	27.1	541	30.3	442	34.0	533	39.0	4.5
Jewellers	136	5.9	201	8.4	133	7.4	104	8.0	108	7.9	-20.6
Others	292	12.7	388	16.3	431	24.1	338	26.0	339	24.8	16.1
SUBTOTAL Luxury & Others	428	18.5	589	24.7	564	31.6	442	34.0	447	32.7	4.4
TOTAL	2308	100	2380	100.0	1786	100.0	1301	100.0	1365	100.0	-40.9

Source: The Census of Artisans in the study area.

than this would be to hide important features of the transition and disguise the complexity of the change. The growth in the number of workers who work with 'ordinary metals' includes not only repair mechanics in general but also car mechanics, radio and TV repairers, computer repair engineers, plumbers and electricians. These 'service' firms are of course different from the personal services that fall into the 'other' category, such as barbers and hairdressers, for they are mainly repair services that depend on the built-in obsolescence of the products of the large-scale capitalist sectors of the economy, both in manufacturing and construction.

The changes in the fortunes of different artisans in Quito has led to a substantial restructuring of the artisan workshops in the city (Figures A.3.2 and A.3.3). As the numbers of shoemakers, tailors and carpenters have fallen, mechanics have emerged as the largest sector of the artisans. As a proportion of all artisans, they have almost doubled, as has the category of 'others', mainly because of the growing demand for the services of hairdressers and beauty salons.[3]

The percentage decline and rise in different artisan activities can be seen in Figure 3.1. The large fall in the number of workshops of tailors, shoemakers and carpenters and a smaller decline amongst painters, printers and jewellers is slightly offset by mechanics and others. These changes, however, have not been uniform over time. For most of the activities, expansion and contraction have moved in different directions at different times over the past 40 years (Table 3.2). The overall changes that have taken place between 1975 and 2015 are the result of the changing balance of the internal component parts of the structure of artisan

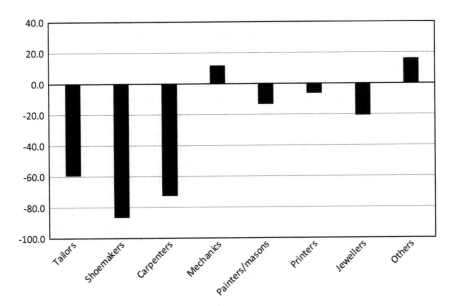

Figure 3.1 Percentage change in artisan activities, 1975–2015

activity as the Ecuadorean economy has grown, stagnated or declined. Comparing the situation in 1975 with that in 2015 provides an oversimplified account of changes that can be observed between two points in time. The comparison disguises an astonishing underlying complexity involving the impact of social and economic forces on the artisans. Different artisan activities have responded to macro-economic changes in different ways and they can be likened to human beings swimming in a sea of strong tides and undercurrents. Nevertheless, the forces created by the two phases of neoliberalism stand out.

The moving components of the structure of artisan production

There are two levels of detail in Table 3.2. The first refers to the different types of artisan activities as discussed above (tailors, shoemakers, etc.). The second level combines these activities into the three different types of artisans referred to in the previous chapter: producers of the means of subsistence (MoS), producers of the means of production (MoP) and the producers of luxury goods and others. The first of these, the group of traditional producers of the means of subsistence (MoS), brings together tailors, shoemakers and carpenters. This group has produced the clothes, footwear and the basic furniture for the homes of the population of Quito from colonial times through to the middle-to-end of the twentieth century. All three activities in this group are oriented towards individuals as clients, they have been in serious decline and at the same time, as we will see later in this chapter, they have increasingly become involved in repair of consumer goods, rather than their manufacture.

The second group is composed of artisans whose labour was traditionally incorporated into industrial and commercial processes in Quito. In 1975, as mechanical workshops, signwriters, stonemasons and printers, they provided labour and produced goods that local capitalist industry and commerce could incorporate into their own production and distribution processes. Historically, they produced part of the means of production (MoP) for larger enterprises, but now they are more likely to repair the cars, televisions, computers, boilers, washing machines and cookers that increase in volume in a growing economy. They are technology-dependent and the skills that are required have changed as the technology involved in the manufacture of the original products has become more complex. For these occupations there is a constant need for skills upgrading. As new knowledge is incorporated into the products during manufacture, additional knowledge is similarly needed by artisans if they are to reconvert damaged and worthless goods into products that continue to function and be valued. Just as in traditional manufacturing, the repair artisan adds value through his or her labour. The demand for that labour will depend on the cost of the labour compared to the cost of a new product. In this regard, as we will see in Chapter 13, artisans across the city are deeply concerned about the impact of globalisation and the dumping of Chinese and other products. Their numbers have been sustained over time. However, they too are now more oriented towards individual clients than previously.

The third composite category is composed of jewellers, who are involved in the production or repair of luxury goods, along with the category of 'others'. In 1975, the others included the traditional activity of barbers, whose artisan roots go back to colonial times, and a handful of ladies' hairdressers. However, this group has been increasingly dominated by these providers of personal services, particularly in hairdressers' shops and beauty salons.

At both levels of analysis, whether using individual types of artisan activity or with reference to the grouped activities, the overall changes between 1975 and 2015 are the result of differing fortunes for different types of artisan activity. The total number of artisans in the area rose slightly between 1975 and 1982, during the years of the first oil boom. It then crashed through the neoliberal years of austerity, financial collapse and dollarization to 2005. Between 2005 and 2015 there was renewed vigour in the sector and a slight increase in numbers. This overall picture, however, is arrived at through variations in the fortunes of different types of activity. The decline of shoemakers and carpenters has been consistent, year on year, from 1975 to 2015 (Figure 3.2). The fortunes of tailors was on a similar trajectory until 2005, after which there was a slight upturn which, as we will see in Chapter 10, is at least partly due to government interventionist support, curtailing cheap imports and encouraging the local manufacture of school uniforms.

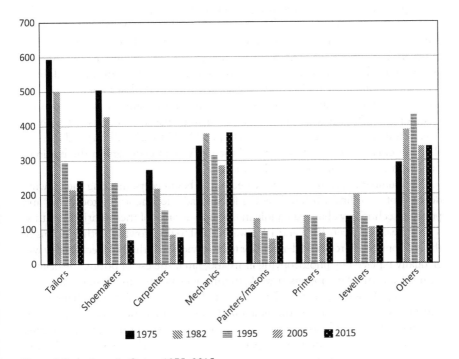

Figure 3.2 Artisans in Quito, 1975–2015

The number of mechanics increased through the oil boom years and then fell away, before recovering between 2005 and 2015. In the early years, the expansion of industry created additional demands for their services; and the growth in the use of private and government cars also stimulated small-scale highly skilled artisans who could not only repair cars when they broke down but also make the parts that were needed to keep them on the road. As car technology changed and sophisticated electronics were introduced, independent mechanics were sidelined by the workshops of the major car dealerships, although they did recover to some extent. More important for this sector was the increasing use of household goods, such as refrigerators, washing machines and water boilers, in the homes of the expanding middle classes, particularly in the years after 2005. This growth of repairable boilers and white line goods created an opportunity for electrical and mechanical repair workshops, whilst the growth in the use of personal computers and peripherals opened up employment opportunities for a college-educated cohort of modern artisan repairers who were able to benefit from the expanding information technology of globalisation.

The human component of the international classification of the workers in 'stone and marble' is mainly composed of painters, signwriters and stonemasons, who also expanded in the boom years. During this period, painters and signwriters in particular benefited from a growth in demand for labour that could be incorporated into the expanding industrial, construction and commercial sectors of the economy. The customers of the workers in 'stone and marble' are diverse – ranging from large-scale enterprises, through small shops and workshops, to the families of the recently dead of the city. The numbers in this artisan sub-group fell away through the years of structural adjustment before a small recovery between 2005 and 2015. The recovery, however, hides changes to the internal structural of the group: signwriters, as artists working with paint on wood, have seen their calligraphy replaced by industrially produced plastics and metal and they have almost disappeared. On the other hand, the number of stonemasons has increased. The growth in the number of stonemasons is consistent with an overall increase in Quito's population (from 600,000 to 2.3 million) and the fact that stonemasons are clustered around the city's main cemetery in the barrio of San Diego, which is included in the study area.

The number of printers also increased in the boom years, meeting the growing demand of local firms, before heading for a steady decline as photocopying and printing technology changed rapidly in the later decades of the twentieth century. The increase between 1975 and 1982 was related to the growth in other sectors of the economy and a renewed demand for their services, but their old technology was gradually replaced by photocopying firms and, later, the use of printers associated with the growth of computers at work, in internet cafes and in urban homes.

The rapid increase in jewellers between 1975 and 1982 was perhaps to be expected in boom years, as the new middle classes had the funds to spend on personal adornment and Quito became an attractive destination for skilled artisans in fine metals from other parts of the country. The subsequent decline through the years of structural adjustment, however, was not only due to a prolonged contraction of personal income but was also related to an increase in personal insecurity in the city and a shift to the purchase of cheaper imported jewellery that was less attractive to thieves. The number of jewellers appears to have stabilised after 2005 but, once again, the internal structure has been changing, this time from jewellery production to watch repair.

The category of 'others', which has come to be dominated by hairdressers and beauty salons, increased rapidly between 1975 and 1995 on the back of a flood of training schemes put on by SECAP[4] and others. This growth was unsustainable as the number of hairdressers' establishments outstripped demand, before thinning out and settling down between 2005 and 2015. Part of the thinning out process was the introduction of cheap and dangerous chemicals from China around the time of the financial crisis and dollazization, which permanently damaged the reputation of some artisans. Those who remain are more careful about their raw materials and about buying cheap tools such as scissors that do not last. Anecdotally, it would appear that there are nevertheless many part-time female hairdressers in Quito who, working for a few hours a week, visit a small number of clients in their own homes.

There were very small increases in the total numbers of artisans in the 1975–1982 and 2005–2015 periods. The first is the period of the oil boom, under the protectionist Revolutionary Nationalist Government of General Rodrigues Lara and the social democrat Jaime Roldos; and the second is the period of rejection of neoliberalism by the populist-socialist administration of Rafael Correa. In contrast, in the years of structural adjustment between 1982 and 1995, when neoliberal government policies were theoretically meant to be operating in support of small business entrepreneurs, there was an across-the-board collapse of artisan workshops. When this was followed by the years of crisis of the neoliberal experiment, exemplified by rampant inflation, the collapse of the financial sector, the dollarization of the economy, and the impact of a rapidly globalising Chinese economy, the situation was even worse. This is confirmed by the average annual rates of growth and decline (Table A.3.1).

There was a decline in the numbers of artisans producing the means of subsistence in the years of the oil boom, as they came into competition with growing industrial and small industry sectors of the economy, but the collapse of this small firm activity was almost wholly during the periods of the neoliberal free market policies. The next question is whether these changes were accompanied by developments in the structure of the internal relations of production, the information for which is contained in the social surveys carried out with a sample of artisans drawn from the census in each year of the study.

Social relations of production

Gender

Artisan workshop owners have always been predominantly male (Table A.3.2). However, the male-female balance has been gradually changing over time and there is a highly significant difference between the situations in 1975 and 2015.[5] Most of this change took place between 1995 and 2005, when the national training agency (SECAP) was extremely active in the training of women as hairdressers.[6] In 1975, there were no female shoemakers, mechanics or printers in the sample and only one carpenter, painter/stonemason or jeweller (Table A.3.3). In 2015, there were no female carpenters, one mechanic, two shoemakers and two jewellers. However, the gender balance amongst garment makers and in printing/photography changed significantly.[7] As tailoring and dressmaking has declined, female garment makers have increased from less than a quarter to more than half of clothes manufacturers. Amongst printers and photographers, whose numbers have held up relatively well, the number of females has gone from zero to 42%. This may be related to changing technology in this sector, as traditional male-dominated printing has been replaced by photocopying. Women in the 'other artisans' category, which includes hairdressers, have grown from 36% to 49% of these micro-firm owners. Overall, however, artisan activity remains male-dominated.

Self-employment

Between 1975 and 2015, there was a slight increase in the proportion of owners who were self-employed and a corresponding fall in the workshops employing additional labour,[8] but this was not statistically significant (Table 3.3). Contrary to what we might expect, in the period of economic growth in particular, and despite a series of government policies and laws aimed at promoting the conversion of the informal artisan sector into 'small enterprises',[9] the proportion

Table 3.3 Artisan self-employment and employers,* 1975–2015

	1975		1982		1995		2005		2015	
	No	%	No	%	No	%	No	%	No.	%
Works alone	78	40.6	131	44.0	145	44.3	138	43.5	120	46.7
With others	114	59.4	167	56.0	182	55.7	179	56.5	137	53.3
Total	192	100	298	100	327	100	317	100	257	100.0

	Chi-sq	DF	p-value
1975–2015	1.6876	4	0.7930
1975–82	0.5309	1	0.4662
1982–95	0.0093	1	0.9233
1995–2005	0.0428	1	0.8361
2005–2015	0.5726	1	0.4492
1975 and 2015	1.6413	1	0.2002

* The self employed work alone and employers work with wage and/or family labour.
Children who are still in education and who work occasionally are not included.

of firms where the owner works alone remained more or less constant over the period. This could be because the size of the firms under study remained the same (up to seven persons) but there was no increase in the proportion of workshops providing employment for more than the owner and, therefore, no indication of the growing importance of employers in these small workshops. Neoliberal policy might have encouraged us to believe that the proportion of employers would have increased, but that was not the case. If anything, the tendency has been in the other direction.[10]

There was also no change in the size-structure of the workshops between 1975 and 2015 (Table A.3.4).[11] However, the change between 1982 and 1995, when the proportion of workshops employing more than two employees declined, is statistically significant (at the 0.05 level). In the period of structural adjustment, when neoliberal economists were promising growth, the size of the workshops fell, never to recover. This decline was also true if we focus on the number of employees, rather than the workshops.

Employees

If we look at the number of workers in each size band, the first thing to note is that *the self-employed account for only around 20% of the total artisan workforce* in any year (Table A.3.5). The growth in micro-firm size was highly significant in the oil boom years, as was the decline through structural adjustment. The average size of the workshops was greatest in 1982, when the proportion of employers was lowest, but by 1995, average firm size had fallen below that of 1975. However, the decline in the size of the workshops continued between 2005 and 2015, when self-employment increased, as did the proportion of workers in two-person workplaces. This was at least partly due to the artisan reaction to the Correa government's attempts to formalise the informal sector, which led to a decline in the employment of wage labour and the growing (sometimes false) employment of paid family labour.

It was argued by the neoliberal proponents of structural adjustment that their policies would provide a macro-economic environment that would be conducive to the modernisation of labour relations and the creation of new wage employment in informal sector enterprises. In Ecuador, the opposite happened. Table 3.4 provides a breakdown of the type of labour found in the workshops and how the relations of production changed. Not only was there no increase in the number of workshops employing labour, but there was a counterintuitive change in the nature of the labour that is employed. The change over the years between 1975 and 2015, which is highly significant, shows that the use of *wage labour* has declined and the employment of *paid family labour* has steadily increased. The direction of travel was supposed to be in the other direction, with a decline in traditional family employment and the generation in new wage employment. However, unpaid family labour has also declined as paid family labour has increased.

The use of *unpaid family labour*, which declined slightly in the boom years and failed to fall after 1982, has declined since 1995, but this is hardly evidence of the

Table 3.4 Artisan self-employment and employment structure

	1975		1982		1995		2005		2015	
	No	%	No	%	No	%	No.	%	No.	%
Works alone	78	40.6	131	44.0	145	44.3	138	43.6	120	46.7
Uses wage labour	79	41.1	112	37.6	105	32.1	92	29.0	58	22.6
Uses paid family labour	20	10.4	47	15.8	60	18.3	63	19.9	67	26.1
Uses unpaid family labour	32	16.7	35	11.7	43	13.1	30	9.5	18	7.0
Total	192		298		327		317		257	

	Chi-sq	DF	p-value:
1975–2015	42.9806	12	2.28E-05
1975–82	5.2037	3	0.1575
1982–95	2.1833	3	0.5352
1995–2005	2.0920	3	0.5535
2005–2015	6.0052	3	0.1114
1975 and 2015	35.7286	3	8.55E-08

	1975–82	1982–95	1995–2005	2005–15
% change in the proportion using wage labour	-9.0	-15.3	-9.6	-22.2
Annual % change in proportion	-1.3	-1.2	-1.0	-2.2

anticipated reorientation of artisan workshops to modern employment practices and the stimulation of wage employment. In fact, unpaid family labour has been converted into paid family labour, which relates to changes in the tax and social security systems. These changes have meant that it is now possible to claim tax benefits through the employment of spouses, while at the same time registering them for social security benefits such as pensions.

If we look at the number of wage earners employed in the workshops, we can see that the size-structure of wage employment did not change significantly when 1975 is compared with 2015 (Table 3.5). Around half of all workshops employed one wage worker in both years. The size-structure of the waged workforce did, however, fluctuate over time. Once again, the change between 1982 and 1995 was particularly important. In this period, the number of workshops employing three or more wage labourers declined significantly. The average size of the waged labour force in artisan workshops rose from 1975 to 1982, during the oil boom, but then declined dramatically through the period of structural adjustment to an all-time low in 1995. The size-structure of the workshops employing wage labour changed substantially as the average size of the workshops fell and the number employing only one worker rose. In 1995, 61% of workshops employing wage labour had only one worker.

Table 3.5 Total number of wage workers

Number	1975		1982		1995		2005		2015	
	No.	%	No.	%	No.	%	No.	%	No.	%
1	40	50.0	42	37.2	64	61.0	43	46.7	28	48.3
2	24	30.0	35	31.0	24	22.9	24	26.1	15	25.9
3	9	11.3	23	20.4	10	9.5	15	16.3	6	10.3
4+	7	8.8	13	11.5	7	6.7	10	10.9	9	15.5
TOTAL	80	100.0	113	100.0	105	100.0	92	100.0	58	100.0
Mean	1.87		2.18		1.68		2.03		1.97	

	Chi-sq	DF	p-value:
1975–2015	17.4121	12	0.1347
1975–82	4.5141	3	0.2110
1982–95	13.2623	3	0.0041
1995–2005	4.8140	3	0.1859
2005–15	1.5275	3	0.6759
1975 & 2015	1.5774	3	0.6645

An examination of the changing social relations of production indicate, therefore, that female ownership has become more important; the proportion of self-employed ownership has not changed; the average size of the workshops has declined and the greatest contraction was during the neoliberal phase when workshops should have been growing; wage labour in particular declined during structural adjustment; and paid family labour has been replacing non-family wage labour, particularly during the neoliberal years but also when efforts were being made by an anti-neoliberal government to formalise the informal sector. We will see in more detail in the next chapter how changes in the external social and economic environment are related to the evolution of the structure of the internal social relations of production. In addition to an evolution of the social relations of production, however, there was also a reorientation of social relationships with customers, which was related to the type of work carried out by artisans.

There was a shift from production (manufacturing) to repair activities in the overall population of artisans, which had two dimensions. First, there was a change that resulted from the evolving balance between the different types of artisan activities that were found (created through the declining importance of tailors and shoemakers and an increase in mechanics and repair engineers, for example). Second, there was a changing balance between production and repair within all types of workshops. These developments, on two levels, provide evidence for a critique of the way the concept of the entrepreneur has been used by neoliberal theorists, as discussed in Chapters 2 and 4. In the next section, we will briefly look at the transformation from manufacturing to repair within the artisan workshops.

Internal changes in the nature of work

Artisans were asked if the major part of their work was production or repair, or if these were equally important. To some extent this is a measure of the balance between manufacturing and service artisans at any point in time, but over time it gives us an indication of any transition between manufacturing and services. The question, of course, does not make sense for the owners of hairdressers and beauty salons. Since they are clearly in the business of providing personal services, rather than carrying out manufacturing or repair activities, the question does not apply. They have therefore been removed from the information that is about to be discussed.

The importance of artisan manufacturing activity has been on a steady downward path since 1975 (Table A.3.6). On the other hand there has only been a slight increase in the proportion reporting that repair work is more common than the production of goods – but it was just enough to push repair above production as the most important type of artisan work in 2015 (Figure 3.3). The growing importance of repair, however, is also expressed in the fact that the greatest increase has been in the number of artisans for whom production and repair are equally important (Figures A.3.4 and A.3.5). The proportion of artisans who fall into this group is now three times what it was in 1975. Artisan manufacturing is gradually being eroded and repair activities are becoming more common – and this change in the type of work done by artisans is statistically highly significant.[12]

The decline of artisan manufacturing started with structural adjustment, but it has not ended. For some activities, the decline intensified with globalisation, as artisans transitioned towards becoming local repair agents of global manufacturing in some sectors of production. They cannot compete with Chinese manufacturing, but the volume and low quality of some of the imported goods creates a new

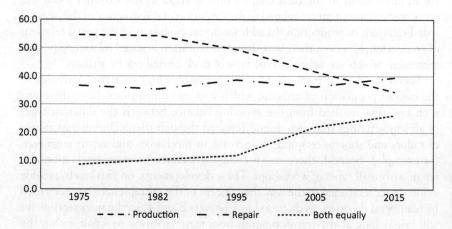

Figure 3.3 Major part of work: production and repair (%)

economic space for repair activities. We saw that the decline in the numbers of artisans was not evenly distributed across all artisan activities, with some faring much worse than others. Similarly, the shift from production to repair was not a uniform experience.

In 1975, tailors, carpenters, painters/signwriters and others were much more likely to report that most of their work was manufacturing, while shoemakers, mechanics and jewellers (which included watch repairers) were already more involved in repair than the production of new goods (Table A.3.7). With the exceptions of printers (who were mainly producing) and jewellers (who were mainly repairing), the proportion saying their main activity was production fell between 1975 and 2015.[13] For shoemakers, who were slightly more likely to be repairing shoes in 1975 than manufacturing them, the importance of repair activity increased even more.

For all three categories of artisan producing the means of subsistence (tailors, shoemakers and carpenters), production declined in importance and repair increased – and in all cases the changes were substantial. The changes that occurred for the other artisan activities were more modest, but the direction of change was the same. However, even if the direction of change between 1975 and 2015 was similar, the activities did not all follow the same trajectories. Through time, the paths taken by the different activities were neither even nor unidirectional.

The decline in the proportion of artisans saying they were mainly involved in production started between 1982 and 1995, the first structural adjustment phase of neoliberalism in Ecuador. This decline then accelerated through the second phase of the crisis of neoliberalism, between 1995 and 2005. Throughout this period, as we will see in Chapter 4, small firm owners were defined as entrepreneurs, they were celebrated as the future of capitalism, and policies and programmes were devised to support their expansion into larger capitalist enterprises. In the face of the theory and the policy that derived from it, artisans declined as producers and increased as repairers of defunct capitalist goods.

However, there are two points we should note here. First, the relationship between the macroeconomic situation and the micro-circumstances of the artisans was not a simple one. For some artisan types, there were internal changes in the type of work that was carried out, which modified these general trends. Some of these changing activities were related to the evolution of technology. Second, this decline in the importance in production continued through the anti-neoliberal period, 2005–2015, when artisans were subjected to the pressures of Chinese competition and globalisation.

In the context of a growing economy, based on the fortunes of oil exportation, and in the face of a difficult international policy agenda – including structural adjustment, the dominance of neoliberal economic theory, periodic financial crises and free market globalisation – Quito's artisans have declined and been restructured. In this process, artisan producers of the means of subsistence have diminished dramatically over 40 years, in spite of overall growth in the economy, whilst the numbers of others such as mechanics and electrical technicians, who can serve the repair needs of the consumers of capitalist production, have held up.

This has led to the restructuring of workshops over time, although the process has not been even or linear. Others have been particularly affected by changing technology (printers), the emergence of negative social change (jewellers), or the over-provision of training (hairdressers). All sectors of the artisans felt the impact of inflation, the banking collapse, dollarization and the globalisation that brought cheap Chinese imports.

Throughout the period, some artisans survived or even prospered. Some are aging survivors of their crafts, the lucky ones, but it remains difficult for artisans in the face of global transformation. Activities that some time ago would have provided stable employment have declined, sometimes leaving the artisans working alone, dependent on the loyalty of surviving clients, who themselves are old and at the end of their lives. As we will see, such artisans cling to their profession, with pride, but they are not entrepreneurs in the Schumpeterian sense. Neither are the new start-ups that are mainly involved in repair. These are not creative product or process innovators. Their work is conditioned by the manufacturers of the products they seek to repair. The nature of their work is built into the design of the faulty items during the process of production, predetermined by the capitalist producer of the car, washing machine or computer. There is little scope for creativity or innovation in a new product, process or route to market – and, as we will see in Chapter 13, they do not seek to expand and grow into larger successful enterprises.

The changes between 1975 and 2015 are the results of different pressures on different types of artisan activities. The pressures on any activity can also change over time. Nevertheless, there are clear trends in most cases, the main one being the downward trajectory of manufacturing activity. The balance of production and repair has been changing, as has the profitability of these activities. The key external drivers of change may be technology, local and global competition, the planning decisions of the council, and so on; all of which affect the key internal driver, which is the relative profitability of production, repair and sales. In the next chapter, we will look more closely at some of the external forces before returning to look in more detail at the internal dynamics of the artisan workshops.

Notes

1 The proposed models were basically the same in that they stressed the importance of reducing income differentials and providing for the 'basic needs' of the poor.
2 This contrasts with recent World Bank research in Ecuador, which defines 'informality' to include capitalist firms with up to 50 workers (World Bank, 2012).
3 It should be acknowledged that this increase in importance is not due to an increase in the population. The boundaries of the study area have not changed and, although there has been some infill, this does not explain the change in demand. The population has not increased substantially.
4 *Servicio Ecuatoriano de Capacitación Professional* (Ecuadorean Service for Professional Training).
5 The Chi-square tests in the survey tables assume that the surveys were carried out with a population of artisans that has been consistently defined over the 40 years of

the study. The tests cover a 5x2 table where all years are taken together (1975–2015); a series of 2x2 tables covering each of the inter-survey periods (1975–1982, etc.); and a 2x2 table where the original situation is compared with the final outcome (1975 and 2015). The same tests are carried out on weighted data in subsequent tables where the cell sizes allow.

6   Barbers have been classified as artisans since colonial times. The numbers of female hairdressers have expanded greatly since the research began and, logically, they too are classified as artisans.

7   When comparing the results for different artisan activities (tailors, shoemakers etc.) unweighted survey data are used. When analysing artisans as a whole, weighted data are used.

8   Including non-family wage labour and family labour, both paid and unpaid, but excluding children who were still in education.

9   Particularly through the Law for the Development of the Artisans (Development Law).

10   It could be argued that this is because firms experiencing growth are no longer in the sampling frame and that, in any case, firms that have grown and employed more workers will have moved out of the area to better premises. Successful firms that will have started in the space-constrained Historic Centre of Quito will have expanded elsewhere. On the contrary, the data from our surveys of what happened to firms that have moved on or disappeared show that this is not the case (Middleton, 1989, 2007.

11   This was true irrespective of how the workers are grouped together, whether the upper limit is three or more, five or more, or six or more. There is also no significant change over the period if all years are taken together.

12   Chi-Sq.= 49.1365; 8 degrees of freedom; p-value=0.0000.

13   As we will see later, the exception of jewellers is explained by the fact that cheap disposable watches have replaced more expensive watches that were more likely to be worth repairing. Watch repair is becoming more expensive than watch replacement.

4 Neoliberalism in Ecuador

Introduction

As discussed briefly in Chapter 1, over the 40 years of the study, the political economy of Ecuador has undergone a number of transformations, from the reformist agenda of the military dictatorship of General Rodriguez Lara after 1972, through the right-wing coup that replaced him, the social democratic government that replaced the generals, followed by a series of governments of the centre, right and left that adopted neoliberal economic policies, before the anti-neoliberal government of Rafael Correa came to power in 2007.[1] Throughout these years, Ecuador remained a middle-income country (Domínguez and Caria, 2016), but there were considerable changes in the national and international economic context, which had an impact on the overall structure of artisan production and the nature of their internal relations of production and exchange.

Before the adoption of neoliberal policies in the early 1980s, the economic development model in Ecuador was characterised by the import substitution model that was promoted by CEPAL and was prevalent in Latin America in the 1960s and 1970s. This model prioritised industrial development for national consumption, which was supported through subsidies for capital goods and raw materials, subsidised interest rates and an over-valued official exchange rate. Following the discovery of oil in Ecuador's Amazon region in the context of an international banking system that was seeking what it thought was relatively low-risk outlets for Middle Eastern oil money, the country found itself embroiled in an external debt crisis (CELA, 2004). In the 1980s, the response of the international financial establishment and a series of Ecuadorean governments was to try to 'stabilise' the economy and introduce structural adjustment. In the 1990s, this was followed by the introduction of further structural changes that were intended to promote the new model of production for the external market. In this chapter, we will see the spectacular failure of this neoliberal model and begin to consider the impact that this had on artisan microenterprises.

There is coherence between the periodicity of the study and the phases of the political economy in the years between 1975 and 2015. As suggested in Chapter 1, the main periods can be described as: the oil boom years (1975–1982); neoliberalism and structural adjustment (1982–1995); globalisation and the crisis of neoliberalism (1995–2005); and the populist socialism of anti-globalisation and anti-neoliberalism (2005–2015). These inter-survey periods reflect blocks of national and international transformation of the economic, social and political landscape. Neoliberal theory dominated the years between 1982 and 2005.

In this chapter we will set out the fundamentals of the impact of neoliberal ideology and practice on the development of Ecuador during the main periods of the research. We should note that no attention was paid by governments to the impact of Structural Adjustment Programmes on the informal sector, either in the design phase or in the subsequent analysis. It was assumed that micro-entrepreneurs of all types would benefit from the reduction of the state and the opening up of the market. We will reflect on the negative impact on the micro-firms that we have been told are the future of capitalism in developing economies.

Neoliberalism

The main assertions of neoliberal economics with respect to the generation and distribution of wealth are as follows:

- The free market is the most efficient means of *generating* wealth.
- The main reason wealth is not generated as much as it could be is government interference with the market – shackling the wealth creators through regulation and red tape.
- The free market is the most efficient way of *distributing* wealth (via 'the hidden hand').
- The main reason that generated wealth is not distributed more evenly is also government interference with the market.

Neoliberals assure us that, left to its own devices, the market will ensure that wealth trickles down. The way to achieve a free market is to enhance the role of the private sector in the economy, reduce the role of the state, support free trade, privatise state assets, cut public expenditure, impose fiscal austerity, deregulate economic activity, decrease business taxation and, insofar as any taxes are required (to support the armed services, for example, or to provide the minimum levels of education and health that are needed to support the growth of the private sector), increase taxes on personal consumption. A fundamental belief in the danger of egalitarian redistributive policy leads to cuts in outlays on public services, combined with the allocation of scarce public sector resources only to those in most need.

The hegemony of neoliberal thinking legitimates vast disparities in wealth, encourages the domination of the state by capital, justifies the commercialisation of 'unethical' practices such as human organ sales and environmental degradation, privatises socialised public goods, and reduces collective rights of access to the benefits of the welfare state. The ethical, the political, the cultural and the social are reduced to an economic register that is no more profound than an accountant's spreadsheet. All human activity is financialised. Competition is everything, it is unquestionably good, and collaboration, outside the family, is a problem.

Because neoliberalism is consistent with the interests of the dominant class, it is not recognised as an ideology. It is assumed to be a scientific economic position, the only rational framework for analysing socio-economic 'facts'. Harvey (2005) argues that the international purpose of neoliberalism is to restore the power of the global ruling class, that it does this by penetrating cultural consciousness, that the neoliberal state creates the conditions for national consent about the values of the neoliberal ethos, and that the freedoms neoliberalism promotes are the freedoms of the global ruling class 'to restore the power of economic elites' (Harvey 2005, 19). In any one country, however, the elite or the ruling class is not always tight-knit or clearly circumscribed. In a country such as Ecuador, for example, it always has been divided and conflicted. It changes over time and the control of power slips from one fragment to another. The divisions and conflicts are based on who should control the levers of economic policy. Ecuador's changing position in relation to the international economic system has had a profound effect on its development. The losers in the process have been the marginalised poor, who have been subjected to powerful economic forces of neoliberalism over decades.

Neoliberalism in Ecuador

Ecuador's transition from an impoverished agro-exporting economy to an oil-exporting member of OPEC was both a blessing and a curse. It was a blessing in that it offered Ecuador a new source of dollar income and a way out of its historic poverty; and it was a curse in that it made the country prey to the international financial sector, which ensured it became one of the earliest victims of neoliberal ideology in the developing world. Throughout Latin America, growing public debt resulted in a debt crisis that was characterised by increasing international interest rates, the sudden flight of capital and the closing off of international finance markets. The net transfer of capital which until this time had been inward, became an outflow. Latin American economies that had been relying on external funding to support development had to confront the difficulties associated with the servicing of the debt and finding the internal resources for investment. A consequence, according to the Inter-American Development Bank, was that across the region there was reduction in standards of living and in the stability of employment for the labour force (CELA, 2004).

In Ecuador, a narrative about the growth of public debt was at the heart of a struggle for control of the state. This struggle for political power, however, was less about reducing the debt than controlling where the borrowed funds were directed and deciding who should pay for it. This was played out in competition between the interests of different social classes and regions. For a short period after a military coup brought General Rodrigues Lara to power in 1972, the marginal masses were the targeted beneficiaries. After the fall of Rodriguez Lara in 1976, the dominant fractions of the ruling classes cut their own taxes and eliminated the public sector expenditure that reduced the cost of living for the marginalised poor, including artisans.

When the first part of the fieldwork for this study was carried out in 1975, there was an emerging feeling of confidence about Ecuador's development potential. However, as the new oil revenues increased Ecuador's attractiveness to the international finance system, since it was seen as a relatively secure place for investment, growth in the main indicators for the economy slowed. Under Rodriguez Lara in 1975, because of the increasing income from oil, the country's external debt was $457 million, or 5.9% of GDP (Table A.4.1), and the cost of debt servicing was declining. However, the fact that that the ratio of total debt to GDP had fallen as oil income had risen was a positive sign for the international bankers. Ecuador's projected oil revenues encouraged both the government and the bankers to increase the volume of public borrowing and lending. After 1975, foreign debt increased dramatically (Salgado, 1987).

When the reforming government of General Rodriguez Lara was overthrown by a military triumvirate in 1976, the government embarked on a policy of 'aggressive indebtedness' for the state. The new government also pursued policies in the interests of the coastal and sierra elites that the administration of Rodriguez Lara had tried to control. In the three years of the right-wing military dictatorship, public debt almost tripled and the debt to GDP ratio doubled. Between 1975 and 1982, the oil-boom years, the average annual growth rate for public debt was 41% and the growth of the debt to GDP ratio was 23% per year (Table 4.1).

This expansion of borrowing was a result of a world economy that was awash with petrodollars. International banks increased their lending to Ecuador, not only based on future oil revenues but also on personal greed. Much of the debt was linked to corruption, as ministers siphoned off 0.5% of contracted loans as commissions for themselves, with the collusion of international banks and construction firms. This ramped up Ecuadorian debt, making a future crash inevitable. The country did not have the institutional capacity to resist this combination of national and international forces.

When the military triumvirate handed over political power to the new democratically elected government of Jaime Roldós in 1979, the structure of newly contracted debt was completely different from what it had been five years previously. International organisations had given way to private banks. In 1974, the international financial institutions had accounted for 92.9% of Ecuador's new external debt but by 1979 their share had fallen to only 13.1%. Over the same period, the private banking sector's share of Ecuador's annual borrowing rose from 2.0% to 70.9% (Hurtado, 2002, Table 2, 250). This change brought with it higher rates of interest, shorter periods of repayment, a shift in investment from infrastructure to other types of government spending, some of which never materialised, and an increase in corruption (Hurtado, 2002, 24). The military dictators' Minister of Finances had by this time fled into exile in London to play polo with his banker friends and avoid corruption charges at home.

International interest rates increased and, as Ecuador's debt grew and the country was increasingly at risk of default, rates for Ecuador were even higher. As the interest rates rose, more borrowing had to be contracted to pay for earlier debts, creating an upward spiral for national costs and a vicious downward spiral

Table 4.1 Selected economic indicators, 1975–2015
Average annual growth rates (2007 US dollars)

	GDP	Government consumption	Manufacturing production	Textiles, clothes and leather	Exports	Traditional agricultural exports	Oil exports	Imports	Public debt*	Public debt/ GDP ratio*
1970–1975	9.4	15.4	9.8	12.5	33.2	11.1	262.7	15.8	n.a.	n.a.
1975–1982	4.0	4.0	7.7	6.7	1.4	9.6	14.6	4.8	40.8	23.0
1982–1995	2.7	1.1	3.4	1.5	7.8	11.0	0.0	1.5	7.2	5.6
1995–2005 (1)	3.0	0.9	2.4	1.2	4.2	-0.4	14.4	4.7	-1.3	-6.4
2005–2013	4.3	8.0	4.1	2.0	2.2	n.a.	12.2	5.7	2.2	-6.3

* After 2007, the accounting methodology changed. The BCE recalculated debt with new methodology back to 1990.

Sources: Tables in the Appendix, as follows:

Tables A.4.1 (GDP); A4.7 (Government Consumption); A.4.15 (Manufacturing and Textiles, etc;
A.4.16 (Exports and Imports); A.4.19 (Trad Exports), A.4.18 (Oil Exports); A.4.20 (Debt).
(1) Unable to borrow 1999–2003, then GDP recovered

for the Ecuadorian economy. By 1982, debt servicing was more than 70% of export earnings, amounting to almost half of the country's GDP (Salgado, 1987). GDP went into decline in 1982 and the same year saw the beginning of Ecuador's adjustment policies, with an increase in interest rates, the creation of two official markets for exchange rates, and devaluation.

It was around this time that a remarkable growth in the global influence of the IMF and the World Bank began, providing these institutions with an unprecedented leverage over the economic policies of the governments of the developing world (Killick, 1996). 'Conditionality' became increasingly important and governments were set preconditions and performance criteria relating to structural adjustment, before they could access financial support from these international organisations. Ecuador was drawn into this system relatively early, with considerable adverse effects on key sectors of the national economy between 1982 and 1995.

The additional debts that had been contracted and the commissions that had been paid were to haunt the economic development of Ecuador over the next 30 years. Employment in Ecuador's public sector had more than doubled in the 1970s, household budgets were supported by food subsidies, the government imposed low prices on other consumer goods, the armed forces were re-armed, money poured into provincial and municipal councils, and salaries across the public and private sectors rose.[2] A reinvigorated trade union movement produced upward pressure on government salaries for the growing number in public employment. Government debt supported private consumption and the private sector responded with an increase in private debt that was double the growth in the debt of the public sector. In spite of structural adjustment, between 1980 and 1989 the government's external debt almost tripled, rising from 20% to 82% of GDP (Table A.4.1 and Hurtado, 2002, 28).

All social classes, including the oligarchy, the military and the marginal masses, became accustomed to the higher levels of public expenditure. No one wanted to return to the pre-oil poverty of the 1950s and 1960s and, with the new revenues, they should have been able to expect progressive improvement in their lives. When the new democratic left-wing government of Jaime Roldós was elected in 1979, these expectations made it difficult to deal with a debt crisis that had run out of control. Instead of progressive development, they got externally imposed neoliberalism, austerity and structural adjustment that were designed to ensure that the international banks did not lose out.

Roldós resisted the increasing dominance of the neoliberal economists that were coming to international prominence, but he was killed in a plane crash in 1981. He was the first in a line of troublesome Third World rulers who died in mysterious plane crashes in the 1980s, including Omar Torrijos of Panama (1981), Zamora Michel of Mozambique (1986) and Muhammad Zia-ul-Haq of Pakistan (1988). Many Ecuadorians believe that 'President Jaime Roldós Aguilera was murdered' by CIA agents (Galarza, 1982, 5) as part of Operation Condor in Latin America.[3] It is no coincidence that when the Christian Democrat Osvaldo

Hurtado took over after his death, structural adjustment and other neoliberal policies were vigorously implemented in Ecuador.

The political context for neoliberalism

Note: For the key events, see Table A.4.2.

Hurtado had served for two years as Vice-president in the populist Roldós government, during which time the Congress had doubled the minimum wage, increased the salaries of teachers and other public sector workers, and increased the budgets of provincial and local governments, but from his perspective, this was a period in which the 'inevitable' policies of adjustment were delayed for 'political reasons' (Hurtado, 2002, 105). Hurtado correctly identified the coming debt storm but he accepted without question that the international banking system should be protected. His actions confirmed that he thought that the needs of the banks took precedence over the needs of any government. It was assumed by Hurtado that the requirements of the banks, whose unregulated and reckless lending and insidious corruption had contributed to the problem, must be attended to.

Hurtado's first message on assuming the presidency was that the country should prepare for austerity. Debt had to be reduced and the mechanism included reducing public spending, eliminating subsidies and increasing taxes. In the face of the opposition of all the important social and economic groups in the country and against the advice of most economists outside the Chicago School, neoliberal adjustment policies were introduced. The outcome over the next decade was a further increase in external public sector debt and a growing debt to GDP ratio.

Hurtado's so-called Social and Economic Stabilisation Programme introduced economic adjustment and paved the way for: increased taxes; the elimination of subsidies for wheat and reductions for milk, sugar, rice, petrol, diesel and gas; increases in the prices of public services such as electricity, telephones and public transport; raising taxes on alcohol and tobacco; reduced public spending; the prohibition of new public sector contracts; limiting the employment of new public employees except in the areas of health, education and the police; devaluation and the recognition of the reality of two exchange rates for the currency; prohibition of the importation of luxury goods such as vehicles; and renegotiation of the debt. Interest rates were increased, the currency was devalued and the IMF took control of the economy.

One effect of the negotiation with the IMF over structural adjustment was that the source of the debt shifted away from the private banking sector and back towards the international organisations and other governments. After the neoliberal adjustment measures were introduced in 1982, one Ecuadorian government after another pursued a similar strategy, to a greater or lesser degree (Acosta, 1996).

Hurtado's initial steps into structural adjustment opened the way for the more extreme forms of neoliberalism that were implemented by the government of Leon Febres Cordero: the reduction of the role of the state, privatisation of state assets, the promotion of competition, letting the free market set prices, the encouragement of foreign investment, the reduction of protectionism, and the repression of wages. Reaganomics came to Ecuador with the support of the IMF and the US government.

Over the next few years, under the neoconservative government of Leon Febres Cordero, a coastal oligarch who was happy to accept the influence of the IMF and the World Bank, interest rates were increased, devaluation became the main means of tackling the balance of payments problem, protection of domestic production was reduced, the control of consumer prices ceased, and taxes on commercial transactions were increased. Nevertheless, the state budget deficit increased by 58% between 1984 and 1985.

Specific changes benefited the coastal agricultural and commercial elite, of which Febres Cordero and his ministers were part: the currency was devalued to promote exports, price controls of basic agricultural products were abolished, and there was a reduction of import tariffs and the elimination of prohibited imports. Manufacturing, which had grown at an average annual rate of almost 10% in the 1970s, declined in the period 1982–84 and throughout the period between 1982 and 1995 the average annual growth in manufacturing industry was just 3.4% (Table A.4.3). At the same time, a growing urban labour force was swelling the numbers in the informal sector (Pita, 1992; Middleton, 2001).

Throughout the presidency of Febres Cordero, the national debt continued to rise. During his four years in office, the debt to GDP ratio almost doubled (Table A.4.1). The government was forced to seek new external credit to finance its operations, despite the sale of government assets and the cuts in services. Whilst Hurtado thought that the main problem for the Ecuadorean economy was the fiscal deficit, for the government of Febres Cordero it was state interference in the working of the free market (Montufar, 2000). Austerity continued through cuts in public expenditure in areas that were designed to help alleviate the worse conditions of poverty and inequality, but in the context of full-blown neoliberalism. In the language of freedom and choice and after deciding the main problem for the Ecuadorian economy was state interference and regulation, the acceptance of the free market doctrine of the IMF was a precondition for the further indebtedness of the country. The austerity of Hurtado had left an inflation rate of 23% but this had increased to 63% by the time Febres Cordero left office in 1988 (Hurtado, 2002, 132).

Corruption and clientelism were rife under Febres Cordero: Public money was stolen by ministers and a great deal was siphoned off to the industries of the supporters of the President. Money was transferred from the Central Bank to private companies and the Development Bank was drained of funds to such an extent that it had to borrow to continue operations. The increase in public spending left the economy in a mess (Thoumi and Grindle, 1992, 65) but it also fed the voracious financial appetite of the coastal oligarchy.

The fears expressed by Rodriguez Lara, when he staged his military coup in 1972 to stop the oligarchy fighting over the new oil wealth, had been partially confirmed by the behaviour of the military government that followed him in

1976, but they became fully realised by the government of Febres Cordero in the 1980s. Rodriguez Lara's commitment to the 'marginados' had become no more than a hiccup in the Ecuadorean struggle for power between the coastal and sierra elites. Rodrigo Borja of the Democratic Left party, took over the presidency in 1988, representing the liberal-left wing of the Sierra's ruling class. He was critical of neoliberalism (Borja, 1982) and his party members included social democrats who had benefited from the boom years of public sector expansion in the 1970s, but austerity continued.

Borja's approach to the control of inflation and dealing with a massive external debt and a record fiscal deficit was more gradual, but subsidies for basic needs were removed and the price of petrol and electricity were raised substantially. In Borja's first year in power, inflation continued to rise, GDP declined, the exchange rate deteriorated and external public sector debt increased, as did the debt to GDP ratio (Table A.4.1). Borja was elected on an anti-neoliberal platform, but his policies continued to follow this theoretical orientation, adding a new dimension to neoliberal practice. In his first year he introduced *El Shock*, which signified a serious economic change, followed by gradual adjustments over time. Immediately, the price of fuel increased by 100% and there were considerable increases in the costs of other goods and services over which the government still had control: electricity, transport, telephones, milk, cooking oil, wheat and some medicines. The sucre was devalued by 56%. Monetarist polices were introduced to contain inflation, and Borja signed a letter of intent with the IMF to ensure that his polices were in agreement with the neoliberal philosophy of the organisation. Borja tried to convince the public that the IMF and the World Bank had no influence over his government, but he continued with their neoliberal model (Thoumi and Grindle, 1992, 72–4).

The debt to GDP ratio continued to rise, from an average annual rate of around 29% during Hurtado's presidency, through 65% under Febres Cordero, to 76% during Borja's period in power. The US dollar, which bought 25 sucres in 1975 and 488 when Borja took office, purchased 1,675 sucres when he left office in August 1992 (Hurtado, 2002, 142). The inflation rate of 63% that he inherited remained stubbornly high at 52%, and it was rising again. In spite of the rhetoric, Borja's legacy was unemployment, poverty and an increase in the concentration of wealth. There was a decline in real wages, per capita income, social expenditure, education spending per head, and education as a proportion of GDP (Hurtado, 2002, 142–3). This round of neoliberal economic adjustment added to the burden of those who could least afford to carry it.

The neoliberal policies of Hurtado, Febres Cordero and Borja sucked demand out of the economy and contributed to the decline of artisan production. At the same time, the ideology was promoting the 'entrepreneurship' of the informal sector but, as we will see, this was in vain.

The application of neoliberal theory continued through a period of continuous social, political and economic upheaval through to 2005. After 1995, as globalisation accelerated, Ecuador entered a new phase of economic instability. Between 1995 and 2005, there were eight presidents of Ecuador, mainly '(neo) populist' actors in the realm of 'political informality' (Verdesoto, 2014) who were nevertheless free marketeers who did not question the dominant neoliberal economic doctrine. Between 1995 and 2005, the country experienced hyper-inflation, the collapse of the financial sector in 1999, and the replacement of the sucre with the US dollar as the national currency in 2000. The neoliberal model in Ecuador was in the grip of a severe crisis.

The neoliberal crash

The failure of the banking system started in 1998 and this led to the freezing of accounts in March 1999 and the closure of two-thirds of the nation's financial institutions (Cevallos, 2004). In 1999, GDP declined by 4.7%. Manufacturing collapsed in 1999 and after China joined the WTO in 2001 the country was flooded with cheap Chinese goods that undermined the production of artisan consumer goods.

In 1999, as output declined, debt soared as a percentage of GDP, from 47% in 1998 to 70% (Table A.4.1). Ecuador's debt represented 366% of its export earnings in 1999 (compared to 1975 when it was a mere 57% of export earnings) (Hurtado, 2002). Inflation, which had fluctuated between 22% and 31% between 1995 and 1998, increased to 42% in December 1999. The country experienced a decline of the sucre against the dollar in the region of 200% in 1999 and in the single month of December of that year it fell by 25.7% (Salgado, 2001, 83–4). The dollar, which was valued at 6,825 sucres at the beginning of 1999 closed the year at 20,243 sucres. It was against this backdrop that dollarization was introduced on 10 January 2000.

The impact of the financial crisis was not shared equally across the economy. Large borrowers with close ties to the banks particularly benefited, while small depositors such as artisans suffered (Halac and Schmukler, 2003). The government set up the Deposit Guaranty Agency (AGD) in December 1998 to return the deposits lost through the closure of 16 financial organisations. The AGD provided an '*explicit guarantee for the international trade-related liabilities* and practically all the deposits of banks taken over by AGD for resolution' (Halac and Schmukler, 2003, 9, my italics). The wealthy were able to take advantage of this by transferring funds out of the country, which exacerbated the situation for microenterprises. Investors with access to foreign-based accounts obtained government compensation and made capital gains, but small companies made capital losses.

In 1999, onshore dollar deposits fell by 15%, while offshore dollar deposits increased by 52%. 'Offshore large depositors withdrew most of the funds as the crisis approached [while] small onshore depositors who did not withdraw their money suffered the deposit freeze and dollarization of their funds' (Halac and Schmukler, 2003, 20). The AGD ensured that the deposits in the private banking system were covered 100% by the state, but four years later there were 103 million dollars of small deposits outstanding. In addition, dollarization converted funds at 25,000 sucres per dollar, rather than at the pre-freeze rate of 10,090 per dollar, which meant the small depositors lost more than 60% of the value of their savings.

The freeze was also applied to most of the deposits that remained in the offshore system, but once offshore they could be further protected. Ecuador's Central Bank provided 2.3 billion dollars of liquidity assistance to onshore banks between August 1998 and December 1999. It appears that the onshore banks were transferring these funds to their offshore affiliates, 'allowing larger depositors to take their funds out of the system' (Halac and Schmukler, 2003, 21). There was capital flight of around 730 million dollars in 1999 and a deposit fall of 1.6 billion offshore dollars during that year, indicating a transfer of funds out of the offshore Ecuadorian subsidiaries.

Some companies with close ties to the banks made large capital gains. They benefited from preferential loan conditions, which allowed them to transfer their risks to the public purse, emerging not only relatively unharmed but in some cases, in profit. Financial and industrial conglomerates linked to the sierra and coastal elites owned the largest banks in Ecuador. This oligarchy included the richest families in the country, whose businesses were financed through preferential credits. The loan portfolios of the banks were concentrated in a small number of large firms and there is evidence that these loans increased as the ADG takeover date approached. Halac and Schmukler (2003, 27–8) explain:

> Anticipating a government bailout, banks took advantage and granted large, cheap loans to their firms. An illustrative example is that of Filanbanco, one of the largest banks in Ecuador. Filanbanco's shareholders, the family Isaias, had reprogrammed loans to 36 companies owned by the family before losing control over the bank. These loans had special terms of two to seven years and subsidized interest rates, and were denominated in sucres (while the currency depreciation was already quite advanced in Ecuador). It was also found that 12 days before AGD took control of Filanbanco, the bank granted a loan of near 2.1 billion sucres with maturity of eight years and zero interest to one of the companies of the conglomerate. After that, Filanbanco not only transferred its liabilities and (non-recoverable) assets to AGD, but also received more than 500 million dollars from the government for recapitalization.

At the same time, artisans had their savings frozen and later transferred into dollars at a considerable loss. The government bailed out the owners of the banks and the wealthy elite and transferred the part of the costs to the people and businesses they celebrated as 'entrepreneurs'. We will see in Chapter 12 that, between the banking collapse and dollarization, many artisans had lost their life savings. Their sucre accounts were frozen and, when they were eventually converted to dollars and paid out, they had lost almost everything.

After 2000, growth was one of the highest in Latin America and foreign debt declined as a proportion of GDP. However, there was a net loss of 570,000 people from Ecuador between 2000 and July 2003, according to official figures, as a result of mass outmigration to the US and Europe. In spite of the economic growth and the decline in population, however, unemployment remained stubbornly high.

After 2005, the economy of Ecuador began to stabilise and grow. Raphael Correa assumed the presidency of Ecuador in January 2007. He introduced a renegotiation of the oil contracts with the transnational oil companies, created new development bonds, renegotiated the country's national debt and set about redistributing wealth to benefit the poorer sectors of society. As the international price of oil rose, he invested in the construction and improvement of the national highway system and the nation's energy supply. As we will see later, between 2005 and 2015, the annual increase in public expenditure was in the order of 7.5% (Table A.4.10).

Behind these broad-brush trends in the Ecuadorian economic, social and political processes there are more detailed data that are important for understanding the context for the transformation of the social relations of production and exchange of microenterprises. The macro-economic issues we will look at are the growth of GDP and the contribution to the economy of oil production, government consumption, manufacturing (which should include artisans but for whom there is no reliable national data), and exports/imports.

First we will see that the growth of GDP was at its lowest during the neoliberal years, particularly under structural adjustment, and that this was not all due to the level of oil production. We will then look at the link between government consumption and GDP, before discussing the performance of different industrial sectors and how these are related to the accomplishment of the stated neoliberal goals for micro-entrepreneurs.

GDP growth

Note: In this section on GDP growth, the relevant tables in the online Appendix are Tables A.4.4, A.4.5, A.4.6, and A.4.7.

The growth and decline of Ecuador's GDP has fluctuated considerably from year to year since the early 1970s (Table A.4.4). The annual fluctuations range from the highest growth rate of 14% in 1973, the year after the oil began to flow in large volumes from the Ecuadorean Amazon region, to a 4.7% decline in 1999, the year in which the Ecuadorian banking system collapsed. The changes in relation to the inter-survey periods are as follows:

1975–1982

Building on the initial three years of the oil boom, the economy grew at an average of 4% per annum in this first inter-survey period. This was not all due to oil growth but in the final year of this cycle, after the price of oil fell by 18% and oil production stagnated, GDP only increased by 0.6%.

1982–1995

During this period, there were two other years of negative growth, in 1983 and 1987. In both years, GDP fell by 0.3%. In 1983, this was related to changes in fiscal policy and in 1987 there was an earthquake that damaged the oil infrastructure and caused a decline in oil exports. After the 1987 crash, the economy bounced back but the annual average for the 1982–95 period was only 2.7%. During these years, when neoliberal theory was enthusiastically applied by a succession of governments and when the rhetoric in support of entrepreneurs was at its loudest, we see the slowest growth rates of the four inter-survey periods.

1995–2005

Between 1995 and 2005, Ecuador's growth continued to be sluggish. The country experienced an average growth of only 3.0% during these 10 years when Ecuador was hit by its crisis of neoliberalism, involving exceedingly high rates of inflation, the banking collapse and dollarization.

2005–2015

Between 2005 and 2014, growth returned to and exceeded the levels of the 1970s, with an annual average rate of 4.4%, before it fell to 3.9% for the decade to 2015. There are two outliers in this period. In 2009, following the global financial crash, when growth fell to 0.6% mainly as a result of a 55% decline in the value of a barrel of oil; and 2011, when a growth rate of 7.9% reflected an increase in the price of oil on the international market.[4]

The two periods of slowest growth of the Ecuadorean economy were the years when, driven by neoliberal policy, growth should have been greatest. The value of oil exports and the price of oil on the international markets will have contributed to this, but the price of oil is only part of the story.

Oil and growth

Since the 1970s, national growth and the fortunes of the non-oil sectors of the economy have been related to the volume of oil production in Ecuador and the price of the commodity on the international markets. However, oil has never been the largest sector of the economy. As a proportion of GDP, oil was at its highest in 1973 when it was 15%, but even at this stage the value of oil output was less than manufacturing output (compare Tables A.4.5 and A.4.8).

The relationship between oil and non-oil sectors of the economy

Between 1970 and 1973, the value added in oil production increased by almost 1,500%. The implications of the growth of the new oil revenues were enormous, but the lag between the increase in the value of oil production and its impact on the wider economy means that it took around three years for the oil bonanza to be felt more widely. The early impact on the economy as a whole can be seen between 1973 and 1975, when there was double digit growth of GDP. This was partly due to the increase in oil revenues, particularly in 1974, but also the 13% and 14% growth of the non-oil sectors of the economy in 1974 and 1975, which occurred as the volume and value added in oil declined. In each of these two years, manufacturing output in Ecuador grew by an unprecedented 15% per annum, as the previous increase in oil revenues found its way into public and private consumption (Table A.4.9).

This growth in manufacturing output had a significant negative effect on the un-enumerated informal artisans producing consumer goods. The outcome was not that artisan production grew to meet the new demand. On the contrary, between 1975 and 1982, as we pointed out in Chapter 3, the new demand stimulated capitalist investment in the national economy, some of it from international firms such as Bata, entering into competition with local artisan production of consumer goods. The result was not, as we discovered in 1982, an expansion of artisan firms to meet the new demand, either in firm size or in workshop numbers. In the face of increased competition from capitalist investment in manufacturing, including multinational corporations from the United States and Europe, artisan production of clothes, shoes and furniture collapsed. However, the growth of capitalist production did, as we have also seen in Chapter 3, offer opportunities for other artisans whose labour could be incorporated by large-scale enterprises.

In three out of the four years between 1974 and 1977, there was a decline in value added in the oil sector, which was related to the fluctuating prices and volumes. Over the decade after 1973, the change in the value added by oil fluctuated between 10% growth and 5% decline (Table A.4.5). Throughout the period after 1982, the non-oil economy was sluggish, mainly because of the impact of structural adjustment policies on national demand. Through the 1980s, there was a discrepancy between the movements in the price of oil, which tended to decrease, with the change in the value of the oil produced in Ecuador, which tended to increase (Tables A.4.5 and A.4.6). This was possible through a substantial increase in the volume of production in Ecuador (Table A.4.7). For the next decade, Ecuador's oil sector was marked by fluctuations in the volume of oil exports and the price of oil on the international markets, but the main features of the Ecuadorean economy were the rampant inflation, the financial crash and dollarization, at the end of about 20 years of neoliberal practice.

The recovering Ecuadorean economy was highly dependent on the balance between the volume of oil and its price on the international markets after 2000. In Table 4.2,[5] we can see that average annual growth of GDP in the 1970s was 7.6%, which fell away to 3% in the following decade and to 2.4% in the 1990s, before recovering again in the 2000s. After 2010, growth increased at an even faster rate, indeed at rates not seen since the 1970s, but the international oil price crash in 2015 put a stop to this.

Oil and non-oil performance between fieldwork surveys

The growth in the gross value added between 1975 and 1982 was greater for the non-oil sector and for the 'other' elements than it was for oil. This was because of the initial impetus given to the non-oil sector as the oil revenues made their way through the state to other sectors of the economy and because of the debt that

Table 4.2 GDP average annual growth in Ecuador, 1970–2015
(Real prices: 2007 US dollars)

Years	Growth rates			
	Value added: oil	Value added: non-oil	Other elements of GDP	GDP
	%	%	%	%
1970–1980	54.6	6.5	8.9	7.6
1980–1990	6.2	3.2	1.1	3.0
1990–2000	3.6	2.2	6.3	2.4
2000–2010	5.0	4.9	-2.7	4.2
1970–1975	71.3	7.2	5.2	9.4
1975–1982	2.9	4.2	4.3	4.0
1982–1995	4.5	2.4	3.2	2.7
1995–2005	3.9	3.0	0.5	3.0
2005–2015	0.0	4.7	-0.6	3.9

Source: Banco Central del Ecuador and Table A.4.5.

was subsequently incurred against future revenues. The overall effect was that the country's GDP grew faster than the oil sector between 1975 and 1982.

In the 1982–95 period, this was reversed. The output of the oil sector grew by twice as much as the non-oil sector and it also outstripped the 'other' elements of the economy. The debt burden and structural adjustment policies had a negative impact on both the state and the private sector during these years. The annual rate of growth of value added in oil was 4.5%, compared to only 2.4% in the non-oil sector. After 1995, oil remained the leading sector for the next decade but the growth rate gap with non-oil narrowed and the growth of 'other' elements almost disappeared.

The government of Gustavo Noboa, who took over the presidency when Mahuad was overthrown following the banking collapse and dollarization, remained under the influence of the IMF and the World Bank, but the country was in no mood for further neoliberal measures. An indigenous uprising that had overthrown Mahuad, with the support of the military and the urban working and middle classes, was still waiting in the wings. The anger and civil unrest generated by the crash was directed towards not only the bankers but also the entrepreneurial class who had been in control as the economy collapsed. They remained in political control through Noboa, but the coup helped calm the neoliberal agenda. The economy stabilised after dollarization, national debt began to fall and, as we will see in the next section, government consumption began to rise.

After 2005, the growth of oil production crashed to almost zero, while value-added in non-oil became more important, increasing by 6% per annum, the highest rate of annual increase in any decade. This was on the basis of annual rates of growth that were on average higher than at any time since the double digit rates of 1974 and 1975. There was also a small recovery of 'other' elements, which probably reflect more efficient tax gathering. However, the growth in government consumption was almost twice that of the GPD. This reflected both a growth of public employment and an increase in social spending, which helped stimulate the demand for some types of artisan production.

Government consumption and GDP

Note: Tables used in this section are A.4.10 and A.4.11.

Over the period between 1975 and 2015, government consumption grew at a slower rate than GDP (by 242% compared to 266%), resulting in an average annual growth rate of 3.1% for government expenditure compared to 3.3% for GDP (Table A.4.10).

In terms of the periodicity of the study, the relationship between government spending and economic growth was as follows:

1975–1982
From 1975, the average annual growth in government spending was 4.0%. This was the same as the growth of GDP over the same period.

1982–1995
After 1981, the rate of growth of government spending fell considerably and for the inter-survey period 1982–95, it grew at an average of 1.1%, compared to a growth of 2.7% for GDP.

1995–2005
In the next decade, the value of government consumption increased by a mere 0.9% per annum, at a time when GDP was growing at a rate of 3.0%. As rampant inflation and the banking crisis created a serious fiscal problem, government expenditure fell in three out of four years between 1998 and 2001.

2005–2015
The recovery in public expenditure began in 2002, before Correa took power in January 2007. Between 2005 and 2015, the annual increase in expenditure was in the order of 7.5%. From 2008, it moved into double figures, before it declined in line with oil revenues in 2014.

After an initial investment in government spending in the early 1970s, the attack on investment in public goods from the government of Hurtado onwards was ideologically driven. Between 1975 and 1982, GDP and Government spending proceeded to grow at similar rates. Debt was incurred that would support the economic interests of the ruling class (both legitimate and illegitimate), creating a crisis that would result in investment in public services being slashed and growth rates repressed. It was not until after the popular uprisings that followed the neoliberal-induced financial crisis that the representatives of the coastal elite in government stepped back from the damaging policies of the 1980s and 1990s. The growth of both GDP and public spending began to recover, but it was only when the international price of oil increased by 63% in 2003 and the volume of Ecuadorian production increased by 25% the following year that the economy reached the levels of growth last experienced in the 1970s and government spending was redirected in support of popular public services.

Gross production by industrial sector, 1970–2015

Note: The tables used in this section are A.4.8 and A.4.12.

Although all sectors of the Ecuadorian economy grew substantially between 1970 and 2015, the growth was not even across all parts of the economy and there were changes in the relative importance of each sector. In 1970, the five most important sectors were, manufacturing, construction, commerce, agriculture and real estate – in that order (Table A.4.8). The advent of oil changed this and by 1975 oil had overtaken agriculture and real estate, becoming the third most important sector.

Throughout the period 1975–2015, contrary to what might be expected of the world's largest banana producer and a member of OPEC, the most important sector has been manufacturing, accounting for between 21% and 26% of national output. At the end of the 1975–2015 period, manufacturing was more important than it was at the beginning, with a 23.6% share of the economy.

The sectors with the greatest growth between 1975 and 2015 were Electricity and Water (999%), Financial Services (718%) and Transport, Storage and Communications (629%) (Table A.4.12). These were followed by Household Services (Health, Education and Leisure – 423%), Hospitality (392%) and Manufacturing (375%).

The relationship between the large growth of financial services and the lower growth of manufacturing points to an aspects of significant structural change in the economy that turned out to be important for artisans and other small firms. We will return to deal with the role of the financial sector in artisan development in more detail in Chapters 11 and 12, but it is worth setting out here the basic elements of the macroeconomic impact of the financialisation of the economy, before turning to the performance of manufacturing.

Financialisation and financial flexibilisation

Financialisation is the process whereby the financial sector becomes the dominant sector of the economy, resulting in the transformation of national economic structures and cultures. *Financial flexibilisation* is the means by which this can be achieved. This involves institutional and economic reforms aimed at minimising or eliminating the controls and regulations of the state over the financial sector, replacing state functions with the 'natural' regulation of the free market.

The results of financial flexibilisation, however, were exactly the contrary to what was intended. There was a transfer of resources from the productive sector to the financial sector, resulting a severe process of disinvestment, new financial barriers to access to credit, an increase in short-termism in lending, and a concentration of financial resources in the hands of those who already had wealth. Between 1995 and 1999, 85% of the authorised loans were for less than one year; one per cent of clients received 63% of all credit; the greatest growth in credit was for high-value loans; and 90% were concentrated in the provinces of Guayas and Pichincha, the seats of political and economic power (CELA, 2004, 45–9). In 1996, Ecuadorian firms registered with the *Superintendencia de Companias* registered a combined net loss and paid more to the financial sector than they did in wages or taxes. In the 1990s, their profits were around one-fifth of what they paid to the banks in interest and commission (CELA, 2004, 50–1).

As we will see later, because the banks were free to set and structure their interest rates on the basis of firm size (where smaller firms paid higher interest rates) this expropriation and regressive distribution of funds had a serious effect on small firms and microenterprises. Financialisation and the flexibilisation of finance allowed banks to increase interest rates, raising the cost of finance and making it more difficult for micro-firms to access credit. Opening up the economy to free trade compounded the problems of financial flexibilisation. Both policies contributed to a contraction of production, insufficient funds for reinvestment, a decline in competitiveness, the closure of small units, increases in unemployment and underemployment, and a deterioration of standards of living.

The outcome was an increase in the importation of consumer goods and a decline in the sales of national production. The combination of these forces had an impact on the structure of capitalist manufacturing in Ecuador, which further impacted on micro-firms.

Manufacturing performance

The impact of neoliberalism can be seen in Table 4.3. From 1975 to 1982, manufacturing growth averaged 7.7% per year. Between 1982 and 1995, growth fell to 3.4% per annum and in the following decade it fell further to 2.4% per annum. After this the situation improved, with average growth at 3.7% between 2005 and 2015.

There have been five years since 1970 when Ecuadorian manufacturing output declined and all are associated with financial crises:

- 1982, the Ecuadorian financial crisis, which was the result of over-borrowing against future oil revenues;
- 1983, the world financial crisis, also known as 'the savings and loans fiasco', combined with local inundations;
- 1997, the Asian financial crash;
- 1999, the Ecuadorian banking crash;
- 2009, the world financial crash.

These years of manufacturing decline are linked to Ecuador's insertion in the world financial system. The issues are structural and systemic. The overall growth in manufacturing over the study period, which was strongest in the anti-oligarchical and anti-neoliberal periods, was severely damaged by the neoclassical and neoliberal economic policies that led to the financial crises. This has affected some manufacturing sectors more than others. There has been growth in all sectors of manufacturing industry but the structure of production has changed over the years.

Historically, manufacturing was based on the processing of the primary products of the rural areas: agriculture, forestry, animal husbandry and minerals extraction. In 1970, processing of agricultural production accounted for 48% of Ecuador's industrial output. This declined to 39% in 2015, but it is still by far the largest sector within manufacturing (Table A.4.13). Over the same period, the growth of Transport Equipment & Manufacturing NEC, which is mainly responsible for the manufacture of capital goods, has been the most significant feature of the changing structure of Ecuador's manufacturing sector. From 1975 to 2015, it was transformed from the second smallest sector of manufacturing to the third largest.

This sector is particularly important for artisans involved in mechanical and electrical repair. It includes the manufacture of machinery and components for industrial, building and civil engineering, agricultural, military or home use.[6] It also produces the tools and machinery that artisans could use,[7] the parts that repair-artisans such as mechanics will use in their work, as well as some of the machinery that will need to be repaired in the future. In the first inter-survey period it grew at a rate of 15% per annum but with the switch from policies of import substitution to freeing up the markets, the growth rates in the production of capital goods slowed down, almost to a standstill.

In 1982, when the government proposed a reorientation away from the policy of import substitution towards the promotion of manufacturing exporters that used national raw materials and other inputs, it was thought that this would favour the generation of employment in the manufacturing sector. In fact, annual growth rates across manufacturing declined dramatically. With the introduction of neoliberal policies in 1982, annual growth in capital goods production halved, whilst all other sectors fared even worse.

Textiles, Clothes and Leather industries have become less important in the country's industrial structure, declining from the third most important sector in 1970 to the sixth in 2015 (Table A.4.14). Production grew at an average annual rate of 12.5% in the five years before the start of the study. This included foreign manufacturers, referred to above, producing downward pressure on artisan production, who were not included in the national statistics. This, however, is also the sector that manufactures raw materials for artisan tailors and shoemakers. There were three years of negative growth during the early years of structural adjustment and very slow overall growth at 1.5% per annum between 1982 and 1995, before the rate fell to 1.2% in the 1995–2005 period of globalisation (Table 4.3).[8] In this process, capitalist investment in the textiles clothing and leather sector first destroyed swathes of artisan production of basic consumer

Table 4.3 Average annual growth of manufacturing sectors (Thousands of dollars, 2007)

Period of growth	Total	Food	Drink and tobacco	Textiles, clothes, leather	Wood	Paper	Oil products	Chemicals, rubber and plastic	Metals, glass and stone	Machinery, transport equipment and manuf. NEC
	%	%	%	%	%	%	%	%	%	%
1970–1975	9.8	6.6	9.3	12.5	14.4	4.4	12.3	15.1	13.9	19.5
1975–1982	7.7	5.3	6.6	6.7	9.2	6.9	10.6	8.6	9.9	15.0
1982–1995	3.4	3.0	0.3	1.5	3.2	4.2	2.4	3.9	4.4	7.4
1995–2005	2.4	3.0	2.1	1.2	4.1	1.8	3.6	1.4	1.9	1.0
2005–2015	3.7	4.6	4.0	1.6	3.9	2.1	0.2	4.0	5.9	3.5
1975–2015	4.0	3.8	2.8	2.4	4.6	3.5	3.5	4.1	5.1	6.1

Source: Banco Central del Ecuador and Table A.4.3.

goods and then this national productive apparatus was destroyed, along with the artisans, by cheap Asian imports.

The periodic crises related to the national and international financial system, the price and volume of oil, natural disasters and political upheavals, all had temporary impacts on manufacturing production in the formal enumerated sector. However, with the exceptions of oil products and paper, the lowest annual growth rates for all manufacturing sectors were experienced in the neoliberal phases of structural adjustment and globalisation.

Growth of exports and imports

Note: The tables used in this section are A.4.15, A.4.16, A.4.17 and A.4.18.
Before the oil began to flow in the 1970s, Ecuador was classified as an 'agro-exporting economy'. In this period, however, imports were greater than exports by a ratio of almost 3:1 (Table A.4.15). This ratio started to decline when the new oil revenues came on stream but the value of imports was always greater than that of exports through to 1988, when there was a surge in oil exports following the pipeline fracture of the previous year. After that, exports were consistently valued more than imports through to 2007, when the international price and the national volume of oil production declined and the balance shifted towards imports again.

In the 1980s and 1990s, the Consumer Price Index grew at a slower rate than the dollar against the sucre,[9] which should have acted as a catalyst for manufacturing exporters. In the 1980s, however, the export of primary products grew at an annual rate of 2.7%, as the export of manufacturing goods fell.[10] Between 1980 and 1990, industrial exports fell by 40% whilst they grew elsewhere in Latin America and across the world (CELA, 2004, 35). In Ecuador the priority was the production of shellfish and wood, alongside support for the interests of the already powerful stockholder groups associated with political and financial power. The result was that, instead of alleviating the national debt, economic policy deepened it and the relationship of debt to exports grew from 183% in 1980 to 490% in 1989 (ibid.).

However, the nature of the imports changed. Rather than a growth of imports of raw materials, the growth was in finished goods, a large proportion of which were products for immediate consumption. Historically, consumption needs were met locally by artisans and small industry. Between 1990 and 1995, the imports of consumer goods increased by almost five times, from 160 to 738 million dollars. In contrast, exports less than doubled; and the same was true of the imports of raw materials and capital goods (CELA, 2004, 42). This had a grave impact on the small industry sector of the economy. Its production, aimed at the local market, was displaced by the importation of consumption goods, leading to the contraction of this sector. The un-enumerated artisan sector, hidden from official statistics, will have fared at least as badly.

In terms of the periodicity of the study, between 1975 and 1982, export growth averaged 1.3% per annum. This is compared with a growth of 4.0% in both GDP and government spending (Tables A.4.5, A.4.10 and A.4.15). The period of structural adjustment, 1982–1995, was the most important for export growth during the study. Consistent with neoliberal theory that encourages nations to concentrate their development efforts on their strongest sectors, which allows them to increase trade with the rest of the world and thereby boost GDP growth, exports increased by an average of 7.3% per annum. However, this compares with only 2.7% for GDP growth and 1.1% for government expenditure. It might be argued that there would be a time lag between export growth and GDP growth but in the following 10-year period, characterised by globalisation and the crisis of neoliberalism, exports increased by an average of 4.1% per annum, compared to 3% per annum GDP growth and 1% growth in government expenditure. There was no evidence that increased exports led to a generalised boost to the economy as a whole. On the contrary, the opposite appears to be true. This may be because the growth of exports in certain sectors, such as agriculture and oil, encourages a flight of capital rather than its reinvestment locally. After 2005, in contrast, during the years of anti-globalisation and populist socialism, export growth fell to 2.4% per annum, while GDP grew at 3.9% and government expenditure at 7.5%.

Oil has been crucial for Ecuador's Export performance, but the distribution of the wealth that was generated also played an important part in the export performance of other sectors of the economy (Table A.4.16). Control of the state, with its capacity to determine tax regimes and distribute subsidies, was a crucial issue for the distribution of the oil wealth. The owners of the haciendas and the modern plantations of the coastal region were extremely effective competitors for the power of the state and the distribution of the wealth generated by oil. In the 1970s, the wealth flowed through Quito, boosting the size of the state and marginalising the coastal elite. By the mid-1980s, control of the oil income was once again firmly in the hands of the coastal oligarchy.

Between 1982 and 1995, oil declined to less than 50% of all export value and the average annual growth rate dropped to zero (Table A.4.17). This happened at the same time as traditional agricultural exports were growing at an average annual rate of 11%, almost four times that of oil (Table A.4.18). This rapid rise in the value of coastal agriculture's exports started with the presidency of Leon Febres Cordero, the coastal oligarch whose government deepened austerity, cut public services, and promoted the interests of his own social class. Between 1984 and 1986, annual growth rates for traditional agricultural exports reached almost 30%. Through the most severe period of structural adjustment, the coastal oligarchy did very well in a stagnating economy.

Between 1995 and 2005, oil dropped again as a proportion of all exports despite the fact that it showed a much higher annual average growth rate than in the previous period. It accounted for around 40% of export earnings, growing at an average of 14.4% per annum. During this period, however, agricultural exports were caught up in the economic crisis, as inflation soared, capital fled the country, the banks crashed, young agricultural labour migrated overseas, and dollarization was introduced. The dollar value of agricultural exports fell by 40% between 1998 and 2000. This contributed to an average annual decline of 0.4% over the 1995–2005 period.

The Ecuadorean Government and the World Bank preferred to see the years between 1995 and 2000 as a period when structural reform stagnated due to an absence of direction, an incoherent economic programme, institutional failure and politicians who blocked all attempts at reform (Naranjo, 1999, 31). In fact, the crisis was the main socio-economic outcome of the neoliberal experiment. The political economy of Ecuador collapsed.

It is not entirely clear why the value of agricultural exports should have declined so dramatically. One could assume that the plantation and hacienda owners and the international companies that supported the export of the agricultural production could have lost their savings when the national banks went down. They were an integral part of the national banking system, but these businesses had dollar bank accounts overseas, a fundamental outcome of financial flexibilisation. The national crisis of soaring inflation and a deteriorating exchange rate would not have had an impact on companies earning in dollars overseas. More likely is that they were involved in transfer pricing, saving their dollar earnings in off-shore banks, waiting out the storm that 18 years of neoliberalism had caused. In 2001, after dollarization, agricultural exports grew by 66% over the previous year. After 2005, the value of oil exports increased as a proportion of export earnings to around 56%, showing an average annual growth of 12.2%. Agricultural exports also recovered, posting an even higher annual growth rate of 15.4%, as Ecuador became bankable again.

As we saw, wealthy landowning families in Ecuador whose earnings were in dollars, along with export-import companies that are often owned by the same families, were able to protect themselves from the collapse by using offshore bank accounts. The families of small-scale employers and the self-employed, who were producing for local customers, were not so lucky. Many of the much-lauded micro-firms serving the national market lost everything.

Notes

1 Ecuador's political history was characterised by swings between dictatorship and democracy from Independence until the election of Roldós in 1979.
2 Some of the investments of the state were in roads, energy, education, housing, and urban water and sanitation. The government provided subsidies for electricity, fuel and telephones. They invested in the production, transport and refining of oil and they supported investment in the private sector through cheap credit from the *Banco de Fomento*, the *Banco Central* and COFIEC.
3 www.telesurtv.net/english/news/Operation-Condor-Docs-Show-US-Wanted-to-Rig-Election-in-Ecuador-20161217-0013.html
4 Energy Information Administration, BLS See Table A.4.6.
5 Calculated from Table A.4.9.
6 https://unstats.un.org/unsd/cr/registry/regcs.asp?Cl=17&Lg=1&Co=29 This division covers the manufacture of machinery and equipment, including fixed or hand-held devices.

7 Although most of their equipment is imported if they buy new machinery.

8 Table 4.3 is derived from Table A.4.14.

9 Between 1980 and 2000, the CPI increased by 524 times and the dollar against the sucre by 899 times (CELA, 2004, 34).

10 USD1,853 million to 2,344 million for primary exports; compared with decline from 626 million to 367 million for manufactured products.

5   Choosing informality

Informal and formal relations

If the categories of formal and informal are accepted as relevant, irrespective of how they are defined, the question of the relationship between the two parts of the duality becomes not only legitimate but also critical for understanding how low-income economies in the developing world function, especially when up to 70% of employment is judged to be informal (Benjamin et al., 2014, 4). However, the confusion over the definition that we saw in Chapter 2 is thrown into sharper relief when we begin to investigate the various dimensions of this dual relationship.

A focus in recent literature has been on the extent to which workers choose to transfer between the sectors in search of employment. While World Bank economists (Maloney, 2004; Perry et al., 2007; Loayza et al., 2009) argue that most are in informal employment through choice, the ILO insist that:

> most people enter the informal economy not by choice but as a consequence of a lack of opportunities in the formal economy and in the absence of other means of livelihood.
>
> (ILO, 2015, 1)

Irrespective of their perception of choice or the lack of it, the promotion of the transition of workers and economic units from the informal to formal economy remains a major goal of all international organisations. It is thought that public policies can speed up the process of transition to the formal economy, and this is seen as an essential feature of sustainable development (ILO, 2015). In this chapter, we will focus on the issue of choice and the extent to which artisans move between formal and informal work. In the discussion that follows, we will accept that there may be a prime facie case for discussing the relationship between formal and informal economic activity, given the theoretical orientation of neoliberal economics, but we will point to the conceptual confusion that exists and argue that there are ideological assumptions about choice that do not survive scrutiny.

Neoliberalism seeks to promote the transition from informal to formal but at the same time insists that it is regulation that holds back the development of small firms into capitalist enterprises. I will argue that this is an amorphous and contradictory ideology, but we will try to disentangle some of it as best we can. In this chapter we will deal with the extent to which the owners of small firms 'choose' informality and the extent to which individuals and firms move between sectors. We will argue that most artisans don't choose to be in the informal sector. At some point they choose to work as a tailor, shoemaker, carpenter, etc. At other points in time, they may decide to be self-employed, or to employ labour. As circumstances evolve, they may change their activity – as markets for their products improve or decline, for instance. When these things happen, they seldom choose to work in a factory, although this also varies over time.

Individuals choosing informality

In contrast with earlier thinking that suggested that the reason people worked in the informal sector was because they could not gain access to or were excluded from the formal sector, Maloney (2004) and other World Bank economists (Perry et al., 2007; Ingram et al., 2007; Loayza et al., 2006; Loayza et al. 2009) have argued that much of the sector is voluntary, in that workers in the informal sector prefer their present job to one in the formal sector. If working in the sector is voluntary, it follows that the workers must have *chosen* to work there. This implies there is something about the sector that is attractive. For Maloney, it is a broad set of job characteristics that substitute the protection and services offered by the formal sector. Informal service workers 'are willing to trade formal protections off for another dimension of job quality' (Maloney, 2004, 1160). Others agree that, while informal workers can be excluded from state benefits and the modern economy:

> many workers, firms and families choose their optimal level of engagement with the mandates and institutions of the state, depending on their valuation of the net benefits associated with formality and the state's enforcement effort and capability.
>
> (Perry et al., 2007)

It is thought that informal sector workers make implicit (if not explicit) cost-benefit analyses about whether to cross the boundary between informal and formal, choosing to remain informal.

The essence of the neoliberal argument is as follows. First, they ask, 'What drives a firm's decision to locate in the informal vs. formal sector?' (Ingram et al., 2007, 5). This question is of the 'when did you last beat your wife' variety: it assumes something that is not known, namely, that small firm owners make such a choice. We will argue that this is an invalid assumption for most informal firms. Second, they hypothesise that this decision is made on the basis of cost-benefit analysis. Once the first assumption is treated as non-negotiable empirical fact, the answer must conform to the economists' belief in 'rational economic man', who makes calculated decisions with the information that is available.

For the World Bank, the decision to formalise involves 'the simple principle of costs and benefits within the informal and formal economy' (Ingram et al., 2007, 5). The costs in the formal economy include registration costs, taxes and bribes, along with government regulations covering the labour force, customs, the environment, and health and safety. The benefits are access to finance, land and utilities, such as electricity, water and telephone services. Paying bribes is also a cost for the informal sector, as is the energy expended avoiding government officials. Benefits include access to some services at a lower cost and access to microcredit. The theory holds that the micro-firm owner takes all of these things into consideration and decides to be informal or formal based on the estimated profits that will derive from this decision.

In this view, high levels of informality derive from massive opting out of formal institutions by individuals and firms who see insignificant or no benefits from engaging with regulatory and tax regimes. This is taken as a 'blunt indictment' of the state's service provision and capacity for enforcement. The relative importance of being excluded versus choosing to remain outside the formal sector become a continuum that excludes other possibilities for explaining how or why individuals, firms and families are identified as informal.

Another possibility is that working in the informal sector has nothing to do with either being excluded from something that is desirable or choosing to be informal on the basis of a cost-benefit analysis (either implicit or explicit). When a 12-year-old child becomes an apprentice tailor, he or she is not thinking in these terms. When a journeyman shoemaker sets up his first business,[1] there is no consideration of the analytical categories of the economist (formal or informal). When a 70-year-old self-employed carpenter decides he will continue as he is, it is not because he has made a cost-benefit analysis of formality versus informality. He continues to do what he knows best, even as his declining business becomes no more than a hobby.

It is not clear why Maloney focuses in on formal sector 'protection' as the main difference between the two parts of the duality, but he goes on to say that we must think less dichotomously about the state of protection 'and more in terms of a broader continuum of jobs that offer different packages of qualities' (Maloney, 2004, 1160). Perry et al. agree that informality is a multidimensional phenomenon where 'agents interact with the state along some dimensions and not others, creating a large grey area between the extremes of full compliance and non-compliance' (Perry et al., 2007, 3). There is no doubt that, no matter how the informal sector is defined, there is a range of relationships between the state and individuals, firms and families in the sector, but it is not clear why we should think about a 'continuum of jobs', rather than a constellation of inter-related economic activities. There is no continuum. The urban economy consists of a network of linked economic activities and these relationships are complicated, but understandable. The elements are heterogeneous, but they can be defined and structured to make sense of what is happening.

In the World Bank's thinking, social protection is elevated from being an issue for informal sector workers to being their defining characteristic. By choosing the informal sector rather than 'formal jobs for which they are qualified', being in the informal sector 'is often the optimal decision for them' (Maloney, 2004, 1160). For some it undoubtedly is, but we need to be wary of assumptions about the transferability of skills between factory work and artisan workshops and, to the extent that some do have a choice, why they make the decisions they come to. We cannot assume it is for social protection; and we should not assume that working in the informal sector reflects any experience of ever having worked in the formal sector.

Firms choosing to be informal

Based on motivational responses from survey data, Maloney (2004) argued that well over 60% of men in informal self-employment left their previous jobs and entered the sector voluntarily, with the desire for greater independence or higher pay as the principle motives. In fact, Maloney's data shows that 37% of men left their last jobs to be independent and 22% left because of low pay. However, there is no indication as to whether these informal self-employed workers were previously employed in the formal sector, rather than the informal sector. Nevertheless, Maloney takes the data as evidence that 'they entered the sector voluntarily' (Maloney, 2004, 1160). We simply do not know how many 'entered the sector' voluntarily, crossing the border between formal and informal. It is assumed that the last job was formal and salaried but there is no evidence that this was the case. Unfortunately, Maloney also uses this 60% figure when referring to *all* informal sector workers and employers, not only the self-employed.

For some authors, choosing informality is seen as the 'response of an economy' that is 'trying to grow', a choice that means giving up some of the benefits of legality (Loayza et al., 2006, 122). In this anthropomorphic narrative, the individual is conflated with the firm and an economy that is 'trying to grow'. The individual is assumed to be making a rational choice and the sum of these choices produces a living, human, rational economy that is choosing informality. But of course if there is anyone choosing informality, it is not 'the economy'. We can agree that *if* an individual does make this choice, it could mean giving up some of the benefits of 'legality', such as the police and judicial protection, access to formal credit and participation in international markets. But this can only be the case if these 'benefits' are meaningful and desired by the individuals concerned. If interaction with the police or getting a bank loan are not seen as 'benefits', they are not being 'given up' and this cannot be a reason for 'choosing' informality.

We should note that in sliding from a discussion of regulations to questions of tax and legality, these writers cannot bring themselves to consider how *some regulations might be beneficial*. In the neoliberal narrative, there are benefits from legality but not from regulations. We should also remember that for the informal sector, particularly those involved in street trade, the police are often seen as a cost, through demanding and receiving bribes, rather than a source of protection. There is also no evidence that, even if an informal 'entrepreneur' does choose informality, they are foregoing much-desired bank credit. As we will see in

Chapters 11 and 12, the unregulated bank can be seen as an even greater cost that the corrupt police officer or local bureaucrat. And why should we think that participation in international markets is on the list of aims and objectives of street traders, small shopkeepers and utilitarian artisans serving local clients? All of these supposed benefits may be no more than a theoretical statement of the perspective of neoliberal economists which, because it bears little or no relation to the real-world experience of artisans or petty traders, becomes no more than pure ideology.

For anyone who has worked with the urban poor in the developing world, the assumptions that combine to produce the world-view of the neoliberal economist are astonishing. They bear no relation to what is going on in the streets and workshops of third world cities. The fundamental driver for the belief system is the idea that regulation 'distorts the normal process of firm creation, growth and disappearance – the Schumpeterian process of creative destruction' (Loayza et al., 2006, 121). In a globalised world, as we will see in Chapter 13, Schumpeter's idea of creative destruction, which is set in the context of a national economy, becomes irrelevant. In countries such as Ecuador, the non-creative destruction of small firms derives from Asian dumping and, in this threatening international context, artisans nevertheless cling on to their workshops.

We have seen that in the developing world, where every self-employed person is conceived of as an entrepreneur, the self-employed poor are seen as small firm creators. It is subsequently assumed that they are innovators who are motivated to accumulate wealth through growing their businesses; that they will enter into competition with other small firms is the pursuit of this objective; and that through the forces of this competition, some will fail and disappear, whilst others will survive and grow. It is further assumed that by trying to escape the control of the state 'many informal firms remain sub-optimally small, use irregular procurement and distribution channels and constantly divert resources to mask their activities or bribe officials' (Loayza et al., 2006, 122).

In this narrative, individuals and firms are choosing to work in the informal sector in order to escape the control of the state. This forces them (against their entrepreneurial and growth-driven will) to remain suboptimally small. They use other informal suppliers, divert scarce resources trying to evade the regulations and they are more likely to have to bribe officials. There is actually no evidence that any of this is taking place on a significant scale. They may divert scarce resources trying to evade regulations, but this may increase as governments try to formalise the informal sector with the support of the World Bank; and they are more likely to have to bribe the police than officials.

It is argued that key economic decisions around the profit motive are 'determinants of firms' decisions to locate in the informal vs. formal sector' (Ingram et al., 2007, 2. There are two things wrong with this. Firstly, there is no evidence from the data that the firms in question 'choose' to locate in any sector of the economy. Their model is based on erroneous assumptions about motivation, decision-making and the knowledge that entrepreneurs have about academic perceptions of the informal and formal sectors. The theory imposes an inadequate academic construct on the reality of the owners of small firms. Secondly, correlation between formality and certain economic conditions does not show that these conditions *determine* anything, least of all decisions about which there is no evidence.

The decisions that artisans make are not only driven by financial rewards – even when they are making decisions that have an impact on their business or on their income levels. The assumption by most economists is that the business decisions they make are dependent on the net income that will be generated. Others argue that the costs and benefits of expenditures on such as health insurance, social security and pensions will also be taken into account, even if these issues cannot be easily monetised. These issues are debated in terms of income levels, taking as evidence national data on wages and self-employed income. Work, however, has social, psychological and cultural dimensions.

We will see in Chapter 8 that the international literature on family firms has shown that they can be distinguished from non-family firms through their pursuit of family-related aspirations and goals, which may be both financial and non-financial (Holt et al., 2016). It is generally recognised that all firms pursue non-economic goals, but family firms also have non-economic goals that respond to the interests of the family (Chrisman et al., 2012).

It has also been clearly demonstrated that when people identify with their work, feel intrinsically motivated by it, find it meaningful in itself and take pride in its outputs, they are less likely to be concerned with material rewards. Volunteers may work for nothing but people in paid employment will often accept lower returns for their labour than they would receive elsewhere if they can continue to perform the work that they love (Ranganathan, 2018). This applies to a range of professions, from musicians through academic researchers to artists and writers. It also applies to artisans, who apply their skills creatively, have high levels of satisfaction in their work but low incomes. Many artisans, who barely earn enough to feed and educate their families, nevertheless prefer to continue to work as artisans when there may be opportunities to earn more in the alienating labour of factory work. This is a 'choice' that neoliberal economists do not consider.

Production for a consumer who appreciates the creativity and aesthetic value of an artisan's output also brings its own emotional rewards for the artisan. When artisan and client display mutual 'product attachment', there is evidence that the appreciative and discerning client will pay lower prices for artisan outputs (Ranganathan, 2018). When artisans who take pride in their work encounter a client who values their outputs in the same way as they do, and will therefore love and treasure the product in the future, they will charge less than they would when selling to a non-discerning customer.

Artisans may behave more commercially or less commercially, depending on the circumstances, but behind this variation is an attachment to their skills and knowledge. It is an attachment to their profession and a pride in their outputs, which begins when they start out as apprentices and continues to validate their worth as human beings in non-financial terms as they decline into old age. The artisan needs to earn an income, but this non-monetary dimension of their economic activity is missing from the debates about the informal sector. There are cases where the choice to become involved in the informal sector is driven by culture and family, not by economic rationality, and these drivers can be important aspects of business behaviour that is not aiming to grow the enterprise.

Some of this commitment by artisans to their profession comes from their experience as children, working with their parents. This was the case of one artisan, whose family had been making hats over three generations and whose father migrated to Quito from Ambato in the 1940s.[2] However, this was not his only work experience. He was also a systems analyst:

> My mother took the decision to educate us [but] I want to be what makes me happy – and I dedicated myself to rescuing my parents' workshop. Now my profession is as a hat maker.

This university-educated artisan was an exception in a number of ways, but his commitment to traditional skills was not unusual. He applied his education to the traditional economic activities of his parents, succeeded in attracting municipal support for his business, and was a successful Schumpeterian entrepreneur in terms of both product innovation and finding new routes to market. He used traditional methods to produce new designs. His market was mainly national, but he also sold to international tourists. In addition to selling his own products, he also sold the work of other hatmakers in his shop. He recognised that the internet offers possibilities for increasing sales and he feels he should embrace it and expand. However, he wants to continue as an artisan. He wants to increase his income, but he also wants to maintain his heritage. He wanted to have 'the best *sombreria* in Ecuador' and to earn more, but he did not want to get involved with a bank. He lost ten years of savings in the banking crash and had no intention of taking out a bank loan to invest in becoming a large formal enterprise. His main problem was not the regulation of an interfering state, but the reckless unregulated behaviour of the private banking system, a sentiment he shared with many artisans.

We cannot assume that all firms want to grow. Being 'formal' may carry costs, but it is the decision to grow that triggers them. Some artisans want to grow, some do not and some are highly ambiguous. Those that do will have to confront these costs. Some may decide not to grow for a variety of reasons. An important question is: how many in the informal sector wish to grow, even marginally?

Their desire to grow may vary over time, depending on their assessment of what the future for their business looks like. On the one hand, they may decide against growth, for example, if they think their market is declining. On the other hand, they may decide to go for growth in an expanding market or if business conditions are otherwise seen as positive. According to Ingram et al., 'a firm will formalize if the estimated profit in the informal sector is less than that in the formal sector' (Ingram et al., 2007, 5). Alternatively, it could be argued that if a firm seeks to increase its profit through growth it will enter the formal sector by necessity. For those firms that have the option of growth and consider it as a possibility, if the costs to the firm of growth are greater than the potential profits, the owner may decide against growth. This, however, may only apply to a very small number of micro-firms, for the conditions for firm growth are often negligible, particularly where there is a hostile financial environment or where other economic conditions do not favour growth.

Artisan choices in expanding and declining markets

We asked the artisans whether they thought the market for their products or services would be better, the same or worse in the coming year. There was an optimism in 1975 that has not been replicated since (Table A.5.1). By 1982, producers of subsistence goods had been squeezed by an expanding capitalist production in the 1970s. For all, the boom years of the 1970s were at an end and, already experiencing a contracting economy, the percentage saying things would get better fell from 41% to 25%. The expectation that things would get worse increased, and it remained high through to 2005, before declining again in 2015. The changes that took place between 1975 and 1982 and between 2005 and 2015 were highly significant, but in opposite directions. For the first time in 40 years optimism increased under Correa and pessimism about the future declined, but the end result was no significant change over the 40-year period. The pessimism was at its height during the years of neoliberalism.

We might have expected to find a relationship between 'business confidence' and the entrepreneurial intention to grow into small industries. During the two periods of relative optimism about the future, however, the intention to grow their businesses were not the same. We asked what the artisans would do *if the market improved* in the following year, asking them to choose from a number of alternatives (Table 5.1). In 1975, the most popular choice was to grow the business and convert from being an artisan into a formal 'small industry'.[3] In this period of high levels of confidence about the future, 47% said they would expand into a small industry, compared to 30% who said they would continue as artisans. By 1982, these figures had completely reversed. Confidence in the future had declined and only 29% said they would create small industries if there was an increasing demand for their products or services. This did not change through to 2015. In the final year of the study, when artisans were less likely to think that things were about to get worse than at any time in the previous 33 years, they were nevertheless much more likely to say that they would continue as artisans if the market for their goods did improve.

From 1982 onwards, there was a growing orientation towards trade. Most did not want to give up being artisans but it was clear that increasing their trading activities was a possibility if the market were to expand. We do not know if they were considering remaining as informal traders or expanding into capitalist firms, but what we do know is that they gradually became more inclined to develop their commercial activities than to become capitalist manufacturers.

In a declining market, they were much more likely to continue working as an artisan than was the case in an expanding market. If under pressure, around

Table 5.1 What artisan would do if market improved

	1975		1982		1995		2005		2015	
	No.	%	No.	%	No.	%	No.	%	No.	%
Continue as artisan	51	30.2	137	47.1	152	46.9	132	42.2	112	43.6
Expand into small industry	79	46.7	83	28.5	99	30.6	91	29.1	53	20.6
Concentrate or expand commerce	37	21.9	45	15.5	63	19.4	80	25.6	82	31.9
Other	2	1.2	26	8.9	10	3.1	10	3.2	10	3.9
TOTAL	169	100	291	100	324	100	313	100	257	100

	Chi-sq	DF	p-value
1975–2015	72.0599	12	1.32E-10
1975–1982	30.5860	3	1.03E-06
1982–1995	10.5559	3	0.0144
1995–2005	3.5774	3	0.3109
2005–2015	6.2504	3	0.1000
1975&2015	33.5530	3	2.46E-07
1982–2005	16.5926	3	0.0009
1982–2015	25.0051	3	1.54E-05

two-thirds would stick with what they knew (Table 5.2). The period when they were most likely to choose not to continue as artisans was between 1995 and 2005, the era of rapid globalisation, increased competition from Chinese products and the financial crisis in Ecuador. This choice that had nothing to do with social protection, state regulation or Schumpeterian creative destruction. In the following decade, the situation was reversed, with the highest proportion choosing to continue as artisans occurring in 2015 (72%). The change in favour of continuing as an artisan was highly significant between 2005 and 2015.

The artisans who said that they would not continue as artisans were then asked what they would turn to if there *was* a decline in demand. There was a wide range of responses but the most significantly consistent reply was that they would switch to trading activities. Once again, we cannot be certain if they were thinking about informal trade. However, with the level of investment required for anything else, the most likely option for artisans under pressure would be small-scale trade based on their own production plus increased sales of both the output of other artisans and the products of large-scale manufacturers. What is certain is that after 1982, trade becomes by far the most important option. The possibility of taking up factory work reached a peak at 19% in 1982 and this option rapidly declined thereafter (Table 5.3). The change between 1975 and 2015 is highly significant: the importance of trade as an option doubles, and by

Table 5.2 If market declines, would artisan continue as present?

	1975		1982		1995		2005		2015	
	No.	*%*	*No.*	*%*	*No.*	*%*	*No.*	*%*	*No.*	*%*
Yes	124	66.3	187	64.0	223	68.6	186	58.9	184	71.9
No	63	33.7	105	36.0	102	31.4	130	41.1	72	28.1
	187	100.0	292	100.0	325	100.0	316	100.0	256	100.0

	Chi-sq	DF	p-value
1975–2015	12.5036	4	0.0140
1975–82	0.2577	1	0.6117
1982–1995	1.4436	1	0.2296
1995–2005	6.6014	1	0.0102
2005–2015	10.4859	1	0.0012
1975&2015	1.5795	1	0.2088

Table 5.3 If not same activity, what?

	1975		1982		1995		2005		2015	
Factory work/ wage labour	7	11.7	20	18.9	7	7.1	9	7.1	6	9.0
Commerce	16	26.7	24	22.6	54	55.1	55	43.7	36	53.7
Driver	14	23.3	9	8.5	6	6.1	3	2.4	3	4.5
Other	23	38.3	53	50.0	31	31.6	59	46.8	22	32.8
TOTAL	60	100.0	106	100	98	100	126	100	67	100

	Chi-sq	DF	p-value:
1975–2015	60.5549	12	1.79E-08
1975–82	8.7102	3	0.0334
1982–1995	23.8826	3	2.64E-05
1995–2005	6.5730	3	0.0868
2005–2015	3.7858	3	0.2855
1975&2015	14.5675	3	0.0022

the end of the study period the choice of formal factory work was attractive to less than 10% of the small firm owners.

Choosing wage work in the formal sector

Rational choice theory suggests that the artisan will weigh up the costs and benefits of working in a factory as a wage-earner, taking account of salaries and benefits. In the 'exclusion' view, it is assumed that informal workers, either self-employed or waged, 'would prefer the presumed higher wages and benefits of formal work ... [and] ... given the opportunity to move, informal workers would happily take on formal jobs' (Perry et al., 2007, 43–4). We should note that higher wages are 'presumed'. In fact it is not clear that workshop owners would earn more as wage workers in the formal economy. Some would and others would not – and because of the conflation of the self-employed and wage workers in the 'informal economy', along with the unreliability of informal income data, there is no reliable evidence on this. Wage employment can deliver more stability than the constantly fluctuating demand of self-employment. Informal small firm owners have irregular incomes, sometimes they do not know what they earn per week or month, and they often lie.

In order to judge the impact of social protection, regulations and other non-salary considerations on choosing to seek formal wage labour, we need to isolate the income variable. Consequently, we asked the artisans if they would be willing to work in a factory for the same income as they earned from self-employment. In 1975, 94% said they would not (Table A.5.2). Seven years later, only 70% said they would not, a highly significant decline. As opportunities for wage labour increased during the oil boom years, as artisans producing consumption goods came under pressure and as optimism about the future declined, the willingness of artisans to work in factory production grew. However, after 1982, working in a factory became less attractive for artisans, as Ecuadorian manufacturing came under increasing pressure from structural adjustment policies and, as we saw in Chapter 4, growth rates declined.

Nevertheless, the change between 1975 and 1995 was highly significant (p-value = 0.0000). In the latter year, factory wage labour was seen as a much better option than it had been in 1975. By 2015, almost one-third of the small workshop owners would have preferred to have worked in a factory for wages that were the same as their current earnings as an artisan. This could have been because of perceived job security and other benefits that were legally enforced in the capitalist sector of the economy. It may also have been based on the perceived future for artisans and we do not know if the perceived benefits of factory work would be their only option or would dominate their preferences – a choice before all other options. We do know that 69% chose to remain as artisans and that they valued their independence and had pride in their crafts.

From 1982, we asked the artisans if they had ever worked in a factory. Much of the literature assumes that the majority of the informal self-employed do have this experience and they make informed choices between formal and informal on this basis (Maloney, 2004; Perry et al., 2007). The vast majority of artisans have no such experience (Table 5.4). The experience of factory employment increased significantly between 1982 and 2005, before declining slightly, but less than one-third of artisans had worked in a factory at any time in their working lives.

Choosing to be an artisan

The first choice that led most of the artisans to be in the informal sector in Quito in 2015 was a decision to escape the poverty they experienced as children – and it

Table 5.4 Has worked in a factory?

	1982		1995		2005		2015	
	No.	%	No.	%	No.	%	No.	%
Yes	65	21.8	81	24.8	99	31.3	71	27.6
No	233	78.2	246	75.2	217	68.7	186	72.4
	298	100.0	327	100.0	316	100.0	257	100.0

	Chi-sq	DF	p-value
1982–2015	7.8293	3	0.0497
1982–1995	0.7623	1	0.3826
1995–2005	3.4292	1	0.0641
2005–2015	0.9312	1	0.3345
1982&2015	2.5217	1	0.1123
1982&2005	7.0961	1	0.0077

was a choice that was not always made by the future tailor, shoemaker or carpenter. The decision was often made by their parents, who wanted something better for their children than the lives of poverty and hardship that they themselves were suffering. If they had been born in the rural areas or provincial towns, the next decision for the young person might be to migrate to Quito for work and further training, followed by a decision to set up their own workshop, commonly around the time they were married. None of these decisions, which placed them firmly in the informal sector and would determine their future relationship to the formal sector of the economy, had anything to do with the benefits of formality or cost-benefit analyses of these two sectors. These were choices, made by the children and/ or their parents, between becoming apprentices in the informal sector or continuing to work in the brutality of the semi-feudal agriculture of the Ecuadorian Sierra.

These are decisions that bear no relationship to the economic theory that focuses on exclusion from the formal sector or rational economic choices between formal and informal sectors. Artisan choices are influenced by a series of life processes that frame the decisions they make. These processes are embedded in experiences such as childhood, family relationships, master–worker relations, the power that property owners exercise over their lives, and the important social relationships that they create and sustain outside the family and work. Small-firm surveys do not capture this reality. There were four cases in Quito that help tease out the complexities.

The first example is an 80-year-old master-tailor at the time of the interview, who was born in 1934 in a rural area near Latacunga, in the province of Cotopaxi.[4] His parents were peasant farmers, with a small piece of land, and they worked in the fields to feed their six children. As explained by the artisan, 'everyone had their piece of land and the pace of life was planting, working, having something to eat'. Today, it is difficult for outsiders to understand the subhuman conditions in the rural areas of the Ecuadorian Sierra in the 1930s and 40s, when he was attending school in Cotopaxi. A way to escape the extreme poverty of Ecuadorian peasants at the time was to migrate to urban areas and learn skills that would allow a child to gain access to urban employment:

> At the time [our parents] told us that we must learn a trade, and that is what we did, not only me, but my brothers. We went to learn the craft in Latacunga.

For many trainees at the time, family support was very important to get a trade – an uncle who had a tailor's workshop, a grandfather who was a master cobbler, for example. The tailor who offered a job to the young boy was not a relative, but a well-known master-tailor in Latacunga. The young tailor worked in Latacunga for 10 years before migrating to Quito at the age of 25: He needed to continue studying. He knew how to sew cloth, but he wanted to learn how to measure and cut it. His employer had graduated in Quito and, as he could not teach the skills the young man wanted to learn, he recommended that he migrate to the academy in the capital.

He came to Quito as a semi-skilled journeyman to look for work in the workshops of the capital. As a worker in an artisan workshop in Quito, he could live and study – and have a way of life very different from his parents. The young man entered the Academy of master tailors in Quito and, after three years of study, he obtained the title of master tailor. With his new qualification he became independent: 'With the title, you could go out and look for a small workshop and get customers'. When he graduated, he was 28 years old and, two years later, he had a workshop in the Centre of Quito with a good clientele.

He occupied this workshop for a few years but when the owner of the building died, the heirs wanted to sell it. He had to leave. This experience was very common for artisans in the Historic Centre of Quito, particularly through the years of regeneration of the city centre when it was remodelled to make it more attractive for international tourists: artisans and shop owners were displaced, some of them giving up their independence, never to return. This was exclusion from the informal sector, not from the formal sector. Neither was it a 'choice' on the part of the owner of the firm. It was a power-induced involuntary means of exclusion from informal work. In this case, this master-tailor moved to the periphery of the old centre, where he opened up a new workshop, grew the business and remained until he partially retired. He never in his life thought about going to work in the formal sector.

A second example is a carpenter born into poverty in the same year as the master tailor, who had a different career and life trajectory.[5] Born to agricultural wage labourers who worked on the haciendas of rural Imbabura, he and his six siblings were raised by an aunt in the provincial capital, Ibarra. He started working as an apprentice at 14 years of age, moved to another workshop, then got a job in a sawmill, which would have been a capitalist firm in the formal sector. He said he learned nothing there, before moving yet again to another artisan workshop. Following a domestic dispute, he fled to Colombia, where he worked as a carpenter. On returning to Ecuador, he moved directly to Quito, where he was arrested for failure to keep up family maintenance and had further problems with the law, before setting up his workshop at the age of 34 in the 1960s. His choices as a carpenter in the informal sector were intimately linked to the (mainly bad) personal choices he made as a husband and father, and had nothing to do with the choice between informality and formality.

A third case was a tinsmith,[6] born of a single mother in Quito and raised by his grandmother and an uncle, who worked for eight years learning to be a metal worker in his uncle's workshop. He then joined another workshop, where he learned a great deal from a master-tinsmith before getting work as a semi-skilled worker in a steel fabrications factory making metal furniture. This case exemplifies the difficulties in adjusting between artisan and factory work. He says the owner of the artisan workshop was:

> Very precise, a master in the true meaning of the word master. He was very precise in all measures, and all the time taught me that I had to do a job well; do not leave things that would make me a mediocre master-craftsman ... I assimilated all the knowledge that he taught me to be a master. ... I applied all this knowledge at the factory ... I liked the geometry and arithmetic, which served me well in the factory work ... I knew how to read plans.

The move to the factory was because of a shortage of work in the tinsmith's workshop, not because of a rational economic decision based on a cost-benefit analysis. The master had to let him go but his training as an artisan was unusual amongst the workers in the factory and his precise way of working was source of some conflict. He subsequently fell out with his fellow workers and had to leave. He explained that this was for reasons of personal animosity: he had upset his fellow workers. It had nothing to do with economic rationality or his choice of workplace or sector. After he left, the workers went on strike, the factory closed, and the owner then approached him about finishing some of the contracts that remained to be completed. He set up his own workshop to do this. It was an unexpected and serendipitous opportunity, not a decision that weighed the pros and cons of the informal versus the formal sector. This was in 1970 and he has been in the present workshop ever since, working as an artisan for 45 years on the edge of the Historic Centre of Quito. Asked why he had never moved he said:

> It was because I really didn't have another place to go to ... The owner of the house appeared to be annoyed with me at one time and he asked me to go, but I didn't know where to go. I went to see the daughter. Well, firstly, when I first knew her she was a child but when I went to speak to her she was a woman. Well, she said that this was not good, that I had been an example to the barrio, of work, and they could not throw me out.

His future was in the hands of the property-owner and, fortuitously, she allowed him to stay in his workshop and continue to practice his craft. In Quito, the choices made by property owners can often be much more important than those made by artisans.

A fourth case was a watchmaker who was born on the rural periphery of Quito and who said he knew as a child that he had to decide what work he would do.[7] From the age of eight, he sold bananas on the streets of Quito with his mother.

> I finished school in the sixth Grade, at the age of 11 years and a few months, and I went to work with my father as an unskilled farmworker, and I never liked it.

Before he learned to repair watches, he did not know what trade he wanted to learn, only that he did not want to be the same as his father. 'I did not want to be a peon, or to work on the sidewalks or in the streets.'

> I wanted to be a mechanic, a tailor, a hairdresser, whatever, but I wanted to have a trade, to be a hard-working person, and to feel good. Some friends took me on to learn this trade [but] it did not go well. There were setbacks, because they always treated me badly, as I was a child, but I dedicated myself and I learned with the blows of life.

He worked in different workshops across Quito, learning his trade before, at the age of 14, being taken on by the owner of the workshop he now owned. He became a skilled watch repairer at the age of 19, continued to work with his boss until, at the age of 28 and after a robbery in which his boss lost all his stock of expensive watches, the owner offered to sell him the business, lending him the money to get started.

He continued to learn as he practised, but he never again had any interest in learning any other trade or profession: 'With this trade, which is a blessing from God, I don't envy anything of anyone.' When asked if he would like to grow his business, he replied:

> Well, perhaps not. Because I have enough work here and it never occurred to me to open a number of other shops in different parts [of the city].

He does not have as much money as he did before, especially following a series of further robberies, but he has been able to feed and educate his children and build a home:

> My daughters are moving ahead. I was able to build my house. I don't covet more … I am not going to live much more, nor am I going to need a lot of money. My best moments have passed. For what? I am healthy, I am happy. What more could I ask for?

He escaped the poverty of rural Ecuador, learned a trade, ran a successful business, provided for his family and never at any time thought about expanding into a formal enterprise.

These four cases are typical of the decisions that artisans make about where they work. The economic models of neoliberalism do not begin to explain the choices they make. They join the informal sector as children and when they are excluded from employment, it is not necessarily from the formal sector. It can be linked to property ownership and the power of landlords to evict tenants. This may or may not result in artisans seeking and finding work in the formal sector as wage labour, to which they have difficulty adapting. All would welcome higher incomes, but this is not related to choosing to be formal.

The power to choose

The role of power is an element that is missing from the debates about choices that individuals, firms and families make about entering or leaving the informal sector. The only time the concept is floated is when there is a reference to the power of trade unions to distort markets. When informal workers are excluded from the formal sector, it is assumed that they wish to gain access but cannot for economic reasons related to rigidities in the labour market. It is argued there are not enough jobs at the right skill levels for them to be absorbed and informal workers are 'forced to queue for preferred formal jobs' (Perry et al., 2007, 44). Wage rigidities in the formal sector, created by minimum wages or trade union power, create labour market segmentation. A wedge is driven between the two sectors, whereby identical workers receive higher earnings in formal sector jobs. These jobs are coveted by workers in the informal sector, who have to find alternative employment in the low-wage, low-productivity sector of the economy. However, none of the above cases support this argument.

There are other sources of power in the labour market that create exclusion and/or impact on the well-being, earnings and livelihoods of workers in the informal sector. In addition to the capacity of property owners to eject informal tenants, there is the power of employers to fire formal workers from both the private and public sectors. There are many cases where formal sector workers have been fired for being a member of a trade union or for trying to improve health and safety at work. Blacklisted, they 'chose' to work in the informal sector.

Structural adjustment policies in the 1980s forced many workers out of the formal public sector, who then 'chose' to become self-employed taxi drivers by using severance pay and preferential automobile import tariffs. Most did not have the skills to become artisans, although some did return to renew the traditional family skills that they may have learned as children, whilst others took over small firms where they either became owner-managers or learned the skills of the trade.

The exclusion of trade unionists from capitalist enterprises has a long history in Ecuador. An example is a 53-year-old dressmaker who was born in Quito to a mother who was a street trader and a father who made and sold charcoal that he brought to Quito for a hacienda owner.[8] Her first experience of work was as a child, selling cleaning cloths in the streets to be able to pay for her education, which her mother was unable to afford. When she left school, she studied dressmaking at a technical college before going to work in a shirt factory at the age of 18. She worked there for eight years, before leaving to set up her own workshop, which was located in her own home at first. Behind this 'choice' to join the informal sector there were forces at work related to the conditions at the factory and why she 'left'.

> When I started, around 60 people worked there. It was a big factory. Like everything else, when you start, work is hard. It is difficult to learn the rhythm of industrial manufacturing, because industrial manufacturing is one thing and another thing is the making of [clothes] garment by garment. It is totally different.

Making a garment to the order of a client, which is what she will have been taught at the academy, is not the same as the repetitive work that results from the division of labour that is found in a factory production line. In the factory, one worker may cut a sleeve, another create a button hole, yet another sew on the button, and yet another sew the sleeve together, before a different worker sews the sleeve to the body of a shirt. The transition from artisan creativity to mind-numbing repetition is difficult, but moving in the other direction is almost impossible because of the difference in the level of skills required.

When she was asked why she left, she explained:

> I was in the union. It had been unionized for a long time as it was a large factory. They sacked all the officers of the union.

Her 'choice' to leave the factory and set up her workshop was driven by the conditions at the factory and the fact that she was sacked and blacklisted for being a trade union officer. Other influences included her circumstances at home:

> It was very difficult for me, for I had to maintain my home – the rent, the food, my brothers and sisters; my father was already dead and [I] was the head of the household, my God, how was I going to manage?

Blacklisted for factory work, she was ill-prepared for setting up on her own. She had no capital, other than what she had received for being sacked, which was the legal minimum. She did not have any knowledge about the market. For her, it was 'a totally different world from the one that was unravelling'. She nevertheless set up on her own, employing a friend she knew from school, and started to build up a stock of clothes that she did not know how to sell – shirts, pyjamas, body warmers, etc. This was the beginning of 'good, good, good, times'. From being excluded from factory work for her trade union activity, she set up a successful small firm, allowing her to educate her children in the process, which was her primary objective in life.

Influences on artisan decision-making

The main influences on the choices artisans make emerged through their life histories and they included:

- Their commitment to their crafts;
- The decision to be a self-employed artisan rather than a wage-earning journeyman in another small workshop;
- The impact of delinquency and insecurity;
- The impact of old age on the choices they can make;
- The advance of technology in their fields;
- The effects of globalisation on their crafts; and
- The overriding importance of their families in all the decisions they make.

These influences were found through all types of activity but were expressed succinctly by jewellers who explained that they continued to work as artisans into old age 'because we like our craft'.[9] They originally started their businesses 'because as a journeyman the pay was very low'.[10] Robbery dissuades clients from spending money on expensive jewellery. The technology of the mobile phone has replaced timepieces and 'replacing a battery is more expensive than buying a new Chinese watch'.[11] Their future rests in their families, which they no longer have responsibility for. Their health begins to fail:

> [Age] is also affecting the sight, so there is a limit to being able to work. I have seen that there are older people who can no longer practice the profession because they are not able to.

Nevertheless, they continue to create jewels and repair watches because it is what they know and love.

Notes

1 Shoemakers are almost inevitably male.
2 Interview C2. This and all subsequent interviews with artisans were carried out in 2015, unless otherwise stated.
3 Small industries at that time were defined in the *Ley de Fomento de la Pequeña Industria y Artesanía of 1965*.
4 Interview AM1.
5 Interview BC2.
6 Interview BC6.
7 Interview MJ1.
8 Interview C1.
9 Interview C-7.
10 Interview C4.
11 Interview C4.

6 Formal-informal relations
Backward linkages

Introduction

In spite of the early literature on the informal sector emphasising the lack of linkages between the informal and formal sectors (ILO, 1972; Weeks, 1975; Sethuraman, 1975a), it has long been recognised that informal activities were 'linked intimately' to the formal sector (Leys, 1973 and 1975; Bromley, 1978; Birkbeck, 1978). When the ILO and others agreed that 'the formal and informal parts of the economy are so interlinked that it is misleading to think of two distinct sectors of the economy' (Chen et al., 2002, 2), they were correct to insist that they were parts of a single complex system. However, this realisation did not lead to an improved understanding of the ways in which capitalist and non-capitalist forms of production and distribution were connected, how these connections influenced the distribution of profits and incomes, and how this affected the accumulation of wealth. Chen went on to point out that 'many informal firms and workers are linked to formal firms through complex chains or networks of production and exchange' (Chen, 2014, 413). The literature on informality, unfortunately, has failed to interrogate this complexity in any depth beyond the narrow field of outsourcing in global supply chains.

Chen also recognises that informal firms provide routes to market for formal industrial production, not only through street sellers and market traders, but also through the purchase and use of equipment and raw materials by informal manufacturers. However, these relationships are seen as subordinate and dependent features of capitalist development and there is little discussion of what they mean for patterns of distribution of income and wealth. The focus of Chen's analysis relates to '*market exclusion* on unfair and unequal terms' and the 'emblematic case' of 'subcontracted industrial outwork for global value chains' (Chen, 2014, 414). These, however, are cases of forward linkages, which we will discuss in the next chapter – where we will argue that they may be exceptional rather than emblematic. When artisans buy equipment and materials from capitalist producers or their agents, these are cases of backwards linkages.

The backward linkages are an important part of the complex relations of production and exchange between the firms classified as formal and informal. Because of the widening of the definitions of informality that we saw in Chapter 2, however, the analysis of the contribution of micro-firms to the national and international economies has been relegated to a discussion about subcontracting of homeworkers. We will see in Chapter 8 that the source of raw materials is a defining issue in the discussion of the difference between homeworkers and the self-employed (ILO, 1996; Chen et al., 2002; Homenet South Asia Group, 2016). However, the variety of sources, along with the quality and price of raw materials and equipment, helps determine profits, household incomes and the potential for accumulation of informal manufacturers.

Artisan raw materials and equipment are normally the products of formal, national and international, manufacturers – and their cost and quality has a profound influence on the long-term relationship between micro-manufacturers and their customers. They create profit for capitalist firms and they help determine the level of profit for informal firms. There are complex purchasing networks, local and global chains that are more pervasive than global chains of production and subcontracting. These purchasing networks, through which capitalist manufacturing firms realise profit, change over time as the world economy develops. They have received scant attention in the theoretical literature, but generalised assumptions have been made about them with little evidence to sustain what is claimed.

In the process of buying tools and materials, a part of the artisan's income passes to the industrial capitalist who makes the inputs and a part may pass to traders who sell the products to the artisans. The traders may be wholesalers, shopkeepers, the owners of market stalls or, occasionally, street traders. Sometimes, the producer of the goods or the wholesaler, who may be the commercial outlet for several capitalist producers, will sell to the artisans through sales representatives who visit their workshops on a regular basis. These travelling salespersons will normally earn both salaries and commission from the large-scale capitalist operations. Some may be wholly reliant on commission and may be classified as 'self-employed' for the purposes of workers' rights and benefits. That is, they have none.

Any discussions of these purchasing patterns inevitably make two fundamental assumptions: first, that the micro-firm *uses* materials and equipment; and secondly, that they *purchase* any goods that they use. As artisans, by definition they will use raw materials that will be converted into another product, but they may not *buy* the materials. While we might also assume that all artisans will use tools to bring about this conversion, this is not always the case; and if they do *use* equipment, they do not always *buy* it.

The clients of some artisans, such as tailors and dressmakers, choose to buy their own materials for artisans to convert into made-to-measure clothes. These customers may buy their cloth locally, from retailers who sell national and imported fabrics, or they may buy them on overseas trips to destinations such as Colombia, the USA and Europe. Today, fashionable materials can be imported by clients through the Ecuadorian diaspora in these places or they can be bought over the internet. Clients buying cloth themselves, however, is a declining source of raw materials for tailors and dressmakers. As one octogenarian tailor said:

In the past, each client came with their own material; now the maestro has to hold a good selection of fine soft woollen cloth, they choose the material and I make the clothes. That is the way it is at the moment, times have changed.

Part of the reason for this change is the closure of national textile factories such as *La Internacional*, through global competition.[1] This factory had its own retail outlets in Quito, where clients would buy their own materials, before it closed in 1990 (Cuvi, 2011, 72). Now, the majority of cloth is imported, the clients prefer the quality of this cloth, and the artisans are resigned to the fate of national production:

La Internacional does not exist anymore. People used to buy a lot of raw material from *La Internacional*; I used to use materials made here in Ecuador, in Quito. Now the factories in Quito are closed. They suffered from international competition – that's what happens.

Nevertheless, most artisans, including tailors and dressmakers, buy their material locally, including the materials that are imported.

The same is true about sources of tools and machinery but the experience of a small number of individuals from 1975 who said they did not use hand tools points to a complex world of social relationships that condition their actions as workshop owners. Their experience illustrated the danger of oversimplification of the social and economic relations involved in even the least complex of artisan activities. These are interesting cases which need to be acknowledged, although they should not lead to us generalising from them and giving them too much weight in the overall analysis. They are also important in that they highlight the limits of any methodology that focuses on firms rather than individuals or households – and they caution us against relying totally on formal interview schedules and data analysis that does not explore the complexities of the lives of those trying to eke out an existence in the cities of the developing world.

The artisan as individual, family member and firm owner

The following cases, which came to light when we were gathering information about the use and sources of tools and machinery, provide a cautionary note before we turn to the survey analysis. They highlight a number of non-firm linkages of some petty producers to the formal sector of the economy, both private and state, without which individual and household survival would not be possible. They point to non-enterprise, sometimes family, inter-relationships which indicate a complexity that is often ignored. To focus on inter-firm relationships and to ask the question about formal–informal relations purely at the level of the firm can easily miss the fact that economic relations are only one set of relations that are embedded in a wider social network and culture.

The point of entry into this complexity was a number of questions about the use of tools and machinery. We asked workshop owners if they *used* hand tools and/or electric hand tools and/or fixed machinery, followed by questions about where they *bought* their equipment and whether they bought *new or used* tools and machinery.

In 1975, there were five cases where the workshop owner said they did not use non-electric hand tools. Two of these respondents were radio and television repair workers who said they used only electric tools. In the twenty-first century, it is difficult to conceive of how they might carry out such work without a screwdriver, but in 1975 this work mainly involved unclipping the back of the TV or radio and replacing valves or renewing or soldering condensers.

Another case was the 66-year-old owner of a shoe repair workshop, who employed a 60-year-old worker in a small rented space that had no external sign to attract business. The owner of the workshop was blind and, since he did not actually repair the shoes, he did not *use* tools. He nevertheless *owned* the small number of antiquated hand tools which were present and the worker, who effectively ran the workshop, used them – as he did not have any of his own. The case raised a number of interesting methodological points, not the least of which was the question as to who should have been interviewed as the owner of the workshop. The worker paid who he thought to be the owner of the business a percentage of his earnings. It could be argued that this was effectively a rent for the premises (and tools) and that the worker was in fact the owner of the business. However, the 'owner' also bought all the materials and paid someone else for the rent of the workshop, which was located in a single small room in a large building on the edge of the historic city centre. In a sense, the worker and the owner were linked into the formal property sector of Quito through the rent they paid. On the other hand, the owner also had a retirement pension from previous employment in the formal sector and he also owned other properties which earned him rental income.

In trying to analyse links to the formal sector through the use and purchase of tools, we therefore uncovered a complexity of personal circumstances and relations which urged caution against simplistic unidimensional analysis. It reminds us that focusing on the firm, rather than the individual, household or the family, only provides us with part of the economic story.

This is reinforced by another case which involved a candle-maker who did not use tools. This 66-year-old woman operated from inside her home, which she shared with her 74-year-old husband. In the same house, but in separate family and household units, lived three of their children. Two of these children, who were in their forties and who worked as a soldier and a policeman, supported their parents every month with a payment that was twice what they earned from the candle-making. Their salaries from the formal sector were, in fact, more important for the daily sustenance of their parents than the activity in the workshop.

Nevertheless, the woman, who worked at a table in the home, said that the candle-making was her full-time occupation. For raw materials she used other people's candle waste and she bought a few things at the local market in San

Roque. She gathered the candle-grease residues from churches in central Quito and spent around 100 sucres per month on wicks, dyes, purple paper and glue, which she bought from informal traders in the market place. The main part of her raw materials, therefore had no value at the point at which she gathered them. She converted this into between 100 and 200 candles every month, which she sold directly to worshippers for two sucres each. Her clients were mainly people who came to her home/workshop and asked for specific sizes and designs of candles to be made especially for them.

This woman's work also offered insight into the spiritual life of Quito at the time and pointed to a relationship between this non-material context and her economic well-being. Her market was in decline, because 'people don't use as many candles as in the past'. There was no continuity in her sales and her standard of living was in decline because of the rising cost of living, and she indicated that she would be willing, even at her age, to work in a factory if she could make the same money as she was earning making candles.

Another case where the owner of the workshop said he did not use tools helps to illuminate the complex relationship between legality and formal–informal relations in 1975. It is assumed by de Soto and his followers that a distinguishing feature between the formal and informal sector is that the former is legal and that the latter is illegal (de Soto, 1989). This case is that of a 75-year-old man who made dusters and cloths. His enterprise was mainly legal, except that he relied on an illegal relationship with the formal sector. This old man, working inside his home with the assistance of his 67-year-old wife, had run his workshop for 20 years. Both had migrated from the rural province of Cotopaxi 42 years previously. A hatmaker before he came to the city, he had hoped to get work with a distributor of *aguardiente* (alcohol distilled in the rural area) but his first job was in the large textile factory referred to above, *The Internacional*. He opened his workshop before retiring from *The Internacional* and he retired with a pension of 750 sucres per month (US$ 30). In the course of his time with the company, he had introduced his son to the firm and the son continued to work there.

When asked about his tools and machinery, he said he did not use tools. When prompted about the use of scissors and needles, he said he only washed wool and cotton, which he said he bought from wholesalers, to make cleaning cloths and dusters (*guaipe*). However, as the interview progressed, it became clear that he was using raw materials that came from the textile company where he had worked most of his life and where his son was still employed. He would not be drawn on this and, realistically, no amount of probing in a cold-calling interview would entice him to clearly admit that his material was illegally obtained by his son, since this would put his employment in jeopardy. It should perhaps be assumed that the cloth which he used was waste from the factory, but we do not know this for sure. It may have been cut to size in the factory, before being washed in the workshop. This source, however, whether it was waste or not, was illegal. His forward linkages to the market, on the other hand, were through the owners of shops who came to his workshop to buy his *guaipe*. He converted illegally obtained factory waste into goods that were distributed through what were probably mainly informal retailers, to all social classes in Quito.

In the course of this man's life and work history, he had been a rural artisanal hatmaker; the employee of one of the largest firms in Ecuador; the owner of a petty production workshop while still working in the capitalist firm, perhaps relying on the labour of his partner at this time; a self-employed workshop owner while drawing a retirement pension from the company, still dependent on the unpaid labour of his wife; someone who built his business on the illegal relations he had with the capitalist firm whilst still employed there; a small-scale producer who was reliant on the procurement activities of his son who still worked there; a manufacturer of goods that were bought and distributed by other small-scale retailers; and, through these shops, the supplier of goods into the homes of the middle classes (and others) in Quito. The man had many economic roles, some in series and some in parallel, some legal and some illegal, all of them involving relationships that were changing over time.

In summary, when we focus on enterprises, we miss a wealth of complexity that helps explain how the poor survive in Third World cities. However, we should also note that in many respects these cases were exceptions to the general rule, in that they emerged as interesting cases because the owners said they did not use tools. They are colourful, but there is always a danger of making unwarranted generalisations when we focus on the most interesting cases. Perhaps the most important message from these cases is that we should be cautious when we attempt to generalise from the results of a methodology which excludes this complexity from the analysis.

We are nevertheless seeking to analyse structures and discover trends in structural changes over time and in space. It is also possible to investigate relations between artisans and capitalist manufacturers, by looking into the complexity of these underlying structures and processes. At the level of the firm, there is a variety of relations between informal activities and formal enterprises, which are channelled through backwards linkages with various types and sizes of firms when the artisans buy their inputs. Artisans who use tools and raw materials often obtain these directly from international conglomerates or through their agents in cities such as Quito, but they also use other firms in the informal sector. As the direct type of relationship is the product of first-hand interaction between micro-producers and other enterprises, information about this can be obtained by asking the small producer about his or her experience.

The investigation of the direct experience of the purchase of inputs provides insight into the types of relationship that exist between artisans, capitalist producers, large-scale merchants, other non-capitalist producers and small traders. The mechanisms for the transfer are varied, as are the patterns of value transfer. In the case of raw materials, for example, the micro-producers can buy them directly from the factory or from representatives of the producers who visit them in their workshops. However, most artisans buy their raw materials from traders, who themselves could be classified as formal or informal sector distributors. Wholesalers, who have made a substantial investment in the purchase of raw materials from producers, exist alongside hardware stores and other retailers who may stock small supplies of nails, screws, threads, paints, etc. and who themselves may obtain the materials from either the wholesalers or the producers themselves. These different types of traders create a structure of distribution which is not dissimilar to that which is found in the developed world, but a significantly higher proportion of the smaller traders may be operating from a room of their home and there are some who operate in the streets or in urban market places. In addition, the structure of supply of artisan materials changes over time.

Through survey research, it is possible to aggregate different relationships to see which are prevalent at any point in time and how the significance and nature of the linkages change over time. These relations determine the transfer of value and the generation of profit. It is widely recognised that people may move in and out of different types of work, that there may be life-cycle effects that influence this movement, and that backward linkages between different types and sizes of firms may be transitory. However, different types of relations between individuals, families and firms may also coexist at any one time.

Micro-producers in Quito represent an important market outlet for a variety of activities in the formal sector. They are a channel through which the formal sector reaches final demand. Tailors, for example, rely on the textile industry, both national and international, for the cloth which they fashion into clothes for men, women and children of all social classes in the city. Shoemakers buy cured hides which mainly have their origins in a modernising cattle-ranching rural economy, although peasant farmers also find an outlet through the same slaughter-houses and tanneries. Carpenters use wood that can be traced back to large-scale timber-producing enterprises, which are often involved in the de-forestation of the Amazonian rain forests. Mechanics, who historically were accomplished in making parts from otherwise worthless scrap metal, now often work with raw materials and spare parts that are produced by some of the world's largest multi-national corporations. Painters and signwriters use materials that are produced by national and international chemical firms, increasingly using the plastics which are derivatives of oil and the products of multi-national oil and chemical giants. Jewellers have traditionally worked with the precious stones and metals of Ecuador and the rest of the Andean Region, but increasingly they fashion their jewels out of cheaper materials produced by the extraction and manufacturing activities of international capital. Printers work with paper, which only the formal sector can produce.

These micro-producers are therefore intimately tied to formal capitalist production, offering large-scale capital a route to a fragmented popular market. However, in functioning as market outlets they can also become *dependent* on large-scale capital. This relationship can be one of subordination and control but, despite what some neo-Marxist analysis has proposed (Le Brun and Gerry, 1975), it is not exploitative according to the labour theory of value. When an artisan buys equipment or materials, s/he is paying for the value of the labour of the factory worker that has gone into the manufacture of goods. It helps the factory owner realise the surplus value generated by the exploited factory labour.

The artisan is helping the capitalist generate a profit, but it is the labour of the factory worker that is exploited.

The artisans' dependence on large-scale production for inputs can be expressed in a number of ways: concentration of capitalist ownership and monopoly supply can push up their costs, making the artisans less competitive in a market that is increasingly penetrated by capitalist production of consumer goods. If supply is cut off, by strikes or the closure of national firms, artisan production can be disrupted. The purchase of inputs using supplier credit increases artisan dependency on their suppliers. Some artisans are also dependent on finance capital for the expansion of their business through investment in equipment, raw materials or the commercialisation of their production.

All of these relationship exist in a developing national and international context, which influences the changing availability and use of different types of equipment and materials. In the next section, we will investigate the use of different types of equipment, the investment that is made, and the structure of supply. We will then look at sources of raw materials, before considering the forces underlying changes in the structure of supply.

The use of tools and machinery

For the purposes of the analysis in 1975, we distinguished between hand tools, electric hand tools (such as electric drills) and fixed machinery. The propensity of different types of artisans to use each of these types of equipment is different and we might expect different trends in their use over time. As an indicator of economic development, for example, we might expect the use of electric hand tools and fixed machinery to increase over time. Indeed, this is what happened, but the changes did not happen in a smooth trajectory.

In 1975, when we asked artisans what tools they used in their work, 95% said they used hand tools and it is no surprise that this level of use continued throughout the 40 years to 2015 (Table 6.1). Over the period of the research, the use of *electric* hand tools increased substantially (from 38% to 81%) as did the use of fixed machinery (from 20% to 63%). The use of electric hand tools increased year by year, but the growth of fixed machinery was irregular throughout. The use of fixed machinery increased in the oil boom years, collapsed during the years of structural adjustment and recovered after the decade of the neoliberal crisis. These changes were highly significant in the relevant inter-survey periods.

We also have to remember, however, that these firms are survivors and that the number of firms in the study area declined after 1982. If we apply the percentage usage from the survey to the number of firms in the census of each year, we find that the *number* of firms using electric hand tools fell in the 1982–95 and 1995–2005 periods (at an annual rate of -2.3% and -1.5% respectively). The decline in the use of fixed machinery during structural adjustment was even greater: following almost 12% per annum growth in 1975–82, there was a 10% decline every year between 1982 and 1995. Although there was a 1% p.a. growth through the crisis

Table 6.1 Tools used by artisans

(Using samples)	1975		1982		1995		2005		2015	
	No.	%	No.	%	No.	%	No.	%	No.	%
Hand tools	183	95.3	295	99.0	313	95.7	305	96.2	249	96.9
Electric hand tools	73	38.0	185	62.1	230	70.3	250	78.9	209	81.3
Fixed machinery	40	20.8	131	44.0	94	28.7	143	45.1	163	63.4
Does not use tools	7	3.6	1	0.3	1	0.3	3	0.9	0	0.0
TOTAL	192		298		327		317		257	
Census Total	2308		2380		1786		1301		1365	

Average annual change (using percentages)

	1975–1982	1982–1995	1995–2005	2005–2015	1975–2015
	% P.A.	% P.A.	% P.A.	% P.A.	% P.A.
Hand tools	0.5	-0.3	0.1	0.1	0.0
Electric hand tools	7.3	1.0	1.2	0.3	1.9
Fixed machinery	11.3	-3.2	4.6	3.5	2.8

Table 6.1 (Cont.)

Extrapolated to censuses

	1975		1982		1995		2005		2015	
	No.	%	No.	%	No.	%	No.	%	No.	%
Hand tools	2200	95.3	2356	99.0	1710	95.7	1252	96.2	1323	96.9
Electric hand tools	878	38.0	1478	62.1	1256	70.3	1026	78.9	1110	81.3
Fixed machinery	481	20.8	1046	44.0	513	28.7	587	45.1	866	63.4
	84	3.6	8	0.3	0	0.0	12	0.9	0	0.0
	2308		2380		1786		1301		1365	

Average annual change (using absolute numbers)

	1975–1982	1982–1995	1995–2005	2005–2015	1975–2015
	% P.A.	% P.A.	% P.A.	% P.A.	% P.A.
Hand tools	1.0	-4.5	-2.4	0.6	-1.3
Electric hand tools	7.7	-2.3	-1.5	0.8	0.6
Fixed machinery	11.7	-9.7	1.0	4.0	1.5

of neoliberalism, the data suggest an overall catastrophic decline in investment by micro-firms during the neoliberal years. It would appear that the policies of successive neoliberal governments produced downward pressure on investment by microenterprises. After 2005, the use of machinery grew rapidly again, during the period of Correa's anti-globalisation government.

Even when artisans *use* different types of equipment, some may not *buy* tools or machinery over long periods, whilst others inherit most of what they use from family or retiring masters. To the extent that we are dealing with a poor population where there is a high turnover of small firms, and where the life of tools is extended through repair, we might expect second-hand sources to be important. In a buoyant economy with expanding enterprises, these sources might diminish. Increased demand should bring about a contraction of second-hand supply and a growing investment in new equipment. Technological change in the context of rapid development would encourage the use of sources of new equipment, although some old tools which were being replaced could find their way back on to the market.

Investment in equipment

Note: The data that support the following sections can be found in Tables A.6.1, A.6.2 and A.6.3 of the online Appendix.

Artisans who did buy tools and machinery purchased them from a variety of sources, formal and informal, including, retailers, market stalls, wholesalers, representatives of manufacturers and directly from the manufacturers themselves. In a developing economy, particularly where the nature of artisan production is evolving, we might expect the aggregated structure of supply to respond to changing patterns of demand. For example, as traditional shoemaking declines in importance and modern car repair increases, the types of tools used by artisans in general will change and the new structure of equipment supply will respond to the growing sophistication of modern automobiles and their maintenance. This could profoundly change the way commerce is organised, in this case increasing demand for electronic testing equipment that needs to be imported, and alter the relationship between suppliers of equipment and informal producers.

We asked artisans if, when they purchased tools and machinery, they bought new or used equipment. One would expect almost all artisans to buy hand tools, less to buy electric hand tools and less still to purchase fixed machinery. When artisans buy equipment, they mainly buy new but they are consistently less likely to buy new machinery than new hand tools. Over the whole study period, 1975–2015, those buying second-hand hand tools declined, the proportion buying second-hand electric tools increased, and those purchasing second-hand machinery halved.[2] The aggregated figures, however, were arrived at through different trends in the inter-survey periods. The change in the proportion buying different types of used equipment was as follows:

1975–1982: The oil boom years
Decline in buying used hand tools
Little change in new/used proportions for electric tools
Large decline in buying used fixed machinery

1982–1995: Structural adjustment
Increase in buying used hand tools.
Increase in buying used electric hand tools.
Increase in buying used machinery

1995–2005: Neoliberal crisis and globalisation
Decline in buying used hand tools
Little change in buying new and used electric tools
Little change in buying new and used machinery

2005–2015: Anti-globalisation
Little change for hand tools
Decline in buying used electric tools
Small decline in buying used machinery.

There was new investment in the oil boom years but since then the artisans have consistently been less able to invest in new tools and machinery. For all three types of equipment, the proportion of artisans who bought only *used* equipment *increased* during structural adjustment (Figure 6.1). Significantly, the proportion *using* fixed machinery not only fell during structural adjustment (Table 6.1), but

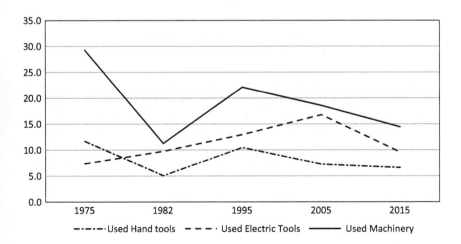

Figure 6.1 Artisans who bought used equipment

there was also an increase in the proportion buying used machinery. As workshops failed during this period, surviving workshops bought their old equipment.

The structure of equipment supply

The supply of hand tools

There was no evidence of widespread 'dependence' on particular suppliers of tools in 1975, when the largest group of suppliers were retailers. Comparing 1975 with 2015, there were important changes in roles of both retailers and the representatives of large-scale producers. The retail outlets grew in importance and company representatives declined, which suggests even less dependency than in 1975 (Table A.6.1).[3] However, the nature of retail was changing over the period. In 1975, artisans bought from street traders, market traders and small shopkeepers, most of whom paid no taxes and were unregulated. By 2015, many of the small suppliers had been drawn into the government's net, using electronic equipment to record not only purchases of materials from formal suppliers but also sales, wages and VAT. They were still small-scale, but it is debatable if they would still be considered to be informal in the original sense of the word.

The changes were not uniform over time. Between 1982 and 1995, there was a collapse in the importance of representatives and a growth in the role of wholesalers, changes that were highly significant. This was consistent with the capitalisation of large-scale importers who were the suppliers of new equipment and who were promoted by the government of Febres Cordero during structural adjustment. By 1995, wholesalers had overtaken retailers to become the main suppliers of hand tools.

Between 1995 and 2005, there was an influx of Asian retail traders who were linked to their homeland through supply chains of international wholesalers who bought from Chinese and South Korean producers. The wholesalers were selling cheap and inferior tools to small retailers who were linked to the wholesalers ethnically as well as economically. They were also dependent on these international suppliers through the provision of credit.

After 2005, there was a large growth in retail at the expense of wholesalers. Global suppliers were emerging and their position was consolidated through an expansion into retail outlets that were less ethnically homogenous. By 2015, as the technology of retail was also changing and small-scale traders were increasingly incorporated into the state's systems, the artisans were obtaining almost 60% of their hand tools from retailers, compared to just 31% in 1995. The significant changes over the 40-year period, however, were not linear. They were a consequence of conflicting forces in the wider economy and the changing use of electronic technology in the supply chain, from producer of inputs to final demand.

The supply of electric hand tools

When asked who the suppliers of electric hand tools were, we found that the initial structure of supply was not the same as for non-electric hand tools. In

1975, the main source was through company representatives who, as agents of mainly international manufacturers from Europe and North America, were much more important than wholesalers and retailers (Table A.6.2). By 2015, however, retailers were by far the most common source of supply and the structure of supply was the same as for ordinary hand tools. As the use of electric hand tools increased, the nature of the suppliers changed from large-scale to small-scale enterprises who were linked to growing Asian production.

The changes over time were highly significant and the trends were similar to what happened in the market for hand tools. There was a steady decline in representatives; an initial decline of retailers in the boom years followed by gradual increase to 2005 and then a particularly pronounced growth between 2005 and 2015. The initial increase in national wholesale suppliers during structural adjustment was reversed in the decade of the neoliberal financial crisis as Asian suppliers took over.

The supply of fixed machinery

The initial structure of supply of fixed machinery was different from that of hand tools, both electric and non-electric, but the changes in the types of supplier between 1975 and 2015 was, once again, highly significant (Table A.6.3). The predominant suppliers in 1975 were representatives and wholesalers, and if we include the small numbers who bought directly from producers, large-scale formal capital accounted for 82% of suppliers. By 2015, wholesalers and retailers had become the most important sources and representatives had declined from 45% to only 12% of suppliers.

At the beginning of the study period, a small number of artisans said they bought their machinery from 'other' sources[4] – from unspecified individuals, other artisans or a pawnshop.[5] By 1982, the proportion using 'other' sources had increased from 3% to 13% and by 1995 this had reached 28%. In the 1982–1995 period, the changes were highly significant, with a surge in the importance of retailers and 'others', including other artisans. Those who bought from other artisans included every type of artisan activity, the largest groups being shoemakers, carpenters and tailors – the main producers of subsistence goods, which were the three groups with the largest rates of decline in the numbers or workshops between 1975 and 1995. Half of the 28 workshop owners who cited 'other' sources said they had bought their machinery from other artisans whose workshops had closed. All the shoemakers had obtained their equipment in this way during structural adjustment.

By 1995, therefore, the failure of artisan workshops was a major contributing factor to the diversity of sources of machinery. Around 14% of artisans who bought machinery had obtained their equipment from failed businesses. Much of this machinery will have been obsolete and may have contributed to the business failure of the original owners.

The general trends in the evolution of retail firms as sources of tools and machinery can be seen in Figures 6.2 and 6.3. If we reclassify the suppliers into large-scale and small-scale,[6] this provides an impression of the balance between

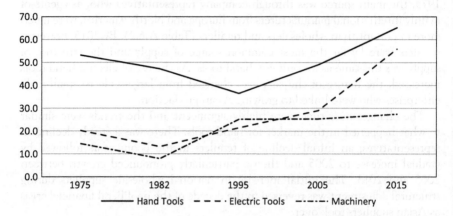

Figure 6.2 Artisans who buy equipment from retailers (including market stalls)

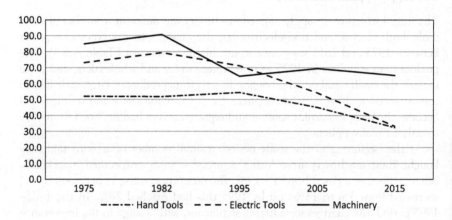

Figure 6.3 Use of large-scale sources of equipment

formal and informal providers in the early years of the study. The change in size of suppliers of hand tools, electric hand tools and fixed machinery are highly significant between 1975 and 2015 (Tables A.6.4, A.6.5 and A.6.6). For both types of hand tools, suppliers changed from being majority large-scale to majority small-scale. For machinery, large-scale suppliers remained the majority, but the switch to small-scale was highly significant. However, the decline in the large formal sector suppliers of machinery took place between 1982 and 1995.

The importance of large formal traders in the supply of machinery is much greater than for the purchase of hand tools – and that is to be expected. Small-scale commercial capital cannot make the type of investment needed to stock larger machinery. This implies that the greater the investment made by the small producer, the less is the relative importance of the contribution s/he is making to the non-capitalist sector of the economy. If it were possible for small producers to enter into a phase of sustained development through capital investment, this would reduce the contribution to informal trade. Investment in labour saving machinery not only means labour replacement in artisan production, but also in small-scale trade.

However, we need to be clear that small-scale suppliers in 2015 are not the same as in 1975. In 1975, there would be little doubt that small-scale suppliers would have been classified as informal, in the sense that shops and market stalls were outside the influence of the state, operated on the margins, paid no taxes, were not affiliated to the social security system, relied on unpaid family labour and had other characteristics of the informal sector. These small-scale traders were non-capitalist forms of distribution, whilst the large-scale sources were capitalist in nature, employing waged and salaried labour. In 2015, this distinction was no longer true. Reflecting some of the changes that have taken place globally, the nature of retail has changed. The new retailers have modernised, are linked into a sophisticated wholesale sector of the economy, are larger than they were in 1975, are more likely to use paid family workers, have greater capital investments, are connected to suppliers electronically, have electronic links to the banking system, have electronic systems for wages and benefits, and are also electronically connected to government sales tax systems. This is also true for small-scale suppliers of raw materials.

The supply of raw materials

The structure of the supply of artisan raw materials changed dramatically after 1975 (Table 6.2). With the exception of 1995–2000, the changes in each inter-survey period were highly significant. In 1975, the two main sources of raw materials were wholesalers and retailers, each providing inputs to around 28% of artisans. Between 1975 and 1982, wholesalers increased in importance, as was the case for hand tools. The role of wholesalers then increased rapidly to 1995, before levelling off in the following decade. The years between 2005 and 2015 saw a resurgence in the importance of retailers, as was the case for the modernised suppliers of equipment (see also Table A.6.7).

The shift towards large-scale commercial capital between 1975 and 1982 contrasts with a transition in the opposite direction between 2005 and 2015 (Table A.6.8). In 1975, supply was dominated by national production and in the decades of neoliberal dominance between 1982 and 2005, the growing importance of the local capitalist suppliers of raw materials stalled and stagnated, contrary to what neoliberal theory would predict. These trends can be seen in Figure 6.4.

In the majority of cases throughout the study period, the part of income created in small manufacturing that goes towards the purchase of raw materials passed directly to large-scale merchants and on to industrial capital. This fraction contributes nothing to the growth of informal trade. On the other hand, since 41% of small producers bought raw materials from small-scale traders in 1975 and

Table 6.2 Sources of raw materials

	1975		1982		1995		2005		2015	
	No.	*%*	*No.*	*%*	*No.*	*%*	*No.*	*%*	*No.*	*%*
Representatives	36	19.0	44	15.4	21	6.4	34	10.9	29	11.6
Markets	11	5.8	9	3.2	7	2.1	10	3.2	3	1.2
Retailers	54	28.6	48	16.8	60	18.4	64	20.5	88	35.3
Wholesalers	52	27.5	88	30.9	144	44.2	133	42.6	92	36.9
Other	14	7.4	44	15.4	32	9.8	33	10.6	18	7.2
Combinations	22	11.6	52	18.2	62	19.0	38	12.2	19	7.6
	189	100.0	285	100.0	326	100.0	312	100.0	249	100.0

	Chi-sq	*DF*	*p-value*
1975–2015	99.0669	20	1.85E-12
1975–1982	19.6826	5	0.0015
1982–1995	23.3649	5	0.0003
1995–2005	9.6408	5	0.0861
2005–2015	19.3407	5	0.0017
1975&2015	17.4042	5	0.0038
1975–1995	55.0978	10	0.0000
1975–2005	62.7470	15	0.0000

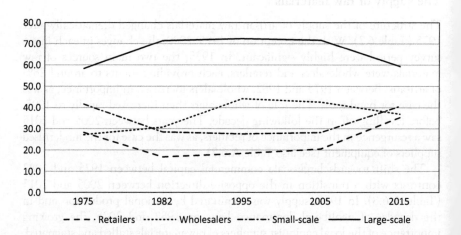

Figure 6.4 Sources of raw materials

2015, a part of their surplus remained within the sphere of small-scale circulation. Artisans therefore not only provide a market for capitalist production, they have also been an important market for some small traders.

As the economy developed, the sources of supply also evolved, but the main changes were within the formal sector. Between 1982 and 1995, the significance of wholesale supply increased and the importance of sales representatives declined. Between 1995 and 2005, there was no significant change in the structure of supply, in spite of the fact that the importance of sales representatives grew again and the number mentioning combinations of sources declined. Between 2005 and 2015, however, the structure changed again and the change was highly significant. In this decade, there was a resurgence of the importance of retailers but, as was the case for equipment, many retailers supplying raw materials to artisans are now highly modernised and regulated. Retail supply has, to a large extent, been formalised.

Individual choice and structural pressures

In deciding to use one or other source of supply, artisans make individual decisions based on their personal circumstances but these preferences are conditioned by a structural context that influences the outcomes. Their personal decisions take place in an economic context that is changing all the time. As a consequence, their preferences are constantly being modified by a variety of pressures beyond their control. The structure of supply for a seamstress, however, is different from the structure of supply for a printer and the relative importance of different types of suppliers has changed over time for these types of activity. The aggregated choices that individual artisans make at any time are a result of economic forces that create a variety of evolving structures of supply for different activities.

The changes in the sources of tools, machinery and raw materials can mainly be attributed to five sets of underlying forces:

a. Changes in the structure of the manufacturers of inputs
b. Changes in the structure of artisan production
c. Changes in the technology of the production of inputs
d. Changes in the technology of tools and equipment
e. Social changes in Quito

Examples of these can be found in different sectors of artisan production and, if we focus on how they affect the sources of raw materials, we can see how they influence relations between the spheres of micro-production and exchange.

Changes in the structure of the manufacturers of raw materials

In 1975, in the case of tailors, the tendency for buying materials from large-scale producers was the opposite from what was found for artisans in general. As suggested earlier, many clients provided their own materials and the majority of tailors bought from retail outlets. This was partially explained by the fact that the largest part of the raw materials bought by tailors were purchased from the retail outlets owned by large national manufacturers. Following the collapse of the textile industry, most of these factories, and their retail outlets, have closed down. Now, textile shops are mainly selling imported goods.

Shoemakers in 1975 relied on the production of hides by traditional haciendas in the Ecuadorean Sierra, which were then cured in tanneries that had changed little in hundreds of years. The representatives of these tanneries of rural Ecuador were important sources of raw materials in the 1970s. The capitalisation of Ecuadorean agriculture, starting in the 1970s as the rural elite captured a large share of the country's new oil wealth, also led to the modernisation of the manufacture and distribution of rural outputs, including the leather that was used by Quito's shoemakers. Capitalist shoe manufacturers, such as Bata, opened factories in Ecuador to respond to the increased demand in the 1970s and, although these factories have now disappeared under the same international pressure that closed the textile factories, the demand for shoes continued to increase, as did the need for repair. The organisation of the market for the shoemakers' raw materials responded by the setting up a network of retail outlets for not only national leather but also imported leather and other materials that service the repair needs of shoemakers. The manufacture of heels, which were previously made of wood and created by hand by artisans, has also been mechanised and, now made of plastic in larger factories or imported, they are distributed through the same retail outlets.

The changing structure of the manufacture of raw materials is perhaps the most important influence on the relations between the artisans and their suppliers. However, the structure of artisan production, which changes for different reasons, is also significant.

Changes in the structure of artisan production

Some of the changes in the sources of supply are related to the evolution of different types of economic activity within a grouped category or subtype of artisan activity. We have noted that artisans are classified internationally according to the materials they use. We also saw that the artisan category of 'stone and marble', for example, includes painters, signwriters, glaziers, stonemasons and ornament makers. This group of artisans predominantly work in glass and stone and many are linked to the trade of shop-fitting, including the creation of signage.

In Quito in 1975, the sector was dominated by signwriters and painters, who benefited from the expansion of the economy in the 1970s as the demand for their skills increased with the growth of the formal sector. However, it later came to be predominantly represented by stonemasons making marble headstones. This, and the changing technology used by signwriters, contributed to a change in the nature of the structure of supply for raw materials. In 1975, two-thirds of them used small-scale sources for their raw materials. Over the next 20 years, the signwriters' materials changed from painted lettering on wooden boards, which was the main method for creating signs in 1975, to neon or plastic lettering on plastic boards, products that have been created and developed by subsidiaries of the oil industry.

By 1995, this had created a demand for new materials that could only be supplied by capitalist manufacturers or their agents. After 1995, the regeneration of the Historic Centre of Quito began to influence signage in the city centre and the role of the *Municipio* as a promoter of cultural heritage caused wrought iron methods to be introduced, which later spread to other areas of the city that were considered worthy of conservation. The shift to plastics and then to wrought iron led to the displacement of the traditional painter/signwriters. This category of artisans, which is internationally defined as 'stone and marble' and included stonemasons who were to be found in the streets around the San Diego cemetery, changed in its composition. As the population of the city grew, and more people died, the demand for the work of the stonemasons came to dominate the subsector. Reliant on industrially produced marble, the links to capitalist enterprises logically increased for this group of artisans.

The work of glaziers also changed, as hand-made window frames were replaced with mass-produced plastic and metal frames, allowing the glaziers to work with industrially produced materials rather than hand-crafted frames and further tying the sub-sector into capitalist production of inputs. In 1975, only 33% of painters, etc. obtained their raw materials from the capitalist sector but this had risen to 71% in 1995 and to over 80% in 2005 (Table A.6.9). By 2015, this group of artisans had gone from the least likely to use large-scale sources of supply for their raw materials to become the most likely to do so.

Changes in the technology of raw material production

Not all cases fit easily into the categories used. Carpenters buy their wood from sawmills, wood depositories and factories. There is little to distinguish wood depositories from sawmills and both were counted as wholesalers of wood in the survey.[7] Sawmills cut logs into timbers and the carpenters turn these timbers into furniture. However, the nature of furniture-making has changed and the production of materials for furniture-making is a modern, high-technology manufacturing enterprise. In 1975, there was no industrially processed wood such as MDF, and very little plywood. Now, the carpenters obtain their raw materials from the agents of new factories producing these industrial materials. The growth of capitalist supply is a function of the technology of the production of raw materials, allied to changing fashions and demand in the emerging middle classes.

Changes in the technology of tools and equipment

An example of the importance of the influence of the change in technology in the tools used by artisans is the case of photographers. Traditionally, photographers obtained their raw materials directly from the makers of film, such as Kodak, or the producers of photographic chemicals, but this has now changed with digital photography. Photographers survive through enlarging photos taken by their clients and restoring and enhancing old photographs, using software such as Photoshop. Their tools are digital technology and computers, and their raw materials are the reams of paper that are to be found in retail outlets across the city.

Social changes in Quito

Quito is a much more dangerous city than it was in 1975. Because of the prevalence of robbery of workshops and their clients, Jewellers have seen the demand for their raw materials change dramatically, from gold, silver, emeralds and other precious stones to imitations of fine metals and other less valuable stones. The jewellers used to buy precious metals through their federation; now they are more likely to obtain gold and silver from individuals who come to the workshop to sell them. These include other artisans as well as traders and, in some cases, thieves.

To summarise, the reality of backward linkages for artisans is much more complex than the duality of the formal–informal model would suggest. An understanding of the changing relations of artisans to the suppliers of equipment and raw materials requires an appreciation of the changing structures of both capitalist and artisan production, changes in the technology of production of both raw materials and tools, as well as social changes that influence demand for artisan outputs. Analyses that are stuck in discussions of the duality of formal–informal relations cannot begin to uncover the complexity of networks and processes that drive capital accumulation and the process of development. Likewise, analyses that lump artisans together with precariously employed wage labour in the capitalist sector cannot begin to tease out these structures and processes.

The activity of the small producers is an important factor in the process of accumulation of large-scale commercial capital and industrial capital. Over time, for a variety of reasons, the nature and structure of the supply of raw materials changes. The provision of goods on a small scale continues to contribute to the accumulation of capital outside the sphere of small-scale production, through the purchase of raw materials, tools and machinery. Artisans are customers for capitalist production. An important question now is the extent to which formal enterprises are customers of artisan activity.

Notes

1 *La Internacional* was set up in 1924 in *Chimbacalle*, one of the barrios where the artisan research was carried out. It transferred to an area close by, which is now *El Recreo* shopping mall, in 1947. It closed in 1990.
2 All were statistically significant.
3 The table refers to 'mentions'. Combinations have been disaggregated and placed in the six categories in Table 6.2.
4 There were five cases, four of whom were printers/photographers and one was a jeweller. When the data were weighted, these accounted for just 3% of the sample.
5 *Monte de Piedad*, which is a not-for-profit international pawnshop, set up in Mexico City in 1775.
6 Classifying representatives, wholesalers and producers as large-scale and market traders and shopkeepers as small-scale.
7 The sawmills could also have been classified as manufacturers of wood that is ready for use in construction and furniture-making. In any case, the sawn wood remains a raw material for the carpenter, albeit an intermediate good.

7 Customers, clients and formal markets

Introduction

Artisans have a variety of different relationships with their customers, who can be individuals, firms or other organisations. The commodities produced or the labour provided by artisans may be consumed directly by the customer, may re-enter the process of production through their incorporation as raw materials or intermediate goods by the private sector, or they may be purchased by the state, either to be consumed in the provision of services or in the production processes of nationalised industries. To reach these consumers, goods may be transferred directly from the artisan to the final user, or they may arrive via intermediaries. The levels of demand for different types of artisans may vary according to the buoyancy or depression of the different segments of the economy to which they are oriented; and their capacity to extend their customer base may be restricted by a narrow structure of access to markets.

We have seen that there were early theoretical disagreements about the extent of linkages between the formal and informal sectors and whether the links were benign or exploitative (ILO, 1972; Leys 1973, 1975; Weeks, 1975; Bienefeld and Godfrey, 1975; Bromley 1978). Part of the argument in favour of the 'exploitation' perspective was that cheap inputs produced by the informal sector made profits in the formal sector higher than they otherwise would have been. Through the exploitation of the informal workforce, capitalist firms were able to increase their profits. The informal sector was integrated and thoroughly exploited and, rather than there being competition for markets, the informal sector only provided for residual markets in which large firms were not interested (Quijano, 1974; Souza and Tokman, 1976; Tokman, 1977; Bienefeld and Godfrey, 1978).

Authors who perceive the relationship with formal firms to be beneficial for micro-firms, argue that it expands the range of market opportunities, allows them to specialise, raises efficiency, improves the use of productive capacity, leads to technology upgrading, minimises business risks and provides enhanced opportunities for access to credit from financial institutions (Sahu, 2010). Sometimes there are technological relations that involve the transfer of tools and machinery, the sharing of technological knowhow and the transfer of related skills. When the capitalist-firm-as-customer is a supplier of raw materials to a subcontractor, this is also seen as an additional benefit for the smaller unit.

It is acknowledged that there are also benefits for the larger or parent firm, such as cost advantages through lower wage costs, more labour flexibility, risk reduction and the avoidance of the problems of labour management. From the exploitation perspective, however, these characteristics of the relationship would confirm the validity of their viewpoint. They would be evidence of power and exploitation, forcing down wages, creating precarious work, transferring risk to the smaller company, and stoking tensions in their labour–management relations. In addition, the provision of raw materials would be evidence of a larger firm's effective control of the production process. It would be argued that there is very little transfer of equipment, and it would be pointed out that credit is not normally made directly available by the firm that controls the contractual relationship. We will return to the relevance of access to bank finance for the artisan in Chapters 11 and 12, pausing only to note here that the precarious nature of these subcontracting arrangements might not instil confidence in formal financial institutions.

Where an author thinks that, on balance, the relationship is benign, it is also conceded that there are exploitative practices such as delayed payments, stringent quality control, undue reductions in prices, sudden cuts in orders, lack of continuity of work, and unjustified termination of contracts (Sahu, 2010, 69). In addition, in what Sahu refers to as the 'unorganised manufacturing sector', productivity levels are higher in non-subcontracting units. Labour in subcontracted manufacturing firms is low-paid, precarious, temporary and less productive than the rest of informal manufacturing.

As globalisation expanded towards the end of the twentieth century and into the twenty-first century, the issue of subcontracting grew in importance (Cunningham and Gomez, 2004; ILO and WIEGO, 2013; Chen, 2014). The exploitation of the impoverished workers of sweatshops in the developing world by enterprises that sold clothes and shoes to the wealthy in developed countries caused outrage in the United States and Europe (Anner, 2000; Appelbaum, 2000). Examples of working conditions in such workshops made headline news, causing global brands to modify their procurement practices. It was assumed that such conditions were widespread, but information that might support or negate these assumptions was lacking.

For some authors, the traditional artisans who produce for local customers are treated as a minority economic activity in informal economies, which are seen to be dominated by multinational corporations that subcontract outwork to 'self-employed' manufacturers. This type of subcontracting was a feature of the development of capitalism in the UK (Clapham, 1929, Thompson, 1968) and, without wishing to deny its existence as part of what is now defined as the 'informal economy', there is an unjustified assumption that, as self-employment has persisted and expanded in developing countries, the production of goods and services has been increasingly subcontracted to small-scale informal firms.

It is argued that, through these relations, the informal economy has become a permanent and dependent feature of capitalist development (Portes et al., 1989; Chen, 2014). The focus is on subcontracted workers who work in or around their own home, producing goods for national or global value chains. Like the self-employed, they absorb many of the costs of production (other than the cost of raw materials) and are not directly supervised by those who contract work to them. 'Subcontracted home-based workers are neither fully independent nor fully dependent and should be considered semi-dependent' (Chen, 2014, 409).

The main difficulty for this type of analysis is that it is not clear whether the formal manufacturer is being treated as an employer or a customer. It can be agreed that most informal workers do not fit neatly into employer–employee relationship categories and, in developing countries, there is a constantly changing mix of traditional, industrial and global forms of production and exchange. However, less certain is the idea that artisanal forms of production 'have not changed significantly over the past century' (Chen, 2014, 409). While it is recognised that classical modes of artisan production still persist, whereby artisans own the means of production, work in their own premises 'with the help of household labour and (as needed) hired workers, and produce for sale in the market' (ibid.), the emphasis is on new modes of artisan production that have emerged, whereby they lose their independence and work partially or exclusively under contract to a larger firm. It is argued that 'production is often subcontracted to informal enterprises or to industrial outworkers who work from their homes' (ibid.). 'In the manufacturing sector, informal firms and industrial outworkers/subcontracted workers produce goods for formal firms through domestic and global value chains' (ibid., 410).

It is also pointed out that many informal firms are linked to formal firms through complex chains or networks of production and exchange. We have already contested the idea that subcontracted industrial outwork for global value chains is an 'emblematic case' of 'market inclusion on unfair and unequal terms' (ibid., 414), without denying the unequal power relations of the situation. Unfair market inclusion is found in subcontracted outwork, through which domestic and global networks of outsourcing link informal firms and their workers to formal firms. One can also agree that certain firms 'tend' to behave in a certain way, that production is 'often' of a certain type and that 'some' relations of production and exchange exist, but it is difficult identify the scale and importance of what is being observed and analysed. The nature and extent of the different relations of production and exchange are unclear.

Many firms operate with a mixture of relations of production, depending on the demand from customers, some are involved in both production and repair, and links to the market may be of a variety of types, including sporadic subcontracting to larger firms as well as to other artisans when they have lots of work.[1] The key issue is about how their labour time is used. The artisans are selling their labour time and some of it is incorporated into relations of subcontracting, but the question is whether the contracting firm is a 'customer' for the outputs of the petty producer.

Defining the customer

The word *customer* is a generic term for anyone, whether an individual or organisation, who buys the artisan's goods or uses their labour. The concept of the *customer* will therefore be applied to clients, shoppers, intermediaries, cooperatives, capitalist manufacturers, other private sector firms and the state. These customers can be broadly described as follows:

- **Clients:** Private individuals who personally ask for the creation of the work.
- **Shoppers:** Individuals who purchase goods that have already been made.
- **Intermediaries:** Individuals and firms (formal and informal) who buy the outputs to re-sell them.
- **Cooperatives:** organisations that are owned by a collective of artisans.
- **Capitalist manufacturers:** Capitalist (formal) forms of production that incorporate the artisan goods or labour into their own production processes.
- **Other private sector firms:** such as builders, banks, transport companies and other service sector firms.
- **The state:** Local authorities, ministries and other organisations of the state, including the armed forces and police.

Artisans have different relations of exchange with each of these customer types and, as we will see, these relationships vary for different types of artisans. Tailors and carpenters, for example, have a different balance of relations with clients, shoppers and intermediaries, and the relationships with the market change over time. When we discuss these relationships for micro-producers as a whole, therefore, the composite data disguise a variety of different underlying trends that respond to changes in the macro-economy and society.

The concept of the *client* refers to those customers who approach the artisan to make something to their own personal specification, such as a made-to-measure suit or a bespoke pair of shoes. The concept of the *shopper* is a shorthand for those who purchase off-the-peg or off-the-shelf goods, such as clothing or footwear. *Intermediaries* may be other artisans, retailers or wholesalers who buy goods for resale to other customers (who in turn may be shoppers, retailers or other wholesalers). The artisan can also be directly contracted to wholesalers in a relationship that is more likely to involve 'buying-up'. In *buying up*, the small-scale producers become dependent on larger-scale commercial capital to reach the market with their goods. Multiple commodities of the small producers are bought complete, for resale to third parties. The artisan provides the raw materials and the details are left to him or her. Intermediaries may therefore be small-scale or large-scale, non-capitalist or capitalist forms of exchange, and classified as informal or formal. Artisans sometimes organise themselves into *cooperatives* for the sale of their goods, in order to minimise contact with intermediaries and retain more of the value of their products for themselves. These are more likely to be rural organisations than urban but they do exist in the urban areas, particularly when artisans in the periphery of cities may be isolated from the main market centres.

The relationships with larger capitalist firms are mainly with manufacturers and wholesalers and they tend to be of three types: in addition to *buying up* by wholesalers, artisans can have social relations of production such as 'subcontracting' and 'direct contracting', mainly with larger manufacturers. *Subcontracting* involves the use of the labour time of a small producer by another larger manufacturer in the production of goods for consumption by a third party. The final consumer is not the larger firm. The subcontractor may provide all or part or none of the raw materials, but the details of the finished product are agreed before the work begins.

In *direct contracting*, the larger firm is the consumer of the product of the artisan's labour, whether this is in the form of goods or a service. A capitalist firm (whether in manufacturing or another sector of the economy) may employ an artisan signwriter, for example, to create signage for the firm. This type of relationship can exist with industrial, commercial or finance capital. Another example could be where a large-scale producer of artisan inputs, such as cloth or leather, may employ an artisan mechanic to maintain and repair their factory machinery. In these cases, the consumer of the artisan's labour is the larger firm. The artisan is not involved in the capitalist transformation of raw materials into new products, but the value of his or her labour is incorporated into the price of the products of the capitalist firm. Some of these products may then be sold as raw materials for other producers, including artisans. In direct contracting, the small producer will normally supply the raw materials and once again the details of the finished product will be agreed before the work begins.

Artisan *relations with the state* are complex and multi-layered, as we will see in Chapter 10. In this chapter, we are only concerned with the situation where the state is a customer for the goods or labour of the artisan. This direct face-to-face relationship could be for signage for an office or the repair of equipment, but there is also an Ecuadorian tradition whereby artisans were contracted to produce gifts or awards for officers of the municipality or a government ministry. For example, artisans could be engaged for the production of awards for long service. There is also a history of jewellers making gifts at Christmas or for someone's birthday. These cases in the public sector were often used to reinforce relations of patronage, or they were sometimes linked to some other form of corruption. In 1953, the Defence Law promised that the state would buy artisan production but, for moral reasons, these practices were banned by the Correa administration, with serious consequences for some of Quito's jewellers.[2]

In the context of global production, an important aspect of the system of distribution is the types of location that are available for the artisan to sell his/her products or services. Some, like artisan furniture-makers, may go to the homes of their clients, where they will make the furniture that the client has ordered. Others will sell only from their workshops or, because of recent planning and health and safety regulations that forbid certain toxic manufacturing methods in city centre workshops, they may have separate manufacturing workshops and commercial outlets. Others may have their own outlets in local markets – something that was historically significant for carpenters, who made furniture for the urban poor and sold it in a local street market.

Where there are intermediaries, these can also be of a variety of types. In addition to the wholesalers who supply a number of small retail outlets, other small-scale non-capitalist, or informal, outlets trade in artisan products. There are other artisans who may be better placed in the geography of demand. With a workshop that also serves as a shop in the city centre, these artisan-traders may be better located than a producer-artisan who is located in the periphery. There are local retailers, who may have a shop in the city centre or even in one of the new modern shopping malls in the north and south of the city. There are also market traders, who may have one or more stalls in the city's covered markets. All of these small-scale retail outlets may also sell industrially manufactured goods.

What then is the structure of artisan distribution in Quito and how has it been changing over time, if at all? If the relations of distribution are changing, is this uniform and unidirectional? Are the changes related to the changing structure of production and does the technology of production influence the relations of exchange? We will see that there is very little subcontracting, formal traders are hardly relevant, there has been a slight growth in sporadic relations with the formal sector, and that the aggregate figures do disguise a variety of relations for different artisan activities.

The most important customers

Throughout the period of the study, the artisans were asked who their customers were and they were asked to put them into order of importance. Since 1975 through to the present time, there has been a consistency in the artisans' response: in that the vast majority of customers have been *clients* who approach the artisans to have their goods made to order. With the development of the Ecuadorian economy, we might have expected the role of clients to decline and, as the city expanded and the open market for consumption goods became more important, the role of *shoppers* to increase. That was not the case. We might also have expected the role of intermediaries to increase but, once again, that was not the case. Artisans continue to be dependent on clients who request the work to be undertaken according to their personal brief. Behind this consistency, however, there are a number of shifting circumstances.

If we directly compare 1975 with 2015, there is a significant difference in the main customers of the artisans (Table 7.1). In addition, in each inter-survey period with the exception of 2005–15, the type of customer changed significantly. In 1975, three-quarters said they produced primarily for private individuals who directly asked for the work to be done to their own specifications – goods made to order or repairs to be carried out. Twelve per cent said they had customers who bought goods that the artisan had already made and intermediaries accounted for 11% of customers. By 2015, the importance of clients had increased (to 82%), the importance of shoppers had not changed and the role of intermediaries had

Table 7.1 Most important customers, 1975–2015

	1975		1982		1995		2005		2015	
	No.	%	No.	%	No.	%	No.	%	No.	%
Clients (made to order)	157	74.8	258	65.8	269	74.9	260	83.1	209	81.6
Shoppers (buy ready made)	25	11.9	91	23.2	49	13.6	39	12.5	31	12.1
Intermediaries (who resell)	24	11.4	35	8.9	36	10.0	4	1.3	7	2.7
Others and combinations	4	1.9	8	2.0	5	1.4	10	3.2	9	3.5
	210	100	392	100	359	100	313	100	256	100

	Chi-sq	DF	p-value
1975–2015	68.5655	12	5.9363E-10
1975–1982	11.5490	3	0.0091
1982–1995	12.1093	3	0.0070
1995–2005	25.5270	3	0.0000
2005–2015	1.6374	3	0.6509
1975&2015	14.8807	3	0.0019

declined (to 3%). Subcontracting, was captured under the heading of others, along with those who could not identify a main customer. It was so low as to be insignificant.

Over 40 years of development, the importance of the artisan–client relationship had increased, rather than declined, whilst intermediaries who bought the artisan output for resale had declined significantly. Contrary to what the literature on subcontracting suggests, capitalist manufacturers barely registered. As we will see, this has at least partly to do with the growing importance of repair work amongst artisans, replacing manufacturing, which is in turn a reflection of the changing structure of the various types of artisan activity.

With the exception of 2005–15, the changes are also significant (at the 0.01 or 0.05 level) in each inter-survey period. Between 1975 and 1982, for example, the importance of shoppers who bought ready-made goods doubled and clients who had their work done to order declined – as did the proportion who sold to intermediaries. The theory assumes that intermediaries will become more important with development but in these years when the Ecuadorean economy was growing rapidly, there was a decline in the importance of intermediaries who bought goods for resale. In the next decade, the significance of these traders remained more or less constant, before declining rapidly between 1995 and 2005. This was the first decade of the growth of the Asian traders in Quito, when artisan production was squeezed out of the market by cheap imports. There is no evidence that, as an economy develops, there will be growth in the importance

Table 7.2 Most important places where goods and services are sold

	1975		1982		1995		2005		2015	
	No.	%	No.	%	No.	%	No.	%	No.	%
Artisan workshop	156	90.2	272	87.2	272	88.0	287	93.5	240	93.8
Homes of customers	12	6.9	29	9.3	36	11.7	13	4.2	11	4.3
Other	5	2.9	11	3.5	1	0.3	7	2.3	5	2.0
	173	100	312	100	309	100	307	100	256	100

Table 7.3 Most important intermediaries*

	1975		1982		1995		2005		2015	
	No.	%	No.	%	No.	%	No.	%	No.	%
Other artisans	11	27.5	10	20.4	6	10.5	5	15.2	10	38.5
Wholesalers	5	12.5	3	6.1	4	7.0	13	39.4	5	19.2
Retailers	20	50.0	25	51.0	35	61.4	10	30.3	6	23.1
Other	4	10.0	11	22.4	12	21.1	5	15.2	5	19.2
	40	100	49	100	57	100	33	100	26	100

	Chi-sq	DF	p-value
1975–2015	37.6208	12	0.0002
1975–1982	3.4955	3	0.3213
1982–1995	2.2621	3	0.5198
1995–2005	16.3925	3	0.0009
2005–2015	5.4687	3	0.1405
1975&2015	4.9502	3	0.1755

Note: * This question was asked of anyone who mentioned intermediaries, not only if most important.

of traders who will buy the artisans' goods for resale in another location. Rather, as the market for goods such as shoes increases with development and the growth of population, traders will step into this market by selling the cheaper goods manufactured by capitalist enterprises.

Artisans who sold to clients and shoppers mainly sold their goods directly through their workshops (Table 7.2). This was the case for 90% of artisans in 1975 and, despite some minor modifications, there was no significant change over time.[3] The workshop remains the main outlet for artisan production, in spite of the changes we have seen in the structure of production (Chapter 3, Table 3.2).

The artisans who mentioned intermediaries as a customer (whether they were the most important customers or not) were asked to identify the intermediaries and to put them in order of importance. With the development of commodity production, the role of intermediaries is thought to become more important and the size of intermediary firms is thought to grow, but this is not the case. The intermediaries are not principally large-scale traders (Table 7.3). In 1975, the main traders were small-scale retailers who themselves would form part of the informal sector. The second most important were other artisans, some of whom would buy complete pairs of shoes, for example, for resale in better-located workshops in the centre; whilst others would buy partly completed final products for finishing in their own larger workshops.

Artisans with shops in the city centre, where footfall is stronger, may sell the shoes of other artisans, as well as their own products. The usual basis of this relationship is that artisans who work in more remote locations will visit a known city centre artisan with a selection of their products and the more favourably located artisan will take what is on offer and/or will place an order. This is an artisan–artisan commercial relationship that is different from the buying-up that takes place in a trader–artisan relationship, where the trader will normally visit a variety of artisan workshops to select the best of their products.

An example of an artisan incorporating the work of another artisan to complete a finished article could be a tailor with an order for a jacket asking another to make the sleeves, which he will later attach to the body of the jacket. For a suit, the artisan who takes the order may make the whole jacket, but ask another artisan to make the trousers. A shoemaker might subcontract another artisan to cut and sew the upper parts of the shoe together, which he will then attach to the soles. A small number (2 in the sample, or 5%) also sold through intermediaries with market stalls, which meant that over 80% of the intermediaries could be identified as informal traders in 1975.

Commercial capital and buying-up

The fact that that the most important customers for 87% of artisans were clients and shoppers while only 11% had intermediaries as their main outlet, suggested that buying-up was little developed in Quito in 1975 (Table 7.1). While the producers of subsistence goods were more likely to rely on traders for the sale of their goods, they mainly depended on other small enterprises which were themselves part of the 'informal sector', or they sold to other artisans. That only 13% of the small producers who had intermediaries amongst their customers sold their wares to large-scale commercial concerns (Table 7.3) also meant that less than 3% of the total artisan universe relied on this type of outlet for the sale of their products.

What we found, therefore, is that in Quito in 1975 there was very little forward linkage to the capitalist or 'formal' sector of the economy through buying-up. Any idea that informal producers were dependent on capitalist merchants for the sale of their products had to be rejected. As we move through the decades, the role of wholesalers within the pool of intermediaries changed, declining to 1982 and then remaining constant at around 7% through 1995. We have seen that after 1995 the role of all intermediaries declined dramatically (from 10% to 1.3% of primary outlets). Within this group of intermediaries, the importance of wholesalers increased from 7% to almost 40% of those who sold to intermediaries.

However, it remained the case that only 3% of all artisans said their main customers were wholesalers and by 2015, this had fallen to 2%.

The argument that small-scale production means small-scale marketing is upheld and any idea that small producers in Quito are dependent on capitalist merchants for the sale of their products has to be rejected. There is very little linkage between the formal and the informal sector through the commercialisation of the product of the small-scale enterprise. Consequently, the proposal that the transfer of value from the urban artisans as a whole to the capitalist sector through the commercialisation of their products is important or is a factor for explaining the impoverished condition of petty producers, also has to be rejected.

By 2015, the extent of the reliance on informal customers had changed, but not significantly. Compared with 1975, the importance of small-scale intermediaries declined but, within this category of customer, the relative importance of other artisans increased. The only significant change in any inter-survey period was in 1995–2005. In this decade, when the role of intermediaries as a whole declined, it was as a result of the collapse of retail customers (and to a lesser extent other artisans) along with a growth in the relative importance of wholesalers. It would appear that Asian competition considerably reduced the role of retail trade in artisan goods in the city centre, a situation that may have been exacerbated by the planning and redevelopment that was taking place in the HCQ at that time. As retailers of cheap Asian goods increased, retailers of artisan goods were being displaced by the remodelling and regeneration of the Historic Centre of Quito.

Over time, there was a decline in the numbers of artisans reporting that their main customers were intermediaries and the majority of the intermediaries were small-scale, with retailers dominating at the beginning of the period and other artisans becoming more important later. However, some artisans do work for the formal sector, even if they are not their most important customers.

Subcontracting, direct contracting and buying-up

In order to understand the extent of producer-customer relations with the formal sector of the economy, we asked the artisans if they *ever* worked for either large-scale private sector firms or the state, rather than who their main customers were. In our sample in 1975, we found that only 17% of the producers reported that they had ever worked for these types of formal organisations (Table A.7.1). This percentage, however, increased consistently over the decades to 33% in 2015. The artisans were significantly more likely to have worked for formal organisations by 2015. These relations, however, tended to be sporadic and they were divided between the private sector and the state.

We asked how frequently they worked for either private firms or state institutions: whether they worked for them often (once a month or more), sometimes (less than once a month) or never. All through the study period, the artisans were more likely to work for the private sector than the state (Tables 7.4 and 7.5). Through to 2005, there was a small but highly significant and consistent growth in the relationship between the artisans and the private sector as a

Table 7.4 Frequency of relations with the formal private sector

	1975		1982		1995		2005		2015	
	No.	%	No.	%	No.	%	No	%	No	%
Often	6	3.3	18	6.0	20	6.1	38	12.0	21	8.2
Sometimes	20	10.9	39	13.1	49	15.0	52	16.5	40	15.6
Never	158	85.9	241	80.9	258	78.9	226	71.5	195	76.2
Total	184	100	298	100.0	327	100.0	316	100	256	100

	Chi-sq	DF	p-value
1975–2015	21.7814	8	0.0053
1975–1982	2.5651	2	0.2773
1982–1995	0.4762	2	0.7881
1995–2005	7.6051	2	0.0223
2005–2015	2.4798	2	0.2894
1975&2015	7.2916	2	0.0261

customer, after which there was a small decline. Between 1975 and 2015, there was a significant increase in the proportion of artisans saying they worked for the private sector but three-quarters of artisans had never worked for the private sector and less than 10% had worked once a month or more. Artisans rely on capitalist firms for their inputs, as we saw in Chapter 6, but not for the sale of the products of their labour.

Working for the state was less common and less regular (Table 7.5). In 1975, only 2% said they worked for the state once a month or more, compared to 9% who said they sometimes did; and in 2015, the figures were 6% and 12.5% respectively.[4] The proposition that informal activities are 'intimately' linked to the formal sector through the provision of low-priced goods and services as inputs for capitalist industry does not apply. By 2015, one-quarter said they had worked for formal organisations, which is not exactly negligible, but less than 10% said they worked for them once a month or more. Through this mechanism, the micro-producers as a whole contributed very little to large-scale capitalist profit making and accumulation, for what strikes one is the overall lack of subcontracting.

The customers of different types of artisans

It was suggested above that different types of artisans have different relations with the market, that these relationships change over time and that any changes may be related to macro-economic forces and wider social pressures. In 1975, when asked who their main customers were, with the exception of shoemakers and carpenters, more than 80% of all other types of artisans produced for clients who ordered bespoke goods and services (Table A.7.2). Over the period to 2015, however, for some artisans, clients became more important and for others

Table 7.5 Location and frequency of working for the state

	1975		1982		1995		2005		2015	
	No.	%	No.	%	No.	%	No	%	No	%
Often	4	2.2	8	2.7	14	4.3	21	6.6	16	6.2
Sometimes	16	8.7	32	10.8	31	9.5	51	16.1	32	12.5
Never	163	89.1	257	86.5	282	86.2	245	77.3	209	81.3
Total	183	100.0	297	100.0	327	100.0	317	100.0	257	100

	Chi-sq	DF	p-value
1975–2015	20.2887	8	0.0093
1975–1982	0.6674	2	0.7163
1982–1995	1.3727	2	0.5034
1995–2005	8.7226	2	0.0128
2005–2015	1.6257	2	0.4436
1975&2015	5.9442	2	0.0512

they declined. The greatest growth in clients as their main customers was for shoemakers and carpenters, whilst there was a decline for jewellers, printers and tailors. A similar pattern emerged for artisans who mentioned clients (whether most important or not). The complexity of the evolving relations of exchange, however, can be illuminated by looking more closely at the influences on the structure of exchange for specific types of artisans. These influences included the changing technology of production, the transition from production to repair activities and contingent events over which the artisans had no control.

Carpenters

In 1975, carpenters were mainly involved in the manufacture of furniture but only 48% produced furniture that was made directly to the order of clients. The market for furniture in Quito was bifurcated: the production of the carpenters in the study was mainly cheap furniture for the lower and working-class market, although there was also some fine quality hand production for the upper-class market. At the beginning of the research, the carpenters were more likely to produce outputs for shoppers and intermediaries than was the case for other artisans (Table A.7.3). One of the features of the carpenters' relationship to their market was an organised trading cooperative that operated in one of the city's open markets two days a week.[5] This traditional market helps explain the relatively high importance of the category of producers whose customers were shoppers who bought already-finished products and intermediaries who were mainly trader-artisans who owned some of the market stalls.

By 2015, clients were much more important than they were in 1975 and shoppers were less important. This was partly because their street market was closed by the city council's planner-architects as part of an urban design exercise that was aimed at improving the tourist experience in the Historic Centre of Quito. However, there were other technological influences such as the growth of factory production of cheap furniture using materials such as MDF. As factory production displaced artisan carpenters, repair work grew in importance for the carpenters who survived.[6] Capitalist production reduced the overall number of artisan carpenters by capturing their market, but it also increased the opportunity for artisan repair work. There was a dramatic decline in carpenter numbers (Chapter 3, Table 3.2), they became much more involved in repair work (Chapter 3 and Table A.3.16) and their orientation to clients who commission their services increased (Table A.7.2).

Shoemakers

At the time of the 1975 survey, factory production of shoes was in its infancy, with recent investment by international firms such as Bata. Only 70% of shoemakers said they produced for clients and a quarter produced for intermediaries, who were mainly trader-artisans with outlets in the city centre. A part of the market was controlled by relatively small commercial capital in the centre of the city. Smuggling of Colombian footwear also existed. As factory production increased we might have expected the growth of a dual market for shoes, with small-scale production becoming increasingly reserved for individual clients who commissioned the work, and for repair.

By 2015, shoemakers were more likely than any other activity to say their most important customers were clients. This was because of the decline of shoe manufacturing in Ecuador by international firms, along with an increase in repair amongst artisans. By 2015, there were only two shoemakers producing for intermediaries. Over the period, as was the case for carpenters, their numbers declined, repair activities increased and clients became more important.

Jewellers

For jewellers, the process was different. The importance of shoppers and intermediaries increased substantially, without diminishing the importance of clients. A more diverse set of customers evolved for jewellers. They still practise their craft, making jewels and repairing watches for clients, but the demand for ready-made jewels has become more important than in the past. The persistence of jeweller shops and workshops in the city centre, serving tourists and the middle classes, has amplified the routes to market for more peripherally located jewellers, but at the cost of a part of the value created passing to the intermediaries. Artisan outlets in the HCQ subcontract older jewellers on the periphery.

Tailors and seamstresses

Between 1975 and 2015, the proportion of garment makers who sold to intermediaries tripled and those who said they sold to shoppers more than tripled.

The increase in the importance of intermediaries occurred mainly between 2005 and 2015, which coincided with government support for national production of school uniforms, which we will return to in a moment. The increase in those selling ready-made clothes to shoppers mainly occurred in the 1975–82 period, when the market for factory-made clothing increased and a large number of garment makers went out of business and were not replaced.

The fact that only 7% of garment makers produced for intermediaries in 1975 was related to the fact that there were three distinct sources of clothes in Quito and three related systems of commercialisation. There was factory production of clothes, which found their way onto the market through mainly large-scale (and some small-scale) enterprises. There was also a considerable black market in smuggled clothes from Colombia, where the price of factory produced garments was much cheaper than in Ecuador. The smuggling of these clothes was a large-scale operation, but the outlets were mainly small-scale – and of particular importance was one of the city's market places. Finally, the small-scale production was demand-specific and the products passed directly to the consumer.

The changes in relationship with clients, shoppers and intermediaries were not unilineal for any category of artisan across the different survey periods (Tables A.7.4 and A.7.5). Each branch of activity has a different story to tell. It is clear that the total (weighted) figures in Table 7.1 are the result of a constant flux in the types of outlets for different types of activity. This fluidity in the number of times that clients, shoppers and intermediaries are mentioned reflects the experience of artisans in their evolving markets, the development of technology in their spheres of action, and the role of the local state in the city. It points to a level of complexity that is too difficult to deal with adequately here. The question that follows, however, is whether the generalised contact that the community of artisans have with the formal sector (Table A.7.1) is also based on an evolving variety of experiences for different types of artisans.

Relationship of different activities to the formal sector

We saw that there was a steady increase in the relationship between the informal artisans and the formal sector. This overall situation of gradual increase was arrived at through an uneven process of change for different types of artisans (Figure A.7.1, based on Table A.7.6). In 1975, the main activities working for private enterprises or the state were mechanics and printers. Some activities, such as shoemakers, jewellers and others, had practically no examples of working for the formal sector in 1975 and each showed a small but relatively steady increase in informal-formal linkages over the period.[7]

The three activities that had the highest levels of informal–formal relations in 1975 (printers, painters/stonemasons and mechanics) continued to hold their top spots in 2015, but their trajectories were uneven and dissimilar (Figure 7.1). These three activities were discussed as 'producers of the Means of Production (MoP)' in Chapter 3, meaning that their outputs or labour power could be absorbed into capitalist production processes. Their work for the formal sector, however, did not follow the same timeline. They come together to create a substructure

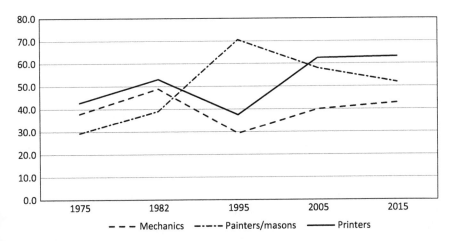

Figure 7.1 Working for the formal sector

of relationships that is constantly changing, responding to forces beyond their control. They provide a selective insight into how macro-forces can influence the relations of exchange that micro-producers have with the state and private sector organisations.

Printers, who were most likely to carry out work for the formal sector in 1975, remained in top position in 2015, but they suffered substantially between 1982 and 1995, when the demand for their services declined and, as pointed out above, the technology of printing was undergoing a transformation. As office technology changed, with the introduction of personal computers and photocopiers, the use of stand-alone office printers spread and small-scale photocopying became much more common. As a result, work with the formal sector declined.

In 1995, the printers were superseded by the artisan category that is classified in the international literature as workers in 'stone and marble' – a category that in fact includes such diverse activities as painters, signwriters, glaziers and stonemasons. The workers in this sector perhaps best exemplify the complexity of the relations between artisans and the formal sector. The changing pattern of demand was in part due to the changing balance of the internal composition of this sector, as well as changes in technology in the three main subsectors of 'stone and marble' artisans. It is worth repeating some of what we have said, above.

The demand for painter/signwriters increased through the boom years but they later suffered from changes in technology, whereby industrialised signage in plastics and metal replaced hand-made signs painted on wood, causing formal sector demand to decline. The new technology displaced the traditional art of the signwriters. The production of glaziers, who traditionally would create windows in wooden frames that were manufactured by artisan carpenters, was replaced by industrially produced systems of metal and plastic windows. In this process, the artisan glaziers were increasingly reduced to repair activities (see Chapter 3).

It is also significant that in early 1995, the Ecuadorean army went to war with Peru and during this conflict, lasting a month, around 500 Ecuadorean soldiers are estimated to have lost their lives. This appears to have produced an increase in the relations between artisan makers of marble headstones and the formal sector, but it was with the state rather than the private sector.

After 1995, the printers recovered their position as the group most likely to have relations with the formal sector, as the relationship between the stonemasons and the formal sector declined. The demand for stonemasons has grown as the population of Quito increased, died, and were buried. Demand continues to be higher than in the pre-1995 period, but they are gradually being replaced by industrial production of marble gravestones and other funereal artefacts.

The development of the trajectory for mechanics followed that of printers, but for different reasons. The mechanics are included in the category of 'ordinary metals'. In 1975, they were already heavily involved in repair activities, including the repair of cars, radios and televisions, but around a quarter were mainly involved in production, rather than repair. These were small mechanical workshops, locksmiths, metal-bashing producers of aluminium pots and pans, manufacturers of spare parts for cars, and so on. As demand in the economy increased after 1975, the producers of pots and pans were replaced by industrial production. With the increasingly sophisticated computerised technology of the modern motor car, the agents of multinational automobile companies gradually squeezed out the micro-manufacturers of spare parts. Car importers became involved in replacing parts, rather than repairing them. In addition, the traditional skills of the locksmith gave way to key cutting related to the expansion of Yale locks and, later, more sophisticated electronic security. By 1995, automobile importers had cornered the market in car repairs based on their exclusive command of the new technology but after this, artisans began to recover on the back of relatively large-scale investment in repair and maintenance technology, which allowed them to forge new relations with the formal sector.

These links, however, have not been particularly strong. The numbers saying they worked 'often' or 'sometimes' for private enterprise were too small to say anything definitive (Table A.7.7 and Figure A.7.2). Combining these two frequencies shows that printers, painters/stonemasons and mechanics are again more likely to have relations with large-scale enterprises that the others (Figure A.7.3). These producers of the MoP can be compared with the producers of the MoS in Figure 7.2.[8] The trajectories are once again uneven but the subsistence producers show an increase to 2005, largely due to the changing nature of the work of carpenters, as they move from the production of furniture to construction-type work. The decline of the MoP between 1982 and 1995 confirms the decline of printers and mechanics during this period. By the end of the period in 2015, only the mechanics were showing a decline, which was consistent with the growing importance of repairs to household white line goods.

Working for the state is another matter. Once again, the numbers are too small to distinguish between those who work 'often' or 'sometimes' for government organisations. Combining these two categories, the trajectories of the three groups

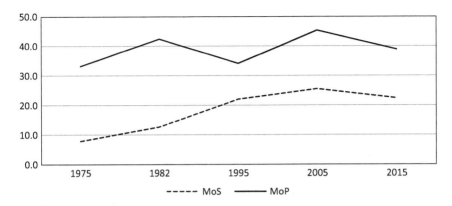

Figure 7.2 Working for the private sector ('often' and 'sometimes')

who work most for the state (printers, painters/stonemasons and mechanics) are quite different (Table A.7.8 and Figure A.7.3). The contribution of the mechanics and printers increases between 1975 and 1982, while that of painters/stonemasons falls. In the period of structural adjustment, the contracts between the state and the printers and mechanics falls, while those of the stone and marble workers increases. In this moment, the painters/stonemasons are outliers, with 50% saying they at least sometimes worked for the state in 1995. As mentioned above, this was related to the Cenepa War with Peru earlier in 1995 (26 January–28 February 1995).[9] If we remove the stonemasons, who will have benefited from the consequences of this war, the trend in relations with the state is almost uniformly downwards in 1982–95, rising again to 2005, then declining for almost all activities.

The one exception between 2005 and 2015, was for tailors, for whom there was no decline. This was related to the government decree relating to school uniforms that was mentioned previously.

Government policy for school uniforms

The Correa government introduced two policies that were important for small-scale production of school uniforms in Ecuador. The first was a policy of demilitarisation of schools, reducing support for any activities that involved behaviour that could be interpreted as promoting the military. School marching bands came into this category. The second was a policy that supported the national production of school uniforms, supplanting the importation of clothing from China. Neither policy was particularly helpful for the artisans.

School marching bands needed uniforms and some of this demand was met by artisan tailors and seamstresses. As the bands were disbanded, this removed an important market for these artisans. A seamstress who produced the uniforms for the band of the Mejia High School said:[10]

There were 500 students in the band and I attended to around 400. I didn't have an exclusive workshop where I could look after the kids ... There was a queue that stretched to the corner ... Now that they have withdrawn access to the college bands, there is not much [work] ... Now there are not even 100 students.

Correa also decreed a change in the purchasing systems of state institutions so that small firms would be encouraged to bid for state contracts. This had two sets of implications for the artisans: first, existing contracts that artisans had with schools were drawn into state purchasing procedures; and second, the new system, which supported small-scale manufacturing, created sweatshops rather than opportunities for the artisans.

Prior to these changes in policy, a number of artisans already had arrangements with schools to provide school uniforms and there is little doubt that these were under threat from cheap Chinese imports. However, existing local arrangement could be unfair to parents or even corrupt, with individuals or schools siphoning off profit from a system that ensured that parents had to buy the uniforms through the school. The same seamstress who provided the uniforms for the band also supplied other schools with everyday uniforms and she described how the arrangement worked:[11]

You remember how a few years ago each institution sold their uniform; well, I remember a Mother Superior came and asked me to carry out some small pieces of work for her. I sewed for her. She said, could you help with the school uniforms? I said, of course ... So I made a uniform for the Mother Superior. The model worked out well, there was a budget, we came to an agreement and she set me to work. I took the order for a number uniforms and I delivered.

The following year, surprise, the Mother was no longer there. I had a surplus on the order she had given me ... I went to present myself to the new Director. She said, leave them with me, but since we are now prohibited from selling uniforms in institutions, let's see if I can sell them and, if I can, I'll give you your money. Well, there was no guarantee ... With caution, with fear, because it was likely that the nuns were going to do something to me, I took them back. I put up a sign, 'School Uniforms Here', and the people began to arrive ... It didn't provide great wealth. Now is another matter. Nothing is happening here now.

Since the government was promoting its school uniform policy as something that was helping artisans, she was then asked about the effect of this policy on her business. She argued that the whole process was beyond the means of artisans.

You have to buy the cloth in a certain place; they will give it to you at such and such a price; the material has to be of a certain quality; well, to have a contract you need to produce a number [of uniforms]. What is it going to earn per article: 25 cents, 50 cents per piece? Do me a favour! How am I going to make 5000 articles of clothing? With a time limit of 45 days to deliver the articles. What does this imply? People, material, which is not cheap, to earn 50 cents per article. No, no, it doesn't work. Also, if I don't deliver on time, there are fines, daily fines. Do me a favour, what world are you living in!

She added that even with a team of artisans getting together and collaborating to provide for the needs of the schoolchildren, they could not meet the exigencies of the government system. The policy may be beneficial for small firms employing up to 20 people, which is the legal definition of artisans, but not those employing less than seven people, even if they try to combine their resources. The only other way that the small artisan tailor could benefit from the policy was if they became part of a system that involved intermediaries or contracting out.

The result is the setting up of sweatshops and some home-based artisans going underground for a few weeks. The sweatshops use Fordist production systems for the manufacture of, for example, jackets or body warmers. Some workers would be cutting the cloth for bodies and others cutting for the sleeves; other workers will sew the cut cloth into sleeves; others will sew the bodies together; yet others will sew the sleeves to the bodies; there will also be others sewing zips or buttons to the bodies and sleeves. The process will be repeated in similar systems for the production of shirts, blouses, trousers, sportswear and socks – and the whole uniform will be delivered by small capitalist sweatshop industries claiming to be artisans.

Another system is where a person organises a number of people working from home, under the radar of the authorities, to produce whole uniforms or parts of a uniform. Part of the uniform can be a shirt, while someone else produces trousers. Alternatively, a homebased artisan can produce bodies of shirts and another the sleeves, which can then be sewn together by another artisan or by someone in the sweatshop. In both cases, however, the sweatshop is working for the state, not the international private sector.

This is a very small part of the artisan customer base, but it is significant for tailors and it may explain the small growth in numbers of artisan tailors and the growing importance of intermediaries, who were mainly other 'artisans', in the 2005–15 period. In the longer term, it may as the seamstress fears, lead to the further demise of independent artisans as surely as Chinese competition would bring this about. However, this is a policy intervention that affects a small number of artisans and we should be wary about generalising its effects to all artisans. As we will see in Chapter 9, it is only possible with the collaboration of the *Junta Nacional de Defensa del Artesano*, who represent the larger workshops that might benefit.

Notes

1 We will return to this in the next chapter.
2 The government of *Alianza Pais* stopped the practice of using state funds to buy Christmas presents and other gifts or prizes for state employees. There was a

tradition of managers in state institutions using government funds to buy presents for other managers in the same organisation or for people they worked with in other government institutions. There was also a custom of presenting prizes to employees for 'achievements' in the course of their work. Many of these gifts and prizes were of jewellery, trophies or other artisan products.

3 In none of the inter-survey periods was the change significant.

4 If we combine the 'often' and 'sometimes' responses, the change between 1975 and 2015 does become significant: p-value= 0.0267.

5 On *Avenida 24 de Mayo*.

6 Artisans who are involved in repair are more likely to carry out the work for people who ask for a specific job to be done than artisans involved in production.

7 The numbers were too small to test for significance. Carpenters started out from a slightly higher level of interaction and relationships also grew.

8 This figure is based on Table A.7.7.

9 This was over a long-standing territorial dispute that dated back to the first decades of the nineteenth century, when both countries came into being after the Wars of Independence of the Spanish colonies, but this dispute was exacerbated by a conflict between British and US oil interests in the Amazon in 1941 (Galarza, 1974). The figures for human losses during the war vary widely. Ecuadorian military sources initially put the number of Ecuadorians killed at 34 while ALDHU, a human rights NGO, has claimed that the total number killed on both sides was around 500, a figure that has since been accepted by Ecuadorean senior officers.

10 Interview C1.

11 Interview C1.

8 Family firms, homeworkers and home-based enterprises

Introduction: family firms in the informal sector

In Chapter 2, we saw that over a period of around 40 years, researchers investigating the informal sector have been unable to agree as to whether the unit of analysis should be the individual, the firm or the household (ILO, 1996; World Bank, 2003, Guha-Khasnobis et al., 2007, WIEGO, 2016). When the firm is taken as the unit of analysis, self-employment is thought to dominate, but the focus on self-employment leads analysts to confound the individual and the firm. Analysis of the firm focuses on the attributes and characteristics of the owner and this leads to accounts of the informal sector that present the small firm owner as a heroic micro-entrepreneur confronting an overbearing regulatory state (de Soto, 1989; Guha-Khasnobis et al., 2007).

The self-employed work of these owners, however, sometimes comprises only a part of their personal earnings; and their enterprises often contribute only a portion of the total economic activity of household production units. The individual may have more than one source of income and there may be others within the household who make a contribution to total family income – and therefore to the consumption and subsistence of the individual who is the owner of the small enterprise. Some of the others in the household or family may help by working in the firm of the person who conceives of him/herself to be self-employed. They may or may not be remunerated for this. The firm may be but one element of a family's ambitions or strategy for survival.

The role of the individual and the performance of the firm may be judged differently by the small firm owner and the academic theorist. For the owner, his or her work may be more important as elements of a strategy for maintaining family well-being and cohesion, rather than for achieving entrepreneurial ambitions. Much of the debate about the main characteristics of family firms revolves around what makes them a success or a failure (Holt et al., 2017; O'Boyle et al., 2012; Amit and Villalonga, 2014). Some authors find that family firms perform better than non-family firms, others conclude that the non-family firms perform better, while others report that family involvement makes little or no difference to performance (O'Boyle et al., 2012). It has been suggested that these conflicting findings are a result of a mismatch between the aspirations of family firms and the outcomes that are measured by researchers (Amit and Villalonga, 2014). Family firms pursue non-financial outcomes, while researchers measure financial or other outcomes that do not correspond with the broad range of aims and objectives of the owners of family firms. There is a disconnection between the theory of the firm and the aspirations of the family.

In addition, as we also saw in Chapter 2, there is no agreement about the relationship between the family and the household or the role of home as a location for work. Informal firms are, by most definitions, 'family-owned firms'. They are also treated as 'household enterprises'. For the purposes of national accounts, informal enterprises are counted as household enterprises, irrespective of whether or not they employ family members (ILO, 2013a). Unpaid family work in a family enterprise is seen as typical of informal enterprises, but in the national accounts, household enterprises need not be located in the home. They are treated as family firms and household enterprises but, paradoxically, they need not involve family members of the owner, nor be located anywhere near his or her house (ILO, 1996; Ferrán, 1998; WIEGO, 2016).

Part of the problem is that, in the context of this complexity, there is no clear consensus about the definitions of *family firms, home-based enterprises* and *homeworkers*. The development literature is confused, these concepts overlap, the empirical work in the field is partial, there is no discussion of how the relationship between home and work might change over time, and little attention is paid to what might drive variations in the relationships between the family, home as a location for work and the wider economic system.

The concept of the *family firm* has been defined in a variety of ways by different authors. Chua et al. (1999) in a review of 250 papers produced a list of 21 different definitions dealing with the nature of family involvement, mostly relating to issues of ownership and management. Eight types of controlling owners were identified, ranging from the individual through nuclear and extended families to the public. There was general agreement that a business owned and controlled by a nuclear family was a family business, but beyond that there was widespread disagreement.

The concept is commonly used to refer to the ownership of the firm, as in a 'family business' where ownership may be passed down from generation to generation. It is also used to refer to control of a business, even where a family may not be a majority owner. In addition, it is often used in relation to a firm's internal relations of production, where the production process is dependent on family labour. Family-owned businesses, where the firm is family-owned and managed, are contrasted with non-family owned businesses, where the firm is owned and managed by a founder with no other relative involved in the business (Miller et al., 2008). Most commonly, it refers to some combination of ownership and internal labour relations, whereby control of the business is in the hands of members of one family.

It has been argued that 'family businesses represent a dominant form of economic organisation throughout the world' (Chrisman et al., 2003, 441) but the definition of the family firm varies from country to country. Ownership patterns in the United States have led to the concept of the 'family business' being used to describe the key characteristics of American capitalism. In the last part of the twentieth century, 98% of all firms were estimated to privately owned and operated and more than 90% of the one million corporations were privately owned family businesses (Alcorn, 1982, ix). In the UK, the percentage of businesses that could be classified as family firms varied from 15% to 78.5%, depending on how family business was defined (Westhead, Cowling and Storey, 1997, 17). In Germany, where 'substantial family influence' over business affairs was taken to define family businesses, whether this influence derived from ownership, control or management, around 58% of enterprises were estimated to be family firms (Klein, 2000, 158–9). Since the new millennium, the rapid expansion of self-employment and the 'gig economy' will have greatly increased the number of family firms in the developed world according to most definitions.

It is recognised that family businesses are heterogeneous and that variance within family firms needs more detailed examination (Chrisman et al., 2012; Chua et al., 2012; Evert et al., 2016). There have been attempts to address the problem of a lack of a comprehensive overview that ties together the various dimensions of family heterogeneity, aiming to show how they are relevant for family business research and how these dimensions affect family business behaviour and outcomes (Jaskiewicz and Gibb-Dyer, 2017). Family firms are distinguished from non-family firms through their pursuit of family-related aspirations and goals, leading to both financial and non-financial outcomes (Holt et al., 2017). All firms can pursue non-economic goals, but only family firms have non-economic goals that reflect the interests of the controlling family (Chrisman et al., 2012).

Research on family firms attempts to discover how family involvement influences firm performance (Chrisman et al., 2012). Most of the literature tends to deal with larger family-owned firms, mainly because they are more likely to be registered, identifiable and able to be sampled; and even when small firms are the focus of attention, they are seldom the smallest enterprises. Chrisman et al. (2012), for example, used a sample of firms who were clients of the Small Business Development Centre in the US, only 10% of whom employed more than 20 workers – but none had less than five. For these 'larger small firms', the power of the family to control decision-making within the firm could be an issue, but in microenterprises with less than five workers, that is unlikely to be the case – the owners are in control, except in cases of subcontracting where capitalist customers may specify the processes as well as the outputs of the family firm.

In micro-firms, all the firms would be family firms on the basis of the generally accepted basic definition that the owner manages the work within the enterprise. It has been proposed that the ever-growing 'informal sector' in developing countries constitutes a 'family mode of production' (Lipton, 1984) and it is true that it is entirely composed of 'family firms' if the criterion of ownership is used. Control is another matter. All businesses function within regulatory and tax regimes which exercise some control over formal businesses and although a defining feature of informal enterprises is taken to be their existence outside the regulatory system, it is seldom the case that they can be free of all national and municipal statutes. The street trader, for example, spends a great deal of time and energy trying to avoid municipal regulations. Local statutes vary from one local authority to another and the spectrum of effective control that results from their implementation is even wider.

In the cases where work is subcontracted to small-scale manufacturers, effective control of the production process is under the control of a larger firm. Non-capitalist forms of production are subordinated to capitalist firms and integrated into the capitalist mode of production. As we have noted, in these cases the larger firm usually determines the design and quality of the smaller firm's output. When the activities of the informal firm is subordinated to the owner of another larger firm, which may also be a family firm, the link between ownership and control is broken. The small firm, however, does not cease to be a family firm.

If the regulatory regime is taken as given, irrespective of its content and effect, does the owner of the micro-firm exercise control over the operations of the business and make strategic decisions for the future of the firm within this regulatory context? For the most part the answer to this question is 'yes'. Within the statutory framework, the informal firm owner exercises control over decision-making, both strategic and ad hoc. Similarly, if subcontracting is taken as context, the small firm owner still has some control over the workforce and the production processes. The owner of the firm manages the informal enterprise within the constraints of the power that is exercised by local authorities and contracting firms. They can still be categorised as family firms on the basis of ownership and (partial or potential) control, but they may or may not involve other members of the owner's family.

If, on the other hand, the definition of the family firm is based on *the internal labour relations* of these microenterprises, the role and importance of family firms in the informal sector is even less certain. The conceptual confusion surrounding the family firm increases when we try to tease out the relationships within and between firms. When we discuss the family in this context should we, for example, be concerned with the extended family or the nuclear family? If we wish to clarify what we mean by family labour, who should define the concept of the 'family'?[1] Should it be the social scientist whose western concept of science seeks logical coherence and mutually exclusive categories, or the people who are being investigated and who, for different purposes, may employ a variety of definitions of who is and who is not in the family? In addition, there are the questions relating to the extent to which family firms are located inside or outside the home; whether independent home-based workers use family labour; and whether this paid and/or unpaid family labour works inside or outside the family home.

Family enterprises in the informal sector should not only be defined by their ownership. The use of family labour distinguishes some firms from others where, for example, no labour is employed or there is only wage labour. Since the use of family labour is seen to be an important feature of the informal sector (ILO, 2013a), there are also questions about the extent to which firms actually employ family labour. Do members of the family contribute to the process of production, paid on unpaid? Is there a relationship between employing family labour or not and whether or not firms are home-based. An important question becomes whether there is an identifiable relationship between Family-based Enterprises (FBEs) and Home-based Enterprises (HBEs); and to what extent are FBEs and HBEs located within the home of the owner; or to what extent do HBEs involve family labour? If such relationships between family and home exists, do they change over time? If so, why? What are the socio-economic processes influencing the evolving relationship between the family and the home of micro-firm owners? Before considering these questions, however, we need to discuss the concept of Home-based Enterprises and how they have been treated in relation to Homeworkers in the international development literature.

Home-based enterprises are generally thought to consist of entrepreneurial business activities that take place in the home. Once again, however, there is no agreement about this in the literature. The concept of *homeworkers*, as used and developed by the ILO, the World Bank and others, is not particularly helpful. They go so far as to suggest that 'homeworkers' are not necessarily working from home and that they may share workshops with other workers, which implies that they are not necessarily a subcategory of 'home-based workers'. Ferrán (1998, 3) proposed that all workers 'who *work outside the establishment to which they sell their products*',[2] whether or not they actually work in the home, are called '*home-based workers*'. In this case, homeworkers were defined by their relationship to the market, rather than their location.

The ILO uses the categories of independent and dependent homeworkers, which are based on the definition of homework used in the 1996 Convention 177 of the ILO and which are still current (ILO, 1996, Article 1; WIEGO, 2016). For the purposes of the Convention, the term *home work* means work carried out by a person, to be referred to as a homeworker (ILO, 1996, Article 1):

(i)   in his or her home or *in other premises of his or her choice*, other than the workplace of the employer;
(ii) for remuneration;
(iii) which results in a product or service as specified by the employer, irrespective of who provides the equipment, materials or other inputs used.

Homeworkers, therefore, may not only work outside the home but may share workshops with other homeworkers (who work outside their home) and they may depend on intermediaries who organise the work but do not commission it. This confuses 'homeworkers' with the 'outworkers', who were intimately linked to large manufacturing firms in the development of capitalism in Europe and North America in the nineteenth century, before being replaced by machinery (Clapham, 1929; Thompson, 1968; Middleton, 1982).

The World Bank and other development agencies (Becker, 2004) have used a modified version of the ILO definition. It proposes that home-based workers consist of dependent home-based workers and independent home-based workers. This classification focuses on location as the primary element of the definition as distinct from social relations of production and exchange.[3]

Dependent home-based workers have the following characteristics:

- They work at home, outside the establishment that buys their products;
- They agree by prior arrangement to supply goods or services to a particular enterprise;
- Their remuneration consists of the prices paid for their products;
- They do not employ workers on a regular basis.

Independent home-based workers are those who work in their home and deliver their products and services to any prospective buyer. Their characteristics are those of the self-employed and are classified as part of the group 'own-account workers'.

In this case, both dependent and independent home-based workers work at home but, in the case of the former, they appear to be the equivalent of the domestic outworkers, providing part of large-scale production's inputs as a part of the development of capitalism in textiles, shoemaking and carpentry in the nineteenth century (Montgomery, 1974, Thompson, 1968; Lenin, 1974).

Given that both types 'do not employ workers on a regular basis' or are 'self-employed', the main difference between these two categories is based on their relationship with different types of customers – the various routes to market for firms in the informal sector that were discussed in the previous chapter. This longstanding confusion about the depiction of outworkers, domestic outworkers, family labour, family firms, home-based enterprises and homeworkers has plagued analysis of the informal sector or the informal economy, concepts about which there is also widespread disagreement. They are also concepts that are used interchangeably and the confusion is not helped by the paucity of empirical evidence that backs up the various theoretical positions, particularly when they are discussing how the relations between family, home and work may change over time.

This chapter offers some evidence that may be relevant for understanding the relationship between family, home and work. In particular, it investigates the relationship between family firms, home-based enterprises and different types of customers. In our sample, control of the decision-making within the firm was not an important issue. The owner was in control of the workshop. The only question of control was about the influence of external customers over the internal processes of production, including the extent of the subordination of informal units and workers to capitalist firms.

Another aspect of the heterogeneity of family firms is whether or not other family members work in the firm (Miller et al., 2008). In this study, this distinction becomes the basis of identifying family-based enterprises and those that are not family-based.

The need for longitudinal research in the field and the difficulties of carrying this out are well-recognised. Chrisman et al. (2012) recommend returning to the same firms again and again, despite the fact that it is difficult to get firms to participate (Evert et al., 2016). Survivor bias is also an issue, for it is even more difficult to return to re-interview owners of firms that no longer exist. In our study of artisans in Quito, for example, in the seven years between 1975 and 1982, 62% of the firms had closed down or moved. By 1995, 87% had gone (Middleton, 2007). Nevertheless, firms were replaced and our periodic random sampling can throw some light on the transformation of the above relationships.

This research is interested in the changes that have taken place in the social relations of production and distribution as a result of failure and survival. We are investigating structural changes, both internal and external, rather than financial outcomes. These structural variations are the unintended consequences of both the behaviour of the firms, as the owners respond to threats and opportunities, and the context of the wider economic system that is in a constant process of transformation.

Traditional artisan–client relationships are thought to be part of a system of production and exchange that is based on household and family production. As we have pointed out above, it has also been assumed by neoclassical economists and Marxists that this is a disappearing feature of production and exchange (Lewis, 1954; Fei and Ranis, 1964; Lenin, 1974). We will investigate the extent to which they persist over time, the extent to which they are dependent on formal sector outlets and how this has changed over time.

To cut through the conceptual confusion, the research adopts the following working definitions:

- *Family-Based Enterprises* (FBEs) are firms that employ family labour, paid or unpaid, including children. The concept of the family was defined by the owner of the firm at the time of interview.[4]
- *Home-Based Enterprises* (HBEs) are firms that are located inside the home or the yard of the owner.
- *Homeworkers*, whether independent or dependent on other enterprises for the sale of their goods and services, work inside their homes or yards.

This chapter tests a number of hypotheses about the relationship of family-based enterprises and home-based enterprises with their customers and with organisations in the formal sector of the economy. We will examine the proposals that:

- FBEs and HBEs are interchangeable concepts.
- FBEs and HBEs have traditional artisan-client relations that are disappearing over time.
- FBEs and HBEs depend on larger capitalist firms to reach their markets.
- Traditional cooperative relations with other artisans are disappearing over time.
- Links between FBEs and HBEs and the formal sector are growing over time.

We have seen that the relationship of the artisans with the market changes over time, as does the extent to which they have links with the formal sector of the economy, both the private sector and the state. In the next section of this chapter, we will examine the relationship between family enterprises and home-based enterprises, before investigating whether the relationship with different types of customers is in any way related to whether the artisan workshops are family firms or home-based enterprises. We will then consider the relationship, if any, between FBEs and HBEs and the formal sector.

The relationship between FBEs and HBEs

An assumption in most of the literature is that there is a clear link between family firms and home-based enterprises. It would be reasonable to hypothesise that small firms employing members of the owners' families should be more likely to be home-based enterprises than enterprises that do not employ family members. In HBEs, the family is at hand and can be called on to help when needed. Throughout the period of the research, however, there was no relationship between whether a workshop was inside/outside the home and whether family labour, paid or unpaid, was used (Table 8.1). Contrary to the assumption that family firms are interchangeable with household enterprises, this was not the case. It is important, therefore, that we look at FBEs and HBEs separately and investigate what has happened to each of them over time.

It is reasonable to assume that with economic development, the incidence of family relations of production and the use of the home as a workplace might decline, as happened in Europe and North America. When the oil began to flow from the Amazon region of Ecuador in the 1970s, all sectors of Ecuador's economy began to modernise and, as a consequence of this, there should have been less reliance on family labour in small firms and an expansion of wage labour, particularly after the introduction of neoliberalism in 1982. Comparing 1975 with 2015, however, there was no significant difference in the use of family labour in artisan workshops (Table 8.2). In no inter-survey period was there a change in the relative importance of the use of family labour. There was therefore no evidence to support the view that family labour was a declining traditional aspect of artisan production.

This contrasts with the changes that took place in the use of the home as a workshop. Over the period of the study, there was a highly significant decline in the use of the home. However, this did not come about because of economic development resulting from neoliberal policies. On the contrary, it can be attributed to the reduction that took place in era of the oil boom (1975–82) and in the period of anti-neoliberalism and anti-globalisation of the Correa administration (Table 8.3). During the years of neoliberal austerity and crisis, the movement of artisans out of the home and into independent workshops stalled. These were years when the ideology that drove government economic policy celebrated the importance of small enterprises for the economic future of the country. In these decades, we should have expected an accelerated modernisation

Table 8.1 The relationship between FBEs and HBEs, 1975–2015

| | 1975 | | | | 1982 | | | | 1995 | | | | 2005 | | | | 2015 | | | |
| | Outside home | | Inside home | | Outside home | | Inside home | | Outside home | | Inside home | | Outside home | | Inside home | | Outside home | | Inside home | |
	No.	%	No.	%	No.	%	No.	%	No.	%	No.	%	No.	%	No.	%	No.	%	No.	%
Uses family labour	29	32.2	31	31.0	69	37.5	38	33.6	80	38.5	47	39.5	58	32.2	52	39.1	66	38.4	34	41.0
Does not use	61	67.8	69	69.0	115	62.5	75	66.4	128	61.5	72	60.5	122	67.8	81	60.9	106	61.6	49	59.0
Total	90	100	100	100	184	100	113	100	208	100	119	100	180	100	133	100	172	100	83	100
Significance	0.85639				0.5000				0.85352				0.2070				0.6910			

Table 8.2 Use of family labour, 1975–2015

	1975		1982		1995		2005		2015	
	No.	%	No.	%	No.	%	No.	%	No.	%
Uses family labour	62	32.3	108	36.2	127	38.8	111	35.0	100	38.9
Does not use	130	67.7	190	63.8	200	61.2	206	65.0	157	61.1
Total	192	100	298	100	327	100	317	100	257	100

	Chi-sq	DF	p-value
1975–2015	3.1914	4	0.5263
1975–1982	0.8041	1	0.3699
1982–1995	0.4479	1	0.5033
1995–2005	1.0093	1	0.3151
2005–2015	0.9261	1	0.3359
1975&2015	2.0876	1	0.1485

Table 8.3 Location of workshops in relation to the home of the owner, 1975–2015

	1975		1982		1995		2005		2015	
	No.	%	No.	%	No.	%	No.	%	No.	%
Outside the home	91	47.5	184	61.9	208	63.6	182	57.6	173	68.1
Inside the home	100	52.5	113	38.1	119	36.4	134	42.4	81	31.9
Total	191	100.0	297	100.0	327	100.0	316	100.0	254	100.0

	Chi-sq	DF	p-value
1975–2015	22.0670	4	0.0002
1975–1982	9.6763	1	0.0019
1982–1995	0.1827	1	0.6691
1995–2005	2.4352	1	0.1186
2005–2015	6.6278	1	0.0100
1975 & 2015	18.9244	1	1.36E-05

as micro-firms expanded into independent workspaces, but the evidence suggests that this aspect of small firm development stagnated during the neoliberal years.

We might also have expected that, with the advent of oil and the development of markets for consumer goods in Ecuador, the traditional artisan–client relationship that is thought to characterise the family-based production units of artisans would diminish in importance. Once again, the processes were not quite as expected. We saw in Chapter 7 that clients have been consistently the main customers of artisans and that 'middlemen' have never been particularly important. There was no evidence of dependency or subordination of the artisans to large-scale commercial capital. The next section will investigate if this is also true of FBEs and HBEs.

FBEs, HBEs and their customers

Family-based enterprises and the route to market

Neoclassical economic theory would expect that, in a developing economy, the historical relationship of artisan FBEs to their customers would be characterised by traditional client-oriented relations but that these might decline with the development of a modern capitalist economy (Lewis, 1954; Fei and Ranis, 1964). Neoliberal theory would expect that this process would be boosted by the application of policies that would support the opening up of markets, the reduction of the state's role in the economy and the promotion of micro-entrepreneurial development in an increasingly commodified economy (de Soto, 1989). In fact, over 40 years, there was no change in the relationship between the structure of the customer base and whether firms were family-based or not (Table A.8.1).

In all years, 'clients' were by far the most mentioned customers for both family and non-family firms. The non-FBEs were more client-oriented, the role of middlemen has been small and declining – and where middlemen have been used, they have mainly been other small workshops and retail outlets, rather than large-scale capitalist enterprises. In only two of the years (1995 and 2005) was there a highly significant relationship between the types of customers and whether the firms were FBEs or not. In both these years, it was the non-family firms that were more likely to be involved in traditional artisan-client relationships and they were much less likely to have customers buying ready-made goods. In contrast, family-based firms were more reliant on informal traders to get their goods to market. This is the opposite of what would be expected of traditional family-based artisan enterprises and non-family firms.

Household enterprises and the route to market

There was no relationship between customer type and whether the workshop was located in the home or not (Table A.8.2). The ILO, the World Bank and others have continually stressed the importance of middlemen for home-based enterprises and 'homeworkers' (ILO, 1996; Ferrán, 1998; Jelin et al., 2000; Tomei, 2000; World Bank, 2003; Cunningham and Gomez, 2004; WIEGO, 2016). What is striking about these data is the small and decreasing number of HBEs who sell their goods through middlemen. In 1975, only 14% of home-based artisans sold their goods to intermediaries, who would then sell them on to either the consumers of the products or other retail outlets. In 2005, only one home-based artisan mentioned middlemen and a decade later there were three.

The relationship between the artisans and their main customers are not what has been suggested by the theory. In four years out of the five, there was no relationship between the customers and the location of the workshop (Table A.8.3). A small and declining number of HBEs sell through middlemen. For the most part, there was no relationship between location and the most important types of customers and in the one year when there was a relationship, it was home-based enterprises that were *less* likely to be selling to the traditional market of clients who ordered bespoke goods. Counter-intuitively, working at home increased the probability that their main customers would be shoppers who visited the workshops to buy ready-made outputs.

Horizontal linkages: artisans working for each other

We have seen that artisan forward linkages with commercial firms tend to be with other microenterprises. We also asked about relations with other enterprises as part of the production process – the extent to which they carry out work for other artisans when they are busy (horizontal integration) or produced goods for the formal private sector or the state (vertical integration). A traditional feature of artisan production, supported through membership of guilds, is that they will share their work during busy times. During periods when they have more orders than they can effectively manage, they will ask colleagues to help them produce the goods. This reciprocal relationship avoids making an investment in equipment and labour that could not be sustained after the order is delivered. It is collaborative, horizontal and reciprocal, but it is also a short-term strategy that avoids long-term risk.

If horizontal linkages are evidence of traditional artisanal behaviour and vertical relationships are characteristic of the integration of small-scale producers in a modern market economy, we should expect horizontal relations to decline over time. In a situation where the market is unsteady and the future is precarious, however, the artisan may decide to share, rather than invest.

In the neoliberal narrative, when demand for the products of artisans increases, entrepreneurs should take this opportunity to expand their businesses. 'Economic man' should pursue self-interest by initially employing more labour and then investing growing profits in new machinery. In a developing economy, we should expect this to produce a permanent process of growth. If it does not happen, the neoliberal narrative is that it is because of state regulations. We should not expect collaboration to increase when neoliberal policy is dominant, but it does. The growth in collaboration through work sharing between 1982 and 2005 is highly significant (Table 8.4). The question now becomes whether this is repeated in family based enterprises and home-based enterprises.

FBEs and horizontal collaboration

If horizontal collaboration is evidence of traditional behaviour from another time, when artisans were more cooperative instead of competing in a neoliberal world,

Table 8.4 Whether or not the owners work for other artisans when they are busy

	1975		1982		1995		2005		2015	
	No.	%	No.	%	No.	%	No.	%	No.	%
Yes	32	17.1	54	18.4	76	23.3	89	28.1	61	24.0
No	155	82.9	239	81.6	250	76.7	228	71.9	193	76.0
TOTAL	187	100	293	100	326	100	317	100	254	100

	Chi-squared statistic	DF	p-value
1975–2015	11.9271	4	0.0179
1975–1982	0.1348	1	0.7135
1982–1995	2.2175	1	0.1365
1995–2005	1.9112	1	0.1668
2005–2015	1.2001	1	0.2733
1975&2015	3.0845	1	0.0790
1982 & 2005	7.8935	1	0.0050

we might expect FBEs to be more likely to behave in this way and for the practice to decline over time. In fact, family-based enterprises were no more or less cooperative that other firms in any single year (Table A.8.4). In addition, between 1975 and 2015, there was no change in the likelihood of FBEs sharing jobs with other artisans when they were busy. There was, however, a significant change between 1982 and 1995, the years of structural adjustment, during which the proportion of family-based artisans working for other artisans *increased*. This growth in collaborative activity for family-based workshops occurred precisely when the situation of family firms was most precarious, when the ideology of neoliberal competition was at its strongest and when the competitive ethos was being promoted through the opening up of the national economy to the free market.

HBEs and horizontal collaboration

We might also expect that HBEs would be more inclined to exhibit these relationships than those that are located outside the home. However, this did not prove to be the case (Table A.8.5). In none of the survey years was there a significant relationship between the location of the workshop and whether or not the entrepreneurs worked for other artisans when they were busy; indeed, in all years there was a tendency for workshops that were *not* based in the home to be more likely to carry out work for other artisans.

There was also no change in the likelihood of HBEs working collaboratively for other artisans over time. There was a steady increase in the likelihood that they would work with others to 2005 (producing a variation that was significant at the 0.05 level compared to 1975) but there was no significant change over the whole study period. There was a tendency for increasing HBE collaboration during the neoliberal period but the results were not statistically significant.

The data therefore suggest that collaboration between artisans as a whole increased during the neoliberal years. There was no relationship between collaboration and whether the workshop was in the home or not, although there was a tendency for them to be more collaborative during the neoliberal years. For family firms there was clear growth in horizontal collaboration during the precarious years of structural adjustment. The neoliberal policies of reducing the role of the state and encouraging free-market competition between small firms coincided with family-based enterprises extending collaboration and horizontal integration.

Vertical linkages: FBEs, HBEs and the formal sector

Examples of vertical linkages are when micro-firm owners provide goods or services for the capitalist private sector or the state. The literature encourages informal firms to have more links with the formal sector, in order to grow. As was pointed out earlier, policy that embraces this thinking tends to assume that there are few links and those that do exist are benign or otherwise supportive of small firms (Guha-Khasnobis et al., 2007; Loayza et al., 2007; ILO, 2015). In contrast, the concept of dependent home-based worker suggests a limit to entrepreneurial free access to markets, imposed by the power of a larger contractor in the formal sector (ILO, 1996; Becker, 2004; WIEGO, 2016). In this perspective, the relationship tends to be exploitative. A question for both perspectives is whether the vertical relations are extensive or not.

We saw in Chapter 7 that when we asked artisans if their services had ever been used by the formal sector, they were much more likely to have links with the formal sector in 2015 than in 1975. This begs the question as to whether there was any difference in this regard between FBEs and HBEs and whether we can say anything about levels of dependency. Just how important is dependent homeworking for family-based and household-based firms?

It is often assumed that the *smallest* family-based firms would benefit from increased links to the formal sector, since they are least likely to have them in the first place. We might also assume that larger firms (non-FBEs and non-HBEs) would be more likely to have these relations with the formal sector. The evidence from Quito's artisans, however, suggests that micro-firms employing family labour have been consistently *more* likely to work for the private sector and/or the state than non-FBEs. In contrast, HBEs are *less* likely than non-HBEs to work for the formal sector. Where the relations do exist, there is also a question about how important they are for artisans. Is there any evidence to suggest widespread dependency?

Since we are interested in the extent of dependency of artisans on the private sector, we will look at the links between formal capitalist enterprises on the one hand and family firms and home-based enterprises on the other. For FBEs and HBEs, however, we will look first at links with the formal sector, including the state, before turning to the social relations of production involved in the links between formal private enterprises and informal artisan workshops. We will see a complex and evolving set of relationships, the reasons for which include a variety of extraneous social and economic forces.

In Chapter 7, we saw that for artisans as a whole, in four out of five years, less than 10% said they worked for the private sector once a month or more. For FBEs and HBEs, there were different patterns of behaviour, but for neither was there evidence of extensive relations that would point to a general state of dependency. There is a growing relationship with the formal sector, but there is no evidence that would justify the classification of artisans as 'dependent home-based workers' or 'household enterprises' whose accounts are indistinguishable from household budgets.

FBEs and the formal sector

Comparing FBEs and non-FBEs, the difference in the relationship to the formal sector was statistically significant in three out of five years (1975, 2005 and 2015) (Table A.8.6 and Figure 8.1). In 1975, workshops employing family labour were more than twice as likely to carry out work for the formal sector as non-family businesses. Between 1975 and 2015, the proportion of FBEs working for the formal sector increased from 28% to 43%, higher in both years than for artisans in general. Most of the growth happened between 1995 and 2005 but in each of the inter-survey periods, the change was not significant. This could be interpreted as FBEs being more dependent on the formal sector, but if we look at relations with the private sector over time, we can see that the evolving relationship is more complicated.

FBEs and the Private Sector

The firms that employed family labour and said they 'often' worked for larger firms (that is, more than once a month) was a negligible proportion of the total sample.

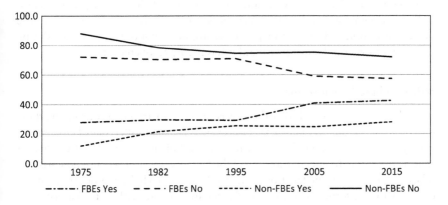

Figure 8.1 FBEs and non-FBEs working for formal sector (FS)

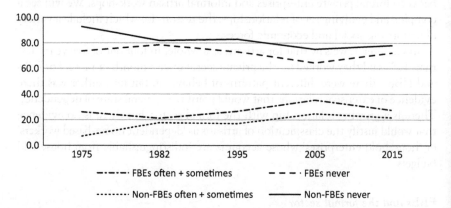

Figure 8.2 FBEs and non-FBEs working for formal private sector

They ranged between 2% and 7% of all artisans (Table A.8.7). In recognition of the small numbers that were involved, we recoded the responses to the question about whether or not they worked for the private sector into those that did (often and sometimes) and those that did not. We then compared the FBEs and non-FBEs and tested to see what happened to them over time (Table A.8.8). There are two points to note. First, the family-based workshops were consistently more likely to say they worked for the private sector than the non-FBEs. This is contrary to what was expected. Second, if we look at the different trajectories of the FBEs and the non-FBEs over time, we can see that they follow different paths (Figure 8.2). There was little change in the likelihood of FBEs reporting private sector links over time, but that is not the case for non-FBEs. For the enterprises that did *not* employ family labour, there were significant variations. In the oil-boom years, there was a highly significant growth in non-FBEs working for the capitalist private sector, which came to an end with structural adjustment. The growing working links between non-family firms and the formal private sector stalled between 1982 and 1995. Over the 40 years, there was an increase in the likelihood of non-FBEs reporting private sector links, but this was set back during the years of structural adjustment and it has hardly recovered since.

HBEs and the formal sector

In both HBEs and Non-HBEs there was an upward trend in artisans working for the formal sector (Figure 8.3). However, very small differences between the two types of workshop at the beginning and end of the period disguise different trajectories through time. In three out of the five survey years there was *no* statistical relationship between the location of the workshop and whether or not they carried out work for the formal sector (Table A.8.9). In 1975 and 2015, only two or three percentage points separated the workshop types. In 1995, however, the difference

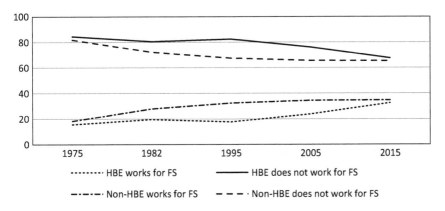

Figure 8.3 HBEs and non-HBEs working for formal sector

was 15 percentage points. Those working for the formal sector were not mainly home-based workers. Firms operating outside the home were around twice as likely to be working for the formal sector, casting doubt on the idea that 'homeworkers', as home-based workers, are particularly dependent on larger organisations.

Between 1982 and 1995, the percentage of HBEs working for the formal sector declined and the proportion of non-HBEs increased. By 1995 the difference between HBEs and non-HBEs was highly significant. By the end of the most intense period of structural adjustment, the workshops located outside the homes of their owners were much more likely to have working links with the formal sector than those located inside. Over the 1975–95 period, therefore, the non-HBEs developed links with the formal sector while there was very little change in this respect for HBEs. By 2005, an increased proportion of both HBEs and non-HBEs were working for the formal sector, but the difference between the two types of workshop remained significant. In 2015, however, a growth in home-based workshops producing for the formal sector meant that there was no relationship between location and working for formal sector firms. The overall outcome of these developments is a highly significant transformation when 1975 is compared with 2015. The steady increase in vertical linkages after 1995 means that 33% of HBEs had links to the formal sector in 2015. However, the assumptions about dependent homeworkers is based on their relationship to larger firms in the private sector.

HBEs and the private sector

After 1975, firms that 'often' worked for large-scale private enterprise were much more likely to be located *outside* the home of the owner (Table A.8.10). In 1975, however, the percentage of home-based artisans who said they worked for larger firms more than once a month represented only 2% of the sample and, at best in 2005, they accounted for only 4% of artisans as a whole.

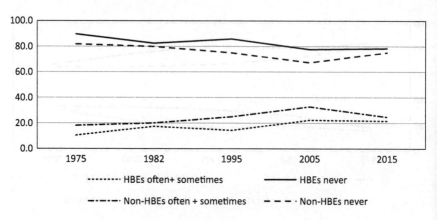

Figure 8.4 HBEs and non-HBEs working for formal private sector

The relationship between location and working for the formal private sector varied in different survey years. Artisans whose workshops were outside the home were consistently more likely to say they worked for the private sector (Figure 8.4), but only in 1995 and 2005 was there a significant difference between the HBEs and non-HBEs (Table A.8.11). The proportion of HBEs working for the private sector fluctuates over the years, but the trend is for a gradual increased relationship up to 2005. There is no significant change in any inter-survey period but when 1975 and 2015 are compared, the difference is significant. Almost all of the increase in HBE work for the private sector happened before 2005 (p-value = 0.0182).

Dependency on the formal sector

The evolving relationship with the private sector was therefore different for family based firms and home-based firms:

- Family-based firms were more likely than non-FBEs to work for the private sector but there was no increase in their involvement over time.
- Non-FBE links with the private sector increased during the oil boom years and then stagnated
- Non-HBEs were more likely to work for the private sector than HBEs. (Firms that would be classified as 'homeworkers' by the ILO and others were more likely to be working outside the home and in the neoliberal years this was highly significant).
- Both HBEs and non-HBEs became more involved over time. For HBEs the difference between 1975 and 2005 was highly significant.
- For the non-HBEs, the change between 1975 and 2005 was significant, but there was a decrease in links in 2005–15.

To explain why these relations should be different at any point in time and to understand why the relationships should evolve in diverse directions and patterns, we need a better understanding of what is happening to the variety of activities that make up the population of artisans. The importance of family-based firms or home based enterprises may be different for tailors and mechanics, for example, and there will be reasons for any variations over time. Unfortunately, it is not possible to be precise about causes and consequences from the survey data, but we can identify the changing relationship of the owners of different types of workshops to the family and the home (Tables A.8.12, A.8.13 and A.8.14).

We can note, for example, that 85% of shoemakers were located inside the home in 1975 but by 2015, this had been reduced to 20%. At the same time, shoemakers employing family labour increased from 20% to 35%. Over the same period, the total number of shoemakers fell by 86% and they declined from 22% to 5% of all workshops. Over the years, the structure of the artisan population changed, which will have had an impact on the aggregated figures for FBEs and HBEs, and therefore on aggregated relations with the private sector. Different levels and changing patterns of attachment to family and home can be identified for all artisan activities covered in the research. The changing structure of production that was identified in Table 3.2 has influenced the aggregated data for artisans as a whole (Table A.8.15).

Behind these statistics there is an indeterminate number of influences that have a differential impact on different types of activities. At his stage, for FBEs and HBEs, it is not possible to disentangle the relative importance of:

- changing activities within the eight artisan activities (e.g. from painters to stonemasons);
- the evolution of productive technology in different spheres;
- cultural changes in relation to gender and female employment;
- changing tax regimes (such that it becomes advantageous to 'employ' a spouse);
- the relevance of toxicity and the fears about health (especially for children);
- the geography of housing (e.g. the move from the centre to the more spacious properties in the south);
- the activities of municipal authorities (who give certain artisans permission to work in some areas and buildings, but not others – the *patente*);
- the changing value that is placed on education for artisan children;
- the wider social networks that can provide access to different types of customers;
- and so on.

All of these affect the social relations of production of microenterprises, have an impact on the relation between the home and the workplace, and influence the growth and accumulation prospects of small firms. The social relations of home, family and work are much more complicated than has been assumed. In the next chapter, we will look more closely at the relevance of artisan social networks beyond the home and place of work.

Notes

1 At the beginning of the research, we defined the family as people who lived in the same house and ate at the same table but, of course, the respondents were not necessarily defining the concept in the same way.
2 Ferrán's emphasis.
3 The other three categories of actors that the Bank and others identify as being part of the informal economy, based on location, are street traders and street vendors; itinerant or seasonal or temporary job workers on building sites or road works; and those between streets and home, e.g., waste collectors.
4 They were asked to identify the numbers of paid and unpaid family workers in their workshops, along with any children still in education who helped them.

9   Social networks and the theft of social capital

Introduction

Analyses of the organisations of the informal sector tend to concentrate on the politics of street traders. Until recently, 'the informal economy was deemed incapable of political organisation' (Meagher, 2010, 46) 'leaving political dimensions largely unexamined' (Lindell, 2010, 1) and, as a consequence, 'very little is known about the organisation of the informal economy or the politics of its external relationship with governments, political parties or with organised labour in the formal economy' (Jimu, 2010, 100). They say that the new interest in and new perspectives on political expression in the informal sector is due to the rapid informalisation of economic activity and the rise of civil society in Latin America, Africa and Asia. A proliferation of popular associations and the political organisation of small-scale unregistered economic actors are thought to be new phenomena. On the contrary, the political organisation of small-scale traders and artisans pre-dates the concept of the informal sector (Middleton, 1982, 2003).

The recent intellectual discovery of organisations claiming to represent actors in the informal economy is to be welcomed, but it tends to marginalise a historical perspective on the changing structures of association in developing economies. In the case of small-scale production units, there are parallels with early industrial organisations in developed countries, as well as significant differences (Middleton, 1982). However, the modern context is neoliberal economics and the political systems that promote free-market capitalism.

In the 1980s and 1990s, capitalism launched a direct attack on labour's capacity to organise, resulting in a reduction in the level of labour organisation in developing countries (Petras and Veltmeyer, 2001). A dramatic expansion of jobs at the lower end of the wage spectrum, a shift away from manufacturing towards services, the introduction of new technologies and other changes in the global economy contributed to this. Self-employed, under-employed and economically marginalised, it was thought that they were not naturally predisposed to the collective action that was evidenced in the labour force of the large-scale capitalist sector of the economy. This encouraged some authors to argue that informal workers lack organisational capabilities (Castells and Portes, 1989), a view that reflected Marx's negative perspective on the lumpenproletariat.

The evidence of this growing mass of informal labour contributed to the academic view that there was no history of economic and political organisation in this segment of the labour force. Following Marx and Latin American neo-Marxists such as Nun (1969 and 2000), Petras and Veltmeyer saw informal workers as a 'reservoir of surplus labour', which undermines organised labour and, in this perspective, artisans and other workers in micro-firms are part of this surplus. Structural adjustment created more precariousness, irregularity and informality, a reduction of jobs in the formal sector of production and the decline of the industrial proletariat (Petras and Veltmeyer, 2001, 85–6). Informal workers, viewed as lacking organisational capacity and motivation, were thought to be contributing to the downward pressure on the wages and conditions of industrial wage labour.

However, the relationship between industrial wage labour, the owners of informal firms and wage labour in microenterprises is more complicated than this perspective suggests. There is, in fact, a long history of small-scale producers allying themselves with the industrial working class. Artisans were involved in nineteenth-century labour struggles in Europe and participated in the setting up of the First International, which dealt with both economic and political issues. This 'stratum of largely self-educated and skilled artisans' with their own culture and intellectuals who were open to democratic and socialist ideas 'provided the base for local, national and international labour organisations' (Waterman, 2001, 17–18). Artisan printing shops were the vehicles for the spread of ideas about the need for the organisation of labour and for the political activity associated with this. By printing leaflets that were written by artisan intellectuals and others, they disseminated information and new ideas of the time.[1]

In order to understand the history and contemporary position of organisations claiming to represent informal workers and how these organisations are connected to other structures and institutions of society, it is helpful to distinguish between informal traders and the producers of goods and services. These groups are often interlinked through their economic activities, but they tend to be organisationally distinct. It is therefore important to treat them separately in the first instance. Traders tend to be organised around local spaces, while small-scale producers are generally organised around the manual skills they possess.

For street traders, the immediacy of the street has organisational primacy and for market traders it is often the passageway around the stall (Middleton, 2003). Relationships between organisations are built up from these basic spatial units to cover a market, a district of the city and, occasionally, the city itself. Lindell (2010, 1) argues that 'our understanding of the politics of informality has been hampered by deeply entrenched views that tend to deprive people in the informal economy of agency'. Seldom seen as political actors, these interpretations allow little space for autonomous action or resistance among informal workers.

Limitations on organisation are said to include lack of leadership skills, material resources and political connections (Lindell, 2010). The political subjectivities of informal workers, however, do not represent a single class interest. Many occupy different class positions at the same time and/or at different times, and they move across class boundaries. The divisions, boundaries and hierarchies are not fixed or permanent, they experience several kinds of injustice and conflict, they have multiple and fragmented identities and their grievances are negotiated and contested:

> The collective identities of organised informal workers are not pre-given or stable, but are rather continuously constructed and reconstructed through multiple struggles and relations in response to wider societal change.
>
> (Lindell, 2010, 14)

The informal workers may also get together with other allies, such as the land movement in the case of Kenya (Lindell, 2010, 21) or the indigenous movement in the case of Ecuador (Middleton, 2003). In some cases their networks extend beyond national boundaries. International NGOs have had a role in organising street traders, locally and internationally. However, there is a question about whether these trader organisations would be sustainable without the active support of international NGOs and it is not clear what their material benefit is for the mass of informal workers. Another important question is whether informal associations 'provide an effective mechanism for political voice' (Meagher, 2010, 47) but this begs the question as to what 'effective' means. It could refer to the ability of the informal sector actors to achieve their aims; but there is a danger that we are trying to compare political outcomes with objectives that these organisations have never professed. When academics discuss 'effective political organisation within the informal economy' (ibid.), it is important to ensure that we do not let academics or NGOs define what this might mean.

The debate about effective political organisation also tends to assume that there is homogeneity in the informal sector, that its members have a common economic interest that can find political expression through their membership organisations, and that they have articulated and distinct political aims for which these organisations can provide a voice. On the contrary, evidence from Ecuador suggests that the informal sector is not politically homogenous, there can be alliances with different political parties, these alliances may be transitory and there may be differences based on religion, ethnicity and class consciousness. These differences can lead to violent conflict between informal workers (Middleton 2003; Zaidi, 2019).

Both artisans and traders in Ecuador would qualify as politically active, but whether or not they are 'effective' depends on their capacity to achieve both short-term and long-term goals as defined by these organisations. As we will see, the organisations are not representative of all informal workers and the interests of some are excluded by the achievements of others. They are subject to elite capture (Reno, 2002) and this leads the informal workforce to question the value and legitimacy of the organisations that claim to represent them.

Artisan guilds and social capital

A major problem with recent debates about the informal sector is that the structural position of the informal labour force is ignored and, beyond formal–informal relations, the social position of this segment of the labour force is not clearly identified in relation to other groups in society. It is recognised that the sector is heterogeneous, but conflicting interests within the sector and between informal workers and others are underestimated.

Work on squatter settlements identifies a community of interest based on identical survival needs within specific social and geographical boundaries. Related organisational activities are examined in the context of state policy for the provision of those needs and in relation to the interests of private landowners or other groups with similar claims on the state's finite resources. In analyses of how poor communities can access these scarce resources and improve their well-being, the concept of social capital has provided an important theoretical focal point (Putnam, 1993, 2000; Fukuyama, 1995). It is a contested concept, with a variety of meanings for different authors (Middleton et al., 2005). According to the World Bank (2000, 128), it is defined as: the ability of individuals to secure benefits as a result of membership in social networks or other social structures.

Brown and Lyons (2010) use the concept of social capital to refer to formally established associations of street traders. The concept is defined as 'the social networks based on norms, reciprocity and trust among their members'. Others have used a similar definition (Carr and Chen, 2002), whilst yet others have extended the concept to cover relations of production and exchange (Lyons and Snoxell, 2005). The popularity of the concept has led some authors to expect too much from social networks or social capital. Meagher, for example, tries to explain 'why social networks have failed to promote economic development in Africa', explain 'the development failures of informal enterprise networks', and show how 'a proliferation of social networks has failed to cope with the challenges of economic reform and globalisation' (Meagher, 2006, 553–4). Perhaps this is expecting too much of social networks but her basic assumption, that 'social networks have not promoted economic development in Africa' (ibid., 556), is crying out for evidence that would support this assertion. It is not clear why we should expect that social networks will promote economic development, what would constitute evidence for this belief, and how we would measure the impact of networks on development. A more modest but nonetheless important contribution is identified by Zaidi (2019), who shows how street traders use social capital to negotiate political structures and ethnic conflict in Karachi.

The World Bank categorises social networks into three kinds of social capital within and between communities – bonding, bridging and linking (World Bank, 2001):

- The strong ties connecting family members, neighbours, close friends and business associates can be called *bonding social capital*. These ties connect people who share similar demographic characteristics.
- The weak ties connecting individuals from different ethnic and occupational backgrounds can be referred to as *bridging social capital*. Bridging social capital implies horizontal connections to people with broadly comparable economic status and political power. A theory of social capital that focuses only on relations within and between communities, however, opens itself to criticism that it ignores power.
- A third dimension, *linking social capital*, consists of the vertical ties between poor people and people in positions of influence in formal organisations (banks, agricultural extension offices, the police). This dimension captures a vitally important additional feature of life in poor communities: that their members are usually excluded – by overt discrimination or lack of resources – from the places where major decisions relating to their welfare are made.

Artisans have a history of social relations outside the workplace that stretch back to medieval times. Their guilds are historical examples of horizontal social relations that defended their interests and promoted their well-being. However, we saw that when they were transported into the New World, they were used to constrain the artisans and impose the will of the ruling colonial elite. Where comparable artisan organisations exist in the developing world today, for example an association of tailors, they can be seen as examples of guilds with *bonding social capital* that connect people with similar demographics and economic characteristics. If the networks connect artisans in different occupational groups or guilds, such as tailors and shoemakers who might come together to oppose council plans for refurbishment and displacement, these relations could be seen as *bridging social capital*; that is, they connect people from different occupational backgrounds through local organisations that are connected horizontally. These organisations, however, are the basis for the creation of a hierarchy of provincial and national federations. When these federations come together in the JNDA, this provides an opportunity for *linking social capital* that connects the individual tailor to national government and the heart of power. However, from the colonial epoch to the present day, the guilds also become conduits for the exercise of power from above.

The creation of this hierarchy of organisations places the artisans at the heart of national and international power politics. As an organised labour force, whose credentials as a social class are disputed because of the master-journeyman relationship inside their workshops, they have been an important component of local democratic movements and the struggle for power.

When the urban poor are analysed as a fraction of the labour force, it is usually assumed that the good of the urban poor is intrinsically tied up with the good of society as a whole or, alternatively, that their needs and interests are the same as those of wage labour in capitalist employment. The assumption of social capital theory is that the relationships involved are positive and they will enhance the well-being of the communities where they exist: higher levels of social capital will increase the standards of living of poorer communities.

If membership of an artisan association is taken as an example of social capital, it is assumed that these relationships will enhance the standards of living of members through the expansion of mutually beneficial activities in fields such as health and welfare. In addition, the participating artisans, through collaboration in the associations and lobbying of government for economic benefits, such as preferential import subsidies and relaxation of employment regulations, will also increase profitability and further enhance the income and welfare of all artisans. Artisan guilds negotiate with those in power, successfully or not, for social and economic advantages that are not available to other sectors of society.

This is a cohesive vision of the artisans as a social group, which coexists with an acceptance that there is competition between them in the marketplace. Market competition does not exclude common interests around which they can organise, in the same way as capitalist employers organise. However, no one would think of organisations such as the Confederation of British Industry or the Engineers Employers Federation in the UK as evidence of social capital. These organisations are more likely to be seen in terms of social class, as the representatives of the owners of capital.

The artisan guilds are different from capitalist employers' federations, in that they include qualified journeymen in their membership. It is assumed, therefore, that they represent all artisans (the self-employed, employers and workers) in the pursuit of common interests. It is also assumed, in line with social capital theory, that membership of guilds are based on social relations that will materially enhance standards of living. In fact, the attraction of membership depends on this. Artisans may be proud of their professions, as we pointed out earlier, but they may also be instrumental in relation to membership of their associations, particularly since they have to pay for affiliation. We should therefore assume that if membership does not enhance the material well-being of the artisans, they will not join or, if the influence of their association wanes, they will cease to be members.

Social capital theory assumes that the relationships involved are benign. The assumption that guilds are mutual benefit associations and can be seen as examples of social capital reinforces the further assumption that increasing membership *will* enhance artisan well-being. But what if the relationships between small workshop owners and wage labourers are neither benign for the majority in the sector nor support the policies and activities that would enhance the incomes of that majority? The relationships involved could be benign for the small masters, but not for their workers and apprentices. If membership assists with keeping wage costs down and supports the exploitation of wage labour through exemption from the benefits of the Labour Code, as has been the case in Ecuador, these membership organisations would not be based on mutual benefit. They would be exploitative of the majority of artisans.

A further assumption in the literature, which often goes unstated, is that the development of workers' representative organisations is a unilineal evolutionary process which proceeds in an even manner as a necessary result of industrial growth.[2] For societies with a large artisan labour force in manufacturing, it is generally thought that there will be a repeat of the British transition from guild organisation through mutual benefit associations to modern trade unionism. However, in countries where the development of manufacturing has been affected by the historical relationship of the local structure of production with an evolving world capitalist system, there is every reason to suspect that the growth of workers organisation should also be affected.

We saw in Chapter 2 that, under the heading of the 'informal economy', international organisations lump together the self-employed, employers, workers in unregulated small firms, and wage workers in capitalist enterprises who cannot access the benefits that should accrue to them by virtue of their employment in the capitalist sector. The lack of access to health, welfare and other benefits is what unites them. However, the historical antecedents and the current structural positions of artisans, whether workshop owners or wage-earning journeymen, are different from factory workers – and this is expressed in different organisational forms. Artisans have different types of horizontal linkages from those created through the trade unions of factory workers. At certain historical junctures the artisans and factory workers have tended to come together, whilst at other times because of conflicting interests, they have stood in opposition to each other.

Artisan networks and trade unions

In Ecuador for most of the twentieth century, in addition to the guilds, there were a host of organisations competing for the allegiance of the artisans. There were federations, associations and chambers that claimed their legitimacy through association with the Law for the Defence of the Artisan (Defence Law) or the Law for the Development of Small Industry and Artisans (Development Law) (Gobierno del Ecuador, 1953, 1965). In addition, there were trade unions such as the Marxist Confederation of Ecuadorean Workers (CTE), the Ecuadorean Confederation of Catholic Workers (CEDOC), and the CIA-sponsored Ecuadorean Confederation of Free Syndical Organisations (CEOSL). These trade unions were at the heart of the struggle for power in Ecuador, each of them claiming to represent the working population as a whole. They had their power bases in different segments of the working class and they were promoted by different national and international interests (Middleton, 1982).

In addition, the artisan guilds, each based on the skills of the artisans and brought together in regional and national federations, such as the National Board for the Defence of the Artisans (JNDA) and the provincial and national Chambers of Artisans, were part of the same struggle for political power. The competition for the allegiance of the artisans, along with their votes in national and regional elections, attracted the interest of other national organisations, such as political parties and employers' organisations, as well as international power brokers such as the USA and her allies, the Soviet Union and the Catholic Church.

The apparently never-ending competition for the hearts and minds of the artisans has been complicated by the class structure of Ecuador and the culture of independence associated with this group of workers. We have seen that the macro-economy of the twentieth century was marked by Ecuador's emergence from the domination of traditional forms of agriculture, which was semi-feudal in the Sierra and an agro-exporting in the Coast, to a dependence on oil exports and the growth of capitalist systems in manufacturing and services. In this process, class conflict has been endemic, but constantly changing in nature, and class alliances have been fluid as the macro-structure has changed. In the context of the changes in the macro-economy, the artisans' relationship to the different elements of the changing system and to the developing configuration of classes has been conditioned by the existence a variety of small-scale employers, the self-employed, wage-earning journeymen and apprentices. Relations between these different types of artisans have their own inherent contradictions.

As discussed briefly in Chapter 3, the present-day federations of artisans have developed out of colonial guilds – but with their own historical trajectories, their developing membership profiles, their unique place in the national social, political and economic system, and their distinct relationship with international capital. Quality control has always been an issue for the guilds, whose accredited qualifications are the passport to the benefits that accrue to artisan employers. Accreditation and professional skills, however, have not stopped non-artisans from taking over or setting up 'artisan' workshops. The guilds have also been evolving, increasingly representing the owners of small capitalist enterprises.

There have been eight themes in the historical development of artisan guilds in Ecuador, some of which have been overlapping in different phases of the country's social, political and economic history. These are:

1. The colonial imposition of guilds;
2. Post-colonial independence and freedom in the market;
3. The emergence of mutual benefit associations;
4. Collaboration in the growth of trade unions;
5. Materially based conflict between small masters and wage-earning trade unionists;
6. Ideologically based conflict with trade unions, in which the artisans were allies of the state and church in anti-communist activities;
7. Emergence as representatives of small capitalist firms;
8. Formalisation under Correa's revised Labour Code.

We saw in Chapter 3 how the relationship between artisans and their guilds developed. In summary we can say that the relationship between artisans and the larger socio-economic structure has always been conditioned by the insertion of the local economy in the world capitalist system. This can be traced back to the colonial times when the system of guilds was transposed from Spain to the colonies as organs of the colonial state. They developed into religious brotherhoods and, in the latter half of the nineteenth century, mutual benefit associations were set up, which became the forerunners of the trade union movement in the early twentieth century. As the unions developed, fundamental differences in the interests of artisans and factory-based wage labour began to emerge: popular consumption needs were met by a two-tiered structure of manufacturing whereby capitalist firms produced the raw materials for artisan production and, as union demands for higher factory wages increased, this affected the costs of artisan inputs. This contradiction made it relatively easy for Conservative politicians, priests and intellectuals to pit the artisan organisations against the trade union movement (Jaramillo, 1962; Elliot, 1970; Hammerly, 1973; Saad, 1974; Hurtado and Herudek, 1974; Moreano, 1975; Hurtado, 1977; Robalino, 1977)

From the 1930s to the 1970s, the artisan organisations were influenced, organised and fought over. In the early 1930s, Velasco Ibarra and a number of conservative intellectuals were active in the promotion of the Catholic Workers Centre and this organisation was to become the basis of the response of the Catholic Church and the Conservative Party to what was seen as 'the communist advance' (Hurtado and Herudek, 1974, 69; Middleton, 1982). The *artisan* associations of the Sierra were initially brought together to form the Ecuadorean Confederation of Catholic Workers (CEDOC) in 1938 (Middleton, 1982). In the same year, the Workers Confederation of Ecuador (CTE) and Marxist intellectuals were active in getting the Labour Code passed into law, regulating relations between employers and workers. CEDOC was dominated by the Church, and each organisation within it had a priest as an adviser (Saad, 1974, 37–8). The CTE was dominated by the Communist Party of Ecuador, with links to the Soviet Union. In the context of the Ecuadorean political spectrum, the proposals of the First Congress of CEDOC were progressive, rather than reactionary and despite the fact that the CTE was basically a union representing wage labour, it still proposed to look after the interests of the small master (see Saad, 1974, 52 and 64).

In the 1970s, intellectuals close to CEDOC argued that the traditional thinking of the artisans made them close to the ideas of the Conservative Party and that the Catholicism of both was a fundamental link (Hurtado and Herudek, 1974, 80). Nonetheless, this idealist interpretation does not stand on its own. The structural contradiction between the small workshop owner and the industrial wage labourer who produces the artisans' inputs provides a sound materialist reason for the conservative-artisans alliance. These differences were exploited by conservative forces who organised the artisans against wage labour, and it was not until the latter became more powerful in an expanding CEDOC that the two opposing union organisations could find common ground.

The position of CEDOC changed through its development in the 1950s and 1960s, as it widened its base to take in more industrial workers. The influence of the Church declined and the Confederation adopted a different ideological perspective, based on a 'Christian humanism', class struggle and socialist objectives (Hurtado and Herudek, 1974, 73). In 1962, the year a CIA-sponsored coup d'état removed the democratically elected government of Carlo Julio Aresomena, the Ecuadorean Confederation of Free Syndical Organisations[3] (CEOSL) was set up under the auspices of AFL-CIO, AID, the CIA and the Labour Attaché of the American Embassy. It mainly organised the urban workers in commerce and services, but it too followed the same path of radicalisation as CEDOC. In 1971, all three unions came together for the first time on a march to celebrate May Day.

Throughout the twentieth century, control of the artisan guilds was an essential aspect of the struggle for power in Ecuador. Artisan social capital was an instrument of power and control, as well as a means of achieving benefits for federation members. This struggle for power resulted in two conflicting pieces of legislation that were constantly being updated. First, in 1953 the Defence Law provided protection and benefits to National Confederation of Professional Artisans of Ecuador and set up the National Board for the Defence of Artisans (JNDA).[4] Second, in 1965 the Development Law, which had the intention of promoting the development of modern capitalist enterprises out of the traditional artisan workshops, set up provincial and national Chambers of Artisans under the control of the Ministry of Industry (Gobierno del Ecuador, 1953, 1965). In the competition between tradition and modernity, which we will return to discuss in more detail in the next chapter, the Development Law could not overcome the main attraction of the Defence Law, which was that the latter freed the workshop owners from employers' obligation under the Labour Code.

Capitalist capture of artisan organisations

At the beginning of the 1970s, despite their lack of membership, the state recognised the Chambers as the legitimate representatives of Ecuadorean artisans. At this time, there was no ideological difference between the two systems of artisan organisation, each being primarily concerned with the 'transformation to small industry'.[5] The main debate was about which Law would best support this aim, a discussion which underpinned a conflict over which system of organisation truly represented the artisans. The artisans preferred the Federations and the Defence Law, mostly because of their status as 'small masters'. The Defence Law exempted the small master from the responsibilities of other employers towards their wage workers under the Labour Code and the Law of Social Security. The attraction of this led to small capitalist firms claiming the status of artisans under the law, with the complicity of the JNDA.

Jewellers' leaders argued that even merchants were masquerading as artisans (*El Comercio*, 5 November 1972), and the Director of the Artisan Section of the Ministry of Social Provision reported that many of the large 'master-artisans' had been petitioning to be classified as 'educators' who were teaching a profession, in order to remain outside the labour legislation (*El Comercio*, 5 December 1972). The guilds, previously perceived to be the representatives of all artisans, were protecting the interests of employers against the demands of their workforces.

Throughout this period after the introduction of the Development Law, in the context of the government promoting a development agenda that was based on the theories of modernisation that were prevalent at the time, the concerns and the perspectives of the artisan organisations were also undergoing a transformation. There was a gradual change in the demands of the artisan organisations to reflect the needs of small industry. In this process, the Defence Board acted in the interests of the small capitalists who had consolidated their grip on the guilds. This not only led to a growing conflict between the interests of the small masters and the labour they employed, but the self-employed producers and the journeymen also found themselves without representation. The CTE tried to step into the organisational space, but the self-employed and journeymen had no organisation to represent their interests. Their social capital was diminished and the artisan workforce had little protection against abuse

Until 1973 a major theme of the artisans' organisations had been the quality and supply of raw materials, along with the lack of training and credit facilities (Middleton, 1979, 240). By 1974, however, these types of demands from the guilds had been declining and a new emphasis was being put on the expansion of individual firms through raising the sales and investment ceilings. The expansion of artisans into small industries has always been a major goal of these small producers but in 1971, when the Defence Law was being revised by the artisans, the concept of the artisan 'class' was prominent in the statements put out by the federations (*El Comercio*, 7 January 1972). The special commission set up to draft the new law was said to have 'made a clear demonstration of class consciousness, laying aside all personalist attitudes and feelings', according to the President of the Federation of Artisans of Pichincha (*El Comercio*, 30 December 1971). The same artisan leader said that to be against the new law 'would be to demonstrate no sense of class' (*El Comercio*, 7 January 1972), and the proposed new law embodied the concept of the 'artisan class' in its statutes.

The idea of the development of the class as a whole, however, was to disappear from the official artisan language after 1972. In its place, the concept of artisan development into small industry increasingly emphasised the needs of the larger capitalist producers, and pressure was increased for a type of legislation which would assist the development of a few producers who had long ceased to be artisans in any normal sense of the word. The Defence Board began to act quite clearly in the interests of these small capitalists and it became clear from the demands of the Federations that they had consolidated their grip. The organisational changes were reflected in the changes that were achieved in the Defence Law in 1974, when the limit of sales was changed to a limit on profit and the limit on capital investment was raised to a level which was quite irrelevant for the needs of the vast majority of artisans.

Under the reformulation of the Defence Law in 1974, 'artisans' could employ up to 13 persons (including four apprentices), own capital to the value of 300,000 sucres (12,000 US dollars) and make a net monthly declared profit of up to 15,000 sucres (600 US dollars). Since the annual average per capita income in Ecuador was only 13,475 sucres (539 US dollars), the changes meant that 'artisans' could be earning (net) 13 times the country's average per capita income. Clearly, the reformulation of the law had very little to do with the needs of 'artisans'. The effect of the redefinition of the 'artisan' was to extend the super-exploitation of this section of the labour force and at the same time it was irrelevant to the needs of small one-person or family enterprises.

Even then, however, the small capitalists were not entirely satisfied. After the law had been changed, the Guayas Federation of Artisans petitioned the Minister of Labour to establish a *minimum* of 250,000 sucres (10,000 US dollars) for capital investment, and they wanted it to be made clear that 'artisans' had no responsibility to receive demands from their workforce (*El Telégrafo*, Mar. 9, 1975).

In addition to both the conflict between wage labour and capital, which was expressed in the growth of the Trade Union movement based on wage labour, and to the contradiction that exists between artisans and industrial wage labourers, which was the basis of the division in workers' organisations, a further source of antagonism had become explicit. It ceased to be the case that both masters and journeymen had a common interest in the quality and price of the product. Rather, leading masters quite clearly had reached a point where they had an overriding interest in reducing labour costs and the journeymen stood in opposition to this. When the self-employed producer and the journeyman found themselves in an organisational vacuum, any attempt to remedy this was swiftly attacked by the small capitalists' organisations. Artisan social capital was diminished when the larger producers captured their organisations and by the late 1990s the size limit for artisan workshops had been extended to 20 workers (Gobierno del Ecuador, 1997).

In the 1970s, the organisations changed from being protectionist with respect to the class of artisans to being exploitative with respect to wage labour, and both the self-employed and the wage workers were left in a situation of being unable to bring any influence (however small) to bear on the state. Firms that would be classified as formal SMEs elsewhere could claim to be artisans and they used the Defence Law to justify the exploitation of workers. This begs the question of where this would leave the relationship between the guilds and artisans as they were originally defined under the Defence Law. To answer this we need to return to the survey research, covering small workshops employing up to seven people including the owner and family labour.

Artisans and guilds, 1975–2015

In 1975, even in the capital city of Quito, the historical heart of organised artisan production, guild membership amongst small-scale artisans was low (Table 9.1). Throughout the period of the study, the majority of artisans did not belong to any organisations but in 1975, almost 70% of artisans had no affiliations. Over the years, membership fluctuated, particularly for the artisan federations. In 1975, 22% of the workshop owners were members of guilds associated with the Defence Law and only 3% were members of the Chambers of Artisans, the modern form of organisation that was associated with the Development Law and was preferred by government. Guild membership increased in 1982 and remained at around one-third of artisan workshop owners through the neoliberal years.

Table 9.1 Membership of groups

	1975		1982		1995		2005		2015	
	No.	%	No.	%	No.	%	No.	%	No.	%
None	133	68.9	168	56.8	185	56.7	184	58.2	178	68.7
Artisan guilds	42	21.8	100	33.8	109	33.4	96	30.4	49	18.9
Chambers of artisans	6	3.1	0	0.0	7	2.1	10	3.2	7	2.7
Chambers of commerce	0	0.0	0	0.0	1	0.3	7	2.2	6	2.3
Producer cooperatives	0	0.0	1	0.3	1	0.3	0	0.0	1	0.4
Trading cooperatives	2	1.0	1	0.3	1	0.3	0	0.0	0	0.0
Trade unions	0	0.0	1	0.3	1	0.3	6	1.9	9	3.5
Political parties	8	4.1	9	3.0	2	0.6	4	1.3	0	0.0
Others	2	1.0	16	5.4	19	5.8	9	2.8	9	3.5
TOTAL	193	100.0	296	100.0	326	100	316	100	259	100

When the artisans were divided into those who were members of guilds and those who were not, over 40 years there was practically no change in the extent to which artisans were affiliated to the associations that claimed to represent them. The periods of significant change in membership were 1975–1982 and 2005–2015 (Table A.9.1). In the first period, when the economy was buoyant following the early years of oil exportation, membership of the guilds increased substantially;[6] and in the last period, when the Correa government insisted that the Labour Code should also apply to artisans who employed wage labour, the decline in membership was highly significant.[7] This suggests that once the guilds were less able to protect members from the labour laws, membership was less relevant.

The level of commitment to the guilds is not the same for all types of artisan (Table A.9.2).[8] At any time, affiliation has varied according to the type of activity of the artisan; and the levels of membership within different sectors have changed over time. Since the guilds associated with the Defence Law had a long historical tradition, we might have expected to find high levels of representation of tailors, shoemakers and carpenters, whose guilds that have roots in the sixteenth century. On the contrary, in 1975, these traditional producers of subsistence goods were less likely to be organised in guilds than, for example, jewellers and mechanics, who are the modern inheritors of the skills of sixteenth-century silversmiths, locksmiths and blacksmiths. Guilds are generally taken to be traditional remnants but the two groups that were most highly organised were also those that were the most *recently* organised at the national level. The jewellers had their first National Congress in November of 1972 (*El Comercio*, 5 November 1972), and the mechanics held only their second congress in July of the same year (*El Comercio*, 26 July 1972).

In all years except 2015, there was a significant relationship between the type of artisan activity and membership of guilds. Over the period, the change was uneven across different activities, ranging from a 40% decline for mechanics and a 28% increase for painters/masons. The membership of all guilds except jewellers increased between 1975 and 1982 (Figure A.9.1). The growth in membership amongst printers, who benefited from links to the expanding private and public sectors, was spectacular. The levels of affiliation after this began to decline for most activities. Mechanics began to decline after 1982, when automobile technology began to change, but jewellers retained high levels of membership until after 2005, when imported goods from China were undermining their businesses.

An important factor in 1975 was that both jewellers and mechanics depended more on state support for importing raw materials and tools than other artisans. While the jewellers relied on the Central Bank for imported gold and platinum, the mechanics imported spare parts and machinery. Mechanics have evolved from mechanical workshops repairing machinery and automobiles to enterprises repairing white line goods; and the balance of painters and stonemasons has shifted from the former to the latter. However, membership amongst jewellers also fell by 27%, a decline related to a fall in demand for precious metals and stones. Over many years, jewellers benefited from special import tariffs for their raw materials, which are available through their federation, but with the decline in the use of imported precious materials, as a consequence of an increase in robberies and a consequent decline in their market, this has made the federation less relevant. However, there were also broader forces at work.

All across the range of activities performed by artisans, a similar process of change has been taking place. The federations have been transformed from organisations that used linking social capital (between poor people and people in positions of influence) to associations of elderly men whose activities provide examples of bonding social capital (between people of similar demographics) (World Bank, 2001, 128). This is true of all the federations linked through the JNDA, but jewellers provide a good example.

Guilds through the eyes of artisans

There were two main guilds representing the jewellers: the Union of Goldsmiths of Pichincha, whose members were the manufacturers and repairers of jewels; and the Association of Watchmakers of Pichincha, representing the repairers of fine watches. Both organisations declined in relevance as they increasingly failed to protect their members from the forces of the market and increased competition from cheap goods and unskilled labour. Both organisations declined, leaving a rump of elderly members who were no more than 'a group of friends'.[9] As one former member said:

> I was a member of the Union of Goldsmiths of Pichincha, but I left because I really could not see any benefit for the members. It exists today. I left about 20 years ago … We asked them to set up a shop, to provide us with parts, raw

materials, for the members – for them to sell material, gold for example, at a good price, but they didn't do it.[10]

For watchmakers, the issues were more about competition that was linked to changing technology. As fine mechanical watches have been replaced by cheap battery-driven Chinese products, the watchmakers' skills have become redundant. As one of the former members of the Association of Watchmakers of Pichincha said:

> Anyone can put a table on a corner and call themselves a watchmaker. To know how to change a battery, or at times to not know how to change a battery, makes you able to call yourself a watchmaker, and that has caused us to decline. It did not used to be like that. They set themselves up on whatever corner to change batteries, straps, whatever … We struggled to get the help of the Federation of Artisans of Pichincha and the *Junta de Defensa del Artesano*, but we never achieved anything, nothing. They spoke about bringing out a law which would not allow them to work in this way, but it still continues. This has damaged us a lot.[11]

Another development has been the conversion of jewellers' workshops in the city centre into commercial outlets. These shops retain some tools to make it appear that they are practising artisans, so that they can continue to claim artisan benefits with the support of the JNDA:

> They make you get a title, they make you learn, they give you courses and everything, in order to work honestly, so to speak. But there are a lot of people who, at the moment, set up premises without knowing anything, nothing. I know a lot of people who have good jewellery businesses, well presented and all, but who know nothing, who bring their work to people like me. And we, shamefully, in order to make money, end up doing the work. I work in this way for several people who own large jewellers shops, well-presented of course, and they know nothing. But what can you do? Work.[12]

A current officer of the association, who came to Quito, followed a course to gain his title and graduated in watchmaking, admits that they have problems:

> The Junta de Defensa del Artesano do not insist that we carry the membership card of the guild, only that we requalify without the obligation to carry the card. For this reason the guilds, and I am not only speaking about watchmaking, but in the guilds of the artisans in general, now do not require the guild membership cards. Well, there is disunity in the guilds; there is no longer attendance at the meetings.[13]

This decline in attendance is seen as being related to both material benefits and cultural aspects in society and it leaves the associations in a precarious position:

When I started work it was more organised, we had a licence, we didn't pay taxes or nothing because the qualified artisan did not pay taxes, nothing. But now, the Association of Watchmakers ... is like a private club ... Eight to ten old watchmakers maintain the headquarters. But now, as far as running courses or doing anything that benefits the artisans in the branch of watchmaking is concerned, nothing. Before, there were things; they ran two courses during the year, there were benefits, but not now.[14]

Not everyone agrees. Another current member thinks that it is important to retain his membership, partially in order to negotiate with the JNDA, but also because he thinks that the social aspect is important:

We are together talking and we are always in agreement about what the JNDA [should do] in their meetings with the state, to see what improvements there are or what obstacles there are, etc. We are in contact, and at the same time with a companion: Hi, how are you, how is it going in your work, come here and we'll eat something, or drink a cola, or we entertain ourselves laughing, or we'll play a game. It is not that we have drunken sessions; that does not exist anymore. We laugh, we chat.[15]

This feeling that the guilds have become no more than social clubs, particularly since the government of Correa reduced the power of the guilds, exists across all artisan activities. A former member of the Association of shirt-makers of Pichincha said that he had left because 'he did not experience any benefit from membership';[16] a shoemaker who is affiliated to his federation said it had 'helped a little with training: almost a little, rather, nothing';[17] an upholsterer said that in order to join he was asked for a million sucres for a membership certificate and he would have to leave them with a fully re-covered suit of furniture, as proof of his skills;[18] a mechanical workshop that was affiliated many years ago claimed that there were 'a lot of procedures, very bureaucratic, the only thing they wanted was money, plus no training';[19] and a member of the Association of Dressmakers of Pichincha said 'I don't see anything good – the association is in trouble, I no longer attend, I have not gone for almost a whole year.'[20]

There always was a social aspect to the guilds, but even that is declining. A now-retired former member of the guild of the Master Tailors of Pichincha travelled overseas for international meetings, congresses, with his brothers, one of whom was President of the federation. He had gone to congresses in Argentina, Brazil and Chile 'for exchange of knowledge' in 1975, 1978, 1980 and 1985. He went as part of a delegation from the guild. A tailors' guild in another country issued an invitation, they met in Quito to select the representatives and the President of the federation chose who will go with him 'to learn a little more'.[21]

Another ex-member praised the opportunity to travel for seminars, although he did not have the opportunity to participate himself: 'there were Maestros, who were already super-elderly, almost little old men, they were involved in this'.[22]

The guilds no longer have the influence they used to have. As examples of linking social capital they have been in decline:

> Previously, some of them helped the artisans. Last century, there were no problems. If you needed something, the President of the guilds went to the President [of the country] and he just helped us. Now, no. The law has changed. Relations between the federations and the government are not good. The federations don't have legal power. Now there are no training centres, there are no societies, because [the guilds] are prohibited by law.[23]

The decline in faith in the federations to represent the owners of these small firms, who were employing up to seven people, took place in the period when the harshest impacts of structural adjustment policies were being felt in Ecuador and when the guilds were increasingly coming to represent the interests of the owners of firms employing up to 20 people, who were registering as artisans to take advantage of the law that freed artisans from the responsibilities of the country's labour laws. However, the consolidation of the grip of small-scale capitalist firms on the guilds is reflected in the continuing decline in their ability to represent the 'artisans' as they were originally defined, and the growing feeling that no organisations were defending their interests.

Who defends the artisans?

Since 1982, the artisans have been asked what institutions defend their interests. Their responses indicate a steady decline in the role of the guilds since then (Table A.9.3). The proportion who believe that no organisations look after their interests has gradually increased over the years and, correspondingly, the percentage who mentioned the artisan federations decreased. The contribution of the Chambers of Artisans was practically zero in 1982 and mentioned by only 3% in 2015. The only other change of any consequence is in relation to the government. While in some years no one mentioned the contribution of the government to the defence of artisan interests, in 2015, 5% said that the Correa government defended their situation.

In order to see if there was any significant change between any of the survey periods the responses were aggregated into none, guilds and others. This showed a highly significant change over the whole period but not between any two years (Table 9.2). Those who thought that no one defended their interests gradually rose from 51% to 73%; those who thought the guilds helped them, fell from 34% to 15%.

The guilds present themselves as the representatives of the artisans and, as such, their claim is to the status of a business organisation. They are no longer representatives of the segment of the urban poor who own microenterprises and consider themselves to be part of the working class. When artisans were specifically asked what these allegedly representative groups had done for them, the answer

Table 9.2 Institutions that defend the interests of artisans

	1982		1995		2005		2015	
	Number	%	Number	%	Number	%	Number	%
None	148	56.3	212	65.6	212	68.6	188	73.7
Federations	99	37.6	92	28.5	69	22.3	40	15.7
Others	16	6.1	19	5.9	28	9.1	27	10.6
Total	263	100	323	100	309	100	255	100

	Chi-sq	DF	p-value
1982–2015	38.4780	6	9.06E-07
1982–1995	5.8090	2	0.0548
1995–2005	4.7013	2	0.0953
2005–2015	4.0406	2	0.1326
1982&2015	32.5032	2	8.75E-08

Table 9.3 What the representative organisations have done for artisans

	1982		1995		2005		2015	
	Number	%	Number	%	Number	%	Number	%
Nothing/critical	122	43.3	198	60.6	225	71.0	157	62.1
Positive response	63	22.3	71	21.7	59	18.6	49	19.4
Don't know	97	34.4	58	17.7	33	10.4	47	18.6
Total	282	100.0	327	100.0	317	100.0	253	100.0

	Chi-sq	DF	p-value
1982–2015	108.1188	6	5.05E-21
1982–1995	25.1527	2	3.45E-06
1995–2005	9.5463	2	0.0085
2005–2015	8.4006	2	0.0150
1982 & 2015	21.9945	2	1.67E-05

was once again mainly negative. In 1982, 34% said they had done nothing, but this rose gradually over the years to 69% in 2005 (Table A.9.4). Around one-third said they did not know what they had done in 1982 but, as those who said this declined over the years, the negativity increased. Part of the argument about the special status of artisans over the years has been that they are educators, training young people for a profession, but the artisans themselves do not appear to give credence to this argument – only around 5% have recognised this as something the guilds have contributed (Table 9.3). A similar percentage acknowledged help with taxes. The change between 1982 and 2015 was highly significant and it was on the basis of increased negativity and declining uncertainty.

Most of the change in the study period was due to what happened during the height of the neoliberal years. The period when successive governments were promoting themselves as the friends of the small businesses, collaborating with business organisations in the spreading of a pro-business ideology and enacting policies that were said to be supportive of microenterprises, the artisans were becoming more and more disillusioned with the organisations who claimed to represent them. As we will see in the next chapter, this was not because the policies were working and the governments of the day were taking the credit. It was not because the government was becoming more successful and the federations were needed less. On the contrary, the declining relevance of the federations goes hand in hand with an increasing hostility to the neoliberal governments.

The decline in confidence in the guilds was confirmed by the maker of musical instruments who said 'the guild is a pure talking shop';[24] the tailor who thought they exist only as meetings of friends;[25] the shirt-maker who did not experience any benefit from membership';[26] the jeweller/watchmaker who thinks something should have been done about people setting themselves up to change watch batteries and calling themselves watchmakers and who complained that 'until recently we had the Asociación de Relojeros de Pichincha, but there are no benefits, there are absolutely no benefits';[27] the shoemaker who is a member and who thinks they have helped with 'nothing';[28] the tailor who had never joined because 'they don't help much, rather they only charged fees';[29] and the shoemaker who spoke more generally to insist that 'the artisan guilds have not helped the artisans, more than anything they involve a paper chase'.[30] These feelings were summed up by a hairdresser who had been a long-term member of the Association of Hairdressers:

> I left recently because they had not helped me with absolutely nothing. I was a member for around 40 years. For around two years now I have not being going to meetings, because they don't help with nothing.[31]

This experience is not confined to the guilds. Artisans who have had relations with the Chambers of Artisans make the same complaints: the mason who said 'they do not offer any assistance';[32] the hat-maker who graduated through the Chamber but who said 'they did not try to help us, no, nothing'.[33]

This feeling of abandonment extends to local and central government. Indeed, as we will see in the next chapter, the state is seen as worse than the guilds for the lack of support. However, there was a button-maker who thought the town council had been more helpful than the guilds;[34] a hat-maker who benefited from working closely with the council in the promotion of tourism;[35] and a shoemaker who praised the government of Rafael Correa for help with setting up an alternative organisation for shoemakers.[36] However, it was the state, and the government of Correa in particular, that put the final nail in the coffin of the artisan guilds.

Notes

1 These means of communication were the equivalent of the internet of their time, now overtaken by new printing and reproduction technologies – firstly by photocopying and then by personal computers and cheap desktop printers linked to the World Wide Web. This artisans' organisational history is well known in the UK and other developed countries, but it is largely unknown across the developing world.
2 Except where they are totally repressed by neoliberal governments in the name of free markets, as happened in Pinochet's Chile.
3 *Confederación Ecuatoriana de Organizaciones Sindicales Libres.*
4 *Junta Nacional de Defensa del Artesano.*
5 In *El Comercio* of Dec. 30, 1971, the National Confederation of Artisans stressed this point in a statement to the newspaper.
6 P-value=0.0050.
7 P-value=0.0011.
8 Using unweighted data.
9 Goldsmith interview, BC-17.
10 Goldsmith interview, C-3.
11 Watchmaker interview, C-4.
12 Watchmaker interview, C-4.
13 Watchmaker Interview, J-1.
14 Interview with jeweller/watchmaker, CU4.
15 Interview with watchmaker, MJ1.
16 Interview with shirt-maker, BC8.
17 Shoemaker interview, BC-7.
18 Upholsterer interview, BC-14.
19 Mechanic Interview, C-2.
20 Dressmaker interview, C-1.
21 Interview with master tailor, AM-1.
22 Tailor interview, MJ-5.
23 Tailor interview, AM-1.
24 Musical instruments, MJ-8.
25 Interview with tailor, AM-1.
26 Interview with shirt-maker, BC8.
27 Interview with watchmaker, C-4.
28 Interview with shoemaker, BC7.
29 Interview with tailor, J-3.
30 Interview with shoemaker, J-2.
31 Interview with hairdresser, MJ-4.
32 Interview with stonemason, BC4.
33 Interview with hat-maker, BC-12.
34 Interview with button maker, BC10.
35 Interview with hat-maker, C-2.
36 Interview with shoemaker, MJ-7.

10 Artisans and the state

Introduction

Since academics first took an interest in the development of firms in the informal sector, there have been two competing perspectives on the role of the state. The neo-Keynesians of the early years were concerned that governments were not active enough in supporting the dynamic small enterprises that proliferated in third world cities (ILO, 1972). It was recognised that there were too many instances of restriction and harassment, but it was also argued that the main issue was that governments did not recognise their existence, policy contained too few elements of support and more state action was needed. Over time, however, the dominant view became that it was a restrictive, interfering and regulatory state that was the main barrier to their progress (de Soto, 1986).

In the theory adopted by the World Bank and the IMF, the rule-bound state became the main reason that the informal sector was failing to develop as part of a successful capitalist economy. The neoliberal solution was to reduce the role of the state and get rid of the regulations that were thought to be holding small enterprises back from realising their full potential. In spite of the fact that in countries such as Ecuador a main aim of the state over the previous three decades was precisely that artisan workshops would develop into small industry, this negative perspective of the-state-as-a-barrier was adopted by successive governments between 1982 and 2007. Legislation benefiting artisans was enacted as long ago as 1953, a law for the development of the artisans had been in place since 1965, and the incorporation of the 'marginados' in the rural and urban areas had been a central concern of national planning since 1972 (Gobierno del Ecuador, 1953, 1965; JNP, 1972a). Ironically, in the name of freeing up the market from state interference, neoliberals have massively interfered in the state and the economy in the interests of the global wealthy against national small-scale enterprise.

There is no denying the existence of laws and regulations that constrain the activities of the informal sector. However, the perspective that is adopted in this research is that new laws and regulations are the manifestation of the dominant ideology and the practical expression of the concentration of power in society at any time. Indeed, the daily experience of some of the most marginalised of the self-employed in the urban streets of developing countries has involved arbitrary violence and repression from the local arm of the state. In many parts of Africa and Latin America, the history of oppression of street traders can be traced back over 100 years but from the 1970s they were increasingly harassed, displaced, beaten, fined, imprisoned and had their goods confiscated without compensation (Skinner, 2008; Jimu, 2010; Middleton, 2003; Brown and Lyons, 2010; Lindell, 2010). This was usually at the insistence of the upper and middle classes. However, it was street traders, rather than micro-producers, who were constantly confronted by the police as they went about their business.

The political history of Ecuador over the past two centuries has been a constant struggle for control of the state apparatus by different fragments of the dominant classes – in order to control the laws and regulations that would affect their capacity to accumulate wealth. There is a fundamental bifurcation of the ruling class that has been brought about by the country's history and geography. The two main fragments are the oligarchies of the Sierra and Coast, who have been the main protagonists in the struggle for control of the state since the declaration of independence in 1809. The sources of wealth of these fragments of class derive from different traditional economic activities and related diversification of economic development. The main historical source of wealth in the Sierra has been the traditional hacienda, producing agricultural goods for the national market. In this case, diversification has followed a path of production of manufactured goods for the local market, largely based on the processing of agricultural outputs, including textiles, leather, wood and other intermediate goods that were reincorporated into the production process by artisans. Capital investment in manufacturing from above confirmed the national orientation of the sierra's industrial production.

In the Coast, the main source of wealth has been the agro-exporting hacienda, where tropical crops such as cocoa and coffee gave way to bananas and later, farmed seafood such as shrimps. Diversification in this case was related to import/export activities, where the small producers of these crops were organised to supply exporters. These exporters were related to the larger-scale producers and to importers who were a source of consumer goods, some of which were in competition with national producers, particularly those located in the Sierra.

In the 1960s, during the era of import-substitution in Latin America, these two fragments of the ruling class were involved in a particularly intense struggle for control of the state (Abad, 1970). With self-interested arguments dressed as economic theory, the sierra elite were vigorous promoters of import substitution, while the coastal elite pursued the end of these policies and the freeing up of markets. When oil began to flow in the 1970s, the competition for control of the state reached fever pitch as the different fragments of the ruling class sought the right to control the new source of wealth and to determine the economic policies that would benefit themselves most. It was in this context that the Revolutionary Nationalist government of General Rodrigues Lara intervened in the name of the marginal populations, promising a more equitable distribution of the new wealth. The artisans were seen as part of this marginal population.

In a country such as Ecuador, with its government constantly veering between democracy and dictatorship for most of its history since Independence, the main fractions of the ruling class have tried to attract the support of other social classes, and this was most evident in state policies in support of artisans in the 1950s and 1960s. The artisans were able to point to the political importance of their large numbers and translate these numbers into a perception of their voting power, which they were then able to use to their advantage. In Chapter 3 we saw that that in the 1960s the artisan federations, through the JNDA, could point out that 89% of the manufacturing labour force were artisans (both urban and rural) and that there were three times as many artisans as factory wage earners in the urban areas. Claiming to control hundreds of thousands of voters gave the artisan organisations significant influence on the competing fragments of the ruling class in the 1970s and this was not lost on an emerging small capitalist manufacturing sector.

We saw in the previous chapter that small-scale capitalist producers began to take over the organisations of the artisans, in order to cloak themselves in the perceived artisan influence and bend the laws in their favour. This resulted in a struggle for power on two levels. The macro level was dominated by a competition of ideas and policies between different fragments of the ruling class and, at the lower level of the social structure, there was a struggle for influence based on the competition between artisans and petty capitalists for a share of the local market for consumer goods. An aspect of this struggle for power was pressure from small-scale capitalists to redefine the artisan in Ecuadorian law and take advantage of the various laws that offered benefits to artisans. We have noted that by changing the definition of the artisan to include small-scale capitalist manufacturers, enterprises that had been defined as small industries were able to claim these benefits. In spite of the historical support for the artisans, the effect of this was to alienate the vast majority from both the guilds and the state.

The neoliberal state and artisans

When artisans have been asked what the government has done for them, the majority have always said 'nothing'. This negative response, usually made forcefully, is an expression of their alienation from the government of the day. However, the proportion who responded in this way has fluctuated considerably between 1982 and 2015, reaching its highest point at 93% in 2005 before declining to its lowest at 58% in 2015 (Table 10.1). In the earlier years of neoliberalism, 1982 and 1995, when around three-quarters were saying the government had done nothing for them, the proportion who were giving more negative responses increased considerably (from 12% to 21%). By far the highest proportion of negative responses was found in the heart of the neoliberal era and the highest proportion of positive responses was during the Correa period of government. When the artisans who said 'nothing' were combined with those who gave other negative responses, the overall negativity during the neoliberal years reached

Table 10.1 What the government has done for artisans

	1982		1995		2005		2015	
	Number	%	Number	%	Number	%	Number	%
Nothing	222	75.3	237	72.9	297	93.4	134	57.5
Positive Response	14	4.7	4	1.2	5	1.6	51	21.9
Negative Response	36	12.2	67	20.6	11	3.5	16	6.9
Don't know	23	7.8	17	5.2	5	1.6	55	23.6
Total	295	100	325	100	317	100	256	109.9

	Chi-sq	DF	p-value
1982–2015	258.887	9	1.3237E-50
1982–1995	14.859	3	0.0019
1995–2005	53.533	3	1.41E-11
2005–2015	136.924	3	1.74E-29
1982 & 2015	113.559	3	1.88E-24

99% (Table A.10.1). It then fell to 75% during the Correa presidency, not exactly a cause for celebration, but it was a decline that was highly significant (p-value = 0.0000).

Neoliberalism's claim to help the small firms that it says are the beating heart of capitalism is not reflected in the artisans' views of the neoliberal state. The rhetoric and the reality do not match up, which is in part due to the artisans' declining power in their struggle to influence legislation.

Artisan legislation and power

Over time, there have been changes in the legal definition of an artisan that reflected how politicians saw the voting potential of artisans. It expressed the relative power of capitalist and non-capitalist firms within artisan federations and it provided an insight into their relative ability to organise and to lobby using networks of friends and family. The relations between the state and artisan federations developed through a form of clientelism, whereby both patron and client gained advantages from each other's support, a form of exchange in which the state sought to trade policy benefits for votes.

This is consistent with what has been found elsewhere with respect to relations with dominating power. While the economists' narrative about informal-state relations has emphasised evading state regulation and disengaging from the state, in many African cities informal associations have actively sought out links with the state by seeking official registration (Lindell, 2010a, 15). Roitman (2004) argues that informal workers are not autonomous from the state, but central to the exercise of state power. While seemingly beyond the reach of the state in many ways, they do not escape its web of domination. Through their organisations, they are drawn into clientelist networks of personal power relations that pervade the state and through which the state extends its power into society. In pursuing their interests, issues of class are important elements in the discourse and conflicts can emerge not only between master and journeyman but also between small and larger masters.

Meager (2010) describes how the interests of the organisations of garment makers and shoemakers in Aba, Nigeria, were dominated by the interests of the better-off producers. The associations' leaders were more interested in their own well-being and interests, rather than those of the sector. For many small producers, the associations were viewed as the enemy and, rather than increasing the political voice of those they claimed to represent, most felt not only excluded but that no one really represented their interests. The associations, pursuing the interests of an elite group of producers, sit between the distrust of their constituencies and the danger of political capture (Meagher, 2010, 63).

A similar situation exists in Ecuador. We have noted that for more than half a century, legislation has supported artisan development, protecting them from the main requirements of the Labour Code and providing considerable financial and tax incentives for development. This is contrary to the neoliberal view of the informal sector that emphasises 'lack of compliance with legal norms'. This latter perspective prompts the question as to why the sector is not in compliance and leads to the view that 'high informality results from a massive opting out of formal institutions by firms and individuals, and offers an indictment of the state's regulations and services and of its enforcement capability' (Perry et al., 2007, 23). The reality in Ecuador and elsewhere is that the owners of larger firms inserted themselves into the organisational structures that claimed to represent artisans and persuaded the state to redefine artisan workshops to include the small factories of non-artisan small-scale manufacturers. As we saw in Chapter 9, state support for micro-producers was diverted towards more wealthy enterprises through the capture of artisan guilds.

Since the middle of the twentieth century, this relationship between the 'artisans' and the state has been embedded in a constantly changing series of laws and other legal instruments that have modified the benefits that the artisans have been able to claim (Table A.10.2). Over time, the Defence Law and the Development Law have been modified, along with several versions of the Constitution, production codes, labour codes and social security laws. Some of these changes have had an impact on the development of artisans. Defining artisans is a political project and the laws are mired in confusion over who precisely is being targeted. This has allowed the small-scale capitalists to highjack the benefits that were supposed be for the artisans, as we suggested in the previous chapter. However, some small-scale employers and their families have benefited from tax and social security laws to the exclusion of wage labour in their workshops. How artisans are defined in the Defence Law and the Development Law have been at the heart of the politics of small-firm development.

Defining artisans: the Defence Law vs the Development Law

Defining artisans has always been a political project. It has been an aspect of the political economy of Ecuador since the first law was set out in 1953, it was an important part of the struggle for hearts and minds in Latin America in the 1960s after the Cuban Revolution, and it became an essential element of the struggle for power in Ecuador in the 1970s, before the development narrative was captured by neoliberalism.

The Defence Law arose from promises made to Ecuadorean artisans by Velasco Ibarra during his presidential campaign of 1952 and the law was jointly promoted by the Conservative Party when he came to power. It created a framework for the *protection* of artisan interests, and it involved a transaction that offered artisan votes in return. The Development Law of 1965 was more specific about promoting the *development* of artisans into small capitalist firms. Responding to concerns that some of the advantages of the Defence Law were so generous that they discouraged artisans from growing into larger enterprises, the new law sought to reduce some of these benefits. Since artisans were able to convince local politicians that they were an important political force, in control of hundreds of thousands of votes, this gave them real power through their guilds. The outcome was that the Defence Law remained on the statute book. Successive governments were caught between the artisans as a political constituency and the economic theory that came to dominate the last decades of the twentieth century. This helped create confusion across a complex network of laws and regulations, which the guilds have tried to manipulate to their advantage.

It is important to distinguish between those who are generally recognised as artisans because of the nature of their work and those who are qualified and categorised as such by the laws of the land. Not all traditional artisans are legally recognised under the law and not all those legally recognised as artisans would be considered as artisans under traditional definitions. The legal definition of an artisan in Ecuador has been in a state of constant change since the 1950s. In Defence Law of 1953, an artisan was considered to be:

A manual worker, a master worker or an independent worker who had invested in his/her workshop, for tools, machinery or raw materials, an amount of not more than 20,000 sucres,[1] who has not more than six workers or employees working under him/her, and who engages in the sale of the articles produced by him/her in an amount of not more than 15,000 sucres per month.

A manual worker who, having invested in tools, machinery or raw materials, an amount of more than 20,000 sucres, also meets the other two conditions specified in the preceding paragraph, and who is declared to be an artisan by the National Board for Protection of Artisans, upon verification that his/her normal work cannot be carried out with tools, machinery or raw materials the value of which is less than 20,000 sucres, shall also be considered to be an artisan.

A manual worker who has not invested any amount in tools and who employs no workers shall also be considered to be an artisan.

The artisans who are members of class or professional organizations having legal status and existing at the time of issuance of this Law, shall also be protected by this Law.

(Gobierno del Ecuador, 1953, Article 1)[2]

The artisan was therefore broadly defined to include workers in the widest possible number of small workshops employing up to seven workers, including the owner, who would also in these circumstances be expected to work 'on the tools'. In terms of their size, all the artisans in our study would have been recognised as artisans according to the Defence Law of 1953.

In the context of international development theory in the 1960s, along with political pressures from within Ecuador, this definition came under scrutiny. The Development Law, as it was conceived in 1965, reflected the thinking of the Alliance for Progress and the American modernisation theories of the 1960s. The mainspring of the Development Law's ideological position was USAID in Quito and the groundwork for its policies was research carried out by the Stanford Research Institute (Stanford Research Institute, 1963). The new law was part of a general strategy that also included a programme for the promotion of artisans and small industry in the 1963 National Plan (JUNAPLA, 1963). The strategy was informed by anti-Castro US policy, which was focusing on pro-capitalist means of reducing poverty in Latin America, shielding the urban poor from communist influence and promoting small-scale capitalist enterprise.

The USAID-supported consultancy for the National Planning Board that was carried out by the Stanford Research Institute proposed that the existing limits on investment and labour force size were holding back development. Their analysis led them to the conclusion that the tax benefits of the Defence Law were acting as disincentives to modernisation, through providing a tax haven for the artisans:

> In a few cases the law has encouraged evasion in the sense that an artisan who elects to expand or mechanise his operations will establish two or more subsidiary artisan workshops, each of which qualifies individually as an artisan workshop and is exempt from taxation (Stanford Research Institute, 1963, 11).

From these 'few cases', they went on to argue that the law established a line of demarcation between the artisan and factory industry, encouraged the artisan to remain small-scale and discouraged investment in new technology.

Although the line of demarcation was real enough in law, information about *the extent* to which the artisans were encouraged to remain as artisans was not forthcoming. There was also no evidence of the extent to which artisans actually wanted to expand into small industries; and an obvious alternative proposition was not considered: even if the artisans *wanted* to expand this was impossible for the vast majority, who did not generate sufficient income for re-investment.

Instead, the lack of growth was held to be the fault of the law and this became a fundamental factor for the formulation of the Small Industry and Artisans Development Law, into which the Stanford team's ideas were incorporated.

Following criticism of the earlier legislation, the provision that the Small Industry and Artisans sectors should not receive more benefits than larger-scale industry were written into the 1965 Development Law. The 1963 Plan, the artisan and small industry development plan in 1969, and the new Plan of 1972 contained the same principal policy statements towards small-scale manufacturing in these years (JUNAPLA, 1963, 1969; JNP, 1972a). The artisans, however, through the JNDA, resisted the new law that was being promoted by government ministries and by the international agencies.

Under the pretence of the 'defence' of artisans, the law made the JNDA the main regulator of artisan activity under the state, giving it power over what was at that time the largest section of the Ecuadorean manufacturing labour force. The requirement that the artisan be recognised and qualified by the JNDA gradually excluded the majority of traditional artisans. The nature and size of the workshop affiliated to the JNDA changed and new laws for artisan development introduced alternative definitions, resulting in conflicting concepts existing side by side within those parts of the legal system that specifically deal with artisans. By the end of the 1970s, the JNDA was already under the control of employers who vigorously defended their right to exploit their labour force and lobbied to extend the size of the labour force that could be exploited. From the 1990s, to be classified as an artisan in Ecuadorean law, the manual worker, workshop master or autonomous artisan had to be qualified as such by the JNDA and registered with the Ministry of Labour and Human Resources. Artisans and their workshops need to be qualified by the JNDA in order to gain the benefits that accrued to artisans under various other laws.

In addition to exemption from some legally enforced employers' obligations, the original benefits of the Defence Law included exemption from sales tax, export tax and tax on income derived from capital equipment operated by workers; favourable terms for the importation of tools and raw materials; long-term government loans; and the purchase of artisan production by Government institutions. Affiliation to the system of social security was to be made compulsory, but the small master was exempted from employers' contributions. While the individual was to contribute up to 8% of his/her earnings, the state would provide a further 13% of the artisan's net income towards the cost of this.[3]

The general tax benefits available under the Development Law were similar to those available under the Defence Law: exemption from or reduction of various taxes such as those on capital reinvested, export of products, and importation of tools, machinery and raw materials. The two main differences between the two laws were that the Development Law allowed no special dispensation to small-scale employers with regard to an employer's obligations to his workforce and did not make any *special* provision for affiliation to the system of social security. The retention of the old law, however, ensured that the artisans remained exempt from certain employers' obligations to their workforce. At the time, such obligations included the payment of two extra salaries in the year, the payment by employers of the equivalent of 7% of the employees' wages to the National Institute of Social Security, and a duty to observe a formal code of conduct for receiving demands from the workforce.

Because of the resistance of the artisans, the Defence Law remained in operation alongside the Development Law. The main reason, however, was not that the Defence Law created a tax haven, as the Stanford report suggested. Rather, it was the provision for the exploitation of labour that was its most attractive feature; and it was attractive not only for artisans but also for small capitalist enterprises where the owners were not artisans in the traditional sense. This led to a subsequent change in the definition of the artisan workshops, which extended this exploitative benefit to capitalist owners and made the situation of workers in small firms worse. The size of the workshops that could be classified as artisan, in terms of both size of the workforce and the amount of investment, was increased, allowing larger enterprises to further increase the scope of exploitation.

As we saw in Chapter 9, the changes in the Defence Law in 1974, meant that 'artisans' could retain their special privileges while employing up to 13 persons, owning capital to the value of 12,000 US dollars and making a net profit that was 13 times the country's per capita income (Gobierno del Ecuador, 1974). These new legal limits had no relevance for 'artisans' as they were originally defined. The JNDA became the promoter of the new limits and the gatekeeper that determined who would benefit from being classified as an artisan. By 1997, the JNDA had succeeded in extending the definition to include factories with up to 20 employees, including five apprentices (Gobierno del Ecuador, 1997). In addition, if the workshop owner also owned a shop through which they sold their goods, both places could be considered as a single unit. The struggle for control of the JNDA was a political project that resulted in small capitalist firms extending their rights to exploit their workforces.

The evolution of the legal framework

In every legal system there are conflicts of laws. The primary logic used to solve these conflicts is the logic of hierarchy. The legal hierarchy in Ecuador is as follows: the Constitution; international treaties and agreements; organic laws (such as the Code of Production and the Labour Code); ordinary laws; regional norms and district by-laws; decrees and regulations; by-laws; agreements and resolutions; other acts and decisions of public authorities. The Production Code and the Labour Code are in conflict over the definition of the artisan and they are constantly upgraded without reference to the conflicts that clearly exist. Ultimately, the Constitution should solve the problem, but Ecuador's Constitution (Article 425) does not foresee the case of conflicts of organic laws among themselves. The constitutional text provides no guidance on organic conflict, and ordinary laws that are in conflict with each other and with different organic laws compound the problem.

By 2015, the work of artisans in Ecuador was directed and regulated by a series of general *codes*, a number of specific national *laws* and a plethora of national and local *regulations* and by-laws (Table A.10.3). These legal instruments use a variety of definitions of artisans, which were not only inconsistent across different areas of legislation but which also changed over time as specific laws were modified and evolved. These laws set different criteria for the recognition of artisans by the state.

The general *codes* that govern the activities of artisans but which also apply more widely include the Constitution of the Republic of Ecuador (Table A.10.4), along with the Labour Code, the Civil Code, the Code for Children and Adolescents, and the Tax Code (Corporación de Estudios y Publicaciones, 2009; Gobierno del Ecuador, 2008b, 2015a, 2005a, 2003, 2005b). There are nine *laws* that apply specifically to artisans or that have sections that do so. Over time, these laws have been changed by a series of government *regulations* that have had an impact on the day-to-day work of artisans (IPANC/MIPRO, 2010; Corporación de Estudios y Publicaciones, 2003). In contrast with the neoliberal ideology that criticised regulations as a barrier to the development of artisans into entrepreneurial capitalists, after 1982 the neoliberal state did not reduce regulations: they increased and modified them.

These laws and regulations have been created since 1953 with remarkable incoherence. There is no consistency in the way artisans are defined in these legal instruments and, within the main laws that apply, the definition has changed over time. The latest version of the Defence Law, for example, defines the categories of artisans that are legally recognised by this law as workshop masters, operatives and apprentices (Gobierno del Ecuador, 2008, Article 2). The latest version of the Development Law, on the other hand, identifies workshop masters, autonomous artisans and artisan guilds as beneficiaries of the law (Gobierno del Ecuador, 2003a, Article 2). There is no mention of workers or apprentices except under 'General Dispositions' where it is made clear that workshop owners are not subject to the obligations of the Labour Code.[4] The number of workers is apparently irrelevant. The existence of apprentices is acknowledged, but only to prescribe wage levels and registration: apprentices, who enter a workshop to gain knowledge, should be paid 60% of the wages of a tradesman and they should register with the JNDA to obtain an apprentice's ID card.

The investment limits have also diverged as they have increased. The latest version of the Defence Law says that the maximum they are allowed to have invested in machinery and raw materials must be less than 25% of the capital that is allowed for companies registered as small firms (Gobierno del Ecuador, 1998). There are, however, major difficulties with this aspect of the definition. It fits with neither the Production Code nor the Labour Code, which also differ from each other when it comes to defining artisans.

Comparing the Defence Law with the Production Code, there are at least two issues. First, the Production Code in Ecuador, which set the size definition for small firms in 2015, made no mention of the capital investment limits that were an essential part of the Defence Law's definition. The Production Code defined micro, small and medium enterprises but these classifications were based on levels of *turnover*, rather than levels of *investment* (Gobierno del Ecuador, 2015b). Second, the Code defines the size of artisan workshops differently from the Defence Law (Gobierno del Ecuador, 2010). Artisans are defined in relation to the main categories of the Code – micro, small, medium and large – but they are not seen as micro-firms, as might be expected. In 2015, the Production Code said artisans could fall into any of these categories. Theoretically, they could have turnovers of up to USD 5 million and up to 199 employees.

The Labour Code, from which the artisans and the JNDA were constantly fighting for exemption, added to this confusion by adopting a definition of an artisan workshop that was different from the definition in the Production Code. When the Labour Code refers to artisans, it uses the Defence Law as its main historical point of reference. However, the definitions used in both documents are not the same and there is little consistency between the latest versions of the laws. In the Labour Code, an artisan can be a master of a workshop, a worker, an apprentice, an autonomous artisan or (an additional category) a subcontractor (Gobierno del Ecuador, 2015a, Articles 285–96). However, it also describes the main categories as the workshop master, an autonomous artisan, an operative and a contractor, with no reference to apprentices (Gobierno del Ecuador, 2015a, Articles 286–9). The contract worker, who is essentially a subcontractor who some would describe as a dependent homeworker, does not appear in any other legal definition of an artisan.

Reflecting the wording in the Defence Law since 1953, the 2015 Labour Code makes it clear that artisans who are qualified according to the JNDA 'are not subject to the obligations imposed on employers by this Code' (Gobierno del Ecuador, 1953, Article 5; Gobierno del Ecuador, 2015a, Article 302).[5] However, they are subject to the part of the Code relating to wages, basic salaries and unified basic minimum payments, and legal compensation for sacking without notice. The workers in artisan workshops also benefit from the right to holidays[6] and maximum working hours per day, but there is no mention of obligatory days of rest every week as set out in the Labour Code. Self-employed artisans inevitably work on Saturdays and sometimes on Sundays, but for their workers Saturdays and Sundays are days of rest and if it is necessary to work on these days they must be replaced by two other consecutive days in the week. The legal working day for adolescents, and therefore for some apprentices, is six hours for a maximum of five days a week.[7] There is no indication that artisans are exempt from the Code's stipulation about days of rest and the Defence Law is not entirely clear about what applies.

As the federations lost their influence and they came to be seen as employers' organisations (particularly during the years of the Correa government) their membership has declined and, as we saw in Chapter 9, they have become more akin to social clubs. Nevertheless, artisans who are members of these organisations still benefit from the exemptions in Article 302 of the Labour Code, which include:

a. The payment of reserve funds with respect to their workers and apprentices;
b. The payment of the 13th and 14th salaries, which are additional payments that are equivalent to one month's salary, paid to other workers at Christmas and, in the Sierra, in August.[8]
c. The distribution of a 15% share of the profits which is paid to other workers under Article 97 of the Labour Code.[9]

There are also benefits under other legislation, but most of them barely apply to utilitarian artisans producing consumer goods for the home market or repairing the imported goods of international capital. They are more relevant for larger firms that are importing machinery and/or exporting their products (see Gobierno del Ecuador, 2003a, Article 9). Nevertheless, artisans are free from the taxes and costs associated with obtaining the *Patente Municipal*, which authorises trades and professions to operate within the municipal boundaries (Municipio de Quito, 2011), and they are not obliged to charge 12% VAT on their goods and services.[10]

Over the years, artisans have been gradually drawn into the tax system, particularly during the Correa years. Like any other worker, artisans are now obliged to pay income tax if they reach the income threshold, after all deductions for expenses (ibid.). However, if spouses or other paid family members are employed by the workshop or in a sales outlet attached to a workshop, their salaries are tax deductible. Artisans can increase household incomes and the family incomes can be set against the tax liabilities of the workshop owner.

We saw in Chapter 3 (Table 3.4) that between 1982 and 2015 there was no increase in the proportion of workshops employing labour, but the nature of that labour was transformed. Instead of growth in the employment of wage labour, as would be expected through economic development, there was a decline. This reduction in wage labour coexisted with a similar decline in unpaid family labour. Over time, unpaid family labour was converted into paid family labour, which replaced wage labour.

The change was at least partly due to the efforts of the Correa government to formalise the informal sector. It was the accumulation of a series of small changes in a consistent downward trend that produced a significant change in the use of wage labour over the 40-year period. However, between 2005 and 2015, the annual rate of decline of wage employment more than doubled and by 2015 more than three-quarters of artisan workshops did not employ non-family wage labour. The greatest movement was during the period of the Correa government, when the tax collection system was modernised and social security contributions for the artisan labour force were not only increased but also enforced.

Defence, development and social security

'Obligatory Universal Insurance' is controlled and regulated by the state (Gobierno del Ecuador, 2008b, Article 369):

Obligatory Universal Insurance covers the contingencies of illness, maternity, paternity, risks at work, retirement, unemployment, old age, invalidity, incapacity, death and other matters determined by the law.

The Ecuadorean Institute for Social Security (IESS) is responsible for the delivery of the social security system and it is funded by contributions from workers, employers and the state.

When discussing the relationship between artisans and the social security system it is important to distinguish between policy and practice. That artisans should be affiliated to the Ecuadorean Institute of Social Security (IESS) is a longstanding feature of artisan social policy but in practice, there has been a low level of take-up. It is also important to identify who has been the target of policy proposals. The workshop owners have been treated differently from workers and apprentices. The policies have not applied equally to all who work in this sector of the economy and, in practice, the application of the policies has discriminated against the wage workers.

The affiliation of artisans to the Ecuadorean social security system is an issue that goes back to a period before the Defence Law in 1953, when there was an almost total lack of social insurance across the sector (Campaña, 1952; Pita and Meier, 1985). This was the context for the workshop masters to push for the introduction of the Defence Law as a means of avoiding their obligations under the Labour Code and the emerging social security system. Once the owners gained their recognition under the Defence Law, through 'qualification' by the JNDA, they were released from all obligations to pay a share of the costs of their workers' affiliation to the social security system. The state took over this responsibility but then failed to provide the funds to support the workers and apprentices. The wage earners were effectively marginalised from the benefits of the system.

Many workshop owners, particularly the poorest, were also excluded because they were not qualified as artisans by the JNDA and most of the qualified labour force were excluded by the failure of the state to live up to their obligations under the law. As time passed, cases were discovered where workshop owners who had contributed monthly quotas for years were found to be not affiliated to the JNDA and therefore not qualified to be covered by the *Regimen Especial*. In these cases, their payments were returned, after the costs of any medical and other benefits already received had been deducted (Pita and Meier, 1985).

When the Development Law was passed in 1965, in addition to offering no special dispensation to artisan employers with regard to their obligations to their workforce, it did not make any special provision for affiliation to the system of social security. In 1971, an updated regime of artisan affiliation to the IESS was put in place. If this had been fully implemented, it would have provided the artisan with medical assistance, income support, medical and financial support around the time of new births, and a system of support for young mothers in the field of preventative hygiene in the first year of a child's life (Gobierno del Ecuador, 1971). IESS would also have provided pensions in old age along with sickness and death benefits. Masters, autonomous artisans, workers and apprentices were to be subject to this amendment to the Law. For the masters, it was to be paid for by a contribution of 13% of their net income – to be paid by masters themselves. Workers and apprentices would be covered by a payment of 13% of their wages, which was broken down into an 8% personal contribution from the workers and apprentices, plus 5% from the workshop owner. In addition, a certain (unquantified) percentage of the artisan funds were to be set aside for the construction of homes for artisans. The Social Security Law was altered to incorporate the changes and some artisan housing was constructed. Once again, however, the new laws on participation and contributions were not enforced.

It was not until 1979 that the Social Security Law was extended to cover artisan wage workers and apprentices, as well as workshop owners (Gobierno del Ecuador, 1979). The master artisan was finally recognised as an employer. However, artisans were still excluded from unemployment benefits, the reserve funds, unsecured loans, insurance against risks, accidents at work and professional illnesses. The new costs of affiliation of workers led to some masters finding new ways to minimise their payments. Since apprentices are paid less than operatives, many workshop owners affiliated their workers as apprentices. Minimising payments also extended to not affiliating all the workers in the workshops and, in some cases, the master increasing their own payments in the last five years before retirement in order to boost their pensions.

In 1986, a new law for Artisan Development was enacted that set out new conditions for the relationship between artisans and the social security system: artisanal social security protection was extended to family members, including spouses, who were employed in any workshop that had previously qualified under the IESS regime. In addition, any new applicant for the affiliation of a workshop could be included if they provided evidence of an artisan qualification authorised by the JNDA (Gobierno del Ecuador, 1986, Article 22). Artisan applications for affiliation were also to be given preferential treatment by IESS under the new law.

In 1990, the IESS resolved that artisan workshops should be no different from other urban businesses (Gobierno del Ecuador, 1990). The workers' contribution was to be 9.35% of their net income, with the employer contributing 12.15% (21.5% in total). The cost for the affiliation of the owner was 20.8%. Consistent with past experience, however, this was not enforced either. The 1990 conditions have carried through to Ecuador's most recent Employment Code, whereby the *maestro*, the workers and apprentices are obliged to be affiliated to Social Security, along with the spouse and any children of the owner if they work in the workshop (Gobierno del Ecuador, 2015a, Article 302). The cost of affiliating workers and apprentices is 20.5% of their income, of which the workshop owner pays 11.15% and the worker or apprentice pays 9.35%.

Throughout the period of the study, therefore, policy has been confusing and conflicting, its implementation has been partial at best. The cost of affiliation has varied considerably, and responsibility for paying the contributions has been gradually evolving. Enforcement of the law is another matter. Practice has been fragmented and, since it depended on affiliation to the JNDA, it had been a minority pursuit – until recently. There has been a substantial rise in the number of workshop owners who are affiliated to the IESS in recent years, but the enforcement of the law that requires workers to be affiliated may also have contributed to a decrease in the number of non-family employees and an increase in paid family labour.

Social security affiliation, 1982–2015

After social security arose as a major issue in the 1975 survey, the owners of artisan workshops have been asked in each subsequent survey if they are affiliated with the government's national social security provision. In 1982 and in 1995, less than one-third of them were members of the scheme and the numbers then started to decline. In 2005, only one-quarter of the workshop owners were affiliated (Table 10.2). Between 2005 and 2015, however, membership more than doubled. For the first time ever, more than half of the artisans interviewed were contributing to the national scheme.

The reason for the increased IESS affiliation is related to the enforcement of the law, a raising of consciousness about the benefits of affiliation and the changing structure of the artisan labour force. Owners who employ wage labour are themselves much more likely to be affiliated than those who work alone or who employ paid family labour (Table A.10.5). Since they are required to enrol their workforce, they too sign up. The probability of the workshops employing wage labour being affiliated increased between 2005 and 2015. More than two-thirds of those employing wage labour in 2015 were affiliated, compared to around 40% previously. Nevertheless, around 30% of those who employ non-family wage labour are still not personally affiliated and, although the affiliation

Table 10.2 Affiliation to social security

	1982		1995		2005		2015	
	No.	%	No.	%	No.	%	No.	%
Yes	94	31.9	102	31.1	79	24.9	133	51.8
No	201	68.1	226	68.9	238	75.1	124	48.2
	295	100.0	328	100.0	317	100.0	257	100.0

	Chi-sq	DF	p-value
1982–2015	49.4983	3	1.02E-10
1982–1995	0.0424	1	0.8369
1995–2005	3.0463	1	0.0809
2005–2015	43.8628	1	3.52E-11
1982 & 2015	22.4339	1	2.18E-06

of the self-employed also rose substantially between 2005 and 2015, the majority were still not affiliated.

A clear dividing line exists between those that are members of guilds and those that are not. Certification by the JNDA is essential for any business that wishes to be recognised as an artisan workshop and seeks to benefit from the advantages that such recognition bestows. Government policy has been mainly aimed at JNDA-registered artisans, relieving these owners of small workshops from the responsibility that other businesses have towards their workforces. However, in recent years, these registered artisans have only accounted for between one-quarter and one-third of all artisan workshops – and practically none of the wage labour force is registered as an artisan.

Although less than 20% of workshop owners were registered with the JNDA in 2015 and only 63% of these members were affiliated to IESS, JNDA-registered workshop owners have consistently been much more likely to be affiliated to the social security system than artisans who are not registered through the federations (Table 10.3 and Figure 10.1). The affiliation of federation members, however, declined during the neoliberal period between 1982 and 2005, as did the gap between the two types of workshop owners. After 2005, during the years of Correa and anti-neoliberalism, affiliation for both federation and non-federation owners increased significantly, with the increased affiliation of the non-federated owners being most dramatic. An important question is whether levels of affiliation are related to the patterns of employment within the workshops.

We have seen earlier that just over half of artisan-owners have consistently employed other workers in their workshops. In 1975, only 40% worked alone and, over the years, there has been no significant change in the population of artisan-owners who work alone or employ other workers. Over the years, there has also been no significant increase or decrease in the total number employed, including the owner.[11] When we look at *who* is employed, however, there is a clear and significant change over the period. We have seen that there has been a decline in the use of wage labour, an increase in paid family labour and a fall in the use of unpaid family members – particularly during the Correa period.

The annual percentage decline in wage employment in the last decade was double what was experienced in the previous 30 years. At the same time, the use of paid family labour increased and most of this increase was not due to growing numbers of artisans or apprentices amongst family members. The new workers appear to be mainly involved in sales and administration. There are questions as to whether they are genuine or full-time employees. The expense of family wages and social security contributions can be set against taxes while at the same time extending social security cover for the family. It would appear that unpaid family members have been moved onto the books, thereby reducing tax liabilities in the context of a more efficient state collection apparatus and increasing access to social security benefits for the family.

Not all artisans are enamoured by their new links to the social security system. Even now, around half of workshop owners are not affiliated and some of those who are do not use it. A 70-year-old hairdresser in the centre of Quito who is

Table 10.3 Membership of federations and affiliation to social security

		Affiliation to social security											
		1982			1995			2005			2015		
		Yes	No	Total	Yes	No	Total	Yes	No	Total	Yes	No	Total
Not federation members	No.	39	154	193	53	164	217	43	179	222	101	107	208
	%	20.2	79.8	100.0	24.4	75.6	100.0	19.4	80.6	100.0	48.6	51.4	100.0
Federation members	No.	55	45	100	47	61	108	35	58	93	29	16	46
	%	55.0	45.0	100.0	43.5	56.5	100.0	37.6	62.4	100.0	63.0	37.0	100.0
Total	No.	94	199	293	100	225	325	78	237	315	130	123	254
	%	32.1	67.9	100.0	30.8	69.2	100.0	24.8	75.2	100.0	51.2	48.4	100.0
		Chi-sq 36.595	df 1	p-value 0.0000	Chi-sq 12.343	df 1	p-value 0.0004	Chi-sq 11.737	df 1	p-value 0.0006	Chi-sq 3.738	df 1	p-value 0.0532

Change in affiliation, 1982–2015

	Chi-sq	df	p-value
1982–2015	32.5796	3	3.95E-07
1982–1995	2.5748	1	0.1086
1995–2005	0.0799	1	0.7775
2005–2015	11.6519	1	0.0006
1982 & 2015	30.5070	1	3.33E-08

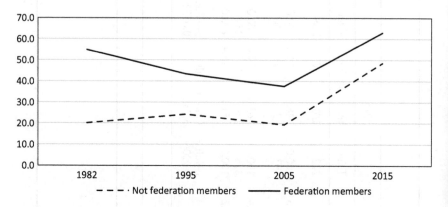

Figure 10.1 Affiliation to social security, 1982–2015

retired and is qualified to use the IESS goes to a private hospital when he is ill because, as he says, 'the social security is a mess'. An upholsterer in the south of the city is also affiliated but he prefers to pay a private doctor. Neither of these artisans is member of any artisan federation or association and they are not therefore affiliated to JNDA. Because of the perceived state of public health, a few artisans have private health insurance.

Others are more positive. A 64-year-old shoemaker, who recently took on a 50-year-old worker, said that the government had given him the opportunity to affiliate to IESS. He had had a business for over 40 years, is not a member of a federation and therefore had no links to the JNDA. A semi-retired 75-year-old tailor, who is not a member of a federation but who recognises the work they have done in the past in defending the rights of artisans, said that he hardly works anymore because of ill-health but that 'thanks to the IESS he does not have any major needs'.

Others are more concerned about the negative impact of social security obligations on their business. One hairdresser, when asked about the number of workers he employed said: 'With the social security they oblige you to pay, there is no way [that workers can be employed].' A 54-year-old mechanic, who is a member of a trade union rather than a guild, said that three years previously he had four or five workers but that he now had only one. For this artisan, 'the issue of social security is a problem' for hiring both workers and apprentices.

For many years, in the context of conflicting and confusing national policies for ensuring that artisans are linked into the national social security system, artisans in Quito largely ignored IESS and its provision. As recently as 2005, only a quarter were affiliated. Many artisans still do not see the benefits of joining the system but in the last decade the number of workshop owners taking advantage of the provision has doubled. At the same time, the number of paid family employees in the workshops has also increased considerably, allowing spouses and other family members to use the service. On the other hand, the number of workshops employing wage labour has declined dramatically, which is in part due to stronger enforcement of the laws relating to the cost of affiliation of non-family employees to the social security system.

Notes

1 Later regulations from June 1957 to April 1961 raised the capital limitation for different artisan sectors: men's tailoring, 30,000 sucres; shoemaking, 30,000 sucres; cabinetmaking, 50,000 sucres; mechanical work, 80,000 sucres; making of gold products, 50,000 sucres; hairdressing, 30,000 sucres; photography, 50,000 sucres.
2 The original English translation was carried out by the Stanford Research Institute in 1963 but this has been updated to include gender-neutral terminology. Stanford Research Institute, 1963, op. cit.
3 Part of the contribution of the artisan was to go towards the provision of low-cost housing for artisans and their families. Artisanal training centres were to be set up, as was a system for the commercialisation of artisanal production.
4 Except for the regulations governing the minimum salary and unfair dismissal.
5 The Defence Law says (Article 16) that artisans protected by the Defence Law are not subject to the obligations imposed on 'business owners in general by current legislation'.
6 In common with other workers, they are due 15 days' holiday, including non-working days, for each year of work (Labour Code, Article 69).
7 Any work carried out between 19.00 and 06.00 must be paid at 125% of the daytime wage.
8 These payments are made under Article 15 of the Labour Code.
9 These exemptions are made under Article 101 of the Labour Code.
10 This reduces the cost of their products and should make them more competitive. They are, however, obliged to provide a receipt to customers, pay VAT on raw materials and other inputs, and provide monthly VAT statements (*Gobierno del Ecuador*, 2014, 123). Many artisans see paying VAT on inputs, without being able to reclaim it in the price of the output, as a cost rather than a benefit.
11 The exception was 1982, at the end of the first oil boom, when artisan firm size was at its peak.

11 Microfinance and micro-firm development in context

Introduction

For the poor in the developing world, particularly those who depend on self-employment and are not directly part of the formal wage economy, their productive assets are an important element for determining family income. For the small firms in the informal sector that employ wage labour, any hand tools that are owned by the employees are also important for the levels of income generated for the employers, as well as being an investment for the generation of the household incomes of the employees. The total sum of these productive assets, when combined with the human capital of the people involved, has a major impact on levels of world poverty.

The distribution of assets is more concentrated than the distribution of incomes and government action, particularly action that is driven by free-market policies, tends to reinforce this concentration. Greater income equality could be achieved if the ownership of private capital were more equally distributed. If this were an aim, then policy would operate in favour of those factors of production owned by the lower income groups and it would attempt to alter the pattern of concentration of physical and human capital. Investment would be redirected towards self-employment and micro-firms, focusing on their stock of physical and human capital, which could also help raises the wages paid by small-scale producers. Opening up access to credit is seen as a way of achieving this outcome.

Changing the concentration of capital, however, is not just a technical exercise. It is not merely a matter of making more credit available in general. In practical terms, it would effectively mean the redistribution of credit away from current beneficiaries to poorer social classes. This is profoundly political. Credit is a scarce resource and, while it is possible to increase the volume of the resource (when, for example, there is a windfall for oil-exporting countries as new oilfields come on stream or when oil prices increase, as has happened in Ecuador) its distribution can be as politically sensitive as the redistribution of wealth itself. There is competition for the scarce resource, which the most powerful usually win. In addition, the lending institutions themselves have no wish to be associated with the insecurity of the losers.

Traditionally, banks have tended to be cautious and risk-averse. In contrast, the entrepreneurial theory of debt is that credit should be vision-oriented, opportunity-targeted, growth-focused and risk-taking. In practice, most banks in developing countries continue to be cautious, despite the proliferation of microfinance institutions over recent decades. The small firms, on the other hand, tend to be wary of bank debt, most of them preferring other sources of investment.

The purpose of small firm credit may be to grow the basic productive activity of the firm or to expand its relationship to the market. Credit may be sought to invest in tools and machinery, to buy raw materials, to increase the number of employees, to increase the wages of existing workers, to finance the ownership or rent of new premises, to develop a new product, to create a new route to market, or to develop a new market.

Properly managed debt can help a small business to finance expansion. Small business owners who have a plan for building up their company's credit rating over time, and who establish good reputations and high credit scores, can have access to larger amounts of future debt at lower interest rates and friendlier fee structures. The ideal balance is to use enough debt to fund various business ventures without exposing the company to too much debt. Finance is seen as an essential enabler of opportunities but too much debt can reduce profit margins. If the company has too much debt, its access to further financing may be restricted, perhaps before the company has had a chance to complete its growth strategy. If revenues decline, the business may not be able to fulfil its obligations. The fixed obligations for repayment, at set intervals and in set amounts regardless of the earnings of the company, can be a threat to the future of the firm, particularly small firms in developing countries whose income streams are irregular. Financial forecasts can predict what the company's sales volumes will be and what kinds of capital expenses they will have, but these are almost impossible to create with any accuracy for artisans. Demand fluctuates and income is unpredictable, often making repayment plans difficult to sustain.

As we saw in the previous chapter, over a long period of time in Ecuador there has been a general consensus amongst artisans, government technocrats and large-scale private enterprise that the expansion of petty manufacturers into small-scale industries should be the main goal of development planning for this sector. In response to long-standing demands for credit from artisan federations, one of the principal means of achieving this has been through policies that attempt to provide generous credit facilities for the small-scale entrepreneur. Internationally, in spite of the overwhelming focus on taxes and regulations as the main inhibitors of growth in the neoliberal narrative, global evidence suggests that the most important constraint is finance.

In a study of mainly formal firms employing five persons or more, surveyed by the World Business Environment Survey (WBES) in 80 developed and developing nations, of 10 obstacles to growth that businesses report, 'only three emerge as binding constraints with a direct association with firm growth: finance, crime and policy instability' (Ayyagari et al., 2008, 484)[1]. Other obstacles, including taxes and regulation, have an indirect association with firm growth, through the binding constraints. Of the three binding constraints, finance is the most important, having the largest direct effect on firm growth, regardless of which firms and countries are included in the sample. Smaller firms are significantly more affected by the finance constraint.

Within the finance constraint, however, not all types of obstacle are constraining. The significant obstacles to growth are high interest rates, collateral, paperwork, special [personal] connections, banks' lack of funds to lend, and lease finance. These perceived obstacles are highly correlated with each other, but 'high interest rates' have the highest economic impact and represent the most significant individual obstacle associated with firm growth: 'High interest rates are the only financial obstacle directly constraining firm growth' (Ayyagari et al., 2008, 506). Contrary to the neoliberal narrative, they are much more important than taxes and regulations.

It is argued that policies that relax the binding constraints 'can be expected to directly increase firm growth' (Ayyagari et al., 2008, 495), which implies that 'financial sector reform should be a priority for governments contemplating reform of their business environments', particularly in relation to high interest rates (Ayyagari et al., 2008, 509). The correlation of other obstacles with high interest rates leads the authors to conclude that 'general access to credit is an important constraint to firm growth' (Ayyagari et al., 2008, 510), which is an unfortunate since their findings do not support this. Even in their formal sector firms, 'general access to credit' is not demonstrated as a significant constraint, whereas high interest rates are. Access to funding has been recognised as an issue for a long time, but it is seldom discussed in relation to the depressing impact of high interest rates on demand.

Access to credit is not the same as access to bank loans. The elevation of the financial sector as the driver of development in developing countries is surprising if we look at the situation in developed countries. In the UK, for example, around 60% of business owners prefer to use personal savings or to re-mortgage their homes to grow their company (BDRC Continental, 2015).[2] Nearly half of UK SMEs are classed as 'permanent non-borrowers' in the BDRC SME Finance Monitor,[3] which means they had not applied for credit in the previous five years and had no intention to do so in future. If the permanent non-borrowers are excluded, the biggest group (76% of other SMEs) had no intentions of seeking credit in the future.[4] The reluctance to involve a bank was greater amongst the smaller firms.

In spite of the lack of demand for bank loans by small firms in the developed world, the provision of bank credit for the support and development of micro-firms in African economies was thought to be an important issue before independence (ILO, 1972, 90). Loan and credit programmes for informal firms were theoretically backed by training and extension programmes as part of the Kenyanisation of the economy following independence. However, there was no evidence that this potential supply of credit was matched by demand for formal finance, nor was there any data on the levels of take-up.

Initial informal funding for informal firms was mainly from personal or family savings. The ILO proposed an overhaul of Kenya's business support systems to make it easier to provide finance for informal firms, but this did not happen. Political reality intervened, as it did in other countries such as Ecuador, where attempts were also made to distribute credit to micro-firms. Around the same time, the institutional sources of small-scale credit in Ecuador expanded, but the practical difficulties of convincing a traditional banking system to allocate funding to informal artisans were immense. Small firms were in competition with a powerful rural oligarchy and an emerging capitalist industrial class.

Small firm finance before microfinance

In Ecuador, it has been assumed that the availability of finance for informal firms is important for increasing their capital investment, improving the levels of technology, increasing productivity and improving incomes (Pita, 1992). The private financial sector, now oriented towards large firms in the modern sector of the economy, traditionally served agriculture, wholesalers (importers and exporters), large industrial firms and other speculative investors. The formal financial sector was deterred from lending to artisans by the relatively high administrative costs associated with providing small loans to informal firms, along with the low levels of return, the lack of guarantees and the related high risks that were thought to be a fundamental characteristic of all micro-firms. There was, however, also a political dimension to the distribution of credit.

It is widely believed that small-scale credit for micro-entrepreneurs started with Yunus and the Grameen Bank. The provision of procedures for credit distribution, however, has been long written into the laws governing artisans and small-scale manufacturing in Ecuador. The 1953 Defence Law stipulated that it was the duty of the Artisan Defence Board 'to apply for the establishment, in the *Banco Popular*, of an artisan credit department or, failing this, to endeavour to have an artisan credit bank established'. The state was to provide economic assistance through 'the granting of long-term loans by the banks of the Development System and the *Banco Popular*' (Gobierno del Ecuador, 1953, Articles 3 and 6). These policies, however, were never implemented.

Nevertheless, through the 1960s, credit was one of the areas where the promotion of small-scale manufacturers was apparently able to make some headway, even if it was not what the state nor the artisans would have wished. The 1963–73 National Development Plan (JUNAPLA, 1963) proposed USD 2.3 million be made available for artisans and a further USD 3.6 million to both Small-scale Industry and Artisans (SI&A).[5] Unfortunately, only one-third of the SI&A loans were distributed and the official statistics do not tell us what these loans were used for or how much actually went to artisans, as distinct from small-scale capitalist industry. According to informal interviews with a number of artisans, the feeling was that these credits did not go to artisans and, as we shall see, there is every reason to believe that the percentage that did was very low. During this period, the majority of the loans were small, short-term and in decline as a proportion of the total loan portfolio.[6]

According to the 1973 *Plan*, the state was to provide 'integrated credit services' for SI&A, and the funds were to be directed towards 'those activities which would be most convenient for the economy of the country' (JNP, 1972a, 280 and 285). From 1973 onwards, the credit allocated by the National Development Bank (BNF[7]) to the SI&A alone greatly surpassed the targets set out in the *Plan*. This was possible because the targets set in the *Plan* were drawn up using the 1972 oil prices of 3.60 dollars per barrel and there was an unexpected bonus the following year when OPEC raised the price to 13.90 dollars per barrel. The finance available for all sectors of the economy increased beyond expectations.

The money was available, but how was it allocated? The figures by themselves hide a complex mechanism of distribution of credit which acts against the less wealthy and less powerful sectors, irrespective of classical policy decisions which take no account of the politics of credit. Oil price rises increased the volume of funds available. USAID loans were contracted, new channels for the distribution of loans were set up in the Ministry of Industry[8] and a list of project applications was created. However, the Ministry did not have the staff to assess the applications. It was quite clear that, in spite of the intentions of the state and the availability of funds, the distribution of credit towards SI&A was not going to be as simple its was at first thought.[9] The romanticism of freely available credit was quite clearly rejected in the pragmatic assertion of the importance of guarantees and 'a real and potential capacity for repayment'.[10]

A number of experts were brought in, who identified a major problem. According to these experts, the money that was available for the development of small manufacturing was lying unused in the banks because there were not enough small producers who could offer the necessary guarantees.[11] Early in 1975 there was already another BID[12] loan arrangement in the pipeline but there remained the problem of two million dollars of the USAID loan still waiting to be distributed and, behind that, the need to break the circularity of 'lack of capital = lack of guarantees = lack of capital'.

From the point of view of the banking institutions, there was only one way out of this situation. Unfortunately, it meant finally renouncing any intention of helping the poorest in the manufacturing sector. Discussion of the plight of the artisans had notably diminished as the official debate on credit reduced the concept of the 'small-scale industry and artisan' sector to refer only to 'small-scale industry'. To bring some financial order to the situation it was necessary to consolidate this tendency formally. The possibility of the vast majority of utilitarian artisans obtaining credit was extremely limited, and at the same time medium-sized industry could use more credit and were better able to offer the guarantees demanded by the financial institutions. In addition, the associations of small-scale industrialists, led by the more successful of their numbers, had been pressing the government to raise the capital ceilings which defined small industries in law, so that their larger industries could access the unused loan facilities that had been targeted at small firms. The apparently non-conflictive solution was to redefine small-scale industries so that larger firms could obtain the credit. Artisans had been excluded and now larger firms would be able to access finance that was meant for small firms. Local power and international banking tradition outplayed emerging entrepreneurialism.

Throughout the second half of 1975, registration of small-scale industries with the Development Law increased. These registrations were not merely of new small-scale industrialists keen to take advantage of the new funds for credit. On the contrary, after the raising of the capital ceiling, there was a rush of medium-sized producers to become classified as 'small-scale industries' to obtain the credit and to claim the 100% tax exemption on any new fixed capital investment that small-scale industry enjoyed. One of the original assumptions of the extension of credit to small enterprises was that, since it was more labour intensive than large industry, its promotion would create additional jobs more cheaply. However, the effect of the solution arrived at for guarantees was that industry that was already more capital-intensive was stimulated to invest in more labour-saving machinery, to the detriment of the smaller producer and, particularly, of the mass of micro-producers whose possibility for obtaining credit had not changed at all.

At the same time, the elite capture of the national development funds surged ahead. Most of the BNF funds were destined for agriculture, but not all recipients used the funds to develop their agricultural production. A known example is a case where a landowner with a *hacienda* just outside Quito obtained a loan from the BNF to start modern chicken production, but used the finance to produce concrete blocks for the booming construction industry in Quito. He received an agricultural loan at 3% interest and erected a building where the indigenous labourers on his hacienda produced the blocks at agricultural wage rates. When the BNF inspector came round, he said that the chickens had all died and that since he had to pay back the loan he started up the present business. He was given an extension on his loan.[13]

In the 1980s, the BNF remained the main channel for national oil income to be directed towards artisan credit. As we have seen above, the category of borrower used by the bank was 'Small Industry and Artisans' (SI&A) and in the banks accounts there was no distinction made between these two quite separate groups. They continued to be defined differently in law and there is little doubt that the main recipients in the category would be 'small industry', rather than artisans (FENAPI, 1985).[14] Between 1977 and 1982, however, there was a decline in the amount that was allocated to the SI&A sector. By 1984, as neoliberal structural adjustment policies began to bite and cheap credit was channelled towards the oligarchy, the volume of credit authorised for SI&A was less than in 1975.

There were problems with 'the requirements of guarantees, the lack of participation of the sector in the Credit Committees [of the BNF], the diversion of credit [away from the sector], the length of time it took to approve or reject applications, and the excess of information that was asked for' (FENAPI, 1985, 11). In addition, interest rates had risen, making credit inaccessible for the majority of small entrepreneurs. FENAPI complained that the participation of small industry was secondary and marginal, and it was declining as a proportion of total lending. They also argued that the situation was even worse than the figures suggested because small industry and artisans were lumped together and 'as entrepreneurs we are suffering a lack of credit opportunities for the development of our small industries' (FENAPI, 1985, 9). There were no separate data for artisans but one should assume that the situation was even worse for them.

The exclusion of micro-firms from credit in the 1970s and 1980s was seen to be a generalised problem across developing countries. Later in the 1980s, however, microfinance became the new buzzword in Asia and Africa. There followed a proliferation of institutions dedicated to the provision of micro-loans to microenterprises. The concept also found its way into the poorly regulated Ecuadorean financial system before the banking crash and before the whole system was regulated by the Correa government. In the next section, we will look at the development of the theory and practice of microfinance, before turning our attention to what happened in Ecuador.

Microcredit and micro-firm growth

Microfinance is commonly understood to be the provision of loans to the poor to help them escape poverty by establishing or expanding income-generating activities (Bateman, 2012). Originally, it was more specifically taken to be the provision of small loans to the owners of micro-firms, to allow them to invest in their businesses and grow both their capital and their income. Through the provision of small loans to impoverished households, mainly headed by women, to help them set up or expand small self-employment ventures, mainly in retail or services, it was thought that the problem of lack of productive capital in informal enterprises would be addressed, there would be a proliferation of micro-capitalist enterprises, and the potential for households and communities to escape poverty would be enhanced. Since the concept was introduced, its meaning has expanded and its application has been extended. It now includes loans to communities and the concept also 'spans a myriad of services including savings, insurance, remittances and non-financial services such as financial literacy training and skills development programmes' (Duvendack et al., 2011, 2).

It is more than 40 years since the first microcredit operations were started in Latin America. As the number of clients and the volume of loans have risen, the trend towards regulating them and converting them into formal banks has grown. The original concept fitted well with the free-market and anti-regulatory narrative of de Soto and others in the 1980s and the setting up of the Grameen Bank by Muhammad Yunus in Bangladesh in 1983 became a cornerstone of the neoliberal pro-poor capitalist adventure. Since the establishment of the Grameen Bank, expanding microfinance has been a key policy intervention for local economic development. Microfinance was the means by which capitalism would be developed in poor communities and poverty would be abolished. The regulatory state would be irrelevant, collective action by trade unions would become an anachronism, and questions of power and social class would give way to a new agenda in which the main issue would be how to expand the microfinance system, in order to help the poor escape their poverty through their own individual efforts.

The early microfinance system, however, presented a contradiction for neoliberalism. The original Grameen model was dependent on subsidies from governments and international organisations, and non-profit-making NGOs were at the heart of the system. Initially, microfinance institutions (MFIs) relied heavily on national and international donors for their sources of funding but in the 1980s, with a growing emphasis on market principles and financial sustainability amongst donors, there was a reduction in reliance on donor support and a transition away from the use of taxpayers' money. The poor were to bear the full cost of any support they received. As the number of microfinance clients rose sharply through the 1990s, there was a growing trend towards formalising MFIs and converting them into regulated banks. Increasingly, MFIs were expected to cover their own costs through market-based interest rates, profit-based incentives for managers, and greater commercialisation of their products and services. By becoming more like private sector firms, it was anticipated that they would become financially sustainable and the volume of low-cost finance to the poor would increase.

After 1990, the number of people with access to microfinance increased dramatically. This trend accelerated through the period of the financial crises of the late 1990s as MFIs were formalised or replaced by 'for-profit' organisations (Conger and Berger, 2004). Latin American MFIs borrowed more money commercially than MFIs in other parts of the world and interest rates escalated accordingly. By 2004, Latin American MFIs were charging the highest interest rates in the world.

The most rapid rates of growth and formalisation appeared to be around the financial crises of 1997–2002, when the NGO share of loans fell below 50% (Conger and Berger, 2004). MFIs weathered the financial storm, offering investors excellent returns. Microfinance became a highly profitable industry and in 2003 the average return on equity (ROE) matched the ROE of the world's largest financial entity, Citigroup (Conger and Berger, 2004). Between 2003 and 2008, the number of microfinance borrowers increased by 21% per annum (Gonzalez, 2010) and in 2007, the Initial Public Offering (IPO) of Mexico's *Compartamos* 'saw its senior managers self-rewarded with windfalls of several tens of millions of dollars effectively paid for by its poor women clients who were being charged up to 195% interest rates on their microloans' (Bateman, 2013). The stock market flotation generated around $410 million for a handful of investors; and external investors and US-based advisors also amassed personal fortunes on the back of Mexico's poor (Sinclair, 2012). By 2012, microfinance was 'a $70 billion industry, employing tens of thousands of people, predominantly managed by a closed group of funds based in the US and Europe acting as gatekeepers of the private capital available, and increasingly some of the public funding as well' (Sinclair, 2012, 3).

The question is, has the microfinance movement been successful? Has it lived up to its own hype? There is no doubt that many individuals and families, as evidenced anecdotally by the MFIs themselves, have benefited. Serious academic research, however, is less certain. A number of authors have argued that this has not had the positive impact on poverty that was hoped for or claimed (Karlan and Zinman, 2009; Banerjee et al., 2015; Roodman and Morduch, 2013; Straus, 2010; Bateman, 2010). Most early evaluations of MFIs reported a positive impact on poverty and income generation (Goldberg, 2005) but these were mainly carried out by or on behalf of the MFIs themselves and have been criticised as methodologically weak and over-reliant on anecdotal evidence (Bateman, 2011). The response of the six leading MFI advocacy bodies was to concede the lack of statistical evidence and reinforce their positive message with more anecdotes about successful cases (ACCION International et al., 2010; Odell, 2010). A review of the evidence carried out for the UK's Department for International Development (DfID), who had been a major investor in the microfinance concept, found that: 'Despite the apparent success and popularity of microfinance, no clear evidence yet exists that microfinance programmes have positive impacts' (Duvendack et al. 2011, 2).

The results of the analyses of the effectiveness of microcredit are, therefore, mixed at best (Haase, 2013). Using different definitions and methodologies, they tend to point to microcredit having little impact on profitability and well-being. Its advocates and practitioners select positive examples to support their arguments and activities, but the methodological complexities mean that academics who disagree with each other are not always comparing like with like. MFIs purposefully select the most promising villages, neighbourhoods and enterprises for their loans; and borrowers already have higher incomes than those who do not borrow.

Coleman (1999, 2006), who found no impact of microfinance for villages in Thailand, was not looking at enterprises; while Alexander-Tedeschi (2008) found that long-term borrowers can have 50% more profits than those who have never borrowed, but that the selection of beneficiaries into microcredit programmes creates a substantial bias problem for impact assessments. Pitt, Khandker and Cartwright (2006) found that microcredit increases women's empowerment, their assets and household consumption, but the impact varies from one lender to another (Khandker, 1998). Pisani and Yoskowitz (2013) found that home-based shops in Nicaragua that received microfinance performed no better in terms of income levels or well-being than shops that did not have access to microcredit.

The growth of clients has been impressive, as have the volume of funds available, the interest rates charged and the rates of profit for MFIs. Are they, however, meeting individual needs any better than any other neighbourhood moneylenders across the developing world? The Grameen Bank charges interest rates of around 20%, which as a mortgage rate would destroy the UK's property owning democracy, but is reasonable enough in the world of microfinance where interest rates can be ten times as high.[15] Helping people to help themselves is now big business, making the promotion of the small-scale entrepreneurial vision a source of a great deal of money for large-scale financial capitalist entrepreneurs.

An important question is the extent to which there is widespread demand for productive microcredit under these circumstances. The growth of clients and of the volume of loans would suggest that the answer is obvious: of course there is demand. However, MFIs lend to individuals who may buy consumption goods such as TVs or clothes for the children, or they may use the money to pay off other debts (Sinclair, 2012, 5). Microfinance is often used to cover basic consumption needs, rather than in small firm investment. The microfinance sector portrays this as 'consumption smoothing', arguing that it reduces risk and vulnerability for the poor. Indeed, when microcredit was banned in Andhra Pradesh in 2010, there is evidence that household consumption fell (Sane and Thomas, 2013). However, it does not increase the productive assets of the poor, which was the original intention of small-scale loans, far less redistribute the stock of wealth in their favour. It also means that a proportion of the income of the poor is siphoned off to pay for exaggerated interest charges, reducing their capacity to invest in income earning opportunities. It removes them from the clutches of loan sharks and in some cases, microcredit debt is used to pay off loan sharks. However, high-interest microfinance can still draw them into unsustainable indebtedness. There are other anecdotal cases (in Andhra Pradesh) where loan sharks have been used to pay off microcredit debts.

An alternative view is that microfinance is so widespread and effective that it has drawn funds away from potentially profitable larger firms. Bateman, for example, argues that the proliferation and expansion of microfinance has had a major negative impact on development in Latin America. In this view, microfinance for the informal sector has reduced the supply of credit to larger firms. He agrees with the IDB (2010) that the informal sector has been sucking scarce financial resources into low-productivity informal microenterprises and self-employment, with too little going to more productive formal small, medium and large enterprises (Bateman, 2013, 22). This misallocation of capital is thought to shield informal firms from competition and reduce a country's productivity. The microfinance market is 'saturated', the informal sector is a serious obstacle to development in the formal sector and the growth of enterprises that are 'right' for development cannot take place because of the amount of finance that is being directed towards 'wrong' enterprises (Bateman, 2013, 16). It is argued that microfinance is supporting unfair competition and causing 'wrong' enterprises to displace the 'right' type of enterprises.

There is, however, absolutely no evidence that the informal sector is displacing capitalist enterprises. The informal sector continues to grow and the formal manufacturing sector has suffered under neoliberalism, but the failure of capitalist development in Latin America cannot be laid at the door of MFIs and uneven competition between the formal and informal sectors. It is grossly overstating the impact of microfinance to say that it is helping to deindustrialise and informalise economies and that it has 'undermined and destroyed' social and economic development trajectories (Bateman, 2013, 26). There is little doubt that the microfinance model has been seriously diverted from its original intention, but this is not a major cause of underdevelopment.

If there is unequal competition based on low-interest-rate loans from MFIs, the failing competitors are more likely to be other micro-producers in the same field, rather than formal enterprises. The woman who borrows to buy a sewing machine will be in competition with other women who own sewing machines. She is also more likely to be involved in repair than production; and if she is a manufacturer, she may be an outworker for a larger firm. However, the extortionate interest rates that have become the norm are more likely to harm the indebted microenterprises, by reducing re-investable income, rather than support uneven competition that benefits these micro-firms.

The high interest rates are a disincentive to borrowing by informal firms. There may be a correlation between the growth of microfinance and the growth of the informal sector, but it is a step too far to argue that the former is a cause of the latter. There is no doubt, however, that microfinance is now an integral part of the global financial system and, as such, it plays a role in the profitability of international financial institutions.

Aitken (2013) explains how microfinance was brought from a reliance on state and philanthropic funding into the mainstream of international finance. It was commercialised, or financialised, through processes of *valuation, intermediation and securitisation*, whereby impoverished borrowers were converted into investable assets and sources of financial profit. Defaults were lower than expected and once it became clear that the poor could be relied on to repay their debts, microcredit was recast in the language of global finance, commercial modes of operation were introduced, microfinance became a way into unregulated local financial systems, and the whole sub-system was absorbed into the neoliberal narrative about entrepreneurialism. It did not matter that most of the credit was used for consumption, rather than income-generating microenterprises (Bateman, 2010). Microfinance in practice became a local variant of the neoliberal crusade.

Financial capitalism is constantly searching for new asset streams and if they fit with international regimes of *valuation*, whereby the assets are attributed with a value, they can therefore be sold on. Poor people who repay their debts become reliable assets for organisations such as *Compartemos*, who can realise their value by selling shares in them on the stock exchange. Through *intermediation*, which involves the setting up of formal routes through which global capital can access the new valuable assets (such as Microcredit Investment Vehicles – MIVs), large institutions can gain access to micro-borrowers 'as an increasingly mainstream financial asset' (Aitken, 2013, 484). The *securitisation* process then separates the loans from the MFIs, transfers them to special purpose vehicles through which the risks associated with micro-loans are channelled into global markets to become accessible to global investors. The apparent reliability of the poor, as disciplined borrowers who will seemingly tolerate ever-increasing interest rates, confirms their security as an investment. The pursuit of high interest rates by MFIs then becomes a strategy designed to attract global capital – rather than a necessary feature of any organisation that carries the high administrative cost associated with the disbursement of a large number of small loans. The high interest rates become a drain on asset accumulation by the poor.

International financial standards have been applied in a realm that initially relied on social capital; and where the international 'assets' (the poor) have accumulated 'debt' rather than their own 'assets' (productive capital). To the extent that they have had access to loans, which we will see is a doubtful generalisation, value has been extracted from microenterprises as a stream of income for capitalist investors in developed countries. Micro-firms have become asset streams that float around formal and informal boundaries at the edges of the international financial system and they are being judged by criteria that may be appropriate in a different world.

The risks, however, are not negligible. Hidden from investors in vehicles that are similar to the sub-prime loan bundles that brought down the world's financial markets in 2007, the rapid growth of commercialised micro-loans has been followed by default crises in a number of countries (Aitken, 2013; Sane and Thomas, 2011; Addae-Korankye, 2014). These crises have come to the attention of governments, who have stepped in to regulate and, in the case of the state of Andhra Pradesh in India, to close the offices of MFIs (Sane and Thomas, 2011). This state intervention against predatory lending, however, encouraged greater defaults.

In other countries the blame for the default is seen to lie with the clients and loose criteria for lending at the local level (Addae-Korankye, 2014; Ofori et al., 2014). In Kenya, where there was 68% default in manufacturing, the blame was clearly seen to rest with the clients and it was proposed that the stakeholders in the microfinance sector should ensure that the loan borrowers have access to adequate relevant technical training (Nguta and Huka, 2013, 5). Apparently nothing had been learned over the 40 years since the ILO came to a similar conclusion (ILO, 1972).

Most of these studies assume that demand for bank loans is a given and that risks to the banking sector can be minimised. In this research, we are interested in the perspective of the owners of micro-firms on the provision of small loans that aim to encourage them to invest in their businesses and expand their income-generating activities. What is the demand from microenterprises at the above rates of interest and what would the money be used for? It is often assumed that all small firms are impeded by a lack of finance, so what proportion of small firms are interested in microfinance loans, how important are they relative to other sources of finance, and would small firms use them, for example, to buy raw materials if 30 days credit is available from suppliers? Microfinance has become a popular concept in the developed world, but does it do anything more than suck profit out of the cities of the developing world as a new form of twenty-first century financial imperialism?

Microfinance for small firms in Ecuador

In the first decade of neoliberalism, as the concept of microfinance was growing in importance, it was assumed that there was a need for the Ecuadorian state to create a number of institutions that would provide finance for the poorly-served informal sector. There was no overall direction. The Central Bank, the National Development Bank, the National Financial Corporation, the Ministry of Labour and Human Resources and the National Corporation for Assistance to Popular Economic Units all had funding streams to support lending to artisans and other small firms. In addition, lines of credit were opened in private banks such as the Banco del Pacífico, and funds were available through the Banco de Cooperativas, OCEPA[16] and from NGOs. However, in spite of the many alternative sources, 'credit for this sector continued to be insignificant' (Pita, 1992, 213). The new sources were hardly used.

The main reasons proposed for the lack of take-up reflected individual and organisational perspectives on supply and demand. From the perspective of those providing the finance, the small workshops had inadequate administrative systems (such as lack of accounts and management systems), low levels of physical capital ownership that could be used as collateral, a lack of a distinction between workshop and family budgets, and a lack of knowledge about what was available and what was required to access it. From the artisan perspective, the main barriers were thought to be the high interest rates demanded of them, the complex bureaucratic requirements and, amongst government officials and NGO officers, a lack of knowledge and understanding about how the artisans operated.

The neoliberal state encouraged the private sector to become more involved in the provision of credit, but the private banks continued to demonstrate scarce interest. Artisans were asked what the main problems were with getting formal credit, but no one asked the 75% of artisans who had not obtained any type of credit in the previous 12 months, whether they had applied to banks and, if they had not, why not.

In the 1990s, the Ecuadorian economy was in crisis, growth was reduced, confidence was low and interest rates, for both savers and borrowers, were extremely high. This encouraged savers to place their money in the banks and dissuaded borrowers from contracting loans. As we saw earlier, in the collapse of the banking system in 1999, accounts were frozen, the value of the sucre collapsed, inflation roared ahead, two-thirds of the nation's financial institutions were closed, debt soared as a percentage of GDP, and dollarization was introduced (Hurtado, 2002; Cevallos, 2004). Around the turn of the Millennium, many artisans lost their savings, along with any faith they might have had in the banks. Interest rates, particularly for small loans, remained excessively high, before the Correa administration was voted into power in 2007.

Correa and microcredit in Ecuador

When the Correa administration introduced reforms to the banking system, they attracted a great deal of international criticism. Branded as ideological by his neoliberal critics, the reforms were introduced to support the broader social and economic development plans of the Popular and Solidarity Economy. With the objectives of increasing social inclusion and social welfare, the government insisted on the separation of consumer banking from the risks associated with the free-for-all neoliberal model that resulted in the global crash of 2008. They established a liquidity fund, to be funded by taxing the banks, and the Central

Bank was brought under the control of the Executive through the Economic Planning Ministry. In 2011, the legal representatives, board members and shareholders of financial institutions were barred from business activity outside the financial sector, leading to banks divesting their interests in insurance, brokerage and pension companies. Interest rates were set and capped, at different levels for different type of activities. Bank profits fell, but the policies led to a more stable banking environment.

The 2008 Constitution confirmed that the Central Bank was responsible for the implementation of credit policy (Gobierno del Ecuador, 2008b, Article 303). The private financial sector was to be brought under more strict government control than in the past (ibid., Article 308) and authorised credit should give priority to economic development as set out in the national development plan, with a particular emphasis on promoting the active inclusion of less favoured groups in the economy (ibid., Article 310). The popular and solidarity financial sector[17] was to receive preferential treatment in order to develop the popular economy (ibid., Article 311).

In 2009, two main types of credit for investment in productive assets were established, based on the size of the turnover of the firm: productive credit and microcredit (BCE, 2009).

- **Productive credit** would be available to firms with annual sales greater than US$100,000. There were three subcategories of productive credit for different sizes of firms. These were loans for:
  - Corporate production
  - Enterprise production
  - SME production.
- **Microcredit** was defined as credit up to US$ 20,000, given to an individual or enterprise with sales of less than US$100,000, a self-employed worker, or groups of borrowers seeking finance for small-scale activities in production, commerce or services. Within microcredit, there were also three subcategories:[18]
  - Extended microcredit
  - Simple microcredit
  - Retail microcredit

All loans above US$20,000 were classified as productive credit, irrespective of sales levels. This would be important when it came to determining interest rates, for microcredit would continue to be much more expensive than productive credit.

The size of the companies who could qualify for these categories and subcategories of credit, along with the maximum interest rates that existed in January 2015, can be seen in Table 11.1. Retail microcredit was the most expensive, with interest rates of 30.5% per annum. For micro-firm owners in the informal sector, interest rates for simple microcredit were three times the rates that were applied for corporate credit. However, for the owners of these micro-firms,

Table 11.1 Maximum interest rates for different types of credit in Ecuador, 2015

Main credit types	Turnover limits	Subcategories of credit	Credit	Maximum
	(USD)		Available (USD)	Interest rates (% p.a.)
Productive credit	More than 100,000	Corporate credit	More than 1,000,000	9.33
		Enterprise credit	200,001–1,000,000	10.21
		SME credit	20,001–200,000	11.83
Microcredit	Up to 100,000	Extended microcredit	10,001–20,000	25.50
		Simple microcredit	3,001–10,000	27.50
		Retail microcredit	Up to 3,000	30.50
Other credit		Credit for consumption		16.30
		Credit for housing		11.33

Source: Banco Central del Ecuador: Boletin Semanal de Tasa de Interes, No. 397, 8–14 23–29 Julio de 2015.

borrowing for consumption and housing was cheaper than loans for investment in their firms. This led a number of artisans to say that they borrowed for items such as furniture and then used the money to buy tools or raw materials. Some borrowed for housing, which they then used both as a home and a workshop. Nevertheless, interest rates were pegged and microcredit borrowing for capital investment and raw materials changed remarkably between 2007 and 2015.[19]

The main changes were a reduction of bank interest rates and a transition from private banking to cooperative banking, which became the finance sector of the government's Popular and Solidarity Economy (EPS). Between 2007 and 2015, as microcredit increased as a proportion of all private credit (from 8% to 12%), private banks were displaced by cooperatives (Table 11.2).[20]

The interest rates charged by the cooperatives did not change much over the period, but those of the private banks fell considerably. In 2007, interest rates for simple microcredit were 10 percentage points higher than for extended credit. In the simple category, private bank loans carried interest rates that were on average 16 percentage points higher than those of cooperatives. Interest rates varied between 16% in one cooperative to 42% in one bank. In July 2015, private banks and cooperatives accounted for around 98% of simple extended microcredit, with average interest rates of 25% and 22% respectively.[21]

By 2017, there were 97 organisations involved in the distribution of microcredit in Ecuador, including 55 cooperatives or credit unions, 23 NGOs and 14 banks (Table 11.3).[22] The banks were national and international, as were

Table 11.2 Microcredit in Ecuador, 2007 and 2015

Financial sectors	2007				2015			
	Simple microcredit		Extended microcredit		Simple microcredit		Extended microcredit	
	APR interest	% of microcredit	APR interest	% of microcredit	APR interest	% of microcredit	APR interest	% of microcredit
Private banks	37.55	65.2	24.97	49.5	26.84	49.4	24.71	33.6
Cooperatives & EPS (1)	21.92	24.2	21.63	50.1	23.52	49.2	21.18	64.1
Mutual societies					20.79	0.0	22.50	0.1
Financial societies	40.19	10.6	19.73	0.4	27.24	1.5	24.00	2.3
Credit cards								
National finance system	34.04	100.0	23.27	100.0	25.17	100.0	22.29	100.0
Percentage of total national credit		**6.5**		**1.9**		**7.7**		**4.6**

Sources:
Banco Central del Ecuador: Boletin Semanal de Tasa de Interes, No. 1, 11–17 Octubre de 2007;
Banco Central del Ecuador: Boletin Semanal de Tasa de Interes, No. 397, 8–14 23-29 Julio de 2015;
https://contenido.bce.fin.ec/documentos/Estadisticas/SectorMonFin/TasasInteres/TasasHistoricoBoletinSemanal.htm

Notes:
(1) EPS is the Popular and Solidarity Economy. After Boletin 397, reporting does not distinguish between the micro-lending of banks and cooperatives/EPS.

Table 11.3 Sources of microcredit in Ecuador, 2017

Sources		
	No	%
Coops and credit unions	55	56.7
NGOs	23	23.7
Banks	14	14.4
Private companies	2	2.1
Others	3	3.1
Total	97	100.0

Sources: www.themix.org; www.smartcampaign.org; www.rfr.org.ec/

the NGOs. The savings and credit cooperatives, which were supported by the Correa Government as part of the Popular and Solidarity Economy, were the most important source of credit for micro-firms and low-income families. Interest rates for artisans remained high, but they were lower and more widely available than previously.

The capped and regulated interest rates produced stability in the financial sector and predictable outlays for artisans. This follows a long period of good intentions but a failure of the state to deliver, from the 1970s onwards, particularly through the neoliberal years. These years were characterised by elite capture of cheap state credit and a lack of realism in the policies that aimed to provide finance for small firms. In the next chapter, we will see what effect all of this had on artisan borrowing, from the perspective of the artisans themselves.

Notes

1 Crime refers to street crime. The other obstacles are anti-competitive behaviour, infrastructure, taxes and regulation, judicial efficiency, corruption, inflation and exchange rates.
2 www.angelnewsletter.co.uk/blog/news/bdrc-continental-publishes-sme-finance-monitor-for-q2-2016/
3 In 2016 the proportion was 47% in Q2. www.bdrc-group.com/
4 This was unchanged before and after the Brexit referendum. It does not appear to be a lack of confidence: more than six in ten SMEs were confident the bank would agree to a future request and eight out of ten that do apply are successful.
5 Between 1970 and 1982 US $ 1 was equivalent to 25 Ecuadorian sucres at the official rate of exchange.
6 The majority of the loans were for less than 1,000 dollars and over a period of less than one year (*El Tiempo*, 4/11/73). BNF credit to SI & A fell from 7.8% of its total credit to only 1.9%. Again, these loans were mainly short term, 66% being for periods of less than two years. Even less private credit went to SI & A and 95% of the loans were for less than one year (PREALC, 1976a, 279).
7 *Banco Nacional de Fomento*, later changed to *BanEcuador B.P.* in 2016.

8 The Programme of Fiduciary Funds for Small Industries in the Ministry of Industry, Commerce and Integration (MICEI).
9 *El Universo*, 15.5.74.
10 *El Comercio*, 23.8.73.
11 Interviews with UN artisan experts. As a result of this problem, the programme turned more towards assisting artistic artisans who were more easily organized into cooperative ventures for the purpose of combining collateral. These were organized mainly outside Quito, and with the expert creation of marketable new designs this programme of relatively modest means was able to make a visible impact on the fortunes of artistic artisans between 1975 and 1978.
12 *Banco Interamericano de Desarrollo*.
13 Interview with recipient, 1976.
14 *Federación Nacional de Cameras de Pequeños Industriales del Ecuador*.
15 In the UK, small short-term loans reached interest rates of over 1200% APR.
16 From 1967, *La Organización Comercial Ecuatoriana de Productos Artesanales* (OCEPA), which was attached to the Ministry of Industry and Commerce (MICEI) promoted the design, production and sales of traditional artisan goods.
17 *El sector financiero popular y solidario*: Article 311 says: 'The popular and solidarity financial sector shall consist of savings and credit cooperatives, associative or solidarity entities, community banks, savings banks. The service initiatives of the popular and solidarity financial sector, and micro, small and medium-sized productive units, will receive differential and preferential state treatment in so far as they promote the development of the popular and solidarity economy.'
18 The relevant concepts in Spanish are *microcredito minorista, microcredito acumulación simple*, and *microcredito acumulación ampliado*.
19 The first weekly bulletin on volume and cost of different types of credit by financial sector and organisation was first published in October 2007 and it continued in more or less the same format until July 2015.
20 https://contenido.bce.fin.ec/documentos/Estadisticas/SectorMonFin/TasasInteres/TasasHistoricoBoletinSemanal.htm
21 The balance was provided by 'financial societies' at similar rates.
22 www.themix.org.; www.smartcampaign.org; www.rfr.org.ec/

12 Artisan perspectives on bank credit

Introduction

Those who propose improving the supply of microcredit make two basic assumptions. First, that micro-firms need and want sources of small-scale formal banking credit, even when evidence from developed countries suggests that small industries do not always wish to get involved with such credit. Second, that the outcome of bank lending is always positive, even when there is little evidence to support this belief.

Micro-firm perspectives on bank credit are more nuanced than the assumption that the problem is one of restricted supply. Their attitudes change over time, as do the attitudes of the banks, and when small firms run into trouble when banks fail, the small firms suffer adverse effects if they apply for future funding. Small-firm failure in the context of bank failure is interpreted by the banks as the fault of the small enterprises, making future loans more difficult to obtain for those who do want them.

This chapter is about the experience of the artisans. It looks at the reality of how they fund start-ups and further development. It is about the demand for loans and how this changes over time. It distinguishes between two concepts: start-up loans and development loans. The latter may be for the purposes of *survival* in difficult times, for example to deal with cash-flow problems between taking an order and delivering it, or it may be for *growth* purposes, such as investment in new machinery or in a larger than normal batch of raw materials. We are classifying both survival and growth loans as *development* loans.

The next section begins with the source of start-up capital and it asks about borrowing after start-up. We then ask the artisans what type of loans they would benefit from and if they would be interested in a loan to expand their workshop into a small industry. The idea of the micro-entrepreneur in search of bank finance for investment and growth is at the heart of the neoliberal narrative about micro-firms in developing countries. It helps sustain the myth of the small informal firm confronting the regulatory state, with its assumption that all small firm owners have ambitions to be capitalist firms and the provision of loans as the route to achieving this. We will see that informal firms' approaches to formal finance are the product of a different set of priorities. The expansion of their business is more of a dream than a serious investment they are willing to commit to through borrowing from banks.

Initial start-up capital

In 1975, three-quarters of artisans said they relied on personal savings alone for setting up their businesses (Table 12.1). A further 12% relied on a loan from a family member, meaning that 86% were reliant on funding from inside the family. Throughout the research, the artisans consistently pointed to personal savings as their only source of start-up capital. However, they also reported the use of a variety of informal and formal sources of funds that do not involve banks, including:

- Savings that came from previous work as artisans in the same field.
- Redundancy money from employment in the formal sector.
- Using tools and other equipment accumulated as an artisan wage labourer.
- Forms of credit that are not seen as loans, such as credit cards.
- Inheritance from a family member.
- Taking over from a boss who died.
- Prepayments by clients for work.
- Supplier credit.
- Savings of a family member who worked elsewhere or had another business.
- Withdrawing paid-up social security contributions that had been accumulated in the course of other employment, such as in the public sector or formal private sector.
- Buying the workshops and paying it off in instalments without an initial payment.
- Having a business partner who provided finance.
- *Chulqueros* – neighbourhood moneylenders or 'loan sharks'.

These sources can be mixed and overlapping, and for a variety of purposes, mostly used at start-up but some also used for development purposes. During the 1975–82 period, there was a significant change in the structure of start-up finance, as bank lending became more important, the numbers relying on personal savings declined, and the relevance of 'other' sources increased.

After 1982, given the rhetoric about the importance of small firms in the neoliberal narrative, we might have expected a further surge in bank lending as an initial source of finance, but there was no change in the structure of finance for setting up artisan workshops between 1982 and 1995. Policies were announced, successive neoliberal governments proclaimed their support for entrepreneurs, international money was borrowed to stimulate small firm capital investment, lending streams for micro-firms were initiated in various government departments and development banks but, consistent with what we found about the supply of credit in Chapter 11, there was no significant change in the relative importance of bank lending, personal savings or family loans.

Table 12.1 Sources of initial capital for the workshop

(MENTIONS)	1975		1982		1995		2005		2015	
	No.	%	No.	%	No.	%	No.	%	No.	%
Personal savings only	139	74.7	179	60.5	202	60.4	226	70.6	147	55.7
Bank loan	9	4.8	37	12.5	34	10.2	43	13.4	67	25.4
Family loan	22	11.8	27	9.1	39	11.6	27	8.4	25	9.5
Other loan	9	4.8	21	7.1	15	4.4	6	1.9	15	5.7
Other (inc. gift)	7	3.8	32	10.8	45	13.4	18	5.6	10	3.8
TOTAL	186	100.0	296	100.0	335	100.0	320	100.0	264	100.0

	Chi-sq	DF	p-value
1975–2015	91.6288	16	1.25E-12
1975–1982	19.3129	4	0.0007
1982–1995	4.7125	4	0.3181
1995–2005	19.3626	4	0.0007
2005–2015	23.0299	4	0.0001
1975 & 2015	34.2158	4	6.73E-07

'Other' sources of start-up funding continued to increase. In 1995, for example, 3.3% of artisans said the source of their initial capital was a gift and a further 3.6% said it was inherited from a father, uncle or brother. Four workshops (1.2%) were set up by using credit from the suppliers of equipment and/or raw materials. Other examples in 1995 involved:

- Severance pay after losing a government job to structural adjustment;
- Surrender of accumulated social security payments after leaving formal factory or government employment;
- A shoemaker who obtained credit from the owner of a shop who bought his shoes for resale in the shop;
- A barber who sold a piece of rural land;
- The owner of a beauty salon whose husband helped finance the business;
- A mechanic who borrowed the machinery;
- A shoemaker who carried out repairs using odds and ends of spare materials;
- A carpenter who received advance payment for his furniture;
- A seamstress whose husband won some money on the lottery;
- The owner of a printer's workshop who called in an outstanding debt;
- A shoemaker whose workshop belonged to his father – who had retired but still owned the workshop.

Between 1995 and 2005, during which time the Ecuadorian banking system collapsed, there was a highly significant change in the structure of start-up finance. This was based on a renewed reliance on personal savings, bringing the importance of savings almost back to the 1975 levels. There was a small increase in bank loans but their relative importance as a source of start-up capital was more or less the same as in 1982. Over the whole neoliberal period, bank lending for artisan start-ups did not improve.

Another main reason for the significant change between 1995 and 2005 was the decline in the relevance of other sources of finance that were squeezed during the financial crisis – including family loans, supplier credit, advance payments and gifts. There was also a decline in the relevance of inheritance. This corresponded with the changing structure of artisan production, which involved a reduction in traditional activities and the emergence of new technologies and skills. As the traditional micro-firms in shoemaking, tailoring and carpentry declined in numbers, so did inheritance of these types of workshops. As these businesses became less and less viable, the children of artisans found work elsewhere, often in professional occupations. The artisans retired or passed away and the businesses disappeared. The new technologies in the workshops that were emerging required investment in new equipment that could not be inherited.

After 2005, when cooperative banking increased and interest rates fell, bank borrowing for setting up new firms increased dramatically. In 2015, artisans were five times more likely to use a bank loan when setting up a business than they were in 1975. This was partially due to the Correa government's support for the financial institutions of the Popular and Solidarity Economy and, in particular, the cap that was introduced on micro-lending interest rates. In the last chapter, we saw the significance of high interest rates as a barrier to small firm investment, along with the reforms that were made to the financial system by the Correa administration. The banking system was stabilised, interest rates were reduced and the impact of Correa's anti-neoliberal stance was to stimulate borrowing by artisans – rather than create another financial crisis, as was predicted. It should be noted that the majority of artisans continued to rely on personal savings alone but a quarter had access to a bank loan, 2.5 times the level in 1995, and artisans relying on their personal savings alone declined to historically low levels. The use of bank loans doubled *after* the years of the neoliberal experiment.

Bank borrowing for survival and growth

It is generally assumed that lack of access to development finance is a major problem for the growth of established firms, but artisans may decide that they do not wish to engage with banks and they may seek other forms of credit. Yet again, they may decide to work without debt of any type. The firms seeking development funding in Quito included artisans who used banks at the point of start-up and those that did not. Some of the artisans who received bank loans to help set up their businesses will have applied for further loans: some of them will have been successful and others rejected. Some of those who did not use a bank loan will have applied when setting up and been rejected; and some of these may have applied for a loan at a later date, and been successful or not.

Table 12.2 Applying for and receiving development loans

	Total no. of workshops	Applied for loan	% of total	Received loan	% of total	% of applied
		No.	%	No.	%	%
1982	298	92	30.9	58	19.5	63.0
1995	327	109	33.3	57	17.4	52.3
2005	317	61	19.2	43	13.6	70.5
2015	257	100	38.9	71	27.6	71.0

In 1975, those who did not use a start-up bank loan were asked if they had ever applied for a bank loan. From 1982 onwards, all artisans were asked if they had ever applied for a bank loan after they had set up their workshops, whatever their initial source of capital.[1] All artisans who had applied were asked about their success or failure in obtaining loans. What emerges is a complex pattern of loan applications and awards that changes over time.

Just over 30% had applied for a development loan in 1982 and 1995 but this fell to around 20% after the financial crisis (Table 12.2). This reflected the negative experience of the artisans during the banking crash. Between 2005 and 2015, the proportion applying doubled, once again pointing to a renewed confidence in the financial system set up by Correa to foster greater financial inclusion through the control of interest rates and the development of the institutions of the Popular and Solidarity Economy.

At no time before Correa's reforms did the proportion of workshops receiving development credit rise above 20%. Indeed, the proportion receiving development loans fell through the neoliberal years when the rhetoric of the times led us to expect an increase in micro-firms benefiting from free-market policies and microcredit institutions. In 1995, just over half of the 17% who applied were successful. In 2005, when less than 20% of artisans applied for a development loan, only 14% of workshops reported they had received financial support. After the crash, owners who applied were more likely to receive a loan than in the past, but the artisans were less likely to apply. After Correa's reforms, when applications doubled, the proportion receiving loans also doubled.

If we break down this analysis of credit applications and outcomes further, there were three groups of artisans who were asked about their experience of bank lending after they had started their businesses. They included:

1. Those who did not mention a bank loan when asked about their start-up capital.
2. Those who said they had obtained a loan at start-up, whether it was a bank loan or another form of loan (from family, friends and others).
3. Those who had obtained a bank loan when they set up the business.

One might assume that firms with a track record with banks might be more likely to apply for and obtain development loans at a later date, but this has not always been the case. The relationship between getting start-up loans and getting loans as an established business, varies over time. First, if artisans had a bank loan at start-up they were more likely than others to apply for a development loan, except in 2015 when others were encouraged to apply under the regime of the Popular and Solidary Economy (Table A.12.1). Second, if artisan had a start-up bank loan, they were *not* always more likely than others to *receive* a development loan (Table A.12.2). In 1982 and 2005, artisans who had *not* had a start-up loan but who had applied for a development loan, were more likely to receive it than others were (Table A.12.3). In the former year, this represents a redistribution of funding that was made possible through the large increase in oil revenues, even if the overall impact of these revenues on artisan lending was not substantial (as we saw in the last chapter). In fact, having a bank loan at start-up did not significantly raise the possibility of receiving a development loan in any year except 1995. In 2005, following the banking crash, having *no* history with banks appears to have increased the possibility of contracting a bank loan for survival and growth. Artisans with a bank history suffered during the crash and then suffered again because of their difficulties during the crash.

Artisans with no bank loan at start-up

Between 1975 and 1995, there were small variations over time in applying for development loans, but considerable differences in the likelihood of receiving such a loan (Table 12.3 and Table A.12.4). After 13 years of neoliberal economic policy and a narrative that eulogised the role of micro-entrepreneurs in the Ecuadorian economy, a small increase in demand for credit for enterprise growth corresponded with a substantial decline in the possibility of obtaining a loan. Despite the rhetoric of the promotion of enterprise and the power of the free market to develop micro-capitalism, bank lending to the artisans declined.

After the collapse of the Ecuadorian banking system in 1999 and the dollarization of the economy the following year, development-loan applications declined. The artisans were more distrustful of the banks and less likely to approach them than in the past. However, the possibility of obtaining a loan increased as the banking sector recovered. In 2015, we saw the highest application and success rates of the 1975–2015 period. As was the case for start-up loans, there is little doubt that the increase in development loan activity is a reflection of Correa's anti-neoliberal banking reforms.

Artisans with a bank loan at start-up

It is not surprising that, for most of the study period, those who mentioned a bank loan at start-up were most likely to apply for another loan at a later date.

Table 12.3 Applying for and receiving development loans (2)

		GROUP 1		GROUP 2		GROUP 3	
		No bank loan at start-up		Mentioned any loan at start-up		Mentioned bank loan at start-up	
		Applied for bank loan later	Received loan	Applied for new bank loan	Received new bank loan	Applied for new bank loan	Received new bank loan
1975	Yes	59	22				
	%	34.1	37.9				
1982	Yes	69	48	41	21	23	10
	%	31.4	70.6	52.6	65.6	63.9	62.5
1995	Yes	94	44	36	22	15	13
	%	37.9	46.8	45.6	66.7	51.7	92.9
2005	Yes	54	39	15	10	7	4
	%	19.7	73.6	55.6	71.4	70.0	57.1
2015	Yes	68	49	52	39	32	22
	%	43.0	77.8	52.0	81.3	47.8	81.5

- In 1982, those who had a bank start-loan were twice as likely to apply for a development loan, compared to those who did not initially borrow from a bank.
- In 1995, they were less likely to apply than in 1982 and the gap narrowed between those who did or did not have a loan.
- In 2005, when overall applications declined dramatically, the data suggest that start-up bank borrowers were much more likely to have applied for a development loan than those who had no start-loans.
- In 2015, the gap between the start-up bank borrowers and others had narrowed considerably.

We might expect that those who borrowed from a bank to set up a business would, with a track record, be more successful than others applying for a development loan. This, however, was not always the case:

- In 1982, start-up bank borrowers were less likely to receive a development loan that those who had no bank loan at start-up.
- By 1995, this was no longer the case. Those with a track record were much more likely to be successful the second time around.
- By 2005, the situation had turned around again, with start-up borrowers less likely to receive development loans.
- In 2015, there was practically no difference in the success rates.

We need to be cautious about the small numbers, but in 2005 the success rate for those with no bank loans at start-up appears to be higher than the success rate of those who did. This supports the conclusion that the firms involved with the banks were most likely to have been damaged by the financial crash and were therefore later judged to be less reliable from the perspectives of the banks. The losses and trauma that resulted from the bank failure resulted in reduced credit ratings for the small firms that were most involved with bank lending.

When the artisans borrowed, it was mainly for equipment and raw materials. However, not all artisans used credit for these purposes and for some, credit was available in a variety of forms. Their approach to debt was best expressed through the life-history interviews of 2015.

The uses of credit

Buying tools

Some of the artisans only use hand tools and have never borrowed to support their workshops. For instance, a 74-year-old jeweller/watchmaker who, when he started at the age of 12, had no more than a tube through which he would blow to control the flame for melting gold, and a hammer to beat it into shape.[2] The tube, or *churumbela*, had a small hole at the end and, according to the force with which the jeweller blew through it, they controlled the size of the flame. Even today, he has no machinery. Everything is done using hand tools.

A 70-year-old tailor who brought his own hand tools with him when he set up the business also never got into debt.[3] His first machine was pedal driven, and he still has it after 45 years. He bought another one, which is now 25 years old, and he expects to have it until he dies. He has grown a successful micro-business purely on the basis of the volume of work he has been able to attract. A goldsmith, who has never sought a loan, imported his rolling machine from the United States 40 years ago and has not needed another one. His work is mainly by hand:[4]

> We work by hand. We don't have to obtain new machines … obviously there are other technologies, but those are in factories that can use them. They have them in Cuenca, for example, but here in Quito the majority of us work manually … The machinery is from overseas … This one was brought from the United States … We already have all the workshop that we need so there is no need to be buying, apart from files and these small saw blades that break.

On the other hand, a 76-year-old shirt maker – who was born in rural Tungurahua, orphaned when he was seven, came to Quito when he was 20 and set up his first workshop when he got married in 1967, still has the machinery he started with. However, he borrowed and he bought quality machinery from Germany and Japan:[5]

> I started the workshop with a loan. And everything was acquired that way: borrowed and paid. I have good quality machinery to produce a good product; and the machines have never been damaged.

Buying raw materials

Paying for raw materials takes a number of forms. Banks will seldom lend for the purchase of goods that are consumed in the production process. In any case, many artisans prefer to pay cash. Others use the credit that is offered by suppliers. Some are encouraged by the suppliers, but there is a great deal of nervous anticipation should they be unable to pay. And some resort to short-term high-interest street moneylenders.

The most common type of credit for raw materials is payment on account, normally within 30 days. A shoemaker in the city centre, for example, buys raw materials from shops and factories, in Cuenca and the *Oriente*.[6] They are provided on credit. The sales reps deliver them to the workshop and they pay for them a month or six weeks later.[7] A shirtmaker in the same area has almost always imported from Mexico, via Guayaquil.[8] 'They don't have the quality here that I need.' He has had the same suppliers for years, who trust him. He pays with post-dated cheques, or he pays in instalments: 'they know me and there are no problems'.

When a pastry-maker in La Ronda was asked if the wholesalers from whom he bought his raw materials had provided the goods on credit, he said:[9]

> No, no, only cash here. I never liked to be in debt, more than anything. I have never worked with credit, no, I have never gone into debt anywhere. I bought according to what I had … Clearly they have offered it to me – look, I get so much material, flour, whatever, but I have not wanted to get into debt.

He had five workers in the bakery and 13 selling in the streets and he had never had any debt. Everything was done by hand so he also never had to invest in machinery in the 14 years he owned the business.

Sometimes payment is made on a credit card, but this is not perceived as debt. Asked if he had ever sought credit for materials, machinery or a small industry, a goldsmith said:[10]

> No, no, no … why? Everything that we would have wanted to buy, for example, merchandise, we asked for at the Bank (the Central Bank, where they would buy their gold); but loans, no. With a card helps.

In this case, the goldsmith never asked for a loan, but he bought goods with a credit card. The credit card was not seen as a source of credit, or a loan.

On the other hand, some jewellers get offered more credit than they can use or would want. One jeweller/watchmaker in the CHQ had difficulty in paying for gold when he started out but he was soon being offered more than he could use. This was based on a level of trust that a bank would never display:[11]

> I had very little capital, but a gentleman who knew me gave me credit for eight days. They saw me coming for, for example, five or 10 grams and they asked me who I was working for. I said I am making such-and-such for this

person or that. Seeing that I was frequently coming for small amounts, they said to me: 'take 20 grams'. I said, I don't have the money. They said: 'Just take it'. Well, 'God will pay you'. I finished the work. Sold it right away, and came back to cancel my debt. In that way I arrived at a situation where they loaned me large amounts.

When I started to work in gold, it cost 3 sucres a gram – gold dust that they brought from the *Oriente*. They gave me the material without me asking and said, 'take it and pay later'. Even now, the Colombian pawn shop owners say 'I'll sell you this'; I say, 'I don't have the money'; they say, 'just take and pay me when you sell it'. They trust me. There is one woman, for example who had a lot of gold. I took 20, 50 grams. One time she said, 'why don't you take more?' I said I don't have the money; she said, how much do you want? I said '100 grams'. 'For how long'? 'Until the end of the week or until the middle of next week and I will pay you back'. She said take it and I took the 100 grams. I sat at the table until midnight seven days a week making the earrings and rings, running to deliver them as they were completed. I had to educate my children.

One time a woman who owned a jewellers shop asked for four pairs of wedding rings of 15 grams each pair. I asked her for half the money [up front] but she said no. I went to the woman who sold the gold. I said, 'I have an order for 4 pairs of rings amounting to 60 grams of gold and I don't have the money. I have hardly enough for 20 grams. 'How many grams do you want?' 'Around 100 grams'. She said 'look, right now I don't have anyone to cut the gold' and because I needed it in a hurry to complete the order by 4.00 that day, the woman brought out the 500 gram bar: 'take it'.

The jeweller, with the assistance of his son, completed the order on time. He bought the gold at $US 38.50, sold 60 grams at $US 55 and returned the balance to the gold merchant, creating an income of around $US 1000 that day. It was the last big order he had, for he now says there is no work for jewellers or watchmakers.

In some cases, as we have seen above, the client provides the credit. An 80-year-old mechanic, born in La Ronda and making cookers in his workshop in the South of the city, initially borrowed money from a family member but later obtained credit from a shop where he sold his goods, but it was not without problems.[12] He started to work as an apprentice in a mechanical workshop age 13, repairing cars. He then worked in industrial textile factories, before returning to work on cars. Some 38 years ago, one of his brothers died and the person from whom he had been renting his workshop sold it to him for 80,000 sucres. Asked whether he bought it with a loan or with savings, he said: 'my brother loaned me the money, without interest, and I paid it back'. He was then asked if he had ever gone to a bank for credit and he replied:

No, no, no – because I had the luck to begin to make industrial cookers. One day, I was passing a shop [selling cookers] and I asked for credit from the owner. I told him I could make better things than he was selling in his shop. I brought one to him and he gave me credit. What happened? You know, I supplied 12 or 13, then one of my own workers offered to make them at a lower price. I was paying his social security as a boss and as a worker he screwed me.

In spite of the need for credit for the purchase of tools and raw materials, artisans are reluctant to engage with the banks and, when they do and get rejected, they feel that the banking system is not for them.

Reasons for not applying for a loan

When artisans were asked why they did not apply for loans, there was a wide range of personal and economic reasons. The main reason for not applying for a bank loan was that the artisans were simply not interested – they had not thought about it, it was not needed (Figure 12.1). There was not a great deal of difference between those who had mentioned bank loan when they were setting up and those where there was no initial loan. However, those who had successfully applied previously continued to be less risk-averse than those who did not have a start-up loan. They were also more likely to give a wide range of other reasons, which were mainly personal, but they also included the fact that they had no trust in banks, the interest rates were too high, they would be unable to repay the loans, or that they had a previous bad experience with the banks.

Towards the end of the neoliberal period, the reluctance to get involved with the banks was based on their experience of the financial crisis at the turn of the millennium and the immediate impact of dollarization on their businesses

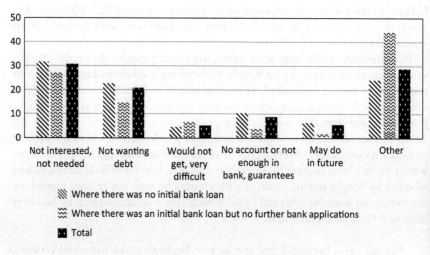

Figure 12.1 Reasons for not applying for a loan, 1975–2015

(Middleton, 2007). Some artisans lost the *savings* they had in the banks when they collapsed and others suffered when the currency changed.

At the time, a baker complained that 'We had a loan in sucres and now we have to pay in dollars.' He had savings when the Ecuadorian banking system collapsed in 1999, he had to take out loans to survive and after dollarization he had to pay back his loans in the new currency. A carpenter said that 'the money I had in the bank in sucres was dollarized and now I have practically nothing. They never returned the money to me.' Savings in sucres were lost in the banking collapse, any that remained were rapidly devalued by inflation, they were then frozen and inaccessible, before being converted into dollars at an extremely low exchange rate. Many artisans lost all their savings during this period.

Reasons for not getting loans

Those who had applied for loans but were not successful were asked why they had been rejected. Their views contrast with the perspectives of the academics and financiers, which tend to blame the recipients as we saw in the previous chapter. From the point of view of the artisans, most of the reasons appeared to lie with the attitudes and behaviour of the banks. The most common reason for outright rejection of the artisan applications was that they could not provide sufficient guarantees or they did not have funds in the bank (Figure 12.2). But there were a host of other reasons. From the artisan perspective the process was like a war of attrition without end. This got significantly worse between 1982 and 1995.

By 1995, after 13 years of neoliberalism, there were too many problems or obstacles when artisans applied for loans, leading to the process to grind to a halt. Artisans complained about the procedures, the processes, the paper chases, the delays, and the inconveniences associated with both the *private and public* sectors. It was all very difficult and complicated and it took so long that the artisans withdrew from the process or, in times of high inflation, the value of the loans was devalued by the time they received them. Sometimes they could not comply with the requirements, but more often they did not want the trouble they had to wade through to get loans that were less than they needed. A number of artisans complained about the high interest rates they were going to be charged by the banks and said they preferred to work with *chulqueros*, who charged 8% interest per month but who provided instant loans and required no paperwork.

If they could get a loan now, what would they use it for?

In each of the years of the study, the artisans were asked what type of loan they thought would be most convenient for their branch of activity at that moment. Their responses changed significantly over time but there was very little evidence of aspirations to grow into formal SMEs. In most years, loans for raw materials and tools and machinery predominated, but there were significant differences from year to year (Table 12.4). In 1975, in the midst of the positivity

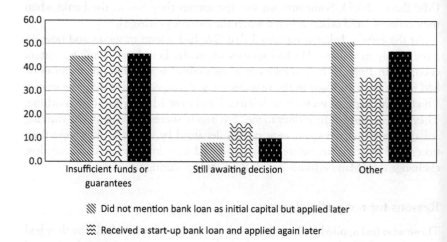

Figure 12.2 Reasons for not receiving a bank loan, 1975–2015

of the boom, there was a good deal of enthusiasm for these types of investment loans, accounting for nearly three-quarters of all loans mentioned. By 1982, as the artisans were restructured and the traditional activities were disappearing, the demand for equipment and materials loans had dropped below half – compared to a surge in the proportion saying 'none' or 'nothing': that is, that no type of loan would be of benefit, confirming that they were not interested in getting one.

There were also significant changes between 1982 and 1995. In this period the demand for credit for tools and machinery declined and was replaced by a demand for funds that would open up commercial possibilities for the artisans: that is, in the years of structural adjustment, they thought it would be more profitable to be a shopkeeper than a small-scale manufacturer and that loans to expand trade would be preferable.

There was a reluctance to get involved in credit but for those who did want credit between 1995 and 2005, there was no significant change in the structure of demand. After 2005, however, there was another significant shift, as the attractiveness of borrowing to set up a small industry declined, as did the demand for funding the expansion of commercial activities. The demand for loans to set up small industries can be a proxy for the entrepreneurial intention to grow the size of the business – and in each of the survey years between 1975 and 2005, around 12% or 13% indicated such a preference. By 2015, this had declined to only 4%.

This is undoubtedly related to the new laws on the provision of social security for workers and apprentices in artisan workshops, as well as the attempts to regularise the sector and bring them into the tax system. The growing importance

Table 12.4 The type of loan that would be most convenient

(MENTIONS)

	1975		1982		1995		2005		2015	
	No.	%	No.	%	No.	%	No.	%	No.	%
Set up small industry	27	13.0	44	13.5	42	11.5	43	11.8	11	4.0
Raw materials	69	33.3	65	19.9	101	27.7	105	28.9	82	29.6
Tools and machinery	82	39.6	94	28.8	67	18.4	85	23.4	79	28.5
Expand commercial activities	12	5.8	30	9.2	88	24.2	83	22.9	37	13.4
Other	3	1.4	25	7.7	14	3.8	13	3.6	23	8.3
Nothing	14	6.8	68	20.9	52	14.3	34	9.4	45	16.2
TOTAL	207	100.0	326	100.0	364	100.0	363	100.0	277	100.0

	Chi-sq	DF	p-value
1975–2015	143.1757	20	1.26E-20
1975–1982	41.0466	5	9.18E-08
1982–1995	44.1673	5	2.14E-08
1995–2005	6.1703	5	0.2900
2005–2015	32.9936	5	3.77E-06
1982 & 2015	43.1177	5	3.50E-08

of repair activity may also have had an impact, and it may also had an effect on the decline of the demand for finance for the expansion of trading activities over the same period. Bank lending increased substantially, but the intention of artisans and the purpose of the expansion of the institutions of the Popular and Solidarity Economy was to improve capital investment in micro-firms, not necessarily grow them to the investment levels that would reclassify them as small industry. This is wholly consistent with the historic lack of priority of borrowing for SME expansion.

Irrespective of what the artisans thought the best use of a loan would be, they were also directly asked, if they could get a loan, would they be interested in setting up a small industry within their branch of activity? There were no conditions attached to this question, so it is independent of interest rates, the paperwork involved, the timescale or even the possibility of repayment. It merely asks, in very broad terms, 'would you be interested'. It is the measure of an un-costed dream, the attractiveness of which varies considerably over time.

The enthusiasm in 1975 was remarkable (Table 12.5). This, however, was a time when anything seemed possible. By 1982, it is the decline in the enthusiasm that is remarkable. The support for the marginal masses, instigated by the reformist government of General Rodrigues Lara, had been replaced by a reinforcement of

Table 12.5 Interested in a loan to set up a small industry

	1975		1982		1995		2005		2015	
	No.	*%*	*No.*	*%*	*No.*	*%*	*No.*	*%*	*No.*	*%*
Yes	129	71.3	142	50.2	161	52.4	200	63.7	125	49.8
No	52	28.7	141	49.8	146	47.6	114	36.3	126	50.2
	181	100.0	283	100.0	307	100.0	314	100.0	251	100.0

	Chi-sq	*DF*	*p-value*
1975–2015	33.9383	4	7.67E-07
1075–1982	20.2198	1	6.90E-06
1982–1995	0.3028	1	0.5822
1995–2005	8.0739	1	0.0045
2005–2015	11.0199	1	0.0009
1975 & 2015	20.0098	1	7.70E-06

the interests of the historic oligarchy, by the triumvirate of armed forces leaders who deposed Rodrigues Lara in a military coup in 1976. At the same time, the artisan producers of consumer goods were being replaced by the production of clothes, shoes and furniture in national and internationally owned factories. As structural adjustment was introduced in 1982, it was not a good time to be a micro-entrepreneur in Ecuador. This was confirmed in 1995 when, despite the pro-entrepreneurial rhetoric of the previous 13 years, there was no increase in the interest in becoming a small industry. This had changed by 2005, five years after the financial crash and dollarization, when interest in this type of growth had recovered again, if not to the levels of 1975. By 2015, however, the dream had once again retreated. Borrowing had increased, but not for growth into formal capitalist enterprises.

In conducting the life history interviews in 2015, we asked if they had been thinking of setting up a small industry or creating a larger business. The creation of a bigger business for many artisans was interpreted as opening up other branches, rather than investing in new machinery and technology – creating new routes to market, rather than product or process innovation. However, they were reticent about the possibilities.

Growing small firms: dreams and reality

Many of those who dream of setting up a formal SME are constrained by the need to be close to their clients or by the costs of growing. In the words of the button-maker who had invested his redundancy money from working in the Central Bank to set up his business:[13]

> The truth, one dreams of these things. But you also have to put your feet on the ground and, for such a thing, you need a lot of money. It is not that the

business rises up, as the majority would have the people believe. No, you also need people behind you to help you. But in our environment it is a little difficult for the people behind you to help … Many people have asked me to set up a branch [in a middle-class area]. Normally, I tell them that when people need something they know where to find me.

This issue of personal clients was also important for the owner of a beauty salon in an insecure barrio near the CHQ:[14]

Do you know what, I have thought about it, but, as I say, my clients have held me here. In the Valle [where she lives] my niece said to me three years ago, 'Aunt, leave the hairdressers there and come here, because I'm setting up large premises, let's set up a spa, and all that, the two of us'. 'Hey', I said, 'no, my clients, my clients; and I am together here with my husband [who works near the salon as a jeweller]. For me to go there, my husband, he alone does not have the means of paying the rent because he doesn't have much work' … I thought about all this and did not do it. Before, I had friends who said to me: 'How awful. If I were you I would hire stylists and I would set up a business in the North'. I said to them, no. I don't know if I was too conformist or I was afraid, I don't know.

According to a goldsmith, it is an impossible dream, even for the middle classes. He had looked at the possibility of moving into a modern shopping mall:[15]

No. At times I have tried to look for my own place in one of the large commercial centres. I tell you, when I went to find out about it they told me that it would cost $US 100,000: $US 50,000 now and $US 50,000 the following year. So, I said no. For the middle class, it is difficult for us to enter into this circle of the gentlemen who have their large shops. That's the reason that only they have everything in the shopping malls. Where am I going to get $US 100,000 to set up my own place in these commercial centres. I was thinking that for around $US 30,000 perhaps I could, selling my car, taking out a loan, but there is no way I could ever do such a thing.

A shoemaker, working in a small rented workshop, carrying out repairs for a declining customer base in a dangerous and insecure barrio, which his clients don't feel safe visiting, considers expansion in terms of moving his workshop into a larger space that would double as a new home. He pays rent for his home in another part of the city and, if he could get a loan, he would move elsewhere:[16]

If some institution would facilitate it, I would look for bigger premises and make one single place. More than anything, I have not asked for it, I've not sought it … I don't know, perhaps I will try to see if they will help me or not … to see if I can get a small place that is bigger. As I say, it would be good: set up the home and the small workshop, instead of paying double rent.

This answer to the question about getting a loan to expand is hardly entrepreneurial. An ambition to expand the workspace can also mean a very modest change for the artisans. A tailor who occupies a space in a mall in the Historic Centre of Quito has never sought formal credit. In the past, she made clothes and sold them on her street stall, before moving into a small space in a renovated commercial centre where, like most tailors in Quito, she now mainly carries out alterations and repairs. For her, expanding the business means finding space for an ironing board:[17]

> Yes we have thought about it and we have an administrator who knows we want to grow. For example, that little stall (pointing cross the passageway) belongs to a friend who has died and the children, seeing that I am working here, came and said that, when they come to sell it, they are going to tell me first to see if I can buy it. So, I said to them, good.
>
> Our administrator has been indicating that we can, as the premises are not open, as they don't want to work, as everything is closed, so we could ask that they give it to us, people who are working. Because, as you see, people come to leave things to be ironed, and I don't have anywhere to do it. I don't have anywhere to iron, because to iron you need space. I have lost this ironing work and I know how to do all this – ironing trousers, suits, whatever. But I have lost it because I don't have anywhere to iron.
>
> So, yes we have thought about it. I wish we could grow and, if it is not open, that they will give us the space opposite. Yes we have thought about this, but, then I don't know. I don't know what will happen with us here in the Commercial Centre, because this is already dead; there is no movement, they don't come to work. Some are closed, some have been turned into store rooms.
>
> Before, we worked with borrowed money, as they say, with *chulquo* money, in the street. All our lives we have worked with this money. But here, now? Not now. We cannot do anything like that, because there is no way we are able to pay daily, weekly – that's the way they pay in the street, daily more than anything. On the other hand, here, no. More than anything we cannot take on debt because there is no way of paying it back.

When pressed on setting up a bigger business, she said:

> The rhythm that I work at, I decided I am going to work like this, because as I say, the business as a trader is no longer functioning, so I am left with this and I'm happy. I am happy to do all this. Because there are some people who say to me: 'The patience of you to carry out repairs, I couldn't repair these things, I couldn't do it.' I work, I repair and I am pleased to do it. I like to do it. I am very happy with this.

Some don't want to expand because of the problems that hiring workers would bring. The owner of a workshop that makes cookers said:[18]

No, no, I had no ambition to set up a larger business because I always had problems with workers who were my friends. Those who came, cost me. One is now in Canada, another in London. I paid what they asked. Another who was an apprentice, every day he went at 5.00 for his studies; but when he wanted, he came to work, when he didn't want to, he didn't turn up; so I said to him, that's enough; he asked me for social security and all that, I told him 'no more', enough.

Other artisans expressed their ambiguity as follows:

- Jeweller-watchmaker: Yes, but no, not now. My idea was to do this, but not now. I don't even think about it because there is no work, neither in jewellery nor in watches.
- Shoemaker: I don't know about this. Amongst us, this possibility does not exist. I've never been interested.
- Hat-maker: No, because for this you need money and you have to be affiliated to a guild, other things, so no.
- Goldsmith: There was an idea, but the opportunity never presented itself.
- Tailor: Obviously I would have liked to, with the experience that I have, since when I began, it would have been another song.

Yet other artisans hang on to the dream. A 65-year-old making spinning tops said:[19]

Yes, the issue is to project to grow, no? So, in the moment of growth, to acquire a good lot of machinery, which I don't have yet, for everything is a process. I still have to adapt a shed. I am in the process because I also don't have the money and, as I don't want to put myself in debt to start, and as I have to produce goods for fairs, I have to put all my efforts into working here [in this workshop]. So I want to do this next year.

I feel fulfilled because I have foreign machinery, and I have machinery of my own invention, national machinery – not just in this workshop but in my house. I have still to adapt a small factory, new sheds, to produce not only spinning tops but also some new things that I have always had in mind. I have my patterns stored away. I took them out once but I didn't return to complete them, and now I want to produce them in the best way possible. This is the project for next year, which is now, since time is flying by, we are only four months to the end of the year. I don't think I am going to manage it, because I have to dedicate myself to work for some fairs that are almost on us.

A restorer of religious images said:[20] 'Certainly, yes. One has always wanted to progress, to own something big.' Asked if it was within his plans, he said 'Yes, to begin making large images, meters high, much bigger.' They did it where he worked before, but he does not have the space. The work is also hazardous, which makes working in a small space dangerous for his health: 'I need space and, since there are chemicals as well, they are very strong.' He was not averse to taking a loan, for he had a loan to start up and has had loans since then, for materials. However, restoring religious images hardly lends itself to expansion into a small industry.

The forces of the market sometimes conspire against ambition. A guitar-maker, whose trade suffered from competition from Chinese imports, was forced to accept cheaper Chinese guitars for resale in his workshop. He had tried to go against the flow and would do so again if had the opportunity:[21]

> Yes. I haven't done it. I have tried. We set up another workshop. People didn't buy. We paid rent for two years. During the time of the Chinese. I set it up, but it was already bad. I had it in Calle Maldonado. We paid rent for nothing.

When asked if he would try again, he said:

> Yes, I have to work out how, where to put myself and try to advance. Rather, not to stay as I am. If there is an opportunity, you have to press ahead.

This possibility of setting up a small industry, of growing their business, is a fairly consistent dream for around half of artisans in Quito. But it is a dream, rather than a practical priority, and the commitment to the dream fluctuates over time. It was strongest before the advent of neoliberalism and it was weakest during the Correa administration, when much of the work of the artisans was regularised, the regulatory system was modernised and expanded and, paradoxically, when loans for development were extended most widely.

Notes

1 Those artisans who had used a start-up loan, including those who had obtained a bank loan, were asked if they had applied for a bank loan after the initial loan.
2 Life history interview BC11.
3 Life history interview BC16.
4 Life history interview CU3.
5 Life history interview BC8.
6 The eastern Amazon region of Ecuador.
7 Life history interview BC7.
8 Life history interview BC8.
9 Life history interview BC13.
10 Life history interview BC17.
11 Life history interview BC11.
12 Life history interview MR2.
13 Life history interview BC10.
14 Life history interview CU8.
15 Life history interview CU3.
16 Life history interview MJ2.

17 Life history interview MJ5.
18 Life history interview MR2.
19 Life history interview CU6.
20 Life history interview CU9.
21 Life history interview MJ8.

13 Major issues and future prospects

Introduction: systems of regulation

Regulatory systems operate to manage risks that individuals and organisations are exposed to when they are involved in transactions with other individuals and organisations. They are a feature of capitalist development that did not exist during its mercantilist phase, when British merchants who were trading across the globe operated on the basis of trust, face to face interaction and letters of agreement (James Finlay & Co., 1951). Before this, artisans in feudal times were tied to large landowners who controlled their activities, a system of regulation that was transferred to the colonies, and persisted in the guilds in modified forms through to the twenty-first century, as we saw earlier. However, as the state has increasingly become involved in regulation, particularly in relation to taxes and employment law, capitalist firms and neoliberal theorists have opposed this, and it has become the focus of attention for most analyses of informal economic activity.

Regulation by the state is a necessary feature in complex democratic societies where business relations are distant and impersonal (Cross and Peña, 2006). In democratic plural societies, trade union pressure and changes in business culture have produced changes in the way workforces are treated. At the same time, capital and labour are constantly trying to find ways to evade the system. In the analysis of this interaction between an emerging set of regulatory procedures and socio-economic groups that are trying to avoid the clutches of the system, two conflicting views emerge about the informal sector, often held simultaneously. Both the World Bank and the left accept that 'informal activity is work outside the regulative ambit of the state' (Harriss-White, 2010, 170) but at the same time, it is argued that regulations are stifling the sector (de Soto, 1989).

The fact that some activities take place outside the government regulatory system is an attribute of informality that has been reified into a defining characteristic. Clearly, not all informal activity is unregulated (unless informality is defined in this way) and the salience of regulation for microenterprises has been overstated. What is salient for these micro-firms is reflected in how they see their lives and their firms changing over time; how they identify their most important problems at any historical juncture; and what needs to happen to improve their situation. We asked the artisans whether their standard of living and their businesses had improved, what were the most important problems they faced and what action was needed to improve their circumstances. As we will see, red tape and regulation are almost invisible. What emerges is a critique of neoliberal financial systems and the free-market propositions of the WTO, the IMF and the World Bank. Regulation is a non-issue for micro-firms – except insofar as they would like to see it applied to financial systems and free market policies that allow unfair competition and the dumping of goods that are priced below the real costs of production.

Changing standards, problems and solutions

There is little to distinguish between the artisans' standard of living and how their businesses are performing.[1] When asked about living standards and business performance over the previous three years, 1975 was the most positive time (Tables A.13.1 and A.13.2). There was then a steady decline in living standards from 1975 to 1995, a decline that accelerated through the years of hyperinflation, the banking collapse and dollarization, before recovering during the anti-globalisation government of Correa (Figure 13.1).

There is a similar pattern for the situation of artisan workshops (Figure 13.2). A decline in confidence by 1982, followed by a deteriorating trend through the neoliberal period, before a recovery during Correa's tenure. While one-third reported a deteriorating trend in 1975, by 2005 this had increased to more than half. In 2015, the artisans were still suffering but their circumstances were better than in 1995 and 2005.

When the artisans were asked why their businesses had changed, whether for the better or worse, the main reason was consistently about the level of demand for their products or services. If things were better, it was mainly because demand had increased, there were more clients, and so on. If things were worse, it was because of a decline in demand, lack of orders, fewer clients, lack of work, etc. The

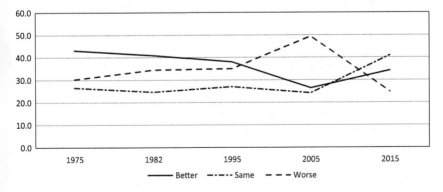

Figure 13.1 Change in living standards

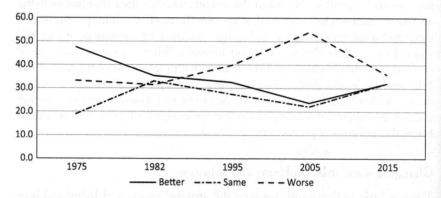

Figure 13.2 Change in business situation

markets for their products declined through structural adjustment, globalisation and the crisis of neoliberalism until it reached its nadir in 2005.

Most important problems

When the artisans were asked about the three most important problems they faced in their work, the answers were more revealing about a range of other issues. The issue that they identified as the most important problems can be seen in Table 13.1. The meanings of these simple categories can be explained as follows:[2]

> **None:** These are artisans who said they had no problems or who could not think of any when asked to identify the main three problems for their business.
>
> **Problems with labour:** included shortages of labour or complaints about their workers, such as low skills, drunkenness and laziness, along with apprentices who did not learn what they were being taught.
>
> **Lack of Capital:** including lack of adequate tools and machinery and the need for new technology.
>
> Problems with the **Workplace** included its location, the rent, its size and the lack of space for expansion.
>
> Problems with **materials** included the supply, cost and quality.
>
> Lack of **demand** was generally expressed as lack of orders, work, clients and access to markets.
>
> Problems with **clients** included their poverty and therefore their inability to buy from them, their inability to pay when they did order something, and their failure to return to pick up goods that were either made to order or had been repaired.
>
> Problems with **government and the economy** were mainly about economic policy, rather than regulations affecting the artisans.

Table 13.1 Most important problems

	1975		1982		1995		2005		2015	
	Number	%	Number	%	Number	%	Number	%	Number	%
None	20	10.6	45	15.1	49	15.3	23	7.5	14	5.6
Problems with labour (incl. shortage)	14	7.4	47	15.8	12	3.6	15	4.7	17	6.7
Lack of capital	34	17.9	33	11.0	17	5.3	18	5.6	2	0.9
Workplace (size, cost, location)	18	9.6	23	7.7	21	6.4	19	6.0	14	5.5
Materials (cost, supply, quality)	37	19.8	68	23.1	20	6.4	21	6.7	30	11.8
Demand	24	12.9	24	8.1	56	17.4	82	26.2	44	17.3
Clients (too poor / don't pay)	14	7.7	9	3.1	13	4.1	4	1.3	5	2.1
Competition	8	4.2	2	0.8	42	13.2	55	17.7	34	13.4
Delinquency	0	0.0	0	0.0	14	4.5	32	10.1	30	11.9
Govt./economy	8	4.3	6	2.2	21	6.5	26	8.4	26	10.2
Not enough time	0	0.0	11	3.6	2	0.6	0	0.0	6	2.3
Finance/debt	0	0.0	4	1.4	5	1.4	1	0.2	1	0.5
Electricity	0	0.0	0	0.0	22	6.9	2	0.6	0	0.0
Other	11	5.8	24	8.0	27	8.4	16	5.6	31	12.2
Total	188	100.0	296	100.0	321	100.0	313	100.0	255	100.0

The question of **competition** included competition with other artisans and national manufacturers, but also with cheap imported goods. These included second hand clothes and shoes, mainly from the United States; and new goods (such as clothes, shoes and watches) that were imported from Korea and China and sold at prices that were less than the cost of repairing them in Ecuador. This 'unfair competition' was linked to the 'dumping' of east Asian goods, sometimes at less than the cost of production, sold via new shops that were owned by Korean and Chinese migrants.

Delinquency first appeared as a problem in 1995, when jewellers complained that 'people do not buy gold now. They prefer to buy cheaper imported jewellery'. The problem has grown over time.

Time was an issue for some in 1982, when a small number of artisans had more work than they could handle and complained that they did not have enough time to complete their orders. It was also mentioned a handful of times in 2015. Being so busy that they did not have enough time to meet demand disappeared as an issue during the neoliberal years.

Lack of finance is thought by economists to be a major issue for small firms. It did not register at all in 1975 and has only been mentioned sporadically since then. In 1982, for example, three artisans mentioned the lack of credit and one pointed to the problem of debt. Over the period of the study, it was identified a major problem by 11 artisans out of almost 1400 workshop owners.

Other problems include mainly personal issues such as old age and the health of the artisan or a member of his/her family, along with lack of skills or training, transport problems, contamination (mainly from urban transport), and so on.

There is no evidence of an overpowering state that crushes enterprise and inhibits the growth of small firms. Following de Soto (1986), their failure to grow into capitalist organisations because of the limitations imposed on them by a regulatory state is seen as a main reason for the failure of capitalism to develop in LDCs. Amongst small firms in Quito, however, the complaints about government were usually about the management of the economy. In 1975, eight artisans (4% of the total) mentioned problems with the government or the economy; but only one of these mentioned taxes and no one mentioned regulations or red tape. The remainder complained about the rising cost of living, which they attributed to government policy. In 1982, only three artisans mentioned unhelpful laws (one specifically mentioned the Labour Code) and no one mentioned either taxes or other regulations. In 1995, only one artisan mentioned bureaucratic procedures as the main issue he was facing. Their main concern with government continued to be the way they were managing the economy, including rising inflation, and to a lesser extent the fact that they were not helping the artisans more.[3]

In 2005, after more than 20 years of neoliberal economic policy, problems with the government and economy were increasing rather than decreasing, but they were still only salient as the most important problem for 8% of small workshop owners. Not one artisan identified red tape, taxes or regulations as their main problem. The problem with government, for three of the five artisans who mentioned the government, was that they did not look after artisans and were not helping enough. One mentioned corruption and another wanted more control by the customs authorities over imports.

In 2015, 10% of artisans mentioned government or the economy as their major problem and most of these referred to the state of the economy or the fact that the government was not giving enough support to the artisans, but seven (out of 255) mentioned problems with municipal paperwork and bureaucracy and five more complained about taxes. These issues were related to the formalisation of the artisans, the electronic modernisation of the retail economy, and the fact that the *Municipio* was enforcing planning controls over such matters as the signage in the historic centre and the health hazards created by some workshops. At this stage, the enforcement of tax policies, the regularisation of the informal sector and the enforcement of municipal by-laws were raising new problems for the artisans. Policies for formalising the informal sector were felt as negative developments by a small but growing proportion of artisans.

The statistical significance of the changes in the main problems for artisans from survey to survey (after those who said they had no problems or who gave a number of other, mainly personal, responses were set aside) can be seen in Table A.13.3 and Figure A.13.1. Moving from year to year, the changes that were taking place were highly significant, with the exception of the 1995–2005 period.

In 1975, the main problems were with the cost, availability and quality of raw materials, followed by a lack of capital. By 1982, after substantial growth in the economy, the problems with raw materials had increased but problems with the labour force, including a shortage of skilled labour, superseded the lack of capital. As the economy grew, the lack of skilled labour increased as a major problem for the artisans.

Lack of demand was an issue for 13% in 1975, but this fell to 8% in 1982.[4] By 1995, lack of demand had become the main issue for the artisans, followed by competition. Structural adjustment had sucked demand out of the economy in the 1982–95 period. The competition was mainly as a result of the free market policies associated with early globalisation. It included competition from second-hand clothes and shoes that were being imported from the United States under WTO free market rules. Almost all tailors and shoemakers mentioned this during the interviews in 1995 and although it did not always appear as the most important issue, it was consistently one of the top three most important problems.

At this time there was also a major issue with electricity and water, which were rationed. As the national economy continued to grow, albeit more slowly, public sector expenditure was slashed, supply had failed to keep up with demand and the failure of these public utilities affected the artisans' productivity and output. This was also a time of rapid technological change. Personal computing and desktop printing had reached Ecuador and artisan printers were confronted by the emergence of sophisticated photocopiers in specialist outlets that imported expensive machines from the United States and Europe. In addition, smaller photocopying machines were appearing in corner shops across the city.

The transformation of the Historic Centre of Quito was underway, with the displacement of street traders a priority in order to make the city centre more attractive as a destination for international tourists (Middleton, 2003). The artisans were also affected by the regeneration. Some were displaced or cut off from their markets by the building of bridges and tunnels. Others suffered from the displacement of the red light district across the Avenue of 24 May, into the heart of the artisan economy. Thieves and other 'delinquents' were also moved out of the HCQ. As the city centre became more secure for the tourists in the 1990s, displaced thieves and prostitutes created insecurity for the artisans in their traditional heartlands. Their customers were scared off.

By 2005, the greatest problem was the lack of demand, followed by (unfair) competition. Together, these issues accounted for 44% of their main problems. The importing of second-hand clothes was stopped in 1999, on health grounds, in the face of strong opposition from the United States and national importers who were allied to the coastal oligarchy. The new problem was that the market for artisan products was flooded with cheap consumer goods manufactured in East Asia.

As the doctrine of free trade took hold globally, problems with demand and competition increased almost five times between 1982 and 2005. Artisans pointed to the economic situation, inflation and dollarization. For 10% of artisans, however, delinquency and lack of security was their main problem in 2005 and this increased further through to 2015 – although lack of demand continued to be the main problem. The difficulties of the years of structural adjustment that had sucked demand out of the economy were compounded by the financial and fiscal crises around the millennium and, while the situation was better in 2015, it had not fully recovered.

We saw in Chapter 11 how access to finance for micro-firms became a major issue in neoliberal thinking from the 1980s onwards – how to provide the capital investment that would encourage the growth of small firms in developing economies and thereby contribute to the alleviation of household poverty. Throughout the 40 years, access to capital was a declining issue for the artisans (Figure A.13.1). From the second most important problem in 1975, it became the least important in 2015, mentioned by only two artisans. This was partly due to the increased access to credit during the Correa administration, making capital investment easier. However, the decline before this had nothing to do with successful applications for finance. As we saw in the previous chapter, applications for credit were relatively flat until after the banking crash, when they declined; and success rates fell in 1995 before rising again in 2005, when the demand for loans fell. The problems deriving from the introduction of free market policies became more salient: the problems of unfair competition and lack of demand soared after 1982, before easing in the Correa era when selective import substitution was reintroduced (COMEXI, 2009; COMEX, 2013).

What is required to improve their situation?

In 1975, the main issue was the need for an improvement in their capital (Table 13.2), was followed by a demand for more credit – which meant that almost half of the artisans mentioned either more credit or capital investment. As Ecuador emerged from being an impoverished agro-exporting economy, the clamour for assets as a way out of poverty for the self-employed was loud and clear. Before the rise of neoliberalism and well before the international surge in the popularity of microfinance, however, the importance of credit declined substantially. From 1982, it never again became the main issue for more than 10% of artisans. In 2015, following Correa's financial reforms, only 4% of artisans said it was the main requirement for improving their situation.

By 1982, the main issue was government policies, by which the artisans meant that they were looking for more government support or that the government was mismanaging the economy. In 1995, however, demand issues were at the forefront: it was an improvement in market conditions that emerged as most important, followed by improvements in levels of income or employment (the amount of work they were commissioned to do), which for the self-employed means other aspects of market conditions. Almost half the artisans referred to these conditions. In 2005, following the financial crisis and a prolonged period of government instability, market conditions and government policies were at the forefront of their minds. In 2015, these remained the two key issues, although government policies declined in importance and issues with the workplace increased.

The two consistent trends are the decline in the importance of new capital and the increase in the need for better market conditions (Figure 13.3). The deterioration of market conditions for these microenterprises, in an era when free-market theory was raised to the level of an international religion for many economists, is remarkable. The surge in the importance of government policies in 2005, however, reflect the perceived failure of the government to deal with the three major economic upheavals around the millennium: the banking crash, which we have dealt with, the dollarization of the economy, and the unfair competition from cheap imports from China.

The impact of dollarization on artisan activities

We saw in Chapter 4 how local elites were able to internationalise their wealth and protect their interests during the banking crash. The government bailed out the owners of the banks and the wealthy elite, whilst the self-employed and others in the informal sector had their savings frozen and later transferred into dollars at a considerable loss. Without sentiment, the costs of the neoliberal crisis were transferred to the sector of the economy that had been celebrated as micro-entrepreneurial saviours of the future.

Table 13.2 What is required to improve their situation?*

	1975		1982		1995		2005		2015	
	Number	%	Number	%	Number	%	Number	%	Number	%
Capital	52	32.3	45	19.4	21	7.7	11	4.6	6	3.5
Other factors of production	12	7.5	28	12.1	25	9.2	25	10.5	19	11.0
Market conditions	18	11.2	29	12.5	75	27.6	81	34.0	65	37.6
Income/employment	24	14.9	25	10.8	55	20.2	3	1.3	11	6.4
Government policies	23	14.3	62	26.7	44	16.2	82	34.5	46	26.6
Credit	26	16.1	17	7.3	26	9.6	22	9.2	7	4.0
Workplace	6	3.7	26	11.2	26	9.6	14	5.9	19	11.0
Total	161	100	232	100	272	100	238	100	173	100.0

*Removed None, NR/DK, other

	Chi-sq	DF	p-value
1975–2015	232.9960	24	3.77E-36
1975–1982	29.9277	6	4.06E-05
1982–1995	42.5268	6	1.45E-07
1995–2005	63.3851	6	9.21E-12
2005–2015	17.4105	6	0.0079
1975&2015	94.5634	6	3.41E-18

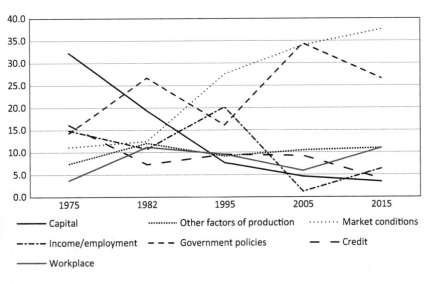

Figure 13.3 What is needed to improve their situation

Shortly after the dollarization of the Ecuadorean economy, the World Bank said:

> Although there is no information about the level of poverty for the country as a whole beyond 2001, we know that the standard of living of households in the urban area has improved significantly since 2000/01, and this has translated into a decline in poverty in these zones. This improvement is due fundamentally to the economic stability created by dollarization
>
> (Banco Mundial, 2004, 7)

and

> There is no doubt that the decision to dollarize the economy improved the investment climate, reassured potential investors and, as a result, potentially raised the capacity of the economy to generate employment and reduce poverty.
>
> (Banco Mundial, 2004, *Resumen Ejecutivo*, i)

However, the World Bank offered no evidence to substantiate these positive assessments of the impact of dollarization on poverty. From the point of view of the artisans in 2005, dollarization was typically described as 'a disaster', 'fatal', 'not only bad but the worst', 'terrible' and 'shattering' (Middleton, 2007). A small number did say the impact was positive and others indicated that there were both

Table 13.3 The impact of dollarization on the business

	2005		2015	
	No	%	No	%
Positive	20	6.8	23	13.2
Negative	234	79.3	95	54.6
Positive and negative	21	7.1	21	12.1
None	20	6.8	35	20.1
Total	295	100.0	174	100.0

positive and negative consequences but the short-term impact of dollarization was overwhelmingly negative.

When the artisans were asked about the impact of dollarization on their businesses in 2005 and 2015, the responses indicated the perceived impact of dollarization in the short term (2005) and over the longer term (2015).[5] Around 80% of artisans described it in negative terms in 2005 (Table 13.3). In 2015, the firms providing positive answers had doubled and those who said there was no impact tripled. Over the longer period, artisans who remembered it in detrimental terms had fallen to just over half. However, we need to keep in mind that these firms are survivors, the turnover rate in the number of firms was around one-third between 2005 and 2015, and the negative impact of dollarization will have been responsible for some of the business failures.

For a very small minority in 2005, dollarization was 'excellent', it meant they could charge what they wanted in a period when where there was widespread confusion over exchange rates and pricing: 'I charge more for the service and now I have a house and the business has grown' [Jeweller]. For others, there was not much impact. A car mechanic said: 'It did not affect me much. At times it is better because one can charge a little bit more in dollars.' This artisan, however, when asked about the most important problem affecting his business said 'dollarization', because his clients could not pay what he was charging.

The points of view of the great majority were expressed as follows:

It was fatal. The change was difficult. Now repairs cost less.

(Jeweller/watchmaker)

We charged more before and it had more value; now we charge one dollar and it is not enough.

(Hairdresser)

It was painful, making everything very expensive. Why would anyone send anything to be repaired when they can buy new for the same price?

(Shoemaker)

The small artisans were most affected because [the price of everything] increased.

(Carpenter)

In addition to the criticism of the way in which dollarization affected the value of the currency and increased the costs of consumption in general, the artisans criticised dollarization in terms of its impact on a range of matters that were important for their businesses and their well-being. These included the increased cost of raw materials; the loss of savings and increase in debt; the incompetent management of the change; the exaggeration of prices by artisans and others; the negative impact on clients; the rising cost of consumer goods; and the negative effect of increased artisan prices on competition with cheaper Asian imports.

The almost universal experience was that 'business declined'. In contrast with the World Bank's assertions about the positive impact of dollarization on poverty, the vast majority clearly said that they were suffering greatly. It would be no exaggeration to say that the effect was traumatic. By 2015, the trauma had eased, but the memories had not faded.

The short-term negativity was not replaced by long-term positivity, but the artisans became more likely to view the economic stability that later resulted as beneficial for their businesses. In response to the same question that was asked in 2005, the stories were similar. A leather goods manufacturer in the CHQ said: 'I lost my savings in the bank; when they returned them to me, I had lost a great deal.' While jewellers in general were more positive than most, for one jeweller, it was even worse: 'I lost some savings and the thing that happened made me lose my business.' Another jeweller complained that 'dollarization affected me strongly, because everything became expensive and I did not have enough money; things cost more than they were worth'. A shoemaker blamed dollarization for an increase in the prices of raw materials: 'Yes, it affected us, because it affected the raw materials; the [imported] raw materials are very expensive.' A baker said that dollarization was unfavourable because 'I lost savings and the price of everything rose exorbitantly.' For the owner of a mechanical workshop dollarization was the low point: 'the savings that I had ended up as nothing'. For others, the effects were not felt immediately: a tailor said: 'at first we did not feel it, but later it got worse'. Most artisans, however, thought that it was worse at first, and then eased as things settled down. More typical was the tailor who said: 'It affected me a great deal, because I did not know how to manage the currency and I lost money; but as things stabilised it got better.'

A television repairman said that 'in the beginning it was better, because people spent; later, it declined'. At first he had his workshop in the more affluent north of the city and he was able to charge what he liked. As television technology advanced after the Millennium, however, TVs lasted longer, parts became extremely expensive and those who could afford new and better, did not get the old ones repaired. He discovered that there was a limit to what he could charge, independent of the costs of imported parts. His over-charging ground to a halt and, at the same time, rents were rising as the new middle classes continued to increase demand for property in the area. Because of the combined effect of dollarization, changing technology, the rising cost of spare parts, demand for property rising, rents increasing and demand falling, he had to move to the less expensive and less lucrative south of the city – where the working-class population still wanted to have their TVs repaired.

On the other hand, a shoemaker whose work was mainly repair and who worked in a lower-middle class barrio in the south of the city said that dollarization 'worked very well for me. Business improved. When they dollarized, I was charging 80,000 sucres (just over US$3 for a repair); after, it was US$5 and now, in the end, its $20.'[6] Another shoemaker in the same area said: 'The change in the currency was a problem. We weren't prepared for the new money. A hand-made pair of shoes cost 250,000 sucres, and at the rate of exchange at the time, that was US$10. But the cost of the raw materials rose and the finished shoes cost US$30. … Although, I had my savings in dollars and when the currency changed, I benefited; I didn't lose.'

Although the experience of artisans was not uniformly bad, it is clear from the life histories that dollarization was part of a series of misfortunes to befall businesses around the millennium – the financial collapse, the increase in delinquency, competition with cheap imports and dollarization came together to make life very difficult. After 15 years, some of these events and processes of the crisis of neoliberalism in Ecuador merged into one and remained in the thoughts of the artisans as a unified bad experience. A jeweller explained:[7]

> In the good times there was more work, with the sucre, we had enough for everything. If you made money you had enough to eat, there was enough to enjoy life, and save … But then came the dollarization, and afterwards, times got difficult, the business deteriorated, we were affected by the amount of cheap watches, the cellular phones, all this, then the robbery of jewels. Before, even although they could be robbed, everyone went around wearing jewels, everyone. Not now. You don't see anyone with good jewels, nobody.

This was a jeweller who thought that the best times his craft were actually during neoliberalism in the 1990s:

> We were not tremendously well off, but there was enough for everything, to save something, to do whatever. … [Dollarization] destroyed us, the devaluation, they took the savings, the banks failed. Haaay, we were the victims of a swindle.

Some artisans feasted on the uncertainty of the times. The owner of a beauty salon said:[8]

> The first two years were excellent, very good. I think this happened with everyone. But I think that after two years we then saw, as you say, the reality.

She, and many others, priced themselves out of the market. For some, the rising prices contained elements of rising prices for raw materials and they found themselves in competition with cheap imports. A shoemaker explained how the combination of dollarization and cheap Chinese imports affected his ability to compete and how it impacted on his living costs:[9]

> Before dollarization, I sold shoes at 185,000 sucres, 200,000 sucres … One month before dollarization I was selling shoes at 250,000 sucres (US$10), and when dollarization started, I sold at US$20, US$25. But when the government of Lucio Gutiérrez[10] came in, he gave free entry. … Senor Gutiérrez gave free entry with the sale of visas to the Chinese, who arrived here with cheap goods.
>
> They sold shoes at US$10, US$12, US$8, beautiful models but they were not leather, rather they were made of synthetic materials. But as our economy was not strong enough to buy shoes at $30, $40, $50, everyone bought their shoes. And what happened was that, for example, in shirts, belts, so many things, the Chinese almost made us disappear. But I'll tell you now, as our economy, the dollar has not served us for anything, we are devalued.

Another shoemaker said:[11]

> For me, yes, it affected me a great deal. Now they don't want to spend, because, in truth, you can get a pair of shoes for US$20, US$15, as low as US10. And to repair a pair of soles can easily cost US$20. So, they say 'why should I pay to repair. Better I buy new'. So they don't leave them to be repaired. [The business has declined] more or less since dollarization … It is hard.

He struggled from day to day, like the tailor who complained that there was no possibility of saving:[12]

> Before, in sucres, we got a lot of money for our work; now, we get little. It goes, when one has a family, it goes just the same.

In the longer term, for some of the survivors, there was a tension between the stabilisation of the economy and the performance of their firms. It was not all negative. A sewing machine repair man said: 'From the sucre to the dollar was absolutely horrible for everyone: there was less work, until we became accustomed to the dollar. A hat-maker said that at the time of the government of Mahuad,[13] 'all this sad era was difficult. In these past eight years of stabilisation, with dollarization, we've been able to live with a certain stability'. A jeweller said things were cheaper before but 'with the dollarization we lost control, but equally, in any case, we kept going'.

Table 13.4 Have cheap imports had an impact on the business?

	2005		2015	
	No.	%	No.	%
Yes	169	53.9	128	50.0
No	145	46.1	128	50.0
Total	314	100.0	256	100.0

The impact of cheap imported goods

The direct impact of cheap imports on artisans is twofold. On the one hand, competition from cheap imported consumer goods eats into their markets and makes their enterprises more precarious. On the other hand, they can reduce the cost of inputs, through cheaper materials and equipment. This should allow the artisans to improve their technology, increase productivity and sell their goods on the market at cheaper prices than would otherwise be the case.

In Table 13.4, we can see that more than half of the artisans thought that cheap imports had had an impact on their businesses in 2005 and by 2015 this had not changed much. In 2015, more than one-third who had been impacted mentioned competition from cheap Chinese imports and a similar proportion mentioned the cheapness and/or poor quality of the imports, without reference to their country of origin.

All types of artisans speak of 'unfair competition' but the traditional artisans such as tailors and shoemakers suffer more than others from cheap imports (Table A.13.4). In 2005, more than 80% of these artisans complained about the effect of cheap imports on their businesses. Between 2005 and 2015, the situation of shoemakers became even worse, while that of the tailors, some of whom may have benefited from the school uniforms policy, had improved. Nevertheless, two-thirds of tailors still said that cheap imports had a detrimental effect. By 2015, the situation of carpenters had also deteriorated, with almost 80% saying they were suffering. The least likely to suffer a detrimental effect were mechanics, stonemasons and printers: mechanics because of the importance of repair activities and masons and printers because there is no international competition for their outputs.

Unfair competition

In 2005, the survey indicated that the artisans thought that the quality of the imports was poor and, for those who pay less for their materials and equipment, the savings were short term (Middleton, 2007). That is, they had to buy new tools and equipment more often than before because of the low quality of the imported goods. However, because of competition and the reduced income they were now receiving, they could not afford to replace the faulty equipment and tools. In addition, because of a mixture of the high investment needed for the repair of items such as new cars with their computerised systems and the cheapness of imported consumer goods such as shoes and watches, traditional artisan repair work was disappearing. As incomes and employment had declined amongst their clients, their markets had disintegrated further.

By 2015, there was no significant change from 2005. The effect of Chinese and other competition was expressed by an artisan manufacturer of leather goods who complained that clients neither came to buy nor to seek repairs. First, they are losing clients because people are buying cheaper Chinese products; Second, because they are of lower quality, they deteriorate quickly and do not last. Third, because they are so cheap, people do not have them repaired – it is almost as expensive to have them repaired as it is to buy new again. They prefer to spend a little more for new goods of poor quality, and the cycle of built-in obsolescence begins again.

These imports affect the artisans, but they also impoverish the buyers. The main argument in favour of cheap imports is that they reduce the costs of consumption for the majority of the population. However, because the products wear out more quickly, they have to buy them more often. Because they are poor, they cannot buy good quality shoes and other products. Because their income is low and intermittent, they take the cheapest option. It is cheaper in the short term, but it turns out to be the more expensive option in the longer term. To buy an expensive pair of shoes they would need to have savings, which they do not have. As a shoemaker said, 'the economy does not allow someone to buy a pair of shoes for US$50. We can't compete with the factories – they can produce them cheaper'.

The growth of the negative effect on the carpenters (Table A.13.4) was mainly due to the mass production of flat-pack furniture. Imported MDF is turned into furniture in Ecuador, through factory production of the materials that can be erected at home by the customer. Local wage labour is created and some carpenters have adapted to offer the assembly of the furniture in middle-class homes, but the traditional skills of the artisan furniture maker are no longer in demand.

The challenges for radio and TV repair workers were different. As the technology of the televisions improved, they lasted longer. The middle classes would transfer their old TVs to another room when they bought the latest technology and when they eventually broke down, they would throw them out. The working class would seek to have them repaired, but they lasted longer, the parts were expensive,[14] and the profits were minimal.

Shoemakers explained how there was no demand for either their manufactured shoes or the repair services they offer. They argued that many customers cannot tell the difference between modern plastic materials and real leather, their ignorance costs them more in the long run, and artisans are going out of business. Some of these artisans will say that repairs can be more lucrative than making new shoes, but lucrative is an inadequate word for their declining economic situation. Many have not made a new pair of shoes 'in years'.[15]

Not since the arrival of Chinese shoes. People see a nice pair of shoes in the window and they buy them, not very expensive. Why repair, when you can buy already made. Now I don't even have a last to make new shoes … So they say 'better I buy a new pair. Why should I pay so much', but they are poor quality'.

The artisans have been resisting, but to no effect. A tailor explained:[16]

When the Chinese imports started, we were all ruined. In every branch of activity we were ruined. Imagine, shirts that for me, I cannot possible make at 3 dollars; not in any circumstances, not even stealing the dollars, would it even cover the raw materials to start with. So they come and sell at 3 dollars … Some two or three years ago we came out in a … protest demonstration in which we gave it to the Chinese, because we were being left without work. A lot of colleagues who are members of the Junta, we are in a bad way.

He was then asked if there was any response to their action:

No, because everything is still the same here. Do you know how many Chinese shops there are? They have cornered the market. Everything: rucksacks, shoes, clothes, imitation jewellery, everything, everything. We, we who work here in the country, what? We can't compete with the Chinese, we can't compete with the imports. There are gigantic containers that arrive; I see them here, just here in [Plaza] San Francisco. There are trucks, three or four containers. The merchandise is coming in.

There are also cheap imported raw materials for tailors but using them, as some customers want, strikes at the pride of the artisan. They prefer to work with better quality imported materials and with good quality national materials, which are being squeezed out of the market:[17]

Before, the imported cloth was expensive, but I always used imported cloth, it was dear but the quality was good; not like now. Chinese cloth is annoying, everything is annoying. No, no, before the quality of the imported cloth was good, the price was also better, but the national cloth was not far behind … some of the national cloth leaves something to be desired, but there is also national cloth that costs a little more but is of better quality.

A few years previously Chinese dacron became fashionable, but he did not like working with it. Another tailor explained that because of the deteriorating state of the economy people will buy clothes for a special occasion, knowing that they will not get much use of them:

Many people don't have the money to buy cloth. They don't have the money to have clothes made. Perhaps many of them, according what they have told me, to attend an occasion, a wedding, a baptism, whatever, they don't have a budget. They say: 'for that night, I'll rescue myself for the occasion, even if it is cheap'. So they prefer to do that. Where am I going to get a budget to have a suit made, a cloth that will cost US$80 or US$100. Where am I going to get money for that. Plus US$100 or US$120 [to have it made up]. We are speaking of US$200. Yes? So I believe this is what is happening with all the artisans, including shoemakers, tailors, shirt-makers, or those who make different articles of clothing.

The Chinese clothes that they bring is beautiful, worn twice it is beautiful, but the cloth is dreadful, and for that matter the manufacture as well. And what can you say, from here on it gets worse.

This tailor adapted to the influx of cheap Chinese clothes by buying them and re-selling them in his workshop. A Chinese suit costs between US$80 and US$100, the same as he has to pay for raw materials, before the cost of labour.[18]

Chinese clothes are very cheap … but cheap ends up being expensive. But … I buy the Chinese suits, I sell them here, it works out better for me.

He also pointed out that they are not only up against Chinese imports, but also cheaper good quality clothes manufactured in Colombia. A couple of weeks before the interview he had gone to Colombia out of curiosity about what was happening there.

There I found a good suit for US$60 or US$70. A ready-made suit. The Colombians have good quality, it is better than the Chinese, much better than the Chinese.

For hat-makers, the competition is also from both the Chinese and Colombians, and it is related to dollarization. The Colombians are also selling cheap manufactured straw hats as 'Panama hats', which is a brand that is world-renowned as products that are hand-made by artisans in Ecuador:

What a shame that Chinese hats and Colombian hats started to come in … They are putting 'Panama Hat' on a hat of poor quality and they come here and sell it for US$8. So how is the artisan making straw hats supposed to compete? So, we need more control of contraband … Or the Chinese hat made of paper, for US$4. That does not even cover the cost of the material. So, when a product is falsified, especially by powers such as China, we cannot compete; and not only in hats but also in shoes, clothes, technology, everything.

Workers in fine metals – silversmiths, goldsmiths, jewellers and watchmakers – have also been affected, particularly after 2005 (Table A.13.4). One watch repairer, who was facing competition from cellular phones with their built-in timepieces also complained about the prices and technology in falsified Chinese watches. As we have already seen, it is cheaper to replace than repair and repairs can be no more than a change of battery, which has implications for businesses that previously supplied spare parts. The decline in demand for parts has meant the closure of suppliers of these parts:[19]

> The Chinese began to import watches from one dollar; from 50 cents; and at the present time there are watches at 5, 6, 7 dollars – beautiful, fantastic. But with the invasion of the Chinese watches and all that, there is not much demand for spare parts and, at the same time, the old watches no longer exist. There are a few hidden away. There are no Swiss watches, which were expensive … They are no longer used … You have to remove a spare part from another that is damaged; the trading houses that sold spare parts no longer exist.

The costs of the poor quality inputs were passed on to customers, sometimes without their knowledge or understanding. Another watchmaker explained to a client that he would be happy to replace her watch battery with one that only cost one dollar but he tried to convince her that she should replace it with one of a better quality that would cost three dollars. He explained that there was no guarantee of quality for the cheaper one and it would not last long, but she bought the Chinese battery.

Cheaper raw materials and tools

The above section refers to the unfair competition between artisan production and cheap imports, but there are also the issues around the importing of cheap raw materials and tools. There were dissenting voices with regard to the problems of cheap imports, mainly referring to cheap imported raw materials or parts from Colombia. In the past, before dollarization and particularly in the 1970s, Colombia was an important source of smuggled contraband, depending on the quality of Colombian factory production and the fluctuation of the sucre-peso exchange rate. Today, the levels of trade depend on the dollar-peso exchange rate. A frame maker said his work was made easier by the cheap imported materials that can be used for modern framing. A tyre repair workshop used imported tyres from Colombia.

Those who work mainly in repair are less concerned about cheap imports. A mechanic praised the poor quality of imports, saying that they were beneficial because 'they make the merchandise cheaper and they have to be repaired when they get damaged'. For a female shoemaker who says she has always worked in repair, rather than manufacturing, importing cheap shoes is 'in part, good, because they bring them here for repair'. She was never involved in making shoes, so importing cheap shoes did not affect her in the same way as it impacted on other shoemakers. Her perspective was that the importing of goods of poor quality was an opportunity, for it signified that there were more shoes to repair. Another shoemaker pointed out that his repair business benefited from the importing of cheap raw materials: 'The Colombian material is good.' A tailor, however, complained of competition from the importing of finished Colombian clothes. Competition 'from Colombia brings cheaper and more beautiful things; I have to go to Lago Agrio[20] to sell, gaining very little'. However, he also buys Colombian clothes for resale in Lago Agrio and another tailor pointed out that his clients were already going directly to Colombia to buy their better-quality clothes.

Another watchmaker complained about the quality of the imported Chinese tools:[21] 'Now there are no good quality tools; now there are many Chinese tools.' This was a common complaint across all sectors. Tailors used poor quality Chinese sewing machines. A sewing machine repairman said he imported spares, which were taxed on entry, pushing up the costs of repair. Chinese machines are cheaper, their spares are cheaper, but they are false economy. Parts used to repair Chinese-made machines, which are more likely to continue to fail, cost more in the long run. The machines he repaired were used both domestically and by artisans, contributing to the costs of production of the latter.

Competition and diversification

Because of the competition, many artisans have 'diversified', as economists would say. Some have started to sell Chinese products, developed their trading activities while still maintaining their artisan production, which economists might interpret as entrepreneurial activity. For many of the artisans, this transition is a measure of their desperation. Ecuadorean guitar making is a skill that goes back to colonial times. These skilled artisans also turned their hands to making other musical instruments, such as maracas or bongo drums, and sometimes they would sell the work of fellow artisans in their workshops. They believe that the Chinese have destroyed all types of artisan activities, including the craft of guitar making:[22]

> The guitar-makers, tailors, everyone. The Chinese market was what caused our decline. It left us dying of hunger. For example, this guitar that my son had, over there; ... that guitar is worth US$350. And to sell a guitar for US$350 is very difficult. So, what I do to maintain my business – support me, pay the rent, everything I have to pay here – is I take in the Chinese guitars and put myself in competition with myself. This is the point we have arrived at. This is good wood, but the people ... I try to explain it to someone 'look, this guitar is such and such, oven dried, the wood is such and such'. People are not interested in this. Because of the poverty we are living in, people are interested in the cost, that it has the shape of a guitar and it shines; this is what interests the majority of people. A good guitar sells for US$300, US$200 ... Only a musician, truly a professional musician, appreciates the sound because they already have it in their hearing. But this is five per cent [of the population] ...
>
> I had to get involved with Chinese guitars ... We only sold national guitars. So, ours were expensive and the Chinese were cheap and I realised that my

neighbour there was selling them and I was not. And of necessity, with my children in high school and paying the rent, I had to take them and sell them. The fact that my son was selling strings and pegs, he sold these guitars. Bring me some, I said. Within a week I had sold all of these Chinese guitars. Bring me more. This was what began to provide something to eat … So, that was it. I myself set up the competition for myself, for I was not going to leave myself to die of hunger … And what was I going to do with my family? … So I took and I sold the Chinese, and with this I am supporting myself.

In the main, the artisans explained how their microenterprises were damaged by the dominant free trade doctrine of international organisations and successive governments. Many artisans adapt, but in doing so they reluctantly abandon their traditional status as artisans. Officially, they hold on, in order to claim the remaining benefits that accrues to them because of their status, but if they cannot make a success of selling cheap Chinese imports they may be reduced to treating their failing business as a hobby in old age.

The neoliberal vision is of artisans who grow into large firms; or they turn to trade because they see an opportunity. The reality is that these artisans are squeezed out of their professions, into commerce; then they give up and start to sell the goods that are killing their professions. To survive, they turn their workshops into shops, sometimes holding on to tools and machinery for display purposes, in case a municipal or government inspector arrives to confirm their artisan status. Even if they continue to produce, their workshops become shops that sometimes start to sell Chinese imports. Some hold on to the pretence that they are artisans by keeping specialist tools and machinery in their shops to avoid charging Value Added Tax (IVA). The artisans suffer and adapt, particularly the older ones whose business lives are behind them.

Notes

1 We tested to see if there was a relationship between standards of living and how the businesses had performed over the previous three years and, up to and including 2005, there was no divergence. In 2015, they were less likely to say their standard of living had deteriorated than they were to say that the situation of the business was worse; and they were more likely to say it had remained the same (significant at the 0.05 level).
2 The question was open-ended and the responses were classified as they appear in the table.
3 One artisan said by lowering the cost of imported materials and another said by buying more of their products.
4 A small proportion said they did not have enough time to keep up with demand or to learn new skills.
5 In 2005, 6% of firms said they did not exist at the time of dollarization in the year 2000; and by 2015 this had increase to 32%. In 2015, three other firms gave vague responses that could not be classified into the headings used in the table.
6 This was a very high cost for a repair. In 2015, the average price would be in the region of US$8.

7 Interview CU4.
8 Interview CU8.
9 Interview MJ7.
10 President of Ecuador 2003–2005.
11 Interview MJ2.
12 Interview MJ3.
13 President between August 1998 and January 2000.
14 For example, parts such as plug-in circuit boards.
15 Interview MJ2.
16 Interview CU1.
17 Interview AM1.
18 Interview MJ6.
19 Interview CU4.
20 The main oil town in the Amazon region.
21 Interview JM1.
22 Interview MJ8.

14 Conclusions
Theory, ideology and evidence

Robert Shiller, Nobel Laureate in Economic Sciences, argues that economics is like all science in that it is searching for truth but, unlike the physical sciences, its subject matter is people, who can change their minds and behave completely differently – in a way that the subjects of the physical sciences cannot (Shiller, 2013). Its qualitative methods lead to a gain in mathematical insights which need to be constantly adjusted to fit the uncertainty that human beings create. He is convinced that, as economics develops, it will broaden its methods and sources of evidence, and the science will become stronger.

The problem with this positive view of an evidence-based future is that all economics is dependent on ideology in a way that science is not. Social scientists bring unspoken assumptions to their work, assumptions about the nature of the social world they are analysing. Their hypotheses are dependent on these personal assumptions, as well as the sometimes conflicting professional theories of their discipline. Economists are also people, as are their subject matter, and they are prone to changing their minds and behaving completely differently. The majority are, unfortunately, locked into a dominant way of thinking at the present time, in their acceptance of the doctrine of neoliberalism.

In his Nobel Prize lecture in 1974, Hayek was critical of Keynesian economists for bringing about accelerating inflation through the policies they had pursued. Their failure to guide policy successfully was, he said, closely connected with their propensity to try to emulate the successful methods of the physical sciences – a 'scientistic' attitude that attempted to transfer mechanically and uncritically the methods of natural science into economics.

> The recognition of the insuperable limits to his knowledge ought indeed to teach the student of society a lesson of humility which should guard him against becoming an accomplice in men's fatal striving to control society – a striving which makes him not only a tyrant over his fellows, but which may make him the destroyer of a civilization which no brain has designed but which has grown from the free efforts of millions of individuals.
>
> (von Hayek, 1974, 5)

This was written before Hayek's thinking became dominant and how ironic it is that much of his critique of neo-Keynesian economics can be applied to his followers. His theories, based on so-called common sense assumptions and devoid of evidence, have created a dominant world view that supports the crushing of the weak and the undermining of the efforts of labour. Since then, Hayek's economic thought has taken a dominant place in the discipline, as the Keynesian habits of thought have been replaced by Hayek's free market ideology, leading to a different set of scientistic errors.

The problem for Hayek is that we all think we know facts that we cannot measure and sometimes, under certain conditions, these 'facts' become ideology. The question is, under what conditions do non-facts or beliefs become accepted as facts? What constitutes a 'valid explanation' for Hayek and who determines its validity? In the absence of factual evidence and sometimes in contradiction with the evidence, what is valid becomes what the most powerful in society say is valid. In the absence of evidence, those who control the means of communication can determine what is valid.

Hayek says the 'correct' explanation for extreme unemployment is derived from 'good qualitative knowledge' and 'the facts of everyday experience' and the logical conclusions drawn from them: 'Few who take the trouble to follow the argument will question the validity of the factual assumptions' (1974, 2). This astonishing statement gives an insight into the mind of Hayek. His assumptions are unquestionable; and he is claiming the deductive logic of his argument confirms his assumptions. He later wants to subject his opponents to the Popperian test of refutability but he wants no such test for his own beliefs.

Hayek is correct in saying we cannot produce all the information we need. Writing before the advent of modern computers and without access to current thinking about the possibilities of artificial intelligence, he is nevertheless right to argue that, because of the 'structures of essential complexity' in which individual human beings relate to each other, we cannot know everything. That, however, is hardly the point. Even if information expanded exponentially and we could compute it, if the assumptions behind the logically deductive model were wrong, the computation would lead to an erroneous conclusion. No matter how sophisticated our computation becomes, it is worse than useless if our assumptions are not valid. It is positively dangerous if scientism, performed by 'charlatans' (Hayek's word) and supported by the powerful and wealthy, determines economic policy. Unfortunately, Hayek's ill-founded theories are the new normal.

It may be impossible to know the total sum of all the facts known by all participants, but it is possible to derive aggregates for different social groups or classes in society and arrive at approximations for their values, attitudes and behaviour. That involves using statistically reliable samples for their views, opinions, aspirations, and so on. We can never know every behavioural detail for every individual for all time, but we can do better than rely on Hayek's 'everyday experience'.

He criticises the uncritical acceptance of assertions that have the appearance of being scientific, proposes that we concern ourselves with the limits to what we can expect science to achieve, and beware of the false belief that the scientific method consists in the application of a ready-made technique. Hayek is not rejecting the use of algebraic equations, but the totality of all information can be 'known only to God', something he wishes mathematical economists would take to heart. This appeal to an all-knowing God is not unusual amongst neoconservatives, but you do not need to ascertain *all* the facts to arrive at a Popperian rejection. You only need the facts that relate to a central aspect of the theory, such as an assumption. If a basic assumption is wrong, the whole theory falls.

I agree with Hayek when he says:

> To act on the belief that we possess the knowledge and the power which enable us to shape the processes of society entirely to our liking, knowledge which in fact we do not possess, is likely to make us do much harm.
>
> (von Hayek, 1974, 5)

However, that is precisely the charge that can be levelled against him and his followers. He is condemned by his own words. Where there is essential complexity, we cannot have full knowledge that would make the mastery of events possible. We cannot subject our human environment to 'the control of human will', but that is precisely what his followers have tried to do.

The emergence of neoliberalism as the dominant narrative in economics in the 1980s owes a great deal to the work of Keith Joseph, the conservative ideologue whom Margaret Thatcher defeated for the leadership of the Conservative party in 1974. In 1979, he wrote (Joseph and Sumption, 1979, 1):

> The object of this book is to challenge one of the central prejudices of modern British politics, the belief that it is a proper function of the state to influence the distribution of wealth for its own sake.

In support of Hayek as 'a formidable but solitary figure' (ibid., 2) in the debate about the role of government in the economy and society, Joseph argued that a high degree of inequality was not only acceptable, but desirable. For him, Hayek, Friedman and others who came to dominate economic thinking in the 1980s, egalitarianism was an emotional preference that had no basis in logical thinking. It was an instinctive premise, a moral conviction for which there is no justification. 'Equality of outcomes', represented by 'fairness', was an 'article of religious faith' (Friedman, 1981, 166). Joseph thought that equality was impossible to achieve in any society that 'reveres and covets material wealth' (Joseph and Sumption, 1979, 5), which he held to be true throughout the west. The position he took was, of course, also emotional, instinctive and moral. It was only logical within the boundaries of his assumptions about the nature of the human condition and, if the assumptions were wrong, his conclusions could not be justified.

There was no doubt in Joseph's mind that the major driving force of British society was the individual accumulation of wealth; and behind every egalitarian mask there was a violent revolutionary who needed to be confronted and defeated. In Joseph and Sumption's book, redistribution is characterised as 'robbing the rich to give to the poor'. It destroys the incentive to create wealth which, it was thought, would trickle down to the poor. Behind this thinking, their assumptions about human motivation are central. While they concede that 'human motivation is elusive' (Joseph and Sumption, 1979, 23), they also argue that the pursuit of wealth is the fundamental driver of human behaviour and to be competitive in this regard is 'human nature'.

It is 'common sense' to believe that redistribution is damaging. The burden of proof for any alternative view requires evidence to refute their core belief, which they say is not forthcoming. Despite this call for evidence, however, it is significant that they nevertheless spend the last chapter decrying statistics as 'damned lies'. Of course, neoliberal thinking in 1979 was not based on evidence. It was a reassertion of a powerful political ideology that had been marginalised in the post-war years and was now being used to fight against the basic tenets of the welfare state in the UK and elsewhere. It was also a weapon in the neoliberal armoury to ensure that the spread of social democratic ideas was confronted in the developing world.

The motivation and capacity to 'exploit opportunities' is not dependent on background or education – institutional factors have no impact – we all equally enjoy opportunities but only some take them. 'Equality of opportunity is the corollary of the liberty of the individual' (ibid., 30) discrimination against the rich is an 'offence against equality of opportunity and therefore against liberty' (ibid., 31). Class distinctions are thought to be a barrier to human brotherhood, but they too are a result of 'human nature' (ibid., 37). They argue that 'one of the few aspirations common to almost everyone [is] the desire to improve [one's] material lot' (ibid., 38). There is no doubt this is true, but the problem is that they confound this with building a large business. Improving one's material lot and building a large business are not coterminous. In their perspective, class distinctions derive from the competitive spirit, which is 'human nature'. To quarrel with competition and class is to quarrel with human nature itself. They believe that an egalitarian must either suppress or frustrate human ambition, the competitive spirit; an egalitarian system suppresses the initiative of an entire population.

Ultimately, however, neoliberalism is a belief system that depends on God-created human nature. Competitive instincts not only exist as human nature, but the basis of this belief is scripture: 'Man has fallen. Original sin exists' (ibid., 99). They have to fall back on God-given human nature. Inequality is natural; people cannot be changed; 'a society of autonomous individuals is the natural condition of mankind' (ibid., 100). Individuals are prior to societies and have rights independent of them. Man has 'natural' characteristics, e.g. to 'pursue private rather than public ends' (ibid., 100) – 'an immutable fact about human nature'. The ambition of the acquisition of private/individual wealth for themselves is 'natural to their humanity'.

The individuals who appear most often in Joseph and Sumption are entrepreneurs. Inherited wealth is obscured, corporate wealth and power are ignored, public servants barely make an appearance and even shareholders are below the horizon. Similar to the position taken by de Soto (1989), tax-avoiding small business owners are celebrated as icons of capitalism. 'Moonlighting plumbers' are involved in 'capitalist acts'. We might ask in what sense they are capitalists, particularly as they are earning incomes informally and off the books, which is not necessarily a capitalist act. Moonlighting plumbers normally work alone, in as much secrecy as possible in order to avoid detection by the authorities. They do not publicise their activities for fear of being uncovered and, as wage labourers in their normal day-jobs, they seldom have ambitions to expand their clandestine work into capitalist firms. It is a non-capitalist form of economic activity, no wage labour being employed.

An a priori assumption is that wealth is created by individuals and taken by societies, not created by societies and taken by individuals. If you take away this assumption, however, the whole edifice collapses. Wealth is created by teams of people in large organisations – workers, not the owners of capital, who are likely to be shareholders sitting at home or working as salaried workers elsewhere. The majority of the wealth that is created is unearned income. Joseph and Sumption (85-6) argue against the idea that wealth should be confiscated and redistributed 'without regard to the different contributions of individuals' to its creation, but the creation of great wealth is not an individual act. They use the example of the self-employed individual, in this case a cake-maker, as the wealth creator, but this misses the point. The artisan cake-maker generates income, but little wealth. It is Mr Kipling, a capitalist organisation, that generates unearned wealth for a community of shareholders.

The same is true of wealth generated by trade. The free market theories of Adam Smith are based on the idea of the trader as an individual carrying out what he says is the activity that distinguishes human beings from other animals: 'Nobody ever saw a dog make a fair and deliberate exchange of one bone for another with another dog' (Smith, 1976, 26). We now know that ants, bees and wasps are social beings, that cleaner fish have a trade-off with whales (food for health), that meerkats and other animals will support each other against common enemies, and that monkeys in lab tests will save tokens as money to spend in the future. Even dogs have the capacity to optimise their food returns by saving for future trades (Leonardi et al., 2012) and chimpanzees can trade between themselves to obtain food (Brosnan and Beran, 2009).

Science has come a long way since Smith but, more importantly, human trade is more likely to be a communal activity. Marx (1967, 351) argued that trade comes into being when collectives with different means of production and means of subsistence in their natural environment come into contact. Historically, it was not private individuals who met on an independent footing, but social organisation such as families, tribes and communities who traded. In Smith's time, this would have included companies with shareholders, such as the East India Company, trading with communities in India and the Americas, albeit through their traditional leaders.

Neoliberals nevertheless believe that large differences in wealth 'represent real differences in economic aptitudes' (Joseph and Sumption, 1979, 88), as well as representing the real differences in the value of individual contributions to the total wealth of society. The owner of wealth owes it to 'his' own talents not to the society in which he lives, and it should not be taken away from him. However, even an entrepreneur who accumulates wealth does so because, if not inherited or stolen, he organised some workers in a firm to accumulate it personally. 'Individuals may owe the retention of their wealth to the state but they owe its acquisition to themselves' (ibid., 5). Here they are confounding acquisition and creation. The wealthy, whether shareholders or entrepreneurs, inevitably owe the creation of their wealth to the work of other people.

Just as Hayek argues that 'the credit with which apparent conformity with recognised scientific standards can gain for seemingly simple but false theories may … have grave consequences' (von Hayek, 1974, 3), Joseph and Sumption go on to deny the validity if any statistics that could be used to counter their arguments. They call for evidence to counter their common sense position and then deny the validity of any evidence that could be used. The pseudo-science of the authors, combined with their anti-science when the evidence does not support them, means that the credit which is given to their unsubstantiated theories are even more dangerous for masses of people.

Neoliberals are also likely to change the evidence, or even the social scientist, when the facts do not fit with their theories. The neoliberal argument is that since the early 1980s, the distribution of income across the world has become more equal and world poverty has fallen. The World Bank, the WTO, the IMF, international think tanks and the financial media, as well as the treasuries of the United States and European countries, have supported this position. Wade (2004) points out that the data that lie behind this thinking come from the World Banks data set that not only contains a large margin of error but which has also led the Bank to come to different conclusions at different times. This is because of methodological issues and political bias. The methodological issues include where the poverty line is set; the extent to which the poorest and wealthiest are reliably included in household surveys of income and expenditure; the fact that China and India declined to participate in the data gathering exercise and their data was largely a matter of guesswork.

The neoliberal argument in favour of national and international free markets is based on one of a number of different ways of measuring poverty and income inequality across the world. Not only is its validity questioned because of a change in the way poverty is measured, but if China is excluded even this measure shows a widening of income inequality since 1980 and if India is also excluded the widening becomes even more pronounced. China and India account for 38% of the world's population and the problem of their non-participation in international price comparisons is compounded by the possibility that China's growth in the 1990s may be overstated. Wade argues that: 'falling income inequality is not a general feature of the world economy, even when using the most favourable combination of measures' (Wade, 2004, 576).

The politics of poverty relies on who controls the data. Wade points out that the World Development Report (WDR) of 2000/2001 says that the number of people living in poverty increased between 1987 and 1998 (World Bank, 2001), before Chief Economist Joseph Stiglitz, another Nobel Prize winner, was sacked. The next major World Bank publication claimed that the number of people living in poverty decreased between 1980 and 1998 (World Bank, 2002).

Conflicting definitions and the question of who decides what they should be is also relevant for the study of the economic activities of the poor in developing countries. European and North American neoliberalism was extended to cover developing countries: an ideology imported and celebrated, and the reality of small firm development distorted (de Soto, 1989). The concept of the entrepreneur, which is central to the neoliberal argument, has been hijacked to refer to anyone who owns or sets up a microenterprise, irrespective of whether they demonstrate the entrepreneurial traits that were identified by Schumpeter (2003). The concepts of the informal sector, economy and employment have been written into the neoliberal narrative in such a way as to promote the entrepreneur as a heroic figure who is constrained by the regulatory state. At the same time, there has been a lack of clarity about the definitions and the relationships between the concepts of homeworkers, family labour, home-based workers, home-based enterprises, outworkers and family-based enterprises. One outcome has been the covering up of the fact that neoliberalism has been detrimental to the interests of the very small enterprises that they claim to be supporting.

The impact of the neoliberal years on the Ecuadorian economy was to drive down economic grown, which had a detrimental impact on the demand for the outputs of the 'micro-entrepreneurs', the socio-economic group who, theoretically, should have benefited most. The years of structural adjustment, with its attack on the role of the state in the economy and the promotion of privatisation at all costs, not only destroyed growth and demand in the economy. It also raised national debt, promoted the interests of local elites in traditional economic activities, and led to a financial crisis that had a major negative impact on microenterprises.

The neoliberal years were the years of slowest growth in GDP, when demand was sucked out of the economy, there was reduced government investment in public services and, paradoxically, the greatest increase in public debt. The growing public debt financed the distribution of cheap loans to rural oligarchs and the wealthiest families. The export of agricultural products grew at the same time as the export of manufactured goods fell. Small-scale industrial production for the local market was devastated by cheap imports. There was a flight of capital, rather than reinvestment locally, which ultimately led to the financial crash.

The manufacturing sector was severely damaged by neoliberalism. Deregulation and the freeing up of financial markets meant high interest rates for small industry, industrial disinvestment, financial barriers to small-scale lending, short-termism in lending, and concentration of resources in the hands of the already wealthy. There was expropriation and regression in the operation of the financial system through a transfer of resources from production to the financial sector. Manufacturing paid more in interest and fees to the financial sector than they did in wages, taxes and dividends. This financial flow supported the economic interests of the powerful groups linked to political and financial power.

The neoliberal experiment led to the failure of the banking system, dollarization and serious pressures on microenterprises that should have benefited through the application of the theory. In this crisis of neoliberalism, local elites were able to protect themselves through offshore banking, while the informal owners of microenterprises lost their savings and saw the value of their debts increase. In almost all regards, the performance of the economy was better under the anti-oligarchical government of Rodriguez-Lara and the anti-neoliberal government of Correa. In these two periods, situated as bookends to the neoliberal years, the artisans of the informal sector also fared better.

The overall structure of artisan production has changed over time as some activities have declined and others have grown. The nature of the work carried out by the artisans has also been in transition, from production to repair. As micro-manufacturers of the means of subsistence have been displaced by global capitalist production, a new space has opened up for the repair of mass-produced goods. However, this is limited by the comparative costs of repairing and buying new. Where the costs of repair are equal to or greater than the cost of new goods, repair will not be the choice of the consumer. In addition, the technology of production determines the technology of repair, which may be beyond the skill sets of traditional artisans. This means that the technology of capitalist production constrains informal entrepreneurial behaviour in the Schumpeterian sense. The changes in these processes have been uneven over time and have not had identical impacts on different types of micro-producers.

At the mercy of external forces that have been driven by an ideology that has made unsustainable assumptions about what drives micro-producers, it is a belief system that has been imposed by global and national elites to the detriment of the socio-economic forces that they pretend to support. In this process, erroneous assumptions have been made about what motivates artisans.

Rational choice theory does not apply when trying to explain why artisans are in the informal sector. The evidence rejects the notion that people make a choice, conscious or otherwise, between the formal and informal sectors. In particular, we reject the idea that workers end up in the informal sector after carrying out cost-benefit analyses that weigh the advantages and disadvantages of membership of what is essentially a theoretical academic construct – a superficial binary imposition on a much more complex reality.

There is no doubt that small firms seek to avoid regulations and taxes, as do larger firms. But raising this to the level of a fetish for small firms does not help to explain the complex processes that lie behind their role in economic development and underdevelopment in the Global South. Social protection is an issue for the self-employed, employers and workers alike. However, there is no evidence that it is a key driver in an assumed choice between sectors. Authors are confounding workers and employers, as well as making assumptions about borders between formal and informal that do not exist. These assumptions bedevil the analysis of the evidence that does exist. Regulation, taxation and corruption are thrown into a mix that is stirred with an ideological spoon to give the answer first thought of: the state is bad and is holding back the entrepreneurial owners of profit-maximising (rather than income-generating) small firms from becoming large-scale capitalist concerns.

Rather than the pursuit of wealth being a natural goal of humanity (Joseph and Sumption, 1979) our assumptions include the proposals that: work has social and cultural dimensions; all firms have non-economic goals; the owners of family firms have specific family-oriented goals that impact on the operation of the enterprises; and artisans in particular have a pride in, and an attachment to, their craft that influence their aspirations for the future. Artisans enter their professions, and therefore the informal sector, as children, often to escape poverty in the rural areas. This is a decision that is often made for them. They set up their own firms after qualifying and around the time they are beginning family life. The future of their children is a major driving force in their working lives. They have an attachment to their craft, sometimes through family history. Their skills may not be transferable to factory production and the skills learned in the factory are seldom transferable to the artisan workshop. They have a fear of banks and of debt, born of experience. Most workshops do not want to grow into larger firms, for reasons related to these characteristics, rather than through them making a rational choice between regulations and benefits.

In Ecuador, pessimism about the future of micro-businesses was highest during the low-growth neoliberal years, but there was no clear relationship between business optimism and the intention of artisans to grow their businesses. In a declining market, a large majority said they would continue as artisans. Of those who indicated that they would not, only a small minority said they would seek factory work, the largest proportion opting to switch to trading activities.

Artisans are not just businesses in competition. They compete and collaborate with each other and sometimes, larger firms exploit them. They are intimately linked to and influenced by the capitalist sector of the economy, particularly with respect to the purchase of equipment and materials. They are customers for the large-scale producers and distributors of tools and raw materials. In this role, they help the capitalist manufacturers to realise their profits, the surplus value that is created by the capitalist workforce, but they also contribute to the profits of traders, both large-scale and small-scale, as they capture some of the manufacturer's surplus value. This is not a relationship that is exploitative of the artisan, although it can be if credit is involved.

The commercial elites were the main beneficiaries of the early neoliberal years, as large-scale traders in both raw materials and tools captured more of the artisan demand. However, the failure and closure of artisan workshops was an increasing source of fixed machinery for surviving artisans during the neoliberal phase. Throughout the whole period, the survival of the artisans depended on sustaining their relations with clients seeking bespoke goods and services.

The historic and current role of small-scale sweatshops in global capitalism is well documented. There is no evidence that artisan production has ever been subordinated to large-scale production in this way in Ecuador. In the development of capitalism in the UK, it was particularly important in the textile industry, shoe-making and carpentry, but it was practically non-existent in any industry in our study. If it was historically an 'organic' part of the development of capitalism, it is certainly not an organic part of peripheral capitalism in Ecuador today.

However, these sweatshops are not the same as domestic industries or home-based industries. They are capitalist forms of production using Fordist production methods. Domestic subcontracting exists as an important part of peripheral capitalism today only if you describe Asian sweatshops that do not exist inside the home as domestic industries and confuse them with artisan production, as has been the case with the ILO, the World Bank and related NGOs.

Subcontracting of artisans is unlikely to be a particularly important aspect of developing capitalism today, given the present level of the development of productive forces on a world scale. The use and abuse of the labour in small-scale manufacturing workshops is integral part of global capitalism, but the owners of these workshops are not artisans – and probably never were. There is a recent policy initiative that may be encouraging the role of sweatshops and buying up: the Ecuador government's policy on school uniforms. This is facilitating both domestic subcontracting and the setting up of factory production employing up to 20 workers, including apprentices, working in line and claiming to be artisan workshops. There is evidence that both domestic subcontracting and small sweatshops claiming to be artisans have increased very slightly as a result of Correa's policy for school uniforms, but is not generalisable across the artisan sector.

It has been argued that in the early development of capitalism, traders in artisan goods developed out of the small producers themselves, expanding their influence over other artisans as markets expanded and eventually subordinating them to the capitalist market. In Quito, some artisans with workshops in the city centre have developed into small-scale traders. These, however, are not large-scale enterprises. They are wealthier than the peripheral artisans and they do capture part of their surplus value, but middlemen have never dominated artisan producers. There was a change in the structure of distribution, but it was the role of clients that increased as the importance of middlemen declined. The role of middlemen collapsed through the Ecuadorean financial crisis and the trading impacts of Chinese imports and globalisation.

Artisans are not dependent on the emergence of a new merchant class who themselves are former small producers. The most important middlemen *are* other artisans, but they represented only 4% of artisan customers in 2015, compared to 6% in 1975. Wholesalers represent only 2% in 2015, practically no change over the period. The threat to the artisans is not subordination to a new set of merchants. It is elimination by competition from the modern Chinese manufacturing system.

Nevertheless, it would be a mistake to focus only on this competition. The decline of artisans and the generalised growth of the relative importance of production for private individuals (clients and shoppers), with a corresponding decline in middlemen, was reflected in the trajectories of most of the artisan subsectors – although the trajectories were not uniform over time. The non-linear routes taken responded to different influences on different sectors. Similarly, the extent of work undertaken for the state and private sectors by artisans over time varied in their volume and direction. One of the influences on these trajectories is the development of technology, inside and outside the artisan sectors, locally and globally.

The growth and survival of subcontracting as a stage in the development of commodity production in England in the nineteenth century was contingent on the development of technology that could replace the labour time of the small producer. At the present time, advanced levels of technology are available in all industrial sectors and they are readily implantable where there are growing markets in the developing world. Today, a much more advanced technology is available in the Third World and wherever there is the development of a sizeable market, which was the precondition for the growth of subcontracting in the nineteenth century, international capitalism and national manufacturing capital can immediately take advantage of it. This has consequences for household and family enterprises.

The literature on the informal sector confuses home-based firms and family-based firms. The relations between home, family and different types of customers are complex and the influences on these relations of production and exchange are extremely difficult to disentangle. However, what is clear is that home-based enterprises and family-based enterprises are not interchangeable concepts. There was no correlation between family-based firms and home-based firms and their growth and decline followed different patterns.

Consistent with development theory, there was a significant decline in the use of the home as a workplace over the 40 years. However, this was not because of economic development during the neoliberal years. It took place during the higher growth years before and after the neoliberal period. In addition, contrary to neoliberal theory, there was no evidence of the opening up of the market for family firms during the neoliberal years and there was no relationship between location of the workshop and access to markets.

Contrary to the theoretical link between homeworkers and subcontracting to formal sector firms, artisans whose workshops were inside the home were consistently less likely to work for the formal private sector. There was a steady growth of HBEs working for the private sector, leading to a significant difference between 1975 and 2015. However, the proportion of HBEs who worked for the private sector more than once a month only accounted for between 2% and 4% of all artisans. That is, dependent home-based working was insignificant.

FBEs were consistently more likely to work for the private sector than non-FBEs, but the FBEs that did so more than once a month accounted for no more than 2–7% of all workshops. There was significant variation for non-FBEs over time, leading to an aggregated increase over the 40 years. This growth, however, was set back during structural adjustment.

More likely was the spread of collaborative activity during the difficult years of neoliberalism. Rather than free-market entrepreneurial investment and expansion, the artisans decided to share more. Generally, family firms were no more or less likely to collaborate than other firms but during the precarious years of structural adjustment, there was a significant increase in collaboration.

Although there was a tendency for more collaboration amongst HBEs than non-HBEs during neoliberalism, there was no significant change in this over time. Nevertheless, there was an overall extension of horizontal integration of artisans during the precarious neoliberal ascendancy.

Artisan organisations are subject to elite capture, which leads members to question the legitimacy of the organisations that claim to represent them. The groups that represent people of the same artisan activities are examples of bonding social capital. When different groupings combine into federations to achieve common goals, bridging social capital is created. When these federations come together in organisations such as the JNDA, the opportunity is created for linking social capital to connect artisans to the heart of power. However, this final process also creates the opportunity for the exercise of social power from above. The artisan can reach the heart of national and international power politics, becoming an important component of national democratic movements and the struggle for power. However, elite capture can be detrimental to the majority of the artisan labour force.

Artisan guilds have a history of negotiating with those in power for social and economic advantages not available to others. Their cohesion as a group means that, despite market competition, they can negotiate around common interests. This common vision assumes that the guilds will represent the interests of journeymen and the self-employed, as well as the small masters. It also assumes that relations between different types of artisans are benign and that guilds operate as mutual benefit associations. If they are subject to elite capture, however, the social networks of linking social capital can be benign for the small masters but not for the majority of workers, apprentices and even the self-employed. The relationships can be exploitative of the majority of artisans.

In this situation, there can be a struggle for power within and between artisan organisations and the artisan guilds become part of the wider struggle for power, attracting the interest of national power brokers such as political parties and powerful international actors, including churches and other national governments. In Ecuador, these processes have evolved over time. As the guilds have increasingly become the representatives of small capitalist manufacturers, it has been relatively easy for conservative politicians, priests and intellectuals to pit the artisan guilds against trade unions.

As the guilds transitioned from being representatives of all artisans into organisations that protected the interests of employers against the demands of their workforces, the JNDA acted in the interests of small capitalist firms that had consolidated their grip on the federations. The guilds ceased to represent all artisans and even the majority of workshop owners who fitted the traditional concept of the artisan did not have representation. Ultimately, the federations were transformed from organisations using linking social capital to extract benefits for small capitalist firms into associations of elderly men whose bonding social capital supports the notion of guilds as no more than social clubs.

The guilds no longer have the influence they used to and artisans have lost faith in them to defend their interests. This decline started in 1982, when the guilds were increasingly becoming the representatives of firms employing up to 20 people. When asked to identify what they had done specifically to help, the growth of negativity through the years of neoliberalism was highly significant. Through the period when neoliberal ideology was celebrating a pro-business ideology and claiming to support microenterprises, the artisans were becoming less supportive of the organisations that claimed to represent them. The neoliberal state, however, was seen in an even worse light than the guilds.

Contrary to the message that emanates from neoliberal ideology, the problem is not that the state has been unsympathetic to or antagonistic towards informal microenterprises. Until recently, governments have been supportive, enacting legislation that would help the artisans to grow into small industries. For more than 70 years, this has been a political project as much as an economic programme. A negotiation of supportive policies for artisans in general became an issue for geopolitics in Latin America in the 1960s, before the majority of the artisans were excluded through elite capture. As the wealthier small manufacturers took advantage of the legislation for their own purposes, the state was unable to identify who the beneficiaries of the policies should be and it failed to live up to its own promises, particularly in relation to health and social security.

When policies for the regulation of the informal sector were introduced after the neoliberal financial crisis, which was consistent with the ILO's exhortation to facilitate 'the movement of informal workers and economic units from the informal to the formal economies' (ILO, 2015, 10–1/6), this inevitably meant more regulation around tax and social security, some of which had unintended consequences. In some regards, it was positive, as more workshop owners and their families registered with the social security system. On the other hand, wage labour was squeezed out of artisan workshops to make way for paid family members, some of whom were registered as employees for tax purposes. That is, formalisation, which probably raised the tax take, also encouraged tax avoidance and a reduction of wage employment.

State policies in support of microenterprises have also included providing sources of finance, but the policies were not embedded in Ecuadorian reality. They were the product of international and regional organisations whose economic theory was out of step with both banking practice and small-firm demand for credit. In spite of the positive policies of different governments, micro-firms were not in a position to realise the benefits of the available resources. There were three main reasons for this. The first was the question of guarantees needed to obtain loans from the formal banking system. The second was the effect of accumulated wealth, not only in making it easier to obtain credit for rational technical banking reasons, but also in permitting individuals and groups to exert influence over state practice. The third was the fact that few of the microenterprises were interested.

Using their informal power networks, it was the agricultural sector that was best able to take advantage of the increased availability of government loans at negative real rates of interest after 1972, while industry still had to rely on the high interest, private financial sector which provided most of the industrial loans. The banks, awash with money, were not lending to small firms and, in particular, artisans. In order to use the money that was available, the upper limits that defined small and micro-firms were raised, encouraging larger firms to compete for the available funds. Both socio-political relations and professional banking practice squeezed the smaller firms out.

After 1982, the concept of microfinance heralded the ascendency of neoliberalism. Originally conceived of as very small low-cost loans to the poor, which would unleash their inner entrepreneur and help them start profitable businesses that would lift their families out of poverty and contribute to community well-being, socially responsible lending developed into a system of predatory financial schemes that sucked funds out of microenterprises and diverted attention away from the deeper structural causes of poverty. Subsidised lending and charitable giving gave way to profit-making international finance; and in this process, part of the income of micro-manufacturers was diverted into international money flows from underdeveloped countries to the financial centres of the world.

Fairly priced micro-loans were replaced by extortionate interest rates, as the commercialisation of the sector led to big banks and neoliberal ideology taking over the system, marginalising concerns about poverty. The poor remained poor, as billions of dollars were extracted and transferred north; and the propaganda machine ensured that investors continued to believe they were behaving ethically by unleashing entrepreneurial flair, rather than skimming a share of the world's wealth that should have accrued to the world's poor and been invested in wealth-creating capital goods.

When the financial system crashed in Ecuador in 1999, interest rates were astronomical, inflation was rampant and the crash took a number of artisans down, which further reduced an already shaky faith in the banking system. In spite of evidence from the developed world that small firms prefer not to deal with formal banks if they can possibly avoid it, the international pressure in favour of artisan indebtedness continued, and continues, to grow.

When the Correa administration took over in Ecuador in 2007, it set in train a series of reforms in the banking sector that reduced interest rates and promoted the Popular and Solidarity Economy. Interest rates for artisans were still relatively high, but they were much lower than the rates charged by private banks and by pay-day lenders in the developed and developing worlds. The capped and regulated interest rates produced stability in the financial sector and predictable outlays for artisans.

The main concerns of neoliberal economists about the failure of microenterprises to develop into larger and formal capitalist firms, namely the stultifying imposition of government regulations and the lack of access to credit, barely register with artisans. Practically no artisans mentioned regulations as an important problem for them or indicated that getting rid of regulations was what was required to improve their situation. Similarly, the obsession with the provision of microcredit as a means of escaping poverty was not reflected in the main issues that were holding back artisans and it was not seen as important for improving their situation.

Neoliberal assumptions about micro-firms are invalid – there is no evidence to support them. What stands out is the rapid deterioration in micro-businesses through the years of the neoliberal dogma that was pursued by successive governments. Their main problems were rooted in international issues that were filtered through national institutions: firstly the opening up of the Ecuadorean economy to the forces of the free market, which produced unfair competition and reduced incomes; and secondly the crisis of neoliberalism in Ecuador, which destroyed investable savings. Anticipated benefits, such as cheaper consumer goods, were in many cases short-term, as they proved more costly in the longer run. This influx of consumer goods encouraged some artisans to become traders, particularly in the city centre, and they created opportunities for an expansion of repair activities. For economists, this is taken as evidence of entrepreneurial behaviour. For many artisans, it is a survival strategy that involves an enforced and regrettable desertion of what it has meant to be a master-artisan.

Bibliography

Abad, G. (1970) *La Lucha por el Poder en el Ecuador*. Tesis de Grado: Colegio de Mexico.

Accion International (2010) *Measuring the Impact of Microfinance: Our Perspective*, www. accion.org/

Acosta, A. (1996) Apuntes Para una Economía Política del Ajuste Neoliberal, *Ecuador Debate* 37: 49–65.

Adachi, T. and Hisada (2017) Gender Differences in Entrepreneurship and Intrapreneurship: An Empirical Analysis, *Small Business Economics* 48(3): 447–86.

Addae-Korankye, A. (2014) Causes and Control of Loan Default/Delinquency in Microfinance Institutions in Ghana, *American International Journal of Contemporary Research* 4(12). www.aijcrnet.com/journals/Vol_4_No_12_December_2014/5.pdf

Ahmad, N. and Seymour, R. (2008) Defining Entrepreneurial Activity: Definitions Supporting Frameworks for Data Collection, *OECD Statistics Working Papers* 2008/01. Paris: OECD.

Aitken, R. (2013) The Financialization of Micro-Credit, *Development and Change* 44(3): 473–99.

Alcorn, P.B. (1982) *Success and Survival in the Family-owned Business*. New York: McGraw-Hill.

Alexander-Tedeschi, G. (2008) Overcoming Selection Bias in Microcredit Impact Assessments: A Case Study in Peru, *Journal of Development Studies* 44(4): 504–18.

Amit, R. and Villalonga, B. (2014) Financial Performance of Family Firms. In Melin, L., Nordqvist, M. and Sharma, P. (eds), *Sage Handbook of Family Business*. Thousand Oaks, CA: Sage, pp. 157–78.

Anheier, H.K. (1992) Economic Environment and Business Behaviour: A Study of Informal Sector Economies in Nigeria, *World Development* 20(11): 1573–85.

Anner, M. (2000) Local and Transnational Campaigns to End Sweatshop Practices. In Gordon, M. and Turner, L. (eds), *Transnational Cooperation among Trade Unions*. Ithaca, NY: Cornell University Press, pp. 238–55.

Appelbaum, R.P. (2000) *Fighting Sweatshops: Problems of Enforcing Global Labor Standards*. University of California at Santa Barbara. https://escholarship.org/uc/item/2693m5pn (accessed 21 May 2019).

Audretsch, D.B., Obschonka, M., Gosling, S.D. et al. (2017) A New Perspective on Entrepreneurial Regions: Linking Cultural Identity with Latent and Manifest Entrepreneurship, *Small Business Economics* 48(3): 681–97.

Awaworyi Churchill, S. (2017) Fractionalization, Entrepreneurship, and the Institutional Environment for Entrepreneurship, *Small Business Economics* 48(3): 577–9.

Ayyagari, M., Demirgüç-Kunt, A. and Maksimovic, V. (2008) How Important Are Financial Constraints? The Role of Finance in the Business Environment, *World Bank Economic Review* 22(3): 483–515.

Banco Central del Ecuador (BCE) (2009) *Regulación No. 184–2009.* Quito: El Directorio del   BCE.   https://contenido.bce.fin.ec/documentos/Estadisticas/SectorMonFin/TasasInteres/RegTasas184.pdf (accessed 21 May 2019).

Banco Mundial (2004) *Ecuador: Evaluación de la Pobreza.* Washington DC: World Bank.

Banco Mundial (2004b) *La Pobreza en el Ecuador: Evaluación y Agenda de Políticas,* Quito, Banco Mundial.

Banerjee, A.V. and Duffo, E. (2007) The Economic Lives of the Poor, *Journal of Economic Perspectives* 21(1): 141–67.

Banerjee A., Duflo E., Glennerster R. and Kinnan, C. (2015) The Miracle of Microfinance? Evidence from a Randomised Evaluation. *American Economic Journal: Applied Economics* 7(1): 22–53.

Bateman, M. (2010) *Why Doesn't Microfinance Work: The Destructive Rise of Local Neoliberalism,* London, Zed Books.

Bateman, M. (2011) Microfinance as a Development and Poverty Reduction Policy: Is It Everything It's Cracked Up to Be? *ODI Background Note, London, ODI.*

Bateman, M. (2012) How Lending to the Poor Began, Grew and Almost Destroyed a Generation in India, *Development and Change* 43(6): 1385–1402.

Bateman, M. (2013) The Age of Microfinance: Destroying Latin American Economies from the Bottom Up, *Ola Financiera.* http://inctpped.ie.ufrj.br/spiderweb/dymsk_4/4-6S%20Bateman-Microfinance%20in%20Latin%20America.pdf (accessed 21 May 2019).

Baumol, W.J., Litan, J. and Schramm, C.J. (2007) *Good Capitalism, Bad Capitalism and the Economics of Growth and Prosperity.* New Haven, CO: Yale University Press.

BDRC Continental (2015) SME Financial Monitor. www.bdrc-group.com/products/sme-finance-monitor/ (accessed 21 May 2019).

Becker, K.F. (2004) *The Informal Economy: Fact Finding Study.* Swedish International Development Cooperation Agency (SIDA). www.sida.se/English/publications/120326/the-informal-economy/ (accessed 31 May 2019).

Benjamin, N., Beegle, K., Recanatini, F. and Santini, M. (2014) Informal Economy and the World Bank, *Policy Research Working Paper* No. 6888. Washington, DC: World Bank.

Bennett, J. (2010) Informal Firms in Developing Countries, *Small Business Economics* 34(3): 53–63.

Bernat, L.F., Lambardi, G. and Palacios, P. (2017) Determinants of the Entrepreneurial Gender Gap in Latin America, *Small Business Economics* 48(3): 727–52.

Bienefeld, M. and Godfrey M. (1978) Surplus Labour and Underdevelopment, *IDS Discussion Paper,* No. 138.

Bienefeld H. and Godfrey M. (1975) Measuring Unemployment and the Informal Sector: Some Conceptual and Statistical Problems, *IDS Bulletin* 7(3): 4–10.

Birkbeck, C. (1978) Self-employed Proletarians in an Informal Factory: The Case of Cali's Garbage Dump, *World Development* 9/10: 1173–85.

Borja, R. (1982) Políticas Neoliberales y Desarrollo, *Seminario International sobre Las Políticas Económicas y las Perspectivas Democráticas en América Latina en las 1980s,* Quito.

Breman, J. (1976) A Dualistic Labour System? A Critique of the Informal Sector Concept, *Economic and Political Weekly,* November–December: 1870–6 and 1905–8.

Bromley, R. (1974) The Organisation of Quito's Urban Markets: Towards a Reinterpretation of Periodic Central Places, *I.B.G. Transactions, O.S.,* 62: 45–70.

Bromley, R. (1978) The Informal Sector: Why Is It Worth Discussing?, Introduction to a special edition of *World Development* 6: 1033–9.

Bromley, R. (ed.) (1979) *The Urban Informal Sector: Critical Perspectives on Employment and Housing Policies*. Oxford: Pergamon Press.

Bromley, R. (1990) A New Path to Development? The Significance and Impact of Hernando de Soto's Ideas on Underdevelopment, Production and Reproduction', *Economic Geography* 66(1): 328–48.

Brosnan, S.F. and Beran, M.J. (2009) Trading Behavior between Conspecifics in Chimpanzees, Pan Troglodytes. *Journal of Comparative Psychology* 123(2): 181–94.

Brown, A. and Lyons, M. (2010) Seen but Not Heard: Urban Voice and Citizenship for Street Traders, In Lindell, I. (ed.), *Africa's Informal Workers: Collective Agency, Alliances and Transnational Organising in Urban Africa*. London: Zed Books, pp. 33–45.

Caliendo, M., Künn, S. and Weißenberger, M. (2016) Personality Traits and the Evaluation of Start-up Subsidies, *European Economic Review* 86: 87–108.

Campaña, A. (1952) Situación económica artesanal y problemas creados por falta de afiliación oportuna de operarios y aprendices, *Boletín del Instituto Nacional de Previsión*, Quito.

Cardoso, F.H. and Faletto, E. (1969) *Dependencia y Desarrollo en América Latina* (México D.F., Siglo XXI.

Carr, M. and Chen, M.A. (2002) Globalization and the Informal Economy: How Global Trade and Investment Impact on the Working Poor, Geneva, ILO. www.ilo.org/employment/Whatwedo/Publications/WCMS_122053/lang--en/index.htm (accessed 21 May 2019).

Castells, M. and Portes, A. (1989) World Underneath: The Origins, Dynamics and Effects of the Informal Economy. In Castells, M., Portes, A. and Benton, L.A. (eds), *The Informal Economy: Studies in Advanced and Less Developed Countries*. Baltimore: Johns Hopkins University Press.

Centro de Estudios Latinoamericanos (CELA) (2004) *Impactos del Neoliberalismo: Una Lectura Distinta desde la Percepción y Experiencias de los Actores*, Quito, Abya Yala.

Cevallos, M.R. (2004) Los callejones oscuros del TLC, *Ecuador Debate No. 63*, 7–20.

Chen, M.A., Jhabvala, R. and Lund, F. (2001) Supporting Workers in the Informal Economy: A Policy Framework, Paper Prepared for ILO Task Force on the Informal Economy, November, WIEGO.

Chen, M.A., Jhabvala, R. and Lund, F. (2002) Supporting Workers in the Informal Economy: A Policy Framework, *Working Paper on the Informal Economy*, 2002-02. Geneva: ILO. www.ilo.org/employment/Whatwedo/Publications/WCMS_122055/lang--en/index.htm (accessed 21 May 2019).

Chen, M. (2014) Informal Employment and Development: Patterns of Inclusion and Exclusion, *European Journal of Development Research* 26: 397–418.

Chrisman, J.J., Chua, J.H. and Steier, L.P. (2003) An Introduction to Theories of Family Business, *Journal of Business Venturing* 18: 441–8.

Chrisman, J. J., Chua, J. H., Pearson, A. W. and Barnett, T. (2012) Family Involvement, Family Influence, and Family-centered Non-economic Goals in Small Firms, *Entrepreneurship Theory and Practice* 36(2): 267–93.

Chua, J.H., Chrisman, J.J. and Sharma, P. (1999) Defining the Family Business by Behaviour, *Entrepreneurship Theory and Practice* 23(4): 19–39.

Chua, J.H., Chrisman, J.J., Steier, L.P. and Rau, S.B. (2012) Sources of Heterogeneity in Family Firms: An Introduction, *Entrepreneurship Theory and Practice* 36(6): 1103–13.

Clapham, J. (1929) *An Economic History of Modern Britain*, Vol. 1, Cambridge: Cambridge University Press.

Coleman B.E. (1999) The Impact of Group Lending in Northeast Thailand, *Journal of Development Economics* 60: 105–41.

Coleman, B.E. (2006) Microfinance in Northeast Thailand: Who Benefits and How Much?, *World Development* 34(9): 1612–38.

Conger, L. and Berger, M. (2004) Latin American Micro-finance: The Debate Heats Up, *Microenterprise Americas*, 22–9.

COMEXI (2009) Resolución No. 446, Suplemento al Registro Oficial, No. 512, Quito, COMEXI.

COMEX (2013) *Resolución No. 116*, Quito, Comité de Comercio Exterior.

Corporación de Estudios y Publicaciones (2003) *Legislación Artesanal*, Quito.

Corporación de Estudios y Publicaciones (2009) *Constitución de la República del Ecuador*, Registro Oficial 449, Quito, 20 de octubre de 2008.

Cross, J.C. and Peña, S (2006) Risk and Regulation in Informal and Illegal Markets. In Fernandez-Kelly, P. and Shefner, J., *Out of the Shadows: Political Action and the Informal Economy in Latin America*. University Park, PA: Pennsylvania State University, pp. 49–80.

Cueva, A. (1974) *El Proceso de Dominación Política en Ecuador*, México, Editorial Diógenes.

Cunningham, W. and Gomez, C.R. (2004) The Home as Factory Floor: Employment and Remuneration of Home-based Workers, *WPS 3295*. Washington. DC: World Bank.

Cuvi, N. (2011) Auge y Decadencia de La Fábrica de Hilados y Tejidos de Algodón La Industrial, 1935–1999, *Procesos* 33(1): 63–95.

de Soto, H. (1986) *El Otro Sendero*. Lima: Editorial el Barranco.

de Soto, H. (1989) *The Other Path: The Invisible Revolution in the Third World*. London: I.B. Taurus.

Domínguez, R. and Caria, S. (2016) Ecuador en la Trampa de la Renta Media, *Revista Problemas de Desarrollo* 47(187): 89–112.

Duvendack, M., Palmer-Jones, R., Copestake, J.G., Hooper, L., Loke, Y. and Rao, N. (2011) *What Is the Evidence of the Impact of Microfinance on the Well-being of Poor People?* London: EPPI-Centre, Social Science Research Unit, Institute of Education, University of London.

Efren Reyes, O. (1974) *Brevísima Historia del Ecuador*. Quito: Lexigrama.

Elliot, J.H. (1970) *Imperial Spain, 1469–1716*. Harmondsworth: Penguin.

Evert, R.E., Martin, J.A., McLeod, M.S. and Payne, G.T. (2016) Empirics in Family Business Research: Progress, Challenges and the Path Ahead, *Family Business Review* 29(1): 17–43.

Federación Nacional de Cameras de Pequeños Industriales del Ecuador (FENAPI) (1985) *Análisis de la Política Crediticia a la Pequeña Industria y Artesanía del Banco Nacional de Fomento, Periodo 1975–84*. Quito: FENAPI.

Fei, J.C.H. and Ranis, G.R. (1964) *Development of the Labour Surplus Economy*. Homewood: Irwin.

Ferrán, L. (1998) *Note on Concepts and Classifications to Improve Statistics on Home-based Workers*. New York: Statistics Division of the United Nations Secretariat.

Frank, A.G. (1967) *Capitalism and Underdevelopment in Latin America: Historical Studies of Chile and Brazil*. New York: Monthly Review Press.

Friedman, M. (1981) *Free to Choose*, Harmondsworth, Penguin.

Fritsch, M. and Mueller, P. (2007) The Persistence of Regional New Business Formation-Activity over Time – Assessing the Potential of Policy Promotion Programs. *Journal of Evolutionary Economics* 17: 299–315.

Fritsch, M. and Storey, D.J. (2014) Entrepreneurship in a Regional Context: Historical Roots, Recent Developments and Future Challenges. *Regional Studies* 48(6): 939–54.

Fritsch, M. and Wyrwich, M. (2014) The Effect of Regional Entrepreneurship culture on Economic Development – Evidence from Germany, *Jena Economic Research Papers*. Jena: Friedrich Schiller University.

Fukuyama, F. (1995) *Trust: The Social Virtues and the Creation of Prosperity*. London: Hamish Hamilton.

Galarza, Z., J. (1974) *El Festín del Petróleo*, Quito, Universidad Central.

Galarza Z., J. (1982) *¿Quiénes Mataron a Roldós?* (2nd edition). Quito: Ediciones Solitierra.

Gartner, W.B. (1990) What Are We Talking about when We Talk about Entrepreneurship, *Journal of Business Venturing* 5(1): 15–28.

GEM (2017) *Global Entrepreneurship Monitor: Global Report, 2016–2017*, Global Enterprise Research Association, London Business School.

Gobierno del Ecuador (1953) *Ley de Defensa del Artesano*, Registro Oficial 356, Quito, 5 November.

Gobierno del Ecuador (1965) *Ley de Fomento de la Pequeña Industria y Artesanía*, Registro Oficial 419. Quito, 20 January.

Gobierno del Ecuador (1971) Decreto Supremo 3641, julio de 1971, Registro Oficial No. 885.

Gobierno del Ecuador (1974) *Ley de Defensa del Artesano*, Decreto No. 1151, noviembre 15, Quito.

Gobierno del Ecuador (1979) *Régimen Especial de Seguro Social*, Decreto No. 3641, Registro Oficial No. 885, Quito, 31 de julio.

Gobierno del Ecuador (1986) *Ley de Fomento Artesanal*, Registro Oficial 446, 29 de mayo de 1986.

Gobierno del Ecuador (1990) Resolución 732 of IESS, 2 julio, 1990.

Gobierno del Ecuador (1997) *Codificación de la Ley de Defensa del Artesano*, Registro Oficial No. 71, 23 May.

Gobierno del Ecuador (1998) *Reglamento General de la Ley de Defensa del Artesano*, Registro Oficial 255, Oficina del Presidente, Quito, 11 de febrero de 1998.

Gobierno del Ecuador (2003a) *Ley de Fomento Artesanal*, Registro Oficial Suplemento 184, Quito, 6 de octubre de 2003.

Gobierno del Ecuador (2005a), *Código Civil*, Codificación No. 2005010, Congreso Nacional, Quito.

Gobierno del Ecuador (2005b), *Código Tributario* (Codificación No. 200509) Congreso Nacional, Quito.

Gobierno del Ecuador (2008) *Ley de Defensa del Artesano*, Ley No. 12, Registro Oficial, Suplemento 20, 7 de Septiembre and Registro Oficial 71, 23-may-1997, Ultima Modificación 14-may-2008, Quito.

Gobierno del Ecuador (2008b) *Constitución Política de la República del Ecuador*, Registro Oficial No. 449, Quito, 20 October; published by Corporación de Estudios y Publicaciones, May 2009.

Gobierno del Ecuador, (2010) *Reglamentos al Código Orgánico de Producción, Comercio e Inversiones*, Registro Oficial 351, diciembre, Quito.

Gobierno del Ecuador (2011) *Ley Orgánica de Economía Popular y Solidaria*, Quito, 28 de abril.

Gobierno del Ecuador (2014) *Ley Orgánico de Incentivos a la Producción y Prevención del Fraude Fiscal*, Suplemento del Registro Oficial No. 405, 9 de diciembre de 2014. In EDICONTAB, *Agenda 2015: Laboral – Tributaria y Seguridad Social*, EDICONTAB, Quito.

Gobierno del Ecuador, (2015a) *Código de Trabajo: Ley Orgánico para la Justicia Laboral*, Registro Oficial 483, abril, Quito.

Gobierno del Ecuador, (2015b) *Código Orgánico de la Producción, Comercialización e Inversiones*, Registro Oficial Suplemento 351 de diciembre, 2010, última modificación, mayo, 2015, Quito.

Goldberg, N. (2005) *Measuring the Impact of Microfinance: Taking Stock of What We Know*. Gameen Foundation USA. www.microfinancegateway.org/sites/default/files/mfg-en-paper-measuring-the-impact-of-microfinance-taking-stock-of-what-we-know-dec-2005_0.pdf (accessed 21 May 2019).

Gonzalez, A. (2010) Is Microfinance Growing too Fast, *Microfinance Information Exchange Data Brief No. 5*. www.themix.org/sites/default/files/publications/MIX%20Data%20Brief%205%20-%20Is%20microfinance%20growing%20too%20fast_0.pdf (accessed 21 May 2019).

Guha-Khasnobis, B., Kanbur, R. and Ostrom, E. (2006) Beyond Formality and Informality. In Guha-Khasnobis, B., Kanbur, R. and Ostrom, E. (eds), *Linking the Formal and Informal Economy: Concepts and Policies*. Oxford: Oxford University Press.

Haase, D. (ed.) (2013) *The Credibility of Microcredit: Studies of Impact and Performance*. Boston, MA: Brill.

Halac, M. and Schmukler, S. L. (2003) *Distributional Effects of Crises: The Role of Financial Transfers*, WPS3173. Washington, DC: World Bank.

Hammerly, M.T. (1973) *Historia Social y Económica de la Antigua Provincia de Guayaquil, 1763–1842*. Guayaquil: Archivo Histórico de Guayas.

Harriss, B. (1977) Quasi-formal Employment Structures and Behaviour in the Unorganised Urban Economy, and the Reverse: Some Evidence from South India, *Institute of British Geographers Conference*, Developing Areas Study Group, London, March.

Harriss-White, B. (2010) Work and Wellbeing in Informal Economies: The Regulative Roles of Institutions of Identity and the State, *World Development* 38(2): 170–83.

Hart, K. (1973) Informal Income Opportunities and Urban Employment in Ghana, *Journal of Modern African Studies* II(I): 61–89.

Harvey, D. (2005) *A Brief History of Neoliberalism*. Oxford: Oxford University Press.

Henrekson, M. and Sanandaji, T. (2013) Small Business Activity Does Not Measure Entrepreneurship, *IFN Working Paper* No. 959, Research Institute of Industrial Economics, Stockholm.

Holt, D.T., Pearson, A.W., Carr, J.C. and Barnett, T. (2017) Family Firm(s) Outcomes Model: Structuring Financial and Nonfinancial Outcomes across the Family and Firm, *Family Business Review* 30(2): 182–202.

Homenet South Asia Group (2016) ILO Convention 177 and Why It Should Be Ratified, Homenet South Asia Trust, Mauritius. http://wiego.org/sites/wiego.org/files/resources/files/HomeNet-C177-advocacy-materials.pdf (accessed 21 May 2019).

Hurst, E. and Pugsley, B.W. (2011) What Do Small Businesses Do? *Brookings Papers on Economic Activity* 2: 73–142. Includes responses by Haltiwanger, J., Lazear, E., Rothstein, J. Schoar, A. and Wolfers, J.

Hurtado, O. (1977) *El Poder Político en el Ecuador*. Quito: Universidad Católica.

Hurtado, O. (2002) *Deuda y Desarrollo en el Ecuador Contemporáneo*. Quito: Editorial Planeta.

Hurtado O. and Herudek, J. (1974) *La Organización Popular en el Ecuador*. Quito: INEDES.

IBRD (1972) *Situación Actual y Perspectivas Económicas del Ecuador, Banco Internacional de Reconstrucción y Fomento*. New York: IBRD.

IDB (2010) *The Age of Productivity: Transforming Economies from the Bottom Up*. Washington DC: IDB.

ILO (1972) *Employment, Incomes and Equality: A Strategy for Increasing Productive Employment in Kenya.* Geneva: ILO (The Kenya Report).

ILO (1993) *Report on the 15th International Conference of Labour Statisticians,* Resolution II Concerning Statistics of Employment in the Informal Sector. Geneva: ILO. www.ilo. org/public/libdoc/ilo/1993/93B09_65_engl.pdf (accessed 2 June 2019).

ILO (1996) *Home Work Convention,* No. 177, adopted at the 1996 General Conference of the International Labour Organisation. www.ilo.org/dyn/normlex/en/f?p=NORMLEX PUB:12100:0::NO::P12100_ILO_CODE:C177 (accessed 21 May 2019).

ILO (2002) *Decent Work and the Informal Economy.* Report VI, International labour Conference, 90th Session. Geneva: ILO.

ILO (2003) *Report of the 17th International Conference of Labour Statisticians.* Geneva: ILO, 19–28 January.

ILO (2013a) *Measuring Informality: A Statistical Manual on the Informal Sector and Informal Employment.* Geneva: ILO.

ILO (2013b) *Report on the 19th International Conference of Labour Statisticians.* Geneva: ILO.

ILO (2013c) *Report III of the 19th International Conference of Labour Statisticians.* Geneva: ILO.

ILO (2015) Recommendation Concerning the Transition from the Informal to the Formal Economy, Adoption: Geneva, 104th ILC session (12 June 2015). www.ilo.org/dyn/ normlex/en/f?p=NORMLEXPUB:12100:0::NO::P12100_ILO_CODE:R204 (accessed 21 May 2019).

ILO and WIEGO (2013) *Women and Men in the Informal Economy: A Statistical Picture* (2nd edn). Geneva: ILO. www.ilo.org/wcmsp5/groups/public/---dgreports/---stat/documents/publication/wcms_ 234413.pdf (accessed 21 May 2019).

Ingram, M., Ramachandran, V. and Desai, V (2007) Why do Firms Choose to be Informal? Evidence from Enterprise Surveys in Africa, RPED Paper No. 134. Washington, DC: World Bank. http://documents.worldbank.org/curated/en/665731468194662235/ Why-do-firms-choose-to-be-informal-Evidence-from-enterprise-surveys-in-Africa (accessed 21 May 2019).

IPANC/MIPRO (2010) *Estudio Propuesta para el Posicionamiento de la Artesanía Patrimonial del Ecuador: Informe Final,* Quito, Instituto Iberoamericano del Patrimonio Natural Y Cultural y el Ministerio de Industrias y Productividad.

James Finlay and Co. Ltd. (1951) *James Finlay & Company Limited: Manufacturers and East India Merchants, 1750–1950.* Glasgow: Jackson Son & Company.

Jaramillo, C. (1962) *Historia del Ecuador.* Quito: Editorial Lasalle.

Jaskiewicz, P. and Gibb-Dyer, W. (2017) Addressing the Elephant in the Room: Disentangling Family Heterogeneity to Advance Family Business Research, *Family Business Review* 3(2): 111–18.

Jelin, E., Mercado, M. and Wyczykier, G. (2000) Home Work in Argentina, *SEED Working Paper,* No. 6. Geneva: ILO.

Jimu, I.M. (2010) Self-organised Informal Workers and Trade Union Initiatives in Malawi: Organising the Informal Economy, in Lindell, I. (ed.), *Africa's Informal Workers: Collective Agency, Alliances and Transnational Organising in Urban Africa.* London: Zed Books, pp. 99–114.

Joseph, K. and Sumption J. (1979) *Equality.* London: John Murray.

Joshi, H., Lubell, H. and Mouly, J. (1975) Urban Development and Employment in Abidjan, *International Labour Review* III(4): 289–306.

JUNAPLA (1962) *Censo de Población y de Vivienda.* Quito: División de Estadísticas Y Censos.

JUNAPLA (1963) *Plan Nacional de Desarrollo Económico y Social, 1963–1973.* Quito: JUNAPLA.

JUNAPLA (1969) *Programa de Artesanías y Pequeñas Industrias.* Quito: JUNAPLA.

JNP (Junta Nacional de Planificación) (1972a) *Plan Integral de Transformación y Desarrollo: 1973–1977, Resumen General.* Quito: JNP.

JNP (1972b) *Filosofía y Plan de Acción del Gobierno Revolucionario Nacionalista del Ecuador.* Quito: JNP.

Khandker, S. (1998) *Fighting Poverty with Microcredit: Experience in Bangladesh.* New York: IBRD/OUP.

Karlan, D. and Zinman, J. (2009) Expanding Microenterprise Credit Access: Using Randomized Supply Decisions to Estimate the Impacts in Manila, *Economic Growth Centre Discussion Paper*, No. 976. New Haven, CO: Yale University.

Kathuria, V., Rajesh Raj, S.N. and Sen, K. (2013) The Effects of Economic Reforms on Manufacturing Dualism: Evidence from India, *Journal of Comparative Economics* 41: 1240–62.

Killick, T. (1996) Principals, Agents and the Limitations of BWI Conditionality, *The World Economy* 19(2): 211–29.

Klein, S.B. (2000) Family Business in Germany: Significance and Structure, *Family Business Review* XIII(3): 157–81.

Krasheninnikova, A., Höner, F., O'Neill, L., Penna, E. and von Bayern, A.M.P. (2018) Economic Decision-making in Parrots, *Nature: Scientific Reports* 8, Article No. 12537. www.nature.com/articles/s41598-018-30933-5 (accessed 2 June 2019).

La Porta, R. and Shleifer, A. (2014) Informality and Development, *Journal of Economic Perspectives* 28(3): 109–26.

Le Brun, O. and Gerry, C. (1975) Petty Producers and Capitalism, *Review of African Political Economy* 3, pp. 20–32.

Leonardi, R.J., Vick, S.J. and Dufour, V. (2012) Waiting for More: The Performance of Domestic Dogs (*Canis familiaris*) on Exchange Tasks. *Anim. Cogn.* **15**: 107–20, quoted in Krasheninnikona et al., 2018.

Lenin. V.L. (1974) *The Development of Capitalism in Russia.* Moscow: Progress.

Lewis, W.A. (1954) Economic Development with Unlimited Supplies of Labour, *Manchester School* 26: 139–91.

Leys, C. (1973) Interpreting African Underdevelopment: Reflections on the ILO Report on Employment, Incomes and Equality in Kenya, *African Affairs* 72(289): 419–29.

Leys, C. (1975) *Underdevelopment in Kenya: The Political Economy of Neo-Colonialism.* London: Heinemann.

Lindell, I. (ed.) (2010) *Africa's Informal Workers: Collective Agency, Alliances and Transnational Organising in Urban Africa.* London: Zed Books.

Lindell, I. (2010a) Introduction: The Changing Politics of Informality – Collective Organising, Alliances and Scales of Engagement. In Lindell, I. (ed.), *Africa's Informal Workers: Collective Agency, Alliances and Transnational Organising in Urban Africa.* London: Zed Books, pp. 1–32.

Lipton, M. (1984) Family, Fungibility and Formality: Rural Advantages of Informal Non-farm Enterprise versus the Urban-formal State. In Amin, S. (ed.), *Human Resources, Employment and Development, Vol. 5, Developing Countries.* London: Macmillan, 189–242.

Little, I.M.D., Mazumdar, D. and Page Jr., J.M. (1987) *Small Manufacturing Enterprises: A Comparative Analysis of India and Other Economies.* Oxford: Oxford University Press.

Loayza, N.V., Oviedo, A.M. and Servén, L. (2006) The Impact of Regulation on Growth and Informality: Cross-country Evidence. In Guha-Khasnobis, B., Kanbur,

R. and Ostrom, E., *Linking the Formal and Informal Economy: Concepts and Policies*. Oxford: Oxford University Press: pp. 121-44.

Loayza, N.V., Servén, L. and Sugawara, N. (2009) Informality in Latin America and the Caribbean, *World Bank Policy Research Working Paper* 4888, Washington, DC: World Bank.

Lyons, M. and Snoxell, S. (2005) Creating Urban Social Capital: Some Evidence from Informal Trades in Nairobi, *Urban Studies* 42(7): 1077–97.

Maloney, W.F. (2004) Informality Revisited, *World Development* 32(7): 1159–78.

Martínez, L. (1994) *Los Campesinos-artesanos en la Sierra Central: el Caso de Tungurahua*. Quito: CAAP.

Marx, K. (1967) *Capital*, Vols I and II. New York: International Publishers.

Mazumdar, O. (1975) The Urban Informal Sector, *World Bank Staff Working* Paper, No. 211. Washington DC: World Bank.

Meagher, K. (2006) Social Capital, Social Liabilities, and Political Capital: Social Networks and Informal Manufacturing in Nigeria, *African Affairs* 105/421: 553–82.

Meagher, K. (2010) The Politics of Vulnerability: Exit, Voice and Capture in Three Nigerian Informal Manufacturing Clusters. In Lindell, I. (ed.), *Africa's Informal Workers: Collective Agency, Alliances and Transnational Organising in Urban Africa*. London: Zed Books, pp. 46–64.

Middleton, A. (1979) Poverty, Production and Power: The Case of Petty Manufacturing in Ecuador. D.Phil. Thesis, Brighton: University of Sussex.

Middleton, A. (1982) Division and Cohesion in the Working Class: Artisans and Wage Labourers in Ecuador, *Journal of Latin American Studies* 14(1): 171–94.

Middleton, A. (1989) The Changing Structure of Petty Production in Ecuador, *World Development* 17(1): 139–55.

Middleton, A. (1991) El Sector Informal y el Neo-Liberalismo en la Región Andina. In Middleton, A., *La Dinámica del Sector Informal Urbano en el Ecuador*. Quito: CIRE.

Middleton, A. (2001) Economic Policy and the Changing Structure of Small-scale Manufacturing in Quito, Ecuador, 1975–99. In Morrisey, O. and Tribe, M. (eds), *Economic Policy and Manufacturing Performance in Developing Countries*. Cheltenham: Edward Elgar, pp. 185–203.

Middleton, A. (2003) Informal Traders and Planners in the Regeneration of Historic City Centres: The Case of Quito, Ecuador, *Progress in Planning* 59(2): 71–123.

Middleton, A. (2007) Globalisation, Free Trade and the Decline of Informal Production: The Case of Artisans in Quito, Ecuador, *World Development* 35(11): 1904–28.

Middleton, A. (2014) *Growth, Productivity and Precarious Self-employment in the UK*. Birmingham: Governance Foundation. www.governancefoundation.org/documents/Growth-Productivity-and-Precarious-Self-employment.pdf (accessed 21 May 2019).

Middleton, A., Murie, A. and Groves, R. (2005) Social Capital and Neighbourhoods that Work, *Urban Studies* 42(10): 1711–38.

Miller, D., Le Breton-Miller, I. and Scholnick, B. (2008) Stewardship versus Stagnation: An Empirical Comparison of Small Family and Non-Family Businesses, *Journal of Management Studies* 45(1): 51–78.

Moncada, J. (1973) *El Desarrollo Económico y la Distribución de Ingreso en el Caso Ecuatoriano*. Quito: Junta Nacional de Planificación.

Montgomery, D. (1974) The Shuttle and the Cross: Weavers and Artisans in the Kensington Riots of 1844. In Stearn, P.N. and Walkovitz, D.J. (eds), *The Workers in the Industrial Revolution*. New Brunswick: Transaction Books, pp. 44–74.

Montufar, C. (2000) *La Reconstrucción Neoliberal: Febres Cordero o la Estatización del Neoliberalismo en El Ecuador, 1984–1988*. Quito: Abya-Yala.

Moreano, A. (1975) Capitalismo y Lucha de Clases en la Primera Mitad del Siglo XX. In L. Mejia et al., *Ecuador: Pasado y Presente*. Quito, Universidad Central, pp. 137–224.

Moser, C.O.N. (1977) The Informal Sector or Petty Commodity Production: Autonomy or Dependence in Urban Development, *Development Planning Unit Working Paper*, No. 3, University College London.

Naranjo, M. (1999) *Marco Introductorio del Estudio 'Aproximación a Impactos de las Políticas de Estabilización y Ajuste Estructural Aplicadas en el Ecuador: 1982–1998'*, Informe Final, Proyecto SAPRI Ecuador, Quito, Gobierno del Ecuador – Sociedad Civil – Banco Mundial.

Naudé, W. (2011) Entrepreneurship is a Non-binding Constraint on Growth and Development in Poor Countries, *World Development* 39(1): 33–44.

Nguta, M.H. and Huka, G.S. (2013) Factors Influencing Loan Repayment Default in Micro-Finance Institutions: The Experience of Imenti North District, Kenya, *International Journal of Applied Science and Technology* 3(3): 80–4.

Nun, J. (1969) Sobre Población Relativa, Ejercito Industrial de Reserva y Masa Marginal, *Revista Latinoamericana de Sociología*, No. 2.

Nun, J. (2000) The End of Work and the 'Marginal Mass' Thesis, *Latin American Perspectives* 27(1): 6–32.

O'Boyle, E.H., Pollack, J.M. and Rutherford, M.W. (2012) Exploring the Relation between Family Involvement and Firms' Financial Performance: A Meta-analysis of Main and Moderator Effects. *Journal of Business Venturing* 27: 1–18.

Odell, K. (2010) Measuring the Impact of Microfinance, Grameen Foundation. https://grameenfoundation.org/

OECD-EUROSTAT (2010) Measuring Entrepreneurship: The OECD-EUROSTAT Entrepreneurship Indicators Programme, *OECD Statistics Brief*, No. 16. Paris: OECD.

Ofori, K.S., Fianu, E., Omoregie, K., Afotey Odai, N. and Oduro-Gyimah, F. (2014) Predicting Credit Default among Micro Borrowers in Ghana, *Research Journal of Finance and Accounting* 5(12): 96–104.

Perry, G.E. et al. (2007) *Informality: Exit and Exclusion*. Washington, DC: World Bank.

Petras, J. and Veltmeyer, H. (2001) *Globalization Unmasked: Imperialism in the 21st Century*. London: Zed Books.

Pisani, M.J. and Yoskowitz, D.W. (2013) The Efficacy of Microfinance at the Sectoral Level: Urban Pulperias in Matagalpa, Nicaragua. In Haase, D. (ed.), *The Credibility of Microcredit: Studies of Impact and Performance*. Boston: Brill, pp. 132–62.

Pita, E. (1992) *Informalidad Urbana: Dinámica y Perspectivas en el Ecuador*. Quito: CONADE.

Pita, E. and Meier, P.C. (1985) *Artesanía y Modernización en el Ecuador*. Quito: CONADE-Banco Central del Ecuador.

Pitt, M.M., Khandker, S.R. and Cartwright, J. (2006) Empowering Women with Micro Finance: Evidence from Bangladesh, *Economic Development and Cultural Change* 54(4), 791–831.

Placencia, M.M. (1986) El Sector Informal Urbano: Notas Acerca de su Génesis y Funcionamiento, *Ecuador Debate* 11: 307–17.

Portes, A. (1978) The Informal Sector and the World Economy: Notes on the Structure of Subsidised Labour, mimeo, Dale University.

Portes, A. (1985) Latin American Class Structures: Their Composition and Change During the Last Decades, *LARR* 20(3): 7–39.

Portes, A. Castells, M. and Benton, L.A. (1989) *The Informal Economy: Studies in Advanced and Less Developed Countries*, Baltimore, Johns Hopkins University Press

PREALC (1976a) *Situación y Perspectivas del Empleo en el Ecuador*. Santiago: PREALC.

PREALC (1976b) *La Estructura del Empleo en el Ecuador; Problemas, Oportunidades y Perspectivas*. Santiago: PREALC.

PREALC (1978) *Sector Informal*. Santiago: PREALC.

Putnam, R.D. (1993) *Making Democracy Work: Civic Tradition in Modern Italy*. Princeton, NJ: Princeton University Press.

Putnam, R.D. (2000) *Bowling Alone: The Collapse and Revival of American Community*. New York: Simon & Schuster.

Quijano, A. (1974) The Marginal Pole of the Economy and the Marginalised Labour Force, *Economy and Society* 3(4): 393–428.

Ranganathan, A. (2018) The Artisan and His Audience: Identification with Work and Price Setting in a Handicraft Cluster in Southern India, *Administrative Science Quarterly* 63(3): 637–67. http://journals.sagepub.com/doi/abs/10.1177/0001839217725782 (accessed 21 May 2019).

Reno, W. (2002) The Politics of Insurgency in Collapsing States, *Development and Change* 33(5): 837–58.

Robalino, I. (1977) *El Sindicalismo en el Ecuador*. Quito: INEDES.

Roberts, B.E. (1976) The Provincial Urban System and the Process of Dependency. In Portes, A. and Browning, H.L. (eds), *Current Perspectives in Latin American Urban Research*. Austin, TX: University of Texas Press.

Roitman, J. (2004) *Fiscal Disobedience: An Anthropology of Economic Regulation in Central Africa*. Princeton, NJ: Princeton University Press.

Roodman, D. and Morduch, J. (2013) The Impact of Microcredit on the Poor in Bangladesh: Revisiting the Evidence, *Journal of Development Studies* 50(4): 583–604.

Saad, P. (1974) *La CTE y su Papel Histórico*. Guayaquil: Claridad.

Sahu, P.P. (2010) Subcontracting in India's Unorganised Manufacturing Sector: A Mode of Adoption or Exploitation, *Journal of South Asian Development* 5(1): 53–83.

Salgado, G. (1987) Ecuador: Crisis and Adjustment Policies. Their Effect on Agriculture, *CEPAL Review* 33: 129–45.

Salgado W. (2001) Dolarización y Globalización: Lecciones de la Experiencia Ecuatoriana. In Marconi, S. (ed.), *Macroeconomía y Economía Política en Dolarización*. Quito: Abya-Yala, pp. 83–100.

Sane, R. and Thomas, S. (2011) A Policy Response to the Indian Micro-finance Crisis, *WP-2011-007*. Mumbai: Indira Gandhi Institute of Development Research.

Sane, R. and Thomas, S. (2013) The Real Cost of Credit Constraints: Evidence from Micro-Finance, *WP-2013-013*. Mumbai: Indira Gandhi Institute of Development Research.

Sauer, R.M. and Wilson, T. (2016) The rise of female entrepreneurs: New evidence on gender differences in liquidity constraints, *European Economic Review*, Vol. 86, 73–86.

Schoar, J. (2011) Comment on Hurst, E. and Pugsley, B.W. (2011) What Do Small Businesses Do? *Brookings Papers on Economic Activity*, No. 2, 73–142.

Schumpeter, J.A. (2003) *Capitalism, Socialism and Democracy*. London: Routledge. Taylor & Francis e-library edition.

Sethuraman, S.V. (1975a) Urbanisation and Employment: A Case Study of Djakarta, *International Labour Review* 112(2–3): 191–205.

Sethuraman, S.V. (1975b) Urbanisation and Employment in Djakarta, World Employment Programme, *Urbanisation and Employment Research Programme Working Paper*, No. 6. Geneva: ILO.

Sethuraman, S.V. (1976) The Urban Informal Sector: Concept, Measurement and Policy, *International Labour Review* 114(1): 69–81.

Shiller, R. (2013) Is Economics a Science? Guardian economics blog: www.theguardian.com/business/economics-blog/2013/nov/06/is-economics-a-science-robert-shiller (accessed 21 May 2019).

Sinclair, H. (2012) *Confessions of a Microfinance Heretic: How Microlending Lost its Way and Betrayed the Poor*. San Francisco, CA: Berrett-Kochler.

Sindzingre, A. (2006) The Relevance of the Concepts of Formality and Informality: A Theoretical Appraisal, in Guha-Khasnobis, B., Kanbur, R. and Ostrom, E. (eds), *Linking the Formal and Informal Economy: Concepts and Policies*. Oxford: Oxford University Press, pp. 58–74.

Skinner, C. (2008) Street Traders in Africa: A Review. *Wiego Working Paper No. 5*. www. wiego.org/sites/default/files/publications/files/Skinner_WIEGO_WP5.pdf (accessed 21 May 2019).

Smith, A, (1976) *An Inquiry into the Nature and Causes of the Wealth of Nations, Vols. 1 and 2*. Oxford: Oxford University Press.

Souza P.R., and Tokman, V.E. (1976) The Informal Urban Sector in Latin America, *International Labour Review* 114(3): 355–65.

Standing, G. (2014) *The Precariat: The New Dangerous Class*. London: Bloomsbury.

Stanford Research Institute (1963) *The Artisan Community in Ecuador's Modernising Economy*. Redwood City, CA: Stanford University.

Straus, T. (2010) A Sobering Assessment of Microfinance's Impact, Stanford Social Innovation Review. https://ssir.org/articles/entry/a_sobering_assessment_of_microfinances_impact (accessed 5 June 2019).

Stuetzer, M. et al. (2016) Industry Structure, Entrepreneurship, and Culture: An Empirical Analysis Using Historical Coalfields, *European Economic Review* 86: 52–72.

Taymaz, E. (2009) Informality and Productivity: Productivity Differentials between Formal and Informal Firms in Turkey, Background Paper, Country Economic Memorandum. Washington, DC: World Bank. http://siteresources.worldbank.org/TURKEYEXTN/Resources/361711-1277211666558/bpg_InformalityAndProductivity.pdf (accessed 21 May 2019).

Thompson, E.P. (1968) *The Making of the English Working Class*. Harmondsworth: Penguin.

Thoumi, F. and Grindle, M. (1992) *La Política de la Economía del Ajuste: La Actual Experiencia Ecuatoriana*. Quito: FLACSO.

Tokman, V.E. (1977) *An Exploration into the Nature of Informal-Formal Sector Interrelationships*. Santiago: PREALC.

Tokman, V.E. (1978) An Exploration into the Nature of Formal–informal Sector Relationships, *World Development* 6(9/10): 1065–75.

Tokman, V.E. (ed.) (1993) *Beyond Regulations: the Informal Sector in Latin America*. London: Lynn Rienner.

Tomei, M. (2000) Homework in Selected Latin American Countries: A Comparative Overview, *SEED Working Paper*, No. 1, ILO, Geneva.

Verdesoto, L.F. (2014) *Los Actores y la Producción de la Democracia y la Política en Ecuador*. Quito: Abya-Yala.

von Hayek, A.F. (1974) The Pretence of Knowledge, Nobel Prize Lecture to the memory of Alfred Nobel, 11 December.

Wade, R.H. (2004) Is Globalisation Reducing Poverty and Inequality? *World Development* 32(4): 567–89.

Waterman, P. (2001) *Globalization, Social Movements and the New Internationalism*. London: Continuum.

Weeks, J. (1975) Policies for Expanding Employment in the Informal Urban Sector of Developing Economies, *International Labour Review* 111: 1–13.

Westhead, P., Cowling, M. and Storey, D.J. (1997) *The Management and Performance of Unquoted Family Companies in the United Kingdom*. Small and Medium Enterprise Centre, Warwick Business School.

WIEGO (2016) Home-Based Workers, Women in Informal Employment: Globalizing and Organizing. http://wiego.org/informal-economy/occupational-groups/home-based-workers (accessed 21 May 2019).

Wolfers, J. (2011) Comment on Hurst, E. and Pugsley, B.W. (2011) What Do Small Businesses Do? *Brookings Papers on Economic Activity*, No. 2, 73–142.

Wong, P.K., Ho, Y.P. and Autio, E. (2005) Entrepreneurship, Innovation and Economic Growth: Evidence from GEM Data, *Small Business Economics* 24(3): 335–50.

World Bank (1991) *World Development Report 1991: The Challenge of Development*. Washington, DC: World Bank.

World Bank (2001) *World Development Report 2000/2001: Attacking Poverty*. New York: Oxford University Press.

World Bank (2002) *Globalisation, Growth and Poverty: Building an Inclusive World Economy*. New York: Oxford University Press.

World Bank (2003) *World Development Report 2004: Making Services Work for Poor People*. Washington, DC: World Bank.

World Bank (2003b) *Ecuador: Las Caras de la Informalidad*, Report No. 67808-EC, Washington, DC: World Bank.

Zaidi, N. (2019) *The Production of Informal Trading Spaces*. PhD Thesis, Cardiff University.

Index

For Product Safety Concerns and Information please contact our
EU representative GPSR@taylorandfrancis.com Taylor & Francis
Verlag GmbH, Kaufingerstraße 24, 80331 München, Germany